THE DISCONTENTED SOCIETY

Interpretations of Twentieth-Century American Protest

Edited by
LeROY ASHBY
Department of History
Washington State University

and

BRUCE M. STAVE
Department of History
University of Connecticut

Rand McNally & Company *Chicago*

For Steven, Eric, and Channing
*Whose protests thus far
have concerned the rights of children*

PREFACE

It was with considerable apprehension and surprise that many Americans reacted to the outbreak of protests in the 1960's, protests that ranged from southern lunch counters to university campuses and urban ghettos. The dissent came from a bewildering variety of sources—students, "doves," "hawks," ethnic and racial minorities, women, homosexuals, hippies—and reflected an equally bewildering variety of grievances, including the Vietnam war, discrimination, values of a consumer culture, and school busing.

By the end of the decade the word "crisis" was much in use, and there was considerable discussion of whether the center could hold. In *Newsweek,* six historians reflected on "What Ails the American Spirit"; *Life* examined the theme of revolution and asked, "Can It Happen Here?"; political scientists such as Hans Morgenthau and Andrew Hacker wrote about "the end of the Republic" and *The End of The American Era;* Katherine Porter's earlier prophecy that America would place a man on the moon before New York City solved its garbage problem assumed a new urgency; and columnist Murray Kempton described "a time when mediation, more nakedly than ever before, is increasingly a sitting-down between the wolf and the lamb." In such a context, the "silent majority" pointed to the virtues of those who do not protest (while ironically lodging its own increasingly vocal protest); automobile bumper stickers proclaimed, "America, Love It or Leave It," and country music star Merle Haggard sang, "When you're runnin' down our country, Hoss,/ You walkin' on the fightin' side of me." Promising to "bring us together again," Richard Nixon won the 1968 presidential election. But within a year, with American campuses in violent upheaval following the Cambodian invasion, *The New Republic* contended that the overriding concern was simply "Staying Alive Until 1973." One historian subsequently entitled his study of the 1960's *Coming Apart,* and a journalist wondered, "Will the cavalry never come?" The question became more pressing when, in 1972, hundreds were arrested during the nationwide protest against President Nixon's decision to blockade and mine North Vietnam's harbors.

A veteran of earlier American protests, without denying that the nation was stumbling through a critical era, and without claiming that history repeats itself, might nonetheless have pointed out that "we've been there before." He might have had in mind the Negro boycotts against segregated streetcars in the South at the turn of the century, the free speech fights of the Industrial Workers of the World several years later in the West, the draft resistance of World War I, the resurgence of the Ku Klux Klan in the early 1920's, the student strike at Columbia in the 1930's, and the sit-downs by American workers in 1937 and by the Congress of Racial Equality in 1942.

Protest was hardly a discovery of the 1960's, even though some Americans apparently believed that this was the case. (Indeed, there were a surprising number of claims that even the protest of the 1960's was a sham, reflecting outside, "un-American" influences rather than genuine, deeply felt grievances.) It seems that on the subject of discontent and protest—nonviolent as well as violent—Americans have short memories or myopia. They have preferred to believe that profound dissatisfaction and social conflict are problems that have marred the history of less successful nations, but have had little place in the United States, with its prosperity, opportunities, unity, constitutional liberties, representative government, mutual trust, and justice. As Robert Finch, President Nixon's first Secretary of Health, Education and Welfare, remarked after governmental reports about the extent of hunger in America, "The real disgrace was not the hunger, but that we didn't know."

This collection of readings is an effort to bring together scholarly and popular analyses of American discontent and protest in the twentieth century. Our view of protest encompasses both its violent and nonviolent forms and deals with the broad range of areas in which dissent has appeared: economic, political, social, cultural, and intellectual.

The book is divided into six sections embracing the protest of discrimination, of economics, of politics and peace, and of values and status. Such distinctions are, of course, arbitrary. Some selections could easily fit under several headings. We have, for example, placed the essay on the fight for women's rights in the section dealing with discrimination; it could also serve as an example of protest that clearly involves matters of status and values. Articles on campus protest appear in two sections. Since Philip Altbach's and Patti Peterson's essay relates pre-Berkeley student activism to larger "political trends in society and in the adult radical movement," we have included it in the section on politics and peace. We have, on the other hand, placed Sheldon Wolin's and John Schaar's discussion of recent university dissent in the section on status and values, because it is their contention that campus protest since Berkeley is part of a larger reaction against the values of a technological society. Some of the selections provide insights into several areas of protest; Stan Steiner's analysis of discontented Mexican-Americans, for example, also probes into unrest in the high schools.

We have been more interested in the analysis of protest than in merely documenting it. As a result, although the essays sometimes focus on particular episodes, they also place their subjects in historical perspective. They provide not only important facts about particular protests, but also make clear historical roots and developments.

In the first and last sections we have included articles that deal with several important conceptual questions regarding American protest. The first two essays point out some of the difficulties that have confronted modern American protest. The last three deal with continuities, especially between earlier protests and those more recently of the New Left. In the section introductions we attempt to provide an overview and to raise pertinent questions.

Our debt to the authors of the selections from which we have reprinted should be clear. We are grateful for permissions to use such material. Our thanks also go to Professors Thomas N. Guinsburg of the University of Western Ontario, Thomas G. Paterson of the University of Connecticut, and Robert H. Zieger of Wisconsin State University at Stevens Point for their helpful advice. Ted Tieken of Rand McNally took an early interest in the project and was most encouraging and helpful, as was our manuscript editor, Charlotte Iglarsh. Two student assistants, Robert Petersen of the University of Connecticut and Judy Fritzen of Illinois State University, helped in the collection of materials. The libraries of the University of Connecticut and Illinois State University were also very cooperative. As always, we wish to thank our wives, Sondra Astor Stave, who compiled the index, and Mary Ashby, both of whom advised at all stages of the project.

We hope that this collection of readings will prove stimulating. If the Seventies, in contrast with the Sixties, are less preoccupied with protest, this book may serve as a reminder of an important aspect of the American experience.

L.A.
Bloomington, Illinois

B.M.S.
High Fields, Coventry, Connecticut

Summer 1972

CONTENTS

THE PROBLEMS
OF
PROTEST

In mid-1969, an advertisement in *The New York Times Magazine* included a picture of Paul Goodman's *Like a Conquered Province,* a book that vigorously criticized America as an "empty society" in which, among other things, middle-class people wandered aimlessly across the barren terrain of a consumer culture. The advertisement, however, was not for the purpose of publicizing Goodman's book. Instead it urged readers to buy a particular brand of women's beach attire. The book was merely a prop in the hands of a leggy model wearing a $32 swimsuit. In this instance, the work of a well-known social critic was part of a come-on for beach wear.

Two years later, on a leading television nighttime talk show, comedian Bob Hope appreciatively noted that Mexican-American golfer Lee Trevino had recently boosted his earnings for the year to a record high of over $200,000. It could only happen in America, asserted Hope in a serious mood. Trevino, whose picture had recently appeared on at least two leading news magazines, echoed Hope's interpretation by enthusiastically pointing out that he—a Mexican-American—had risen from poverty to fame and fortune, something he could have done only in the United States.

These two incidents stand not in isolation, but illustrate related themes in American life that have profound implications for those who would protest or attempt to effect social change through demonstrations of grievances. The first manifests the enormous adaptability of "the system," which has demonstrated an extraordinary capacity to absorb and redirect protest. The second concerns a compelling set of national ideals built around a deeply-rooted faith in progress and in the Poor Richard–Horatio Alger symbol of individual self-improvement and advancement. The assumption is that the natural course of events in America is toward betterment, and that problems point more to the limitations and aberrations of groups and individuals than to the society itself.

An oppressive society might well forbid the publication of such criticism as Goodman's. But in America the response has been (and increasingly so as the mass media have grown) to co-opt it, to render it innocuous by the very amount

1

and kind of attention that it receives. Hence the phrase "Right on!"—popular during the university demonstrations of the late Sixties—ended up coming from "Tony the Tiger," a cartoon dynamo urging children to eat a certain brand of breakfast cereal. In another television ad, at a time when hundreds of antiwar demonstrations were occurring, dozens of women took to the streets in behalf of a particular laundry detergent. In a decade filled with cries of "Black Power," "Brown Power," "Red Power," and "Student Power," there was also the plea for "pucker power," which could be achieved by using the right kind of mouthwash. And for those concerned with the growing ecology crisis, there was the question of what one man could do to combat pollution of the atmosphere; and the answer that he could, if he had the courage of his convictions, make sure that he purchased the appropriate lead-free gasoline.

In somewhat similar ways, a black leader of protest received a White House medal while the ghettos continued to seethe; President Nixon used the phrase "Right on!" during a press conference and called for "a new American Revolution" in his 1971 State of the Union address; and radical spokesmen found themselves on television's talk shows. James Kunen, a participant in demonstrations at Columbia University, described the events in *The Strawberry Statement,* which became an immediate bestseller, appeared in serial form in many newspapers, and was made into a movie featuring Kunen himself. By such means have revolution and protest been rechannelled. Dissenters for the most part have found themselves not in political exile, but collecting royalties and answering invitations to speak on various campuses. "Warner Brothers and Columbia Records have taken over the counterculture," observed Yippee leader Abbie Hoffman.

Under these conditions, what happens to protest? The answer seems to be that it may very well be blunted. The general public may mistake form for substance and believe that grievances have received considerate attention; key leaders may be siphoned off, or both. On another level, protest may dissolve into mere rhetoric and posturing. Professor Robert Brustein has noted the extraordinary freedom of expression of social critics who have constant access to the platforms of establishment theatres, presses, and airwaves. But he has also observed that "freedom of this kind ends no wars and fills no bellies"; to the victims of political and economic injustice, free speech is simply no substitute for their felt needs. As political scientist Philip Green has said, "There is a wide gap between having one's views tolerated and having them consulted; 'free speech' is *not* participation."[1] The end result is what Brustein describes as "our culturally open, politically closed society"—a society open to protest but

---

[1] Philip Green, "Does Disobedience Mean Anarchy?" *The New York Times Book Review* (February 22, 1970), p. 43.

seemingly immune to genuine social change. The danger, as Brustein makes clear, is that protest may become an extension of theatre, a substitute for action.[2]

*   *   *

In the first selection of this reader, Andrew Kopkind deals with this problem. If the process of co-optation makes protest respectable, it may just as easily frustrate protest by creating the illusion of change. After all, someone might observe, has not Mrs. Martin Luther King, Jr., received honorary degrees and has not the black legislator from Georgia, Julian Bond, become a very popular campus speaker? And what, too, of the number of blacks in the fields of entertainment and athletics?

The jump from here to the example of Lee Trevino is a short one. His success story seems to offer proof that American ideals are still reflections of reality, and that the "American Dream" is indeed available to the individual who seeks to realize it. Trevino, just like dozens of black athletes, is supposedly symbolic proof that America does not discriminate and that the nation's minorities really have unlimited opportunities. The fact that thousands of youths in urban ghettos would dispute this falls on deaf ears. Why, after all, listen to complaints if there is no reason to complain? Indeed, who except a malcontent would complain? Could Trevino have made $200,000 in Soviet Russia, or Maoist China, or even Mexico? To ask the question is presumably to answer it. This may help to explain why a report in late 1970 by the Education Commission of the United States discovered that only 12 percent of the adults queried had ever attempted to get any law changed, whether by signing a petition, joining an organization, writing letters to officials, or actively demonstrating. In fact, the study showed that less than half (49 percent) of the adults surveyed could point to any specific law that was unfair or unjust.

This continuing faith in the ideals of equality of opportunity and equal treatment under just laws may thus account for much of the general public's aversion to protest. But, as John William Ward points out in his essay, national ideals may also have a different kind of effect. They may, in fact, have given impetus to much of the discontent, and even violence, in the American past. The bloody uprisings in black ghettos during the 1960's were unquestionably—despite some charges of alien influence—very much outgrowths of American ideals; the ideals helped to raise expectations which, unrealized, exploded into anger at a system seemingly built upon deceit. Moreover, as Ward suggests, the national faith in individualism may also be a source of considerable unrest because of the psychic burdens that it imposes.

[2] Robert Brustein, "Revolution as Theatre," *The New Republic* (March 14, 1970), pp. 13–17.

1 *The problems of protest*

The ideals in which most Americans take pride may, ironically, help to produce the protest that angers many Americans and makes them fearful of the collapse of law and order. "We must," Ward concludes, "act on our ideals, or change our minds."

This raises a number of questions. What indications are there that Americans are genuinely committed to ideals such as equality of opportunity and social justice? To what extent does the nation seem genuinely open to social change? How accurate is the description of a culturally open, but politically closed society? Does America, like a sponge, absorb protest only to return to its original shape? How should one view the process of co-optation? Is it basically a substitute for change, a way in which society experiences change vicariously? Or quite the opposite, is it part of a process that in the long run produces profound social change? Might not co-optation be a way of using the system against itself? If so, who, in the subtle process of co-optation, really has the last laugh? Is co-optation actually little more than a basic ingredient of a viable society that is sufficiently shrewd, resourceful and responsive to adjust and accommodate to new demands and pressures?

Andrew Kopkind

Andrew Kopkind touches upon a
problem that has increasingly plagued
American protest: the immense
capacity of "the system" to co-opt
dissent, giving the illusion of change,
rendering dissent ineffective by
smothering it with attention and
respectability, and turning it into yet
another source of commercialism and
profit. The challenge to American
protest becomes not suppression but,
as Kopkind avers, " 'repressive tolerance'. . . . The dissidents let off steam;
the controllers keep power." Kopkind
is a journalist who has written widely on
American politics and radicalism. After

Protest and the Illusion of Change

a brief career with *Time* magazine, he
served as contributing editor to *The
New Republic* and as Washington
correspondent to *The New Statesman;*
he is an editor of *Hard Times,* now
published as a supplement to *Ramparts.*

Revolution is a serious business. It is not the Dodge Rebellion, the miniskirt revolt, or the [Eugene] McCarthy movement, however beneficial or entertaining those campaigns may have been. People talk now about the coming of the revolution as they would discuss the arrival of the latest hurricane; it is thought to be imminent, or upon us, or just blowing by. But real revolution is a wind of longer passing.

It is at once the most tragic and redeeming social experience. It is what societies do instead of committing suicide, when the alternatives are exhausted and all the connections that bind men's lives in familiar patterns are cut. Death and transfiguration is the ultimate human drama; revolution combines those two acts in a single transcendent scene.

Whatever else may be going on in America, it is not very much of a revolution. Despite some unruliness, a few perilous moments, and a great deal of intramural bickering, the strongest fortresses of "the system" remain in the hands of the same elites that have held power for years. The only change is that the capability of those hands can now be questioned. But Ralph Nader and his irate consumers have hardly dented General Motors. The New Left and the Yippies will find the Cook County Democratic machine still running. All the power of poor people's organizations, community-control projects, and black economic-development schemes have failed to impede the extravagant growth of corporate capitalism at home and abroad in this generation. RAT does not threaten the hegemony of the *New York Times;* Luckies outsell grass; Andrew Cordier still out-ranks Mark Rudd in anybody's hierarchy of power.

By usual definition, revolution means the displacement of the rulers by the ruled, a redress of the imbalance of power in a social system. The classic model—a seizure of the state in violent struggle—is of course unthinkable in America now. Potential revolutionary classes—black people, students, blue-collar workers, hippies—are either ill-placed or ill-disposed for such battle.

If there is a revolutionary program in anyone's head, it involves action along all kinds of fronts to soften the system—by blowing kids' minds, frightening the comfortable classes, organizing the oppressed, questioning the legitimacy of everything. But that would be only a preliminary stage; plans and programs would have to grow out of the experience. The Declaration of Independence detailed tyranny but presented no formula for constitutional democracy. Marx carved up capitalism but laid out only the foggiest conception of a Communist state.

Conventional politics should be the last place to look for revolutionary change, and with only one possible exception—the distressing example of the [George] Wallace campaign—no exercise of electoral politics has carried revolutionary values along with it. As the midnight choo-choo left Alabam', it carried an implausible coalition of rich Goldwaterites, *petit-bourgeois* Birchers, battered blue-collar workers and agonized rednecks. The passengers harangue against the "liberal Establishment," which Wallace identifies quite correctly as the power base of both the Republican and Democratic parties. Wallace supporters may entertain fantasies of replacing the Establishment's welfare bureaucrats, bankers, foundation managers, internationalist businessmen and union leaders with their own numbers. If they could do it, the result would be a revolution of a kind—a kind of American Fascism. But the Wallace movement is strongest where America is least vulnerable—in the decaying rural South or the shrinking near-slums of the blue-collar North—and it can amount only to a permanent (if permanently dangerous) minority.

Across the center spread, the left margin of politics is even thinner. The [Eugene] McCarthy campaign was conceived (if not plotted) as an *anti*-revolutionary reform movement, to "channel protest" into the two-party system, to strengthen the Democratic liberals, and to replace evil and incompetent managers with humane and wise ones—at the head of the same machine.

The effort had many advantages: It gave large numbers of people the opportunity to *fail* in a last "test" of the only political methods they believed effective. Most of those people may never go further than a "peace" campaign within a major party, but they are now concerned enough to set themselves up as a buffer zone between the stern forces of law-and-order and the radicals. But throughout its long winter and spring, the campaign never developed the first plan or promise for dismantling and restructuring the institutions which give rise to white racism and militarism—the effects of which the McCarthyites so clearly disliked.

Understandably, they focused their attack on segregation and unequal opportunity, and on the war in Vietnam. But the war which they sought to end is only the deformed child of too-healthy parents: the Joint Chiefs and the defense intellectuals, Lockheed Aircraft and IBM, the Rand Corporation and the AFL–CIO, the nice and the nasty, the actively conniving and the merely complicit. Sterilization of the parents might have been revolutionary; abortion of the child could not be.

Segregation and unequal opportunity are only expressions of the racist element in all aspects of national life. It may have nothing to do with personal prejudice. The fact that in most big cities most domestic maids are black is a fact of a racist economy in a class society, whether the mistress of the house is a member of a civil-rights organization or not. The certainty that black children will receive inferior educations is determined by racism. Urban riots, however "unpolitical" they may seem, are responses to racist political structures. Though they may be unaware of the relationship, the affluent suburbanites built their comfortable homes and careers at the expense of those in the ghettos. The suburbs get better public services, cheaper insurance, convenient domestic labor, classy culture, good education and political power—and the slums lose out in "competition." To "revolutionize" the role of blacks would require commitments of resources, sacrifices of status and the drastic reallocation of priorities which politics as currently constituted is unable to make. "Socialism" would perhaps be a beginning, but only that. Obviously, McCarthy was far even from that first step, as the Robert Kennedy campaign—with all its "urbanism"—was, too.

The only reallocation of power which the McCarthy campaign seemed to propose was in favor of the suburban liberal "New Class." That would have been small change indeed: The same people have been accumulating power for thirty years. If they are to get even bigger slices of the power pie, they will have to take it away from those without the means to hold on: blacks, poor whites, the underemployed. For example, as McCarthy's well-educated liberals (the candidate's own characterization of his supporters) asserted power in Democratic organizations, they preempted political space from the militant and poor of both races, who had either to stay in subservient positions or else drift into fractional and irrelevant sects. The left is much less cohesive today than it was a year ago, in some measure because the McCarthy campaign took power—in terms of money, energy, publicity and numbers of people—away from the racial base. Last winter, there were perhaps hundreds of thousands of woebegone liberals ready to desert the Democratic party for more militant political action outside the narrow two-party framework. McCarthy successfully stopped the movement of that base—perhaps only temporarily—by giving it creative play therapy in Democratic primaries. But we have only to sniff the air to notice that McCarthy did nothing to reduce the power of the right.

It is where the conscientious and well-surrounded McCarthy liberals find themselves in the social universe—not what they fancy in fashion and style—that gives them an unrevolutionary role. With the best intentions and warmest sympathies, they will work to keep control of resources in their own hands. In a wholly different context, Marx described the same mentality 120 years ago:

> They desire the existing state of society minus its revolutionary and disintegrating elements. . . . They naturally conceive the world in which [they are] supreme to be the best; and they develop this comfortable conception into various more or less complete systems. . . . They wish for a *bourgeoisie* without a proletariat.

Replace the old-fashioned terminology with trendier words, and it is easy to understand McCarthy's list of putative cabinet members: Rockefeller, Gardner, Thomas Watson and the rest of that able crew were aboard. None could be counted exactly revolutionary cadre, and McCarthy had the wit and sensitivity to deny a revolutionary role for himself. But his campaigners were less discreet. Last spring, they were talking about "the McCarthy revolution," which had accomplished, among other things, the termination of the war and a "bloodless coup" in the White House. What they forgot was that even if McCarthy, by some miracle, had won the Democratic nomination, the same interest groups and classes would stay in power. That may be all right, but it's not revolution.

The art of holding onto power is the American system's special grace. The trick is to make reform seem so tantalizingly close as to dull the edge of militancy and force the purest revolutionaries into the peripheries of political action. Dissent has a political function as well as a constitutional position; it legitimizes and supports the status quo. Only the dumbest establishments practice open suppression of dissidence; what Marcuse calls "repressive tolerance" is far more effective: In practice, it is the art of letting dissident minorities say whatever they please within a system loaded in favor of the most powerful elites. The dissidents let off steam; the controllers keep power. A shirt-sleeve walk through a riot area works better than a police charge—and for the same ultimate objective.

America is cleverest when it protects its oppositions and neutralizes them: by buying them (War on Poverty), channeling them (Clean for Gene) or marketing them (turn on with cars). The last method is the most fun—and the most profitable. To a society that is suffering from too much internalized repression already, the sale of vicarious liberation can bring a bonanza in cash returns. Radicals, hippies and "black-power extremists" have only to sit by the phone or collect their mail these days while the invitations pour in. Newspaper syndicates are searching for lefties to run alongside their regular columnists on the editorial pages of a hundred provincial papers. The mass-circulation magazines can't seem to get enough of SDS. Hearst is publishing a head magazine for the straights. The performing rebel is urged to tell it like it is and do his own thing —*pour épater les bourgeois.* Media fortunes will be made or broken on a company's ability to swing with the liberation movements. It is all proof enough that this is not a revolutionary situation; if it were, Tom Hayden wouldn't be on television, Country Joe & the Fish would be underground, and Eldridge Cleaver would be shot.

Sometimes it seems that if Tom Hayden, Country Joe and Eldridge Cleaver did not exist, America would have had to invent them. And so— in a way—America *did* invent them: to satisfy revolutionary longings. They are aphrodisiacs in the air-conditioning system, hallucinogens in the water supply. . . .

John William Ward

Protest and the Ambiguous Role of American Ideals

John William Ward comes to grips with a major question: how is it possible for Americans to reconcile the image of themselves as a peaceful people with the grim historical fact that the nation has suffered a high rate of social violence? The problem, as Ward makes clear, has important implications for American protest. If Americans see themselves as products of a free, egalitarian society, it becomes most difficult for them to understand violent protest except as a break from American tradition and an act of insanity. Violent protest becomes, in effect, un-American. Ward, however, is skeptical. He posits that such violence actually is deeply rooted in American ideals. Ward is a well-known student of American culture. He is the author of *Andrew Jackson, Symbol for an Age,* and a collection of essays, *Red, White and Blue.*

O n July 23, 1892, Alexander Berkman, an immigrant Russian Jew, idealist, and anarchist, forced his way into the Pittsburgh office of Henry Clay Frick in order to kill him. The assassination was, in the anarchist tradition, to be an *attentat,* a political deed of violence to awaken the consciousness of the people against their oppressors. Frick, manager of the Carnegie steel works while Andrew Carnegie was on vacation in Scotland, had crushed the Amalgamated Association of Iron and Steel Workers in the infamous Homestead strike, which ended in a fatal battle between Pinkertons and strikers. Berkman was there to continue the struggle between the workers and their capitalist oppressors. He failed. He failed to kill Frick. He failed to arouse the workers. The outcome, instead, was a book, a classic in the literature of autobiography, *Prison Memoirs of an Anarchist. . . .*

Berkman forces a question on us. Does the terrible violence which has characterized American culture throughout its history, along with our inability to understand it, derive from our best and noblest ideals about the meaning and the promise of American life? Is violence, rather than some mad aberration, an intrinsic and understandable part of America? . . .

When Berkman went to prison, he discovered that no one could understand why he had tried to kill Frick, not even the Homestead workers

From John William Ward, "Violence, Anarchy, and Alexander Berkman," *The New York Review of Books* (November 5, 1970), pp. 25–30. Reprinted by permission of the author.

there in prison themselves. Other prisoners thought there must have been some personal quarrel between Berkman and Frick, or some "business misunderstanding." Or they thought Berkman was simply crazy. Not only those in prison. The union in Homestead immediately dissociated itself from Berkman's act, and sent condolences to Frick with the message that they prayed for his speedy recovery.

But Berkman, in his letter to Emma [Goldman], did not simply resign himself to misunderstanding. He understood with remarkable precision why conditions in America made all the difference.

> In Russia, where political oppression is popularly felt, such a deed would be of great value. But the scheme of political subjection is more subtle in America. And though McKinley was the chief representative of our modern slavery, he could not be considered in the light of a direct and immediate enemy of the people; while in an absolutism, the autocrat is visible and tangible. The real despotism of republican institutions is far deeper, more insidious, because it rests on the popular delusion of self-government and independence. That is the subtle source of democratic tyranny, and, as such, it cannot be reached with a bullet.

By comparing Russia and the United States, Berkman does not, of course, say that there is no oppression in the United States and that there is no need for conflict, but that the real repression in American society, what Berkman names "despotism," derives from the generally shared belief that one *is* independent, one *is* self-governing. Berkman points, in other words, to the ideology which is immune to revolution and violent action, which cannot be "reached with a bullet."

. . . . Berkman is not saying that violence has no place in American life. He is saying that violence cannot be understood by Americans because of the ideology which holds captive even those who are the oppressed. The American creed of an open, egalitarian society means that there can be no violent protest against the conditions of American society because there can be no real cause for it. The act of violence cannot be understood. It must be the act of a deranged and mad individual. It escapes historical understanding.

To say that because of our ideals violence should not happen here is not to say that it does not happen here. Statistically, both in individual and collective acts of violence, the United States far surpasses any other Western society. In the straightforward language of the final report of the National Commission on the Causes and Prevention of Violence, "The United States is the clear leader among modern stable democratic nations in its rates of homicide, assault, rape, robbery, and it is at least among the highest in the incidence of group violence and assassination." In that context, the use of the word "stable" may seem rather heavy-handed irony, but it points to a curious aspect of the phenomenon of violence in America: the violence which has marked our history has rarely been directed against the state. Our political institutions have been little affected by it. Which is what Berkman pointed out: violence has had no political meaning in American consciousness. Berkman hints at why this is so: Americans believe deeply that they enjoy self-government and personal independence.

When Americans insist that American society is free, they generally mean that American society is a society in which each individual, irrespective of extrinsic associations of family, neighborhood, class, race, or ethnic origin, is free to make of himself what he can. More is involved than classical liberalism or laissez-faire capitalism. As Emerson put it, "Government will be adamantine without any governor." That was the millennial promise of America, a benign anarchism in which each individual was to be the bearer of his own destiny and society no more than a collection of individual wills. It was that very dream which drew Berkman to America: "There, beyond the ocean, was the land of noble achievement, a glorious free country, where men walked erect in the full stature of manhood."

A society which believes that it is the result of the actions of free and equal and self-reliant individuals has, logically, no reason to suppose that the state and the institutions of society are important. To the degree one believes that America is a uniquely free society, that each person is unencumbered by forces beyond the determination of his own personality, to the degree such an ideal has power over one's mind and imagination, there is no way to understand violence except as irrational and aberrant. Our difficulty in understanding violence in America is, in part at least, a consequence of our insistence that ours is a society of equality and opportunity and individual freedom. To ask questions about the reality of violence would force us to ask questions about the reality of our ideals.

Furthermore, our ideology, to the degree it is believed in and acted upon, leads to intense frustration which easily spills over into violent behavior when the social situation, the daily, lived experience of actual people, blocks and prevents them from acting out what they are told is ideally possible. After the ghetto riots in Watts and Newark and Detroit, a study was made of those who could be identified as participants. In the Detroit study, blacks who were actors in the riot, that is, those who were apprehended in overt acts from breaking a window to sniping, were asked whether they believed that if one had sufficient will and desire he could make of himself what he wanted in American society. A majority of those ghetto blacks said yes. There is a fact. What is one to make of it?

Not too much, perhaps, without knowing more. Was it a white man or a black man who asked the question? The blacks who answered were in the hands of the police and might well have wanted to assure everyone of their benign disposition toward American society. But to accept the fact on its face, one conclusion is that the most aggressive blacks were precisely those who believed they were free to seize the advantages of American life and, when blocked from doing so, reacted with rage and violence. One sociologist put it, as sociologists like to put it, that violence varies inversely with the presence of avenues to status and power, and avenues of legitimate modes of protest.

At yet a lower level, as Herman Melville put it, our ideals and values are even more deeply involved in the high incidence of violence in America. The traditional American emphasis on individualism and self-determination entails a weakening of institutional forms of restraint with the consequence of a relatively high statistical incidence of aberrant behavior. To put it paradoxically, a liberal, free society must be a repressive society: Freedom from external restraint means that the individual must internalize values of the culture, and restrain himself. He must be, as we say, self-governing; he must repress his antisocial impulses in order to remain free.

A society such as ours, which increasingly rejects the sanctions of tradition, the family, the church, and the power of the state, necessarily must create the kind of personality who is self-governing, self-restraining, self-repressive. The founding fathers, following the Roman model, defined the essential quality as virtue; Emerson called it character; the Protestant evangelical tradition named it benevolence. The tradition is a long one, and we may respond warmly to some of its phrases, but we should not in our self-congratulation ignore the enormous psychic burden such an ideal places upon the individual. Until we reach the millennium of American democratic hopes, we must accept the probable instability of our society, especially when it denies the opportunity and self-respect which its ideology constantly celebrates.

Most interestingly, the rejection of violence as somehow un–American blinds us to the forms of violence, both official and private, which have in fact dominated American history. Consider the occasion of Berkman's deed: the Carnegie Steel Company imported a private army of three hundred Pinkertons, the *condottieri* of industrial warfare in the late nineteenth century. The company held back its ultimatum to labor until it completed an order for steel plate for the United States Navy, whose power was needed to shield American commercial expansion. A lynch mob, after Berkman's assassination attempt, pillaged and destroyed a utopian anarchist community outside Pittsburgh. Finally, the state militia, welcomed by the Homestead workers who believed that the state was a neutral umpire, broke the strike and escorted scabs back to work. Such particulars support an important generalization: violence has been used again and again to support the structure of authority in American society. We are only puzzled when violence is used to attack that structure.

Our ideals are involved even here. The insistence that all men are free and equal leads to the curious consequence of a mass conformity and a mood of intolerance for dissent in any form. Tocqueville provided the classic statement, which still holds, that the energetic individualism and the tyranny of the majority in America both derived from the ideal of equality. The necessary obverse of the belief that "I'm as good as you are,"

13

is acceptance of the fact that "You are as good as I am." The basis of one's own self-trust and self-sufficiency must be extended to all the equal others in society. So, if one is in a minority, one has no claim against a tyrannous majority. The very ideal of the equal worth of every man, which promises a world of manly, independent, and free men, perversely leads to the mind and mood of the mass man who is intolerant of any deviation from what he thinks. That majority may be silent, but it has throughout American history been ready always to wreak its own repressive violence on the rash individual who dares to challenge it or call into question the ideology which creates and sustains it.

The fault, as Berkman would have it, lies in American consciousness: "that is the subtle source of democratic tyranny, and, as such, it cannot be reached with a bullet." . . . . We have failed to see that the ugly violence of our society is not an aberration of an otherwise sound and healthy society, but the unintended and unforeseen consequence of our most cherished ideals. We must act on our ideals, or change our minds. . . .

Interpretations of the problems of
protest in America necessarily involve
certain assumptions about the nature
of the national experience. Literature
on the subject of protest thus often
reflects larger historiographical trends
regarding American history generally.
For example, while Andrew Kopkind
and others in the 1960's described a
system that maintained itself through
a process of co-optation, historians in
the immediate post-World War II
period believed that the system
flourished through a process of
consensus. The politics of consensus
was clearly less invidious than the
politics of co-optation.

The so-called "consensus school" of
historians, which in the 1950's
profoundly influenced interpretations
of the American past, stressed the
harmony, shared values, lack of
divisive ideologies and class conflict,
and continuity of American
development. The focus was primarily
on agreement rather than disagreement,
on contentment rather than discontent,
and on pragmatic adjustment rather
than protest. Helpful summaries and
analyses of "consensus" history appear
in chapter 12 ("Conflict and Consensus
in American History") of Richard
Hofstadter's *The Progressive Historians*
(New York, 1969); John Higham,
"The Cult of the 'American
Consensus,'" *Commentary* (February,
1959), 93–100; and J. Rogers
Hollingsworth, "Consensus and
Continuity in Recent American
Historical Writing," *South Atlantic
Quarterly*, 61 (Winter, 1962), 40–50.

The shocks and anger of the 1960's
evoked questions about the genuineness
of the American "consensus." Partly as
a result of this, historians began to
focus more on the extent to which
conflict and discontent had marked
the nation's past. In a stimulating essay,

THE PROBLEMS
OF
PROTEST

"The Confinements of Consensus,"
Northwestern Tri-Quarterly, No. 6
(1966), 155–58, Robert Wiebe
suggested that much of the apparent
lack of disagreement in American
history might be accounted for by the
gulf that separated groups rather than
by a consensus that joined them: "The
absence of ideological debate, hard
political battle, and armed conflict may
indicate social distance and power
differentials so great that they preclude
any direct confrontation." In an equally
insightful essay, Stephen Thernstrom,
"Urbanization, Migration and Social
Mobility in Late Nineteenth-Century
America," in Barton J. Bernstein (ed.),
*Towards a New Past: Dissenting Essays
in American History* (New York,
1968), 158–75, offered explanations
for the relative absence of working-
class protest in the United States. He
pointed out, in part, that the great
amount of physical mobility in the late
nineteenth century did not necessarily
indicate social and economic success;
indeed, a bottom social layer of "people
who were least successful and who had
the greatest grievances" may have
comprised a floating group of
"permanent transients" who were
clearly discontented but never in one
place long enough to "discover a
sense of common identity and common
grievance."

By the end of the 1960's, there was
a growing literature concerning
discontent, protest and conflict in
American history. For analyses of
one aspect of this literature—that of

the so-called "New Left" historians—see Irwin Unger, "The 'New Left' and American History: Some Recent Trends in United States Historiography," *American Historical Review,* 72 (July, 1967), 1237–63, and C. Vann Woodward, "Wild in the Stacks," *The New York Review of Books* (August 1, 1968).

Richard Hofstadter, author of some of the most significant "consensus" interpretations, concluded by the end of the 1960's that "consensus history . . . no longer seems as satisfactory to me as it did ten or twenty years ago." He noted, for one thing, that it did not explain the racial, ethnic, and religious conflict that marked American life.

One product of Hofstadter's rethinking of the process of America's development is a superb essay, "Reflections on Violence in the United States," in Hofstadter and Michael Wallace (eds.), *American Violence: A Documentary History* (New York, 1970), 3–43. "What is most exceptional about the Americans," he wrote, "is not in the voluminous record of their violence, but their extraordinary ability, in the face of that record, to persuade themselves that they are among the best-behaved and best-regulated of peoples." Hofstadter's essay, like John William Ward's article reprinted here, probes astutely into the more violent aspects of American discontent.

THE PROTEST
OF
DISCRIMINATION

In the 1960's America experienced the shocks of what sociologist Herbert J. Gans has called "the 'equality' revolution." From the black ghettos of Newark and Detroit to the Mexican-American barrios of the Southwest, from demonstrations of Women's Liberation groups at the Atlantic City Miss America contests to a parade of the Gay Liberation movement down New York's Sixth Avenue, from cries of "student power" on college campuses and in high-school classrooms to policemen demanding recognition as professionals, from Indians objecting to the policies of the Bureau of Indian Affairs to Italian-Americans organizing to end stereotyped treatment in the mass media, the Sixties were alive with protest against discriminatory treatment.

As Gans has emphasized, the social protest of the Sixties was less concerned with poverty than "with *inequality,* with the pervasive inequities remaining in American life."[1] While the 1930's witnessed the most dramatic of the twentieth-century upheavals of labor and agriculture, the 1960's provided the setting for a growing concern with *non*economic questions involving the quality and control of one's life, the right of autonomy of neighborhoods and groups, and the redistribution of privileges traditionally limited to the "top dogs" in society.

Although the selections in Section II focus for the most part on manifestations of the "equality revolution" of the Sixties, they demonstrate that the roots of such protest run deep into American history. Martin Duberman, for example, sees significant parallels between the quest for "black power" and the earlier struggles of abolitionists and anarchists. J. Herman Blake reaches back to the early 1800's to trace the development of the idea of black nationalism. He dates its transformation into a mass movement with the establishment of Marcus Garvey's Universal Negro Improvement Association (UNIA) in New York City in 1917, and describes how Black Muslims subsequently sketched out new patterns of militance among black Americans. An important element in the growth of Garvey's UNIA, the Black Muslims, and organizations such as

[1] Herbert J. Gans, "The 'Equality' Revolution," *The New York Times Magazine* (November 3, 1968), p. 36.

the Urban League (founded in 1911) has been the largely urban base of membership and support. Michael Lewis's essay probes into the role of the city in the development of twentieth-century black protest, and places the landmark March on Washington Movement of the early 1940's in historical perspective. In the article, "You've Come a Long Way, Baby," Jane Seitz and Connie Brown point out the relationship of the early women's rights movement to abolitionism, the significance of the famous Seneca Falls convention of 1848, the "new growth of feminism" that followed the Civil War, and the strengths and weaknesses of the suffragettes.

While the fact of such earlier protests is a matter of historic record, it has been, paradoxically, seldom a part of public memory. In fact, perhaps one of the most subtle forms of discrimination for a vast range of groups has been their omission from treatments of the American past. As historic entities they have been for the most part invisible, or, in the case of the Indians, visible only as stereotypes who, in the words of Hollywood's John Wayne, "were selfishly trying to keep it [land] for themselves."

School literature and history books have traditionally contained the names and accomplishments of Anglo-Saxon males. In 1971 a committee within the Organization of American Historians reported that textbooks covering 99 percent of the college market almost totally ignored women; the most extensive coverage in any of the books was only 2 percent. The roles and contributions of black Americans also received almost no attention—a fact which inspired cries for black studies programs and courses in Afro-American history and literature. Professor Michael Novak, whose grandparents migrated to America from Slovakia, has recalled that nowhere in his education was there "an attempt to put me in touch with my own history." The results, Novak observes, were feelings "of unimportance, of remoteness, of not having heft enough to count."[2] In such a context, young Chippewa students on a reservation in the 1960's labored to write essays on the subject that the white teacher had assigned them: "Why we are all happy the Pilgrims landed." Stan Steiner, in a selection reprinted here, describes classrooms in which Anglo schoolteachers, seemingly oblivious of the historical identity of Mexican-Americans, insisted upon the "laying on" of Anglo culture. As Steiner shows, in 1968 some 15,000 Chicano students in Los Angeles high schools decided that they had endured such treatment long enough, and they boycotted their classes. Similarly, it was a reaction to the alleged "laying on" of masculine culture that inspired the Gay Activists' Alliance in 1969 to occupy the offices of *Harper's Magazine*.

The eruption of protest against discrimination in the 1960's was unquestionably a result of social pressures that had been building throughout the nation for

[2] Michael Novak, "White Ethnic," *Harper's Magazine*, 243 (September, 1971), p. 45.

years. Yet, there is little doubt that developments of the decade itself brought those pressures to more explosive levels. There was, for example, the impact of the civil rights movement, whose tactics and rhetoric influenced a wide variety of discontented groups. The deeply divisive Vietnam war produced a crisis in national leadership, pointed up problems of national priorities and stirred a deep uneasiness about the national condition. A rapid and sustained economic boom fused with political rhetoric and attention from the mass media to encourage quickly rising expectations. As expectations rose, there was a growing awareness of the gap between them and social realities. Statistics showed that important social changes were taking place. There were increases, for instance, in the percentage of nonwhites in better paying jobs, in university classrooms, on police departments, and in important political offices. But to nonwhites mired in urban ghettos, government reservations, or migrant labor camps, the pace of change had little direct effect, smacked of tokenism, and was too little too late.

Whatever the relative influence of such factors, an important trend began clearly to emerge: many individuals began to experience what Michael Novak describes as an "inner thaw, a willingness to think about feelings heretofore shepherded out of sight."[3] A growing concern with self-discovery, with defining one's roots and purposes, became a dominant theme of the period. It marked the dance patterns in which the individual could break from his partner and "do his own thing," the cinema in which protagonists such as those in *Easy Rider* went in search of America and their place in it, and the novel in which more and more writers portrayed the desperate struggle of the individual trying to save himself from a paranoid world of dehumanizing, conspiratorial forces. In this context, when author Robert Penn Warren asked in 1964, "Who Speaks for the Negro?", the ever-louder reply was that the black man spoke for himself—a fact that certainly underlay cries for "Black Power" and black studies programs. Similarly, one thousand Chinese students attended a 1969 conference at Berkeley on "Yellow Power"; and women who for years had felt a vague uneasiness and dissatisfaction with "Momism" and the confines of the home, found new meaning in the Women's Liberation movement.

Peter Collier's essay in this section illustrates very well the quest for self-discovery and the mounting sense of one's rights that galvanized so much of the protest of the 1960's. Collier's article traces the path by which a Shoshone-Bannock girl became a participant in what has been called "the last, continuing Indian War." Her road to self-discovery eventually involved her in a student strike at Berkeley in behalf of a proposed program to study Native Americans and, later, in the much-publicized occupation of Alcatraz Island, a superlative example of symbolic protest in which the Indians

[3] Novak, "White Ethnic," p. 44.

established a Bureau of Caucasian Affairs, and offered to buy the abandoned federal prison for "twenty-four dollars in glass beads and red cloth."

When one set of individuals asserted claims, others were quick to follow. If blacks had long confronted outside control of their lives, what about the "student as nigger"? Or, as one homosexual stated, "I think what Gays are asking today is the same that Negroes, Mexicans, Indians, women and other minorities have said. This country claims a national basis of equality. It's about time we got it. We don't want you to take a homosexual to dinner. You don't have to socialize with us, just don't harass us."[4] By the early 1970's, a "Gray Power" movement was underway, seeking "power for the aged." A retired United Presbyterian church member, Margaret "Maggie" Kuhn, mobilized the "Gray Panthers" and advocated demonstrations, sit-ins, and other protests against "our oppressive, paternalistic society [which] wants to keep the elderly out of the way, playing bingo and shuffleboard." To those people who might find the group offensive, she replied: "They can go back and play in their 'golden age clubs' which are nothing but glorified playpens."[5]

Invariably, when some groups felt that they were under pressure to make concessions, the patterns of protest broadened. White ethnic groups of non-English-speaking background joined "backlash" protests against the demands of black Americans that threatened to come primarily at their expense. The concern of some black males with the assertion of black manhood struck some feminists as yet another example of male chauvinism that relegated, in this case, black women to inferior roles. In the same way, homosexuals suspected that the attempt of some feminists to disassociate Women's Liberation from any links with Gay Liberation was only one more expression of assumptions that had made social lepers of homosexuals.

"We like to think," historian Bernard A. Weisberger has written, "that out of the chaffering among factions, justice will emerge—a kind of laissez-faire credo of politics."[6] There are a number of questions concerning the extent to which such jostling among groups indeed produces justice. Does a system that sees competing groups balancing off each other, in fact, operate to the advantage of those groups who pack the most muscle? What, then, of the chances of those groups who find themselves in the weakest position? Should they receive help, and from whom? If government comes to their aid, is this a discriminatory act against other groups, or is some governmental assistance necessary to offset built-in discriminations that load the contest in favor of the well-off or largest

---

[4] Myra MacPherson, "Ulrich vs. the Pentagon: A Homosexual Fights Back," *The Washington Post* (October 10, 1971), p. E6.
[5] *Bloomington Pantagraph* (May 21 , 1972).
[6] Bernard A. Weisberger, "A Vote for Bryan," *Book World* (June 6, 1971), p. 5.

groups? What of the role of coalitions? Bayard Rustin, a leading black spokesman, has argued that since blacks alone cannot force concessions from a white majority, they must look to the white community for alliances. What of the response to Rustin of those blacks who argue that such alliances will inevitably assume the shape wanted by whites and will invariably work to the disadvantage of blacks?

There is also the difficult problem of how one defines discrimination. What, for example, is one to make of the Roper Poll in mid-1971 in which 69 percent of the female respondents denied that "women are discriminated against and treated as second-class citizens"? How does this square with such continuing phrases in school readers as "boys invent things, girls use what boys invent"? Or are women, in effect, first-class citizens because a solid majority apparently think they are? What, too, of the thousands of "nigger," "Polack," "greaser," "dumb broad," or "queer" jokes that are part of the nation's sub-literature? Is it merely a matter of humor (since presumably jokes always come at someone's expense), or deep down is it an instance of discrimination? Is it merely a matter of timing and intent? Or are there some things that are too serious to laugh about?

In what sense can social policies serve as deterrents to discrimination? Or are there limits to what can be expected of social policies? If there are limits, and the struggle is turned back entirely to competing communities and groups, are we not left with the limitations of that "laissez-faire credo of politics" to which Weisberger refers? Are such limitations preferable to those of other alternatives? In American history (during the Progressive era, for example) there have been several important efforts to reduce the confusion and friction of such jockeying among groups by taking issues out of politics and turning them over to nonpartisan experts who can presumably settle problems within the quiet confines of panelled rooms more effectively than in the clamorous give-and-take of the political world. But in what ways is this only an apparent solution to problems? Decision-makers may be experts, but are they really nonpartisan? Are the end results merely decisions which reflect, even if inadvertently, the needs and desires of the groups from which the experts come? If so, is this preferable to the "chaos" of contending factions? In what sense does this desire to remove issues from politics reflect an elitist view that is basically suspicious of democratic processes? Is it perhaps better—both in terms of democratic ideals and in terms of long-run settlement of issues—to keep the issue in the public arena with the full realization that a host of competing groups will seek to promote their own interests, often at the expense of others? Does the position taken on such questions tell a great deal about one's basic views on democracy and the people?

How, in sum, can and should a society handle the protest of discrimination?

Martin Duberman

Black Power and the American Radical Tradition

Few slogans in America's racial history have been as emotionally loaded as that of "black power." Martin Duberman places the term in historical context, stressing that it should come as no shock to a nation that has traditionally relied on organized power as the means to success. The extent to which black

power assumes militant proportions will depend largely, Duberman feels, on the response of white America. As a possible gauge to that response, and as a means of speculating on the development and future of the Black Power movement, he suggests parallels with two earlier examples of radical protest: abolitionism and anarchism. Duberman has written prize-winning biographies of two well-known abolitionists, Charles Francis Adams and James Russell Lowell, has edited a book on American abolitionism, and published a collection of wide-ranging essays. He is also a playwright and drama critic.

The slogan "black power" has caused widespread confusion and alarm. This is partly due to a problem inherent in language: words necessarily reduce complex attitudes or phenomena to symbols which, in their abbreviation, allow for a variety of interpretations. Stuart Chase has reported that in the thirties, when the word "fascism" was on every tongue, he asked one hundred persons from various walks of life what the word meant and got one hundred widely differing definitions. And in 1953, when *The Capitol Times* of Madison, Wisconsin, asked two hundred people "What is a Communist?" not only was there no agreement, but five out of every eight admitted they couldn't define the term at all. So it is with "black power." Its definition depends on whom you ask, when you ask, where you ask, and, not least, who does the asking. . . .

I

If "black power" means only that Negroes should organize politically and economically in order to heighten self-regard and to exert maximum pressure, then the new philosophy would be difficult to fault, for it would be based on the truism that minorities must argue from positions of strength rather than weakness, that the majority is far more likely to make concessions to power than to justice. To insist that Negro Americans seek their goals as individuals and solely by appeals to conscience and "love,"

From Martin Duberman, "Black Power in America," *Partisan Review,* 35 (Winter, 1968). Copyright © 1968 by Martin Duberman. Reprinted by permission of the Sterling Lord Agency, Inc. Footnotes have been omitted.

when white Americans have always relied on group association and organized power to achieve theirs, would be yet one more form of discrimination. Moreover, when whites decry SNCC's declaration that it is tired of turning the other cheek, that henceforth it will actively resist white brutality, they might do well to remember that they have always considered self-defense acceptable behavior for themselves; our textbooks, for example, view the refusal of the revolutionaries of 1776 to "sit supinely by" as the very essence of manhood.

Although black power makes good sense when defined to mean further organization and cooperation within the Negro community, the results which are likely to follow in terms of political leverage can easily be exaggerated. The impact is likely to be greatest at the county level in the deep South and in the urban ghettos of the North. In this regard, the Black Panther party of Lowndes County, Alabama, is the prototype.

There are roughly twelve thousand Negroes in Lowndes County and three thousand whites, but until 1964 not a single Negro was registered to vote, while white registration had reached 118 percent of those eligible. Negro life in Lowndes County, as Andrew Kopkind has graphically recounted, was—and is—wretched. The median family income for whites is $4,400, for Negroes $935; Negro farmhands earn $3 to $6 a day; half of the Negro women who work are maids in Montgomery (which requires a forty- to sixty-mile daily round trip) at $4 a day; few Negroes have farms, since 90 percent of the land is owned by about eighty-five white families; the one large industrial plant in the area, the new Dan River Mills textile factory, will employ Negroes only in menial capacities; most Lowndes Negroes are functional illiterates, living in squalor and hopelessness.

The Black Panther party set out to change all this. The only path to change in Lowndes, and in much of the deep South, is to "take over the courthouse," the seat of local power. For generations the courthouse in Lowndes has been controlled by the Democratic party; indeed there is no Republican party in the county. Obviously it made little sense for SNCC organizers to hope to influence the local Democrats; no white moderates existed and no discussion of integration was tolerated. To have expected blacks to "bore from within," as [Stokely] Carmichael has said, would have been "like asking the Jews to reform the Nazi party."

Instead, Carmichael and his associates established the separate Black Panther party. After months of work, SNCC organizers (with almost no assistance from federal agents) registered enough Negroes to hope for a numerical majority in the county. But in the election of November, 1966, the Black Panther party was defeated, for a variety of reasons—which include Negro apathy or fear and white intimidation. Despite this defeat, the possibility of a better life for Lowndes County Negroes does at last exist, and, should the Black Panther party come into power at some future point, that possibility could become a reality.

Nonetheless, even on the local level and even in the deep South,

Lowndes County is not representative. In Alabama, for example, only eleven of the state's sixty-seven counties have black majorities. Where these majorities do not exist, the only effect independent black political parties are likely to have is to consolidate the whites in opposition. Moreover, and more significantly, many of the basic ills from which Negro Americans suffer—inadequate housing, inferior education, limited job opportunities—are national phenomena and require national resources to overcome. Whether these resources will be allocated in sufficient amounts will depend, in turn, on whether a national coalition can be formed to exert pressure on the federal government. Such a coalition—of civil rights activists, church groups, campus radicals, New Class technocrats, un-skilled, un-unionized laborers, and certain elements in organized labor, like the United Auto Workers or the United Federation of Teachers— would, of course, necessitate Negro-white unity, a unity that Black Power at least temporarily rejects.

The answer that Black Power advocates give to the "coalition argu-ment" is of several pieces. The only kind of progressive coalition which can exist in this country, they say, is the mild, liberal variety which pro-duced the civil rights legislation of recent years. And that kind of legisla-tion has proven itself grossly inadequate. Its chief result has been to lull white liberals into believing that the major battles have been won, whereas in fact there has been almost no change, or change for the worse, in the daily lives of most blacks.

The evidence for this last assertion is persuasive. Despite the Supreme Court decision of 1954, almost 85 percent of school-age Negroes in the South still sit in segregated classrooms. Unemployment among Negroes has actually gone up in the past ten years. Title VI of the 1964 Civil Rights Act, with its promising provision for the withdrawal of federal funds in cases of discrimination, has been used in limited fashion in regard to the schools but not at all in regard to other forms of unequal treatment, such as segregated hospital facilities. Under the 1965 Voting Rights Act, only about forty federal registrars have been sent into the South, though many areas have less than the 50 percent registration figure which would legally warrant intervention. In short, the legislation produced by the liberal coalition of the early Sixties has turned out to be little more than federally approved tokenism, a continuation of paper promises and an-cient inequities.

If a *radical* coalition could be formed in this country—that is, one will-ing to scrutinize in depth the failings of our system, to suggest structural, not piecemeal, reforms, to see them executed with sustained rather than occasional vigor—then black power advocates might feel less need to separate themselves and to concentrate on local, marginal successes. But no responsible observer believes that in the foreseeable future a radical coalition on the left can become the effective political majority in the United States; we will be fortunate if a radical coalition on the right does not. And so, to SNCC and CORE, talk of further cooperation with white liberals is only an invitation to further futility. It is better, they feel, to concentrate on encouraging Negroes everywhere to self-respect and self-help, and in certain local areas, where their numbers warrant it, to try to win actual political power. . . .

The philosophy of black power is thus a blend of varied, in part contending, elements, and it cannot be predicted with any certainty which will assume dominance. But a comparison between the black power movement and the personnel, programs, and fates of earlier radical movements in this country can make some contribution toward understanding its dilemmas and its likely directions.

Any argument based on historical analogy can, of course, become oversimplified and irresponsible. Historical events do not repeat themselves with anything like regularity, for every event is to a large degree embedded in its own special context. An additional danger in reasoning from historical analogy is that in the process we will limit rather than expand our options: by arguing that certain consequences seem always to follow from certain actions and that therefore only a set number of alternatives ever exist, we can prevent ourselves from seeing new possibilities or from utilizing old ones in creative ways. We must be careful, when attempting to predict the future from the past, that in the process we do not straitjacket the present. Bearing these cautions and limitations in mind, we can still gain some insight from a historical perspective. For if there are large variances through time between roughly analogous events, there are also some similarities, and it is these which make comparative study possible and profitable. In regard to black power, I think we gain particular insight by comparing it with the two earlier radical movements of abolitionism and anarchism.

II

The abolitionists represented the left wing of the antislavery movement (a position comparable to the one SNCC and CORE occupy today in the civil rights movement) because they called for an *immediate* end to slavery everywhere in the United States. Most northerners who disapproved of slavery were not willing to go as far or as fast as the abolitionists, preferring instead a more ameliorative approach. The tactic which increasingly won the approval of the northern majority was the doctrine of "nonextension": no further expansion of slavery would be allowed, but the institution would be left alone where it already existed. The principle of nonextension first came into prominence in the late 1840's, when fear developed in the North that territory acquired from our war with Mexico would be made into new slave states. Later the doctrine formed the basis of the Republican party, which in 1860 elected Lincoln to the presidency. The abolitionists, in other words, with their demand for immediate (and uncompensated) emancipation, never became the major channel of northern antislavery sentiment. They always remained a small sect, vilified by slavery's defenders and distrusted even by allies within the antislavery movement.

The parallels between the abolitionists and the current defenders of black power seem to me numerous and striking. It is worth noting, first of all, that neither group started off with so-called extremist positions (the appropriateness of that word being, in any case, dubious). The SNCC of 1968 is not the SNCC formed in 1960; both its personnel and its programs have shifted markedly. SNCC originally grew out of the sit-ins spontaneously begun in Greensboro, North Carolina, by four freshmen at the all-Negro North Carolina Agricultural and Technical College. The sit-in technique spread rapidly through the South, and within a few months the Student Nonviolent Coordinating Committee (SNCC) was formally inaugurated to channel and encourage further activities. At its inception, SNCC's staff was interracial, religious in orientation, committed to the "American Dream," chiefly concerned with winning the right to share more equitably in that dream and optimistic about the possibility of being allowed to do so. SNCC placed its hopes on an appeal to the national conscience, which it expected to arouse by the examples of nonviolence and redemptive love and by the dramatic devices of sit-ins, freedom rides, and protest marches.

The abolitionist movement, at the time of its inception, was similarly benign and sanguine. It, too, placed emphasis on "moral suasion," believing that the first order of business was to bring the inequity of slavery to the country's attention, to arouse the average American's conscience. Once this was done, the Abolitionists felt, discussion could, and would, begin on the particular ways and means best calculated to bring about rapid, orderly emancipation. Some of those abolitionists who later became intransigent defenders of "immediatism"—including William Lloyd Garrison—were willing, early in their careers, to consider plans for preliminary apprenticeship. They were willing, in other words, to settle for gradual emancipation *immediately begun* instead of demanding that freedom itself be instantly achieved.

But this early flexibility received little encouragement. The appeal to conscience and the willingness to engage in debate over means alike brought meager results. In the North the abolitionists encountered massive apathy, in the South massive resistance. Thus thwarted (and influenced as well by the discouraging British experiment with gradualism in the West Indies), the abolitionists abandoned their earlier willingness to consider a variety of plans for prior education and training, and shifted to the position that emancipation had to take place at once and without compensation to the slaveholder. They also began (especially in New England) to advocate such doctrines as "dis-union" and "no-government," positions which directly parallel Black Power's recent advocacy of "separation," and "de-centralization," and which, then as now, produced discord and division within the movement, anger and denunciation without.

But the parallel of paramount importance which I wish to draw between the two movements is their similar passage from "moderation" to "extremism." In both cases there *was* a passage, a shift in attitude and program, and it is essential that this be recognized, for it demonstrates the developmental nature of these—of all—movements for social change. Or, to reduce the point to individuals (and to clichés): "Revolutionaries are not born but made." Garrison did not start his career with the doctrine of immediatism; as a young man, he even had kind words for the American Colonization Society, a group devoted to deporting Negroes to Africa and Central America. And Stokely Carmichael did not begin his ideological voyage with the slogan of black power; as a teenager he was opposed to student sit-ins in the South. What makes a man shift from "reform" to "revolution" is, it seems to me, primarily to be explained by the intransigence or indifference of his society: either society refuses reforms or gives them in the form of tokens. Thus, *if* one views the Garrisons and Carmichaels as extremists, one should at least place the blame for that extremism where it belongs—not on their individual temperaments, their genetic predispositions, but on a society which scorned or toyed with their initial pleas for justice.

III

In turning to the anarchist movement, I think we can see between it and the new turn taken by SNCC and CORE (or, more comprehensively still, by much of the New Left) significant affinities of style and thought. These are largely unconscious and unexplored; I have seen almost no overt references to them either in the movement's official literature or in its unofficial pronouncements. Yet the affinities seem to me important.

But first I should make clear that in speaking of anarchism as if it were a unified tradition I am necessarily oversimplifying. The anarchist movement contained a variety of contending factions, disparate personalities, and differing national patterns. Some anarchists believed in terrorism, others insisted upon nonviolence; some aimed for a communal life based on trade union "syndicates," others refused to bind the individual by organizational ties of any kind; some wished to retain private ownership of property, others demanded its collectivization.

Despite these differing perspectives, all anarchists did share one major premise: a distrust of authority, the rejection of all forms of rule by man over man, especially that embodied in the state but also that exemplified by parent, teacher, lawyer, priest. They justified their opposition in the name of the individual; the anarchists wished each man to develop his "specialness" without the inhibiting interference imposed by authority, be it political or economic, moral or intellectual. This does not mean that the anarchists sanctioned the idea "each against all." On the contrary, they believed that man was a social creature—that is, that he needed the affection and assistance of his fellows—and most anarchist versions of the good life (Max Stirner would be the major exception) involved the idea of community. The anarchists insisted, moreover, that it was not their vision of the future but rather society as presently constructed, which represented chaos; with privilege the lot of the few and misery the lot of the many, society was currently the essence of *dis*order. The anarchists envisioned a system which would substitute mutual aid for mutual exploitation, voluntarism for force, individual decision-making for centralized dictation.

All of these emphases find echo today in SNCC and CORE. The echoes are not perfect: black power, after all, is essentially a call to organization, and its acceptance of politics (and therefore of "governing") would offend a true anarchist—as would such collectivist terms as "black psyche" or "black personality." Nonetheless, the affinities of SNCC and CORE with the anarchist position are substantial.

There is, first of all, the same belief in the possibilities of "community" and the same insistence that community be the product of voluntary association. This in turn reflects a second and still more basic affinity: the distrust of centralized authority. SNCC and CORE's energies, and also those of such other New Left groups as Students for a Democratic Society (SDS), are increasingly channeled into local, community organizing. On this level, it is felt, "participatory" democracy, as opposed to the authoritarianism of "representative" democracy, becomes possible. And in the Black Panther party, where the poor and disinherited do take a direct role in decision-making, theory has become reality (as it has, on the economic side, in the Mississippi-based Poor People's Corporation, which to date has formed some fifteen cooperatives).

Then, too, SNCC and CORE, like the anarchists, talk increasingly of the supreme importance of the individual. They do so, paradoxically, in a rhetoric strongly reminiscent of that long associated with the right. It could be Herbert Hoover (or Booker T. Washington), but in fact it is Rap Brown who now reiterates the Negro's need to stand on his own two feet, to make his own decisions, to develop self-reliance and a sense of self-worth. SNCC may be scornful of present-day liberals and "statism," but it seems hardly to realize that the laissez-faire rhetoric it prefers derives almost verbatim from the classic liberalism of John Stuart Mill.

A final, more intangible affinity between anarchism and the entire New Left, including the advocates of black power, is in the area of personal style. Both hold up similar values for highest praise and emulation: simplicity, spontaneity, "naturalness," and "primitivism." Both reject modes of dress, music, personal relations, even of intoxication, which might be associated with the dominant middle-class culture. Both, finally, tend to link the basic virtues with "the people," and especially with the poor, the downtrodden, the alienated. It is this *Lumpenproletariat*—long kept outside the "system" and thus uncorrupted by its values—who are looked to as a repository of virtue, an example of a better way. The New Left, even while demanding that the lot of the underclasses be improved, implicitly venerates that lot; the desire to cure poverty cohabits with the wish to emulate it.

IV

The anarchist movement in the United States never made much headway. A few individuals—Benjamin Tucker, Adin Ballou, Lysander Spooner, Stephen Pearl Andrews, Emma Goldman, Josiah Warren—are still faintly remembered, but more for the style of their lives than for any impact on their society. It is not difficult to see what prevented them from attracting a large following. Their very distaste for organization and power precluded the traditional modes for exerting influence. More important, their philosophy ran directly counter to the national hierarchy of values, a system of beliefs, conscious and otherwise, which has always impeded the drive for rapid change in this country. And it is a system which constitutes a roadblock at least as formidable today as at any previous point in our history.

This value structure stresses, first of all, the prime virtue of "accumulation," chiefly of goods, but also of power and prestige. Any group, be it anarchists or New Leftists, which challenges the soundness of that goal, which suggests that it interferes with the more important pursuits of self-realization and human fellowship, presents so basic a threat to our national and individual identities as to invite almost automatic rejection.

A second obstacle that our value structure places in the path of radical change is its insistence on the benevolence of history. To the average American, human history is the story of automatic progress. Every day in every way we have got better and better. *Ergo,* there is no need for a frontal assault on our ills; time alone will be sufficient to cure them. Thus it is that many whites considered the "Negro problem" solved by the passage of civil rights legislation. They choose to ignore the fact that the daily lives of most Negroes have changed but slightly, or, as in the case of unemployment, for the worse. They ignore, too, the group of hard-core problems that have only recently emerged: maldistribution of income, urban slums, disparities in education and training, the breakdown of family structure in the ghetto, technological unemployment—problems which show no signs of yielding to time, but which will require concentrated energy and resources for solution.

Without a massive assault on these basic ills, ours will continue to be a society where the gap between rich and poor widens, where the major rewards go to the few (who are not to be confused with the best). Yet it seems highly unlikely, as of 1968, that the public pressure needed for such an assault will be forthcoming. Most Americans still prefer to believe that ours is either already the best of all possible worlds or will shortly, and without any special effort, become such. It is this deep-seated smugness, this intractable optimism, which must be reckoned with—which, indeed, will almost certainly destroy any call for substantive change.

A further obstacle facing the New Left today, black power advocates and otherwise, is that its anarchist style and mood run directly counter to the prevailing tendencies in our national life, especially of conformity and centralization. The conformity has been commented on too often to bear repetition, except to point out that the young radicals' unorthodox mores (sexual, social, cultural) are in themselves enough to produce un-easiness and anger in the average American. In insisting on the right of the individual to please himself and to rely on his own judgment (whether in dress, speech, music, sex, or stimulants), SNCC and SDS may be sol-idly within the American tradition—indeed may be its mainstream—but this tradition is now more central to our rhetoric than to our behavior.

The anarchist focus in SNCC and SDS on decentralization, participa-tory democracy, and community organizing likewise runs counter to domi-nant national trends. Consolidation, not dispersion, is currently king. There are some signs that a counterdevelopment has begun—such as the pending decentralization of the New York City school system—but as yet the overwhelming pattern continues to be consolidation. Both big govern-ment and big business are getting bigger and, more ominous still, are com-ing into ever closer partnership. As Richard J. Barber has recently docu-mented, the federal government is not only failing to block the growth of huge "conglomerate" firms by antitrust action but it is contributing to that growth through procurement contracts and the exchange of personnel. The traditional hostility between business and government has rapidly drawn to a close. Washington is no longer interested in restraining the giant corporations, and the corporations have lost much of their fear of federal intentions. The two, in happy tandem, are moving the country still further along the road to oligopoly, militarism, economic imperialism, and greater privileges for the already-privileged. The trend is so pronounced, and there is so little effective opposition to it, that it begins to take on an irrevocable, even irreversible, quality.

In the face of these monoliths of national power, black power in Lowndes County is pathetic by comparison. Yet while the formation of the Black Panther party in Lowndes brought out paroxysms of fear in the nation at large, the announcement that General Motors' 1965 sales totaled $21 billion—exceeding the gross national product of all but nine countries in the world—produced barely a tremor of apprehension. The unspoken assumption can only be something like this: It is less dangerous for a few whites to control the whole nation than for a local majority of Negroes to control their own community. The Kafkaesque dimension of life in Amer-ica continues to grow.

Black Power is both a product of our society and a repudiation of it. Confronted with the continuing indifference of the majority of whites to the Negro's plight, SNCC and CORE have lost faith in conscience and time and have shifted to a position which the white majority finds infuriating. The nation as a whole—as in the case of the abolitionists over a hundred years ago—has created the climate in which earlier tactics no longer seem relevant, in which new directions become mandatory if frustration is to be met and hope maintained. And if the new turn proves a wrong one, if Black Power forecloses rather than animates further debate on the Negro's condition, if it destroys previous alliances without opening up promising new options, it is the nation as a whole that must bear the responsibility. There seems little likelihood that the American majority will admit to that responsibility. Let us at least hope it will not fail to recognize the rage which Black Power represents, to hear the message at the movement's core. . . .

J. Herman Blake

Black Nationalism

A compelling theme in Afro-American protest has been that of black nationalism. During the twentieth century, dynamic and pivotal leaders such as Marcus Garvey and El-Hajj Malik El-Shabazz [Malcolm X] combined its earlier manifestations— political, economic and cultural—into a broad, integral form of nationalism with mass support. Sociologist J. Herman Blake traces this development and points out recent emerging themes concerning land, self-determination in black communities, unity between black intellectuals and the masses, and black consciousness. He writes that black nationalism reflects "the social conditions which have repeatedly indicated to black people that, though they are in this country, they are not a part of this country." Like Duberman, he suggests that the forms of Afro-American protest ultimately depend a great deal upon the reaction from the white community.

> The price the immigrants paid to get into America was that they had to become Americans. The black man *cannot* become an American (unless we get a different set of rules) because he is black.
> LeRoi Jones, *Home*

It is one of the bitter ironies of American history that the seeds of the contradiction which created black nationalism were sown in the colony of Jamestown in 1619. When the settlers accepted twenty captured Africans as servants—an act which eventually led to slavery—the reality of black inequality in America was established at the same time that the rhetoric of democracy was articulated. Black nationalism has been a major form of protest against this contradiction since the early nineteenth century. Early nationalist protest followed several different emphases, but in the twentieth century these different strands were incorporated into a unified form of protest. The most recent trends in black nationalism reveal some unique features which have significant implications for future developments.

Black nationalist thought is a consequence of the duality of the experience of Afro-Americans, a people who are identified by racial characteristics as different from the "typical" American and denied full participa-

From J. Herman Blake, "Black Nationalism," *The Annals of the American Academy of Political and Social Science,* 382 (March, 1969), pp. 16–25. Reprinted by permission of the American Academy of Political and Social Science and the author. Footnotes have been renumbered.

tion in this society for that reason, while, at the same time, they are expected to meet all the responsibilities of citizenship. It reflects the negative self-image which many black people have unconsciously developed, and the sense of hopelessness that has persisted in the Afro-American community as a consequence of being treated as inferiors.

EARLY TRENDS

The first distinctive form of black nationalism was the desire to separate from America expressed by some free blacks in the early part of the nineteenth century. The proponents of this form of *political nationalism* argued for the establishment of a black nation in Africa or some other territory. Their views were based on a conviction that Afro-Americans would never receive justice in America and that the only hope was to leave the country and establish a political entity for black people. The apex of this development came at the Emigration Convention of 1854, when three men were commissioned to investigate the possibilities of emigration of blacks to Central America, the black Republic of Haiti, or the Niger Valley in West Africa.

The apparent permanence of American slavery and the racial barriers set up against freed blacks led these men to the conviction that true justice and equality for black people would never be reached in this country, and there were other territories to which they might emigrate. Thus, those in favor of emigration argued that the only hope for the black man was to leave this country and establish a black nation in which the emigrants could live free from fear, racial prejudice, and discrimination. The Civil War and emancipation of the slaves brought black agitation for emigration to a halt, and black people devoted themselves to the task of becoming a part of the American society.

Though emancipation increased the hopes of blacks that full participation in the society was forthcoming, post-Reconstruction developments made it increasingly clear that such was not to be the case. The depressing conditions which followed the Hayes compromise led to the development of philosophies of self-help, particularly as expressed in *economic nationalism*. This emphasis called for racial solidarity and economic cooperation as the solution to the problems of the Afro-American. The growing influx of Europeans into Northern cities and factories increased the pessimism of some influential Afro-Americans and led them to look for salvation within the race. Booker T. Washington, a major proponent of economic nationalism, felt that industrial education and the perfection of agricultural skills in the rural South would lead whites to the realization that black people were worthy of equal treatment. In his famous Atlanta Exposition Address of 1895, Washington revealed that he was aware of the impact of European immigration upon American industry, and evidently felt that this trend closed the doors of opportunity in the North to blacks. Therefore, he pursued a policy of racial solidarity and economic self-sufficiency, establishing the National Negro Business League in 1900 for the purpose of stimulating business enterprise. At the 1904 convention of the League, Washington viewed the developments of black businesses through the support of black people as crucial to the removal of racial prejudice in America. Unlike political nationalism, economic nationalism revealed a desire for participation in the society, but in the face of rejection by Americans, the economic emphasis worked on strengthening the internal community as part of an attack upon the racial barriers.

Cultural nationalism was another response to the denial of equality to Afro-Americans. Like economic nationalism, the emphasis was upon racial solidarity, with added attraction given to the development of racial pride and dignity. These goals were sought through the study of the history of the black man and his contribution to mankind. The essential belief of the cultural nationalists was that a scholarly analysis and study of the history of black people throughout the world, particularly in America, would show blacks and whites that Afro-Americans are descended from a proud heritage and have made outstanding contributions to human progress. It was thought that such an understanding would have two consequences: (1) It would give blacks a positive self-image and further the development of racial pride and solidarity; and (2) it would show whites that blacks were no better nor worse than any other race and that because of their contributions, they should be fully accepted into the society.

Although there were attempts to develop the study of Afro-American history before the Civil War, cultural nationalism received its greatest impetus during the latter part of the nineteenth century. The desire to give scholarly attention to the historical past of the black man resulted in the organization of the Association for the Study of Negro Life and History in 1915, and to the establishment of the *Journal of Negro History*.

Political, economic, and cultural forms of black nationalism all had their roots in the social conditions confronting Afro-Americans. During the days of slavery, the desire for emigration and separation increased with the growing conviction that slavery would never be eliminated. It is noteworthy that the emigration movement among blacks reached its most significant point during the 1850's and that such interest declined with the onset of the Civil War. In the latter part of the nineteenth century, economic and cultural nationalism developed as a consequence of continued hostility and repression. The end of Reconstruction, the rise of Jim Crow, the lack of economic opportunity, and similar conditions led to the development of economic and cultural attempts to foster individual and collective strength within the black community while pursuing an attack upon the prejudiced and discriminatory behavior of the larger society. The major proponents of these various emphases came from the upper levels of the Afro-American community. Martin R. Delany, a supporter of emigration, was a physician and Harvard graduate; Booker T. Washington was the undisputed leader of black people from 1895 until his death in 1915; and Arthur A. Schomburg, Carter G. Woodson, and W. E. B. Du Bois were all highly educated and literate men. Black nationalist movements did not develop a foundation among the masses until after World War I.

TWENTIETH-CENTURY PATTERNS

Black nationalism as a mass movement followed the creation of a ready audience and the combination of the various strands of nationalistic thought into an integral whole. When Marcus Garvey, a native of Jamaica, established the Universal Negro Improvement Association and African Communities League (UNIA) in New York City in 1917, he brought *integral nationalism* to a people who were looking for hope in what appeared to be a hopeless situation.

Garvey made his strongest appeal to the many blacks who had migrated out of the South shortly before his arrival in the country, seeking employment in the industrial centers of the North. Agricultural depression and the appearance of the boll weevil in Southern cotton had made living conditions extremely difficult. At the same time, the European war had placed heavy demands on Northern industry, and the supply of European immigrant labor had been cut off. Therefore, Northern industrialists began a campaign to induce blacks to leave the South and work in Northern factories. It is estimated that in one two-year period a half-million black people moved to the North.

The many blacks who made this journey found that though they were often openly recruited, they were seldom welcomed, for they were crowded into urban slums and faced a continual round of unemployment, depression, and indigence. Furthermore, they met the massive hostility of whites—many of them newly arrived in this country—who saw the black in-migrants as threats to their economic security and reacted against them with devastating riots. The continued hardships of the blacks and the intense hostility of the whites created a situation in which Garvey's appeal seemed eminently rational. They were the same conditions which led to earlier forms of nationalism, except that the blacks perceived them in a much more intensified manner than previously. Garvey's integral form of black nationalism flourished in this situation, and its significance was not only that it was the first major social movement among the black masses; it also indicated the extent to which they "entertained doubts concerning the hope for first-class citizenship in the only fatherland of which they knew."[1]

The UNIA program combined previous emphases in black nationalism. Drawing upon the Booker T. Washington philosophy of economic independence, Garvey established various commercial enterprises, among them the Black Star Line, a steamship company designed to link the black peoples of the world through trade, and the Negro Factories Corporation, designed to build and operate factories in the industrial centers of the

[1] John Hope Franklin, *From Slavery to Freedom* (New York: Alfred A. Knopf, 1963), p. 483.

United States, Central America, the West Indies, and Africa. In the tradition of the political nationalists, Garvey sought to have all whites expelled from Africa so that it could become a territory for black people only. He told Afro-Americans that race prejudice was such an inherent part of white civilization that it was futile to appeal to the white man's sense of justice. The only hope was to leave America and return to Africa. His vigorous promotion of racial solidarity and black consciousness was one of his most lasting successes. Exalting everything black, he renewed the assertions that Africa had a noble history and urged Afro-Americans to be proud of their ancestry. Coming when it did, his program had a profound impact upon the black masses, and even his severest critics admit that in the early 1920's, his followers numbered perhaps half a million.

The Garvey movement did not show the dualism found in earlier nationalist sentiment. It was a philosophy that fully embraced blackness and vigorously rejected white America. Although the movement declined after his imprisonment in 1925, the integral form of black nationalism was to continue. In the early 1930's the Lost Found Nation of Islam in the Wilderness of North America was established in Detroit, and began to grow under the leadership of Elijah Muhammad.

After two decades of relative obscurity, the Nation of Islam experienced rapid growth during the 1950's, particularly when the brilliant and articulate ex-convict, Malcolm X, began speaking around the country in the name of the organization. Like the UNIA, the Nation of Islam is an unequivocal rejection of white America and a turn inward to the black man and the black community as the only source of hope for resolving racial problems. Unlike the UNIA, the Nation of Islam contains a strong religious component which is a major binding force in the organization. There is the Holy Koran which provides scriptural guidance, Elijah Muhammad (The Messenger) who provides everyday leadership, an eschatology, and a set of rituals which give the members a valuable shared experience. The rejection of white America involves a rejection of Christianity as the religion of the black man, English as the mother tongue of the black man, and the Stars and Stripes as the flag of the black man. Muslims also refuse to use the term "Negro," their family names, and traditional Southern foods, which are all taken as remnants of the slave condition and a reaffirmation of that condition so long as they are used.

The Nation of Islam places great emphasis upon black consciousness and racial pride, claiming that a man cannot know another man until he knows himself. This search for black identity is conducted through the study of the religious teachings of Islam, as interpreted by Elijah Muhammad, and through the study of Afro-American and African history.

Muslims also follow a strong program of economic nationalism, with their emphasis upon independent black businesses. Muslim enterprises, mostly of the service variety, have been established across the country and have been quite successful. They are now opening supermarkets and supplying them with produce from Muslim-owned farms. There is also some movement now into light manufacturing.

The Muslim emphasis upon a separate territory for black people gave new emphasis to political nationalism. They have never specified whether that land should be on this continent or another, but they have consistently argued that since blacks and whites cannot live together in peace in this country, it would be better if the blacks were to leave the country and set up an independent nation. In the Muslim view, such a nation would be an Islamic theocracy. This new element of political nationalism, emphasizing land rather than Africa, emigration, or colonization, has become a significant element of contemporary black nationalist protest.

The Nation of Islam had a profound effect upon the development of contemporary trends in black nationalism. There are very few ardent black nationalists today who have not had some close contact with the Nation of Islam either through membership or through having come under the influence of one of its eloquent ministers. Even though the Nation of Islam grew rapidly there were many black people who were deeply influenced but were not persuaded by the doctrine of total separation from America or by the religious emphasis. This was particularly true of college-educated blacks. The break between Malcolm X and the Nation of Islam in early 1964 had a profound impact on current trends by spurring the development of black nationalism among countless numbers of blacks who supported the Muslim emphasis upon black consciousness and racial solidarity.

The Universal Negro Improvement Association and African Communities League under Marcus Garvey and the Lost Found Nation of Islam in the Wilderness of North America under Elijah Muhammad have been very successful and influential forms of integral nationalism. Both the leaders and the followers came primarily from among the black masses of the urban North, whose lives had not seen the steady progress toward perfection which characterizes the myth of the American dream of success. These two movements brought the various threads of nineteenth-century black nationalism together, and wove them into a matrix out of which the more recent trends in black nationalist thought have developed. Contemporary trends, however, add some distinctive elements of their own which are shaping black nationalism and the current pattern of race relations in America.

CONTEMPORARY DEVELOPMENTS

The development of black-nationalist-protest thought in recent years is related to the same conditions which produced such sentiment in earlier periods, as well as to some new and unique conditions. In recent years, the urbanization of the black man has proceeded at a very rapid pace. In 1960, a higher proportion of the black population (73 percent) were residents of the cities than ever before, and this proportion exceeded that of the white population (70 percent). Not only are blacks moving into the cities; whites are moving out, so that more of the central cities are becoming all-black enclaves. Between 1960 and 1965, the proportion of blacks in central cities increased by 23 percent while the proportion of whites declined by 9 percent.

It is not simply that black people are now predominantly urban; in recent years, black urban residents have become new urbanites for two major reasons. Not a small proportion of the in-migrants to central cities are younger blacks who are generally better educated than those whites who remain in the cities. Furthermore, a new generation of black people is coming to maturity, young people who were born and raised in the urban black communities. They do not use a previous Southern pattern of living as the framework through which they assess their current situation, but use an urban, mainstream-America framework, usually learned from the mass media rather than experienced. These youth comprise a very large proportion of the urban residents and are less enchanted by the view that, although things are bad, they are better than they used to be. As such, they are very critical of attitudes of those blacks who see the situation of the black man as improving. A small but significant proportion of the new urbanites are young people who have graduated from first-rate colleges and hold white-collar positions in integrated firms. The subtle prejudices which they have encountered, along with the empty lives of the many middle-class whites whom they have met, have increased their awareness that there is a style and tone of life in the black community which gives much more satisfaction than that of the white middle class. The heightened interaction of black youth as a result of urban living, the coming-of-age of a generation of post-World War II youth, and the rejection of some white middle-class values in the attempt to articulate values which grow out of the black experience are some of the internal dynamics of black communities in the 1960's which are producing a new upsurge in nationalism.

The postwar independence movements around the world have also affected the thinking of black people. Earlier generations of black nationalists predicted the rise of Africa as part of the world community. They had preached about the day when "princes would come out of Ethiopia," but the present generation has witnessed that rise. Black urbanites, seeing African diplomats welcomed by American presidents and taking leading roles in the United Nations, became increasingly bitter about the limited freedom and opportunity of Afro-Americans.

While Africans and Asians were gaining independence and taking seats in the halls of world council, the gap between black and white Americans was not changing perceptibly. Since 1960, black males have not made appreciable gains on white males in income and occupation, black communities are more separated from white communities than ever before, and the education of black youth is still woefully inadequate. Even for those middle-class blacks who appear to have made many strides during the 1960's, the evidence indicates that they have made large relative gains over lower-class blacks, but have not reduced the gap between themselves and middle-class whites.

There is one major positive change that has taken place in the past few years, however; a higher proportion of black youth are completing high school and college. Such youth are not following past patterns of individualistic escape from the black community—with their heightened awareness and knowledge, they are becoming more involved in black communities as residents and as activists. An important and new element in black nationalism is this union of black intellectuals and the black masses. While nationalism in the nineteenth century was notable for its lack of mass support, and for its lack of intellectual backing, in the mass movements of the twentieth century in recent years, intellectuals and the masses have combined their skills to give new impetus to nationalist movements. An excellent example is the development of the Mississippi Freedom Democratic Party.

The key figure in the development of the recent trends was the late El-Hajj Malik El-Shabazz. After his break with the Nation of Islam, he began to link the struggle of Afro-Americans with the struggle of oppressed peoples throughout the world, and particularly in Africa. He also emphasized *human rights* rather than *civil rights,* thereby increasing the hope that the Afro-American struggle might come before the United Nations. In this way, he internationalized the conditions of Afro-Americans and increased their awareness of the value of links with the non-Western world.

Malik El-Shabazz gave new emphasis to the possibility of reform in America, an idea which was not contained in the view of either Marcus Garvey or Elijah Muhammad. In his "The Ballot or the Bullet" speech, he expressed the view that it was possible to produce a bloodless revolution in this country. His views were close to those of earlier nationalists who saw the development of the inner strengths of the black community as a first step in attacking racial barriers.

Another key contribution was his ability to appeal to both intellectuals and the masses and bring them together. El-Shabazz was very widely read, and a brilliant and articulate spokesman. His knowledge and logic impressed black intellectuals deeply. He was also an ex-convict and a man of the streets. Consequently, those who were the most deprived could identify as strongly with him as could the intellectual. His dual appeal to intellectuals and the masses, along with his emphasis upon racial solidarity, helped to bring these two elements of the black community into greater harmony.

In addition, Malik El-Shabazz spurred the development of black consciousness and black dignity. He was a living example of the positive effect of black consciousness, and there were few black people who met him who were not profoundly moved by what he was. Said one writer:

The concept of Blackness, the concept of National Consciousness, the proposal of a political (and diplomatic) form for this aggregate of Black Spirit, these are the things given to us by Garvey, through Elijah Muhammad, and finally given motion into still another area of Black Response by Malcolm X.[2]

Another captures the nature of the appeal of El-Shabazz:

It was not the Black Muslim movement itself that was so irresistibly appealing to the true believers. It was the awakening into self-consciousness of twenty million Negroes which was so compelling. Malcolm X articulated their aspirations better than any other man of our time. When he spoke under the banner of Elijah Muhammad, he was irresistible. When he spoke under his own banner, he was still irresistible. If he had become a Quaker, . . . and if he had continued to give voice to the mute ambitions in the black man's soul, his message would still have been triumphant: because what was great was not Malcolm X but the truth he uttered.[3]

In the minds of present-day nationalists, El-Hajj Malik El-Shabazz was the greatest prince to come out of Ethiopia, and he is now the martyred saint of the movement.

The articulation and development of the concept of Black Power continues the emphasis on an integral form of black nationalism, yet with new elements. The political emphasis of Black Power renews the hope for reform in America, but with attention given to a reform of *values* as well as *behavior*. As such, it strikes more deeply at the basis of the problems separating blacks and whites. Black Power advocates also add a strong community orientation to black nationalism. They have not sought to build a unified mass movement around the country, but rather to develop programs and policies relating to the particular needs, conditions, and expressed desires of specific communities. The articulation of Black Power by a student-based organization, along with its community orientation, continued the unified approach of the intellectuals and the masses.

The development of black nationalist thought since the rise of El-Hajj Malik El-Shabazz has brought new emphasis to old issues, particularly the political and cultural forms of nationalism. The political emphasis is developing around the issues of colonization of black people, land, independence, self-determination for black communities, and the accountability of black leaders. When Malik El-Shabazz began to link black people with the Third World—a trend continued by Black Power advocates—black people became more aware that their situation in this country was very similar to that of colonized peoples throughout the world.

[2] LeRoi Jones, *Home* (New York: Morrow, 1966), p. 243. Reprinted by permission of publisher.
[3] Eldridge Cleaver, *Soul on Ice* (New York: McGraw-Hill, 1968), p. 59. Used with permission of McGraw-Hill Book Company.

The large numbers of blacks in central cities, along with the presence
of agencies of social control directed by forces outside of the black communities, bear a strong resemblance to a colonial situation. This awareness has brought many blacks to the realization that such aggregations
are similar to nations in the same way that Indian tribes saw themselves
as nations, and they now occupy a territory which can be viewed as their
own. LeRoi Jones puts it thus:

> What the Black Man must do now is to look down at the ground
> upon which he stands, and claim it as his own. It is not abstract.
> Look down! Pick up the earth, or jab your fingernails into the con-
> crete. It is real and it is yours, if you want it.
>
> All the large concentrations of Black People in the West are al-
> ready nations. All that is missing is the consciousness of this state of
> affairs.[4]

This awareness and consciousness is growing rapidly, and the emphasis
upon self-determination for black communities is evidence of this fact.
Indeed, if one understands this intense desire of black people to control
their own communities and to determine their destinies, the urban in-
surrections of recent years take on another facet. If the community is seen
as a colony and the social control agencies as colonial agents, then spontaneous outbursts may also be interpreted as attempts to reaffirm local
rather than foreign control of the community. An altercation between a
police officer and a black man is an assertion of colonial control, and the
ensuing outburst, however destructive, is a reaffirmation of the view that
such control does not lie exclusively with the colonial agencies. Related
to self-determination is the emphasis upon accountability being developed
by nationalists. This view holds that those who hold positions of power
which affect the black community must answer exclusively to the black
community.

Colonization, land, self-determination, and accountability are the basic
elements in recent developments in black nationalism, particularly the
expansion of its political emphasis. Such views led one group of black
militants, the Federation for Self-Determination in Detroit, to reject a
grant of $100,000 from the New Detroit Committee in early 1968 on the
grounds that there were too many controls attached to the grant. Such
views led the militant Black Panther party, based in Oakland, California,
to begin to develop a political program on the grounds that black men
who represent either of the major political parties cannot be held wholly
accountable by the black community. Similar examples can be found in
black communities across the nation, for these views are crucial aspects
of the present framework of action of black nationalists today.

In recent years, black consciousness has received added impetus in
terms of racial solidarity and a positive self-image. Thus, there is the new

[4] Jones, *op. cit.*, pp. 244 and 249.

emphasis upon black as beautiful, and black youth are adopting African-style clothing and wearing African or natural hair styles. They are seeking to establish black studies and black curricula on college campuses. These courses of study, however, are to have a strong community and service orientation, rather than to become wholly intellectual pursuits. It is unquestionably the development of black consciousness and racial solidarity, along with the attitude of self-determination and black accountability, which has spurred the revolt of black athletes in many colleges and the attempt to obtain a black boycott of the 1968 Olympic Games. This is a new and revolutionary black consciousness, exemplified by El-Hajj Malik El-Shabazz and activated among black communities across the land.

SUMMARY AND CONCLUSION

Black nationalism has been one of the most militant and strident forms of Afro-American protest. It has grown out of the social conditions which have repeatedly indicated to black people that, though they are in this country, they are not a part of this country. The most recent emphases in nationalist thought are clearly developing the inner strengths of the black community through cultural nationalism, and expanding the concept of political nationalism. It may well be that black people will find that after all other barriers between the races have been eliminated, the barrier of color will prove to be ineradicable. Such a realization will give new and revolutionary impetus to black nationalism.

*   *   *

Some of us have been, and some still are, interested
in learning whether it is *ultimately* possible to
live in the same territory with people who seem
so disagreeable to live with; still others want to
get as far away from ofays as possible.
ELDRIDGE CLEAVER, *Soul on Ice*

42

Michael Lewis

Negro Protest in Urban America

In order to understand the nature of much of twentieth-century black protest, it is essential to recognize the extent to which that protest has been an expression of profound disillusionment with the conditions of urban, ghetto life. Massive black migrations northward during and after World War I attested to the lure of the city as a promised land, supposedly full of economic opportunity and free of institutionalized forms of oppression. But as the reality of city life fell far short of the promise, the urban Negro responded with growing bitterness. Michael Lewis discusses here the March on Washington Movement, which more than any other movement of the Forties and Fifties involved the urban masses. He also notes a shift in recent years to more urban-*focused*—as distinct from urban-*based*—protests. In his analysis of some of the implications of that shift, Lewis deals directly with some of the larger problems and difficulties that mark "the creative use of conflict" in America's race relations.

The most impressive development of the Forties occurred early in the decade at a time when the nation was in the throes of its preparation for war. *The March on Washington Movement,* while not in the strictest sense indigenous to urban areas, did derive a major portion of its support in such areas. The MOWM differed significantly from its urban-based predecessors in several respects. In the first place, it was a reformist movement with a single delimited goal—to open up opportunities for Negro labor in the burgeoning defense industries. Second, it was a broadly based movement drawing adherents from across class lines. And finally, it was so loosely organized that there is some question as to whether it was in fact a movement at all.

Although a number of prominent Negro leaders—among them Walter White of the NAACP and Lester Granger of the Urban League—supported the MOWM at one time or another, only one man, A. Philip Randolph, President of the Brotherhood of Sleeping Car Porters, dominated it. It was Randolph (the same Randolph who earlier had been a bitter antagonist of Marcus Garvey) who, in January of 1941, proposed that ten thousand Negroes march on Washington to wrest from a reluctant administration a guarantee of equal access to defense employment.

Excerpted from Michael Lewis, "The Negro Protest in Urban America," in *Protest, Reform, and Revolt: A Reader in Social Movements,* edited by J. R. Gusfield, pp. 172–79, 181, 186–89. Copyright © 1970, by John Wiley & Sons, Inc. Reprinted by permission of publisher. Footnotes have been omitted.

Today, when we have experienced a mammoth march of some 250,000 people to Washington in behalf of civil rights legislation, Randolph's original call seems modest indeed and certainly not a proposal likely to generate a mass movement. Coming when it did, however, the proposal seemed anything but modest and the early reaction to it among the Negro leadership ranged from very cautious optimism to outright pessimism. Only Marcus Garvey approximately twenty years earlier had been able to effect a mass mobilization of black men. Although Negroes, particularly those in the cities, were bitter about their inability to get a real foothold in the defense industries, they had not had the experience of employing organized mass pressure in pursuit of redress. Furthermore, the government was reminding everyone that in this time of crisis it was necessary to put aside special pleas in a show of national unity. Finally, and not insignificantly, Randolph's proposal meant demonstrating against the administration of Franklin Delano Roosevelt, a man revered by most Negroes. By May, however, the reservations of the Negro leadership had given way to commitment to the march, which was to take place on July 1. March committees were formed in a number of cities, street meetings were held to whip up support, and the Negro press undertook a vigorous campaign in support of the proposed venture. This organized restiveness did not go unnoticed in Washington. A mass demonstration of black men seeking equal opportunity—particularly if such a demonstration took place in the nation's capital—would have undoubtedly been a major international embarrassment to a government so close to entering a war for the defense of democracy and human equality. Moreover, such a demonstration might very well have served to indicate to potential enemies that the nation was not unified and that consequently it was unprepared to wage a major struggle. Certainly such a demonstration would have transformed a minority disaffection into a polarizing national issue. Early in June the administration began to "bargain collectively" with Randolph and other MOWM leaders in an attempt to have the proposed march canceled. The leaders demanded that the President issue an Executive Order establishing a Fair Employment Practices Committee empowered to deal with the problems of equal opportunity in defense industries. On June 25th, the President issued such an order and the Washington demonstration scheduled for the following week was called off.

In most quarters the establishment of FEPC was considered a major victory. Those most closely associated with Randolph went so far as to proclaim it the "second Emancipation Proclamation." As it turned out, it was something less than that. The establishment of the FEPC did not eradicate the inequities which moved the Negro leadership to organize the march. In the year following its establishment the President's committee held hearings in several cities. A report issued by the Bureau of Employment Security in March 1942 indicated that many defense employment opportunities during this period remained closed to Negroes. The MOWM leadership maintained that the original march had never been canceled but rather had been postponed, and that given the absence of major gains the time had come to reactivate the movement on a mass basis. Randolph and those associated with him announced plans for a series of mass convocations to be held in cities such as New York, Chicago, and St. Louis. The movement, galvanized by Randolph's charisma, undertook the major organizational effort necessary to ensure a mass turnout for the planned events. Their efforts met with extraordinary success. On June 16, eighteen thousand people packed New York's Madison Square Garden for the MOWM rally, and ten days later twelve thousand more packed a similar rally in Chicago. In the glitter of these successes, it seemed that a militantly reformist Negro mass movement was about to become a major factor in American race relations. However, these rallies represented the high-water mark for the MOWM. The tide was soon to recede. Plans for a similar rally in Washington, D.C., never materialized. In September of 1942, Walter White (NAACP) and Lester Granger (Urban League) withdrew their support from the MOWM, and the broadly based federation no longer existed. Randolph, going it alone, adopted two positions for the MOWM which drew increasing criticism. First, he held that the MOWM should be an all-Negro organization. While not eschewing interracial cooperation, he did maintain that it was important for Negroes to show what they could accomplish on their own. Second, he believed that a strategy of nonviolent civil disobedience might be employed by the movement with some effect. The first position aroused the displeasure of those who saw in it a residue of the kind of nationalism which Randolph himself had so vigorously condemned in his earlier opposition to Marcus Garvey. The second position seemed to many a dangerous gamble with little hope of success. By 1943 the MOWM had ceased to be much of a factor in the Negro protest, urban or otherwise. While Randolph was able to sustain the MOWM throughout the remaining years of the war (the last national conference was held in 1946), it never developed into the permanent protest movement he had so optimistically envisaged.

The MOWM experience, however, is instructive because during its short-lived course the movement demonstrated the feasibility of certain possibilities for the organization and expression of the urban Negro's protest. If nothing else, the MOWM demonstrated that it is possible to mobilize a broadly based Negro constituency. While its following (it would be erroneous to talk of membership) was pre-eminently working class, it did strike a response among middle-class Negroes as well. While most of its following was made up of people who would in some measure endorse the goal of an interracial society, it also attracted those who might be designated as nationalists or racial separatists. In all probability, the MOWM's broad appeal can be attributed to the fact that its leadership focused upon a specific issue rather than upon such global concerns as the general state of the race itself or the possibility (or impossibility) of the Negro's ultimate salvation in American society. The issue, unfair exclusion from job opportunities in defense industries, served as a "common denominator," a condition which every Negro—irrespective of class identity or ideological predisposition—would be likely to condemn. In a very real sense the immediacy of the problem and its delimited scope left no room for factionalism, on any basis, to fully bloom. In this regard it should be remembered that it was only after apparent (if not real) victory that cleavages within the Negro community began to weaken the movement, i.e., the loss of support of the NAACP and the Urban League.

Beyond the question of broadly based mobilization, the MOWM experience also indicates how effective the strategy of mass mobilization might be. FEPC became a reality when and only when government authorities perceived the strong possibility that thousands of aroused black men would dramatize their demands for redress in such a way as to interfere seriously with the pursuit of national objectives. . . . In this case a demonstrable threat of mass action was enough, for a grave international crisis confronted the nation. In less severe circumstances the march leaders no doubt would have had to make good their threat before the government would have taken positive action. Nevertheless, the events which led to the establishment of the FEPC indicate that the representative of the majority polity *will* make accommodations to minority demands when disciplined protest in behalf of those demands threatens to interfere with (or actually does interfere with) the orderly realization of majority interests.

Finally it should be noted that the two positions for which Randolph and his closest followers were criticized—their desire to limit the movement to Negroes and their desire to use nonviolent direct action (civil disobedience)—presaged later developments in the national protest. Although he was accused of fostering black nationalism when he favored an all-Negro MOWM, Randolph maintained that he was really fostering the Negro's sense of his own ability to influence his own destiny. He maintained that, unlike the nationalists, he was not anti-white. He believed, however, that just as other minorities, like the Jews, had their own defense organizations, the Negroes too should have a movement they could feel was entirely their own. As we shall see, this position, more than the exotic anti-white nationalism of such as Marcus Garvey and the Muslim leaders, seems to be the direct antecedent of contemporary Black Power advocacy. The call to a nonviolent direct action was a new and radical departure— a bit too radical for many who previously supported the MOWM. Nevertheless, today, after the "sit-ins," the "lie-ins," and the freedom rides of the late Fifties and Sixties, assertive civil disobedience is commonly associated with both urban and national Negro protest.

Quiescence and resurgence: The localization of the protest. Except for the MOWM no other movement of the Forties and early Fifties seemed to have the capacity for capturing the attention—let alone the loyalties—of the urban masses. . . .

A major characteristic of the earlier urban protest efforts—and in particular those of the nationalists—was their unrelatedness to specific local grievances. They were urban-*based* rather than urban-*focused*. The UNIA, for example, did not involve itself in seeking redress in the cities for the grievances of the Negro. Garvey was a visionary who saw the black man's problems on a grand scale; consequently, he was little interested in solutions which were not equally grand. The sorrows of the Negro's urban condition—the poverty, poor educational and job opportunities, the despair born of being locked into a ghetto existence—Garvey knew and understood, but in his eyes they would only be obliterated by the black man's return to Africa. The result of such a view was the calculated neglect of direct action to force change in the immediate urban environment. The Muslims too have been nourished by the justifiable discontents of the urban Negro without committing themselves to a program for redress. Since their dogma foresees the apocalyptic fall of white society as the result of divine intervention, they have avoided direct remedial action on the local scene. Even the MOWM, with its direct action program, focused upon a national problem—denial of equal job opportunities in defense industries—to the neglect of issues of local genesis.

When viewed against their predecessors, the urban movements of the late Fifties and Sixties appear markedly reduced in scale. Their focus has generally been the community rather than the nation, the obliteration in the present of a specified evil or series of evils rather than the evocation of some future utopia. A few examples will make this abundantly clear.

New York City has been the scene of heightened protest activity since the late Fifties. For the most part this protest has been organized and executed by independent groups (which, on occasion, have been aligned with local NAACP and CORE chapters) focusing upon three perennial problems of ghetto life—inadequate educational opportunities, a limited job ceiling, and the physical decrepitude of available housing.

During the period under consideration the protest against inadequate educational opportunities in New York has grown in intensity as the protesters have come to view the educational "establishment" as lacking in good faith. Many of the protest groups have adopted a nihilistic rhetoric and tactics best described as disruptive, as they have come to view the Board of Education's plans and proposals as demagogic gestures designed to forestall an honest reckoning with the problem. What began as an effort to break the pattern of *de facto* segregation by getting the Board of Education to employ its administrative prerogatives has turned into a struggle for neighborhood control of the ghetto schools. Local parents' groups have gone so far as to demand the right to oversee the school curriculum and the right to select professional staff, including the principal.

In the early Sixties a coalition of protest groups, involving among others local CORE chapters, began to use direct action tactics in an attempt to force the unions to accept Negro members and to open their apprenticeship programs to qualified Negro applicants. In the summer of 1963, the protesters began picketing construction sites, lying down in the paths of trucks in order to prevent them from unloading construction materials, and "sitting in" at the offices of the Mayor and Governor. . . .

For years the majority of New York's Negro population has been forced to live in the teeming slums of areas like Harlem and the Bedford-Stuyvesant-East New York section of Brooklyn. A perusal of available housing statistics indicates in understatement what even casual observation in such areas reveals with shocking force—that the physical condition of the housing is abominable. In Harlem, for example, as of 1960, 49 percent of the available housing was in need of major repair as compared with 15 percent for New York City as a whole. Even these statistics do not convey just how desperate the situation really has been. The need for major repairs would be grave enough, but extensive overcrowding in such dwellings multiplies the seriousness of the situation. When an inadequate dwelling unit houses one family it is bad enough; when it houses two or even three families the wretchedness of the conditions is staggering.

Faced with intolerable conditions which seemed to be getting worse rather than better, the ghetto residents of Harlem and other similar areas decided to take matters into their own hands. During the early Sixties a number of tenants' associations were organized. For the most part, these groups adopted a direct action strategy. On the assumption that the slum-lord will respond only to economic pressure, they have attempted to make ownership of slum buildings unprofitable by withholding rents until needed repairs have been undertaken.

Similar examples of locally focused protest activity may be cited in cities other than New York during this same period. In Philadelphia, Negro ministers organized the *Selective Patronage Movement* (1960), which by using the consumer boycott as a direct action technique induced a number of local companies to start hiring more Negroes while upgrading those whom they already employed. In San Francisco, Negroes organized what might be labeled "shop-ins" against supermarkets which discriminated in their hiring practices (1964). Organized school boycotts and large-scale demonstrations have occurred in Boston and Chicago, where the local school systems have long been segregated on a *de facto* basis. In Cleveland, "lie-ins" have occurred at construction sites in protest against discriminatory hiring practices in the building trades. . . .

The cases cited here—and they by no means exhaust the list—have one major characteristic in common. They all represent attempts to change the course of events within the context of the local community. . . . On the face of it, it would seem that there is a parallel between the MOWM experience and the localized urban protests. For, like the MOWM, the direct action efforts have also focused upon issues of immediate relevance. Thus it would seem that the localized protests should have similar success in effecting a broadly based mobilization. In point of fact, however, this has not been the case in most instances, because on the local level the issues seem most often to directly affect only certain segments of the Negro population. The MOWM's concern was a "bread and butter" issue which—given the direction of the national economy immediately prior to World War II (and during the war)—affected millions of Negroes. The protest was specific in that it was limited to the defense economy, but at the same time it was broad enough to cover various levels within the economy. The skilled and the unskilled, the blue-collar worker and the white-collar worker, could all perceive a gain for themselves in its successful outcome. Typically, the organized local protest has been *overspecified*. Allowing for a number of exceptions, which are striking just because they are exceptions (the school protests for one), the localized protest efforts have tended to focus *not* on an identifiable problem area itself, but on a highly specific *aspect* of the problem area. Thus direct action protest does not attack the full range of discriminatory hiring practices, but job discrimination at specific levels in specific industries, such as the building trades and the retail food stores; it does not lump all housing problems together into a single target, but focuses upon slum conditions in one instance and suburban discrimination in another. The effect of such overspecification is to narrow the affected audience and consequently to limit the potential number of activities. . . .

The Negroes of our urban slums are no longer "invisible." Their increasingly intense protest activities, their articulate indictment of continuing racism, and even their violent expressions of frustration in the summer riots have forced us all to confront the unpleasant realities which are the products of the American racial dichotomy. The issue has been joined but whether or not the protest will ultimately result in racial equity is still a matter of some uncertainty.

We have already noted that the protest has developed outside the constraints of institutionalized politics. The practice of noninstitutional politics in American society is, however, severely limited by historical circumstance. It would seem, for example, that the only strategy available to Negroes with any possibility of success is the evocation and sustenance of *mass dissidence*. Without mass support, an activist vanguard could theoretically achieve its ends by one of two alternative courses. If the committed few, as the result of historic good fortune, have intimate access to the inner circles of power, they may, by various covert activities, bring about the conditions they desire. Lacking such access, the ultimate success of the committed will depend upon their ability to seize power, most probably by acts of disciplined violence. For Negro activists neither of these alternatives is possible. Certainly the vanguard has but very limited access to the inner circles of power. In large part this is what the protest is about. A seizure of power, on the other hand, is inconceivable except in a situation characterized by political anomie. Despite recurrent crises there is nothing now present or in the foreseeable future which suggests an upheaval in American society of such cataclysmic proportions as to enable any group to violently seize power. . . . Thus, unless the protest leadership is willing to settle for the compromise solutions available through institutionalized channels, it would seem that they must ultimately undertake a campaign of mass dissidence.

Essentially mass dissidence refers to the large-scale projection of direct action. It implies the organization of a mass movement committed to large-scale tactical disruption of orderly social process. It would, in effect, unite two previously disparate characteristics of the Negro's urban protest: large-scale organization and participation (the UNIA, the MOWM, and perhaps the Black Muslims) and the techniques of militant civil disobedience (CORE, SNCC, SCLC, and the localized protest groups). The strategic rationale for mass dissidence may be stated as follows. No social system can long endure the disruption of orderly social process even if the system's power structure has the loyalty of the majority. The persistent dissidence of a numerically significant minority would throw the system into a state of crisis. If this occurred two alternatives would be open to the power structure. It must either "break the back" of the dissident minority by acts of repression, or accommodate the demands of the dissidents. On the assumption that repression of a large-scale Negro movement would be effectively impossible without a complete breakdown in the American legal system, the power structure would be forced to make an accommodation.

If mass dissidence is the only noninstitutional strategy which might eventuate in significant gains for the urban Negro, it is nevertheless a course faced with two significant difficulties, either one of which might foreclose the possibility of success. First, there is the problem of developing an ideological repertoire capable of evoking a broadly based activism. As we have seen, there has been only one urban-based Negro protest movement—the MOWM—which, for even a short time, had broad enough appeal to evoke consolidated mass action. . . .

Without the development of ideological solidarity, organized mass dissidence is unlikely to materialize. Without it the protest will continue to be the sporadic product of the alliance between civil rights cadres and those who are touched directly by given concrete issues.

Second, there is the problem of developing a stable leadership coalition. Historically the urban protest leadership has dissipated much of its energy in internecine warfare. In many instances—as was the case with the conflict between Garvey and men like Du Bois, Randolph, and Owen —such struggles have emerged out of meaningful disagreement over ideological postures. In other instances, however, such as the break of White and Granger with Randolph during the MOWM episode or the isolation of Malcolm X by the Muslim hierarchy, the conflicts seem to have been the derivatives of organizational or personal self-interest. If the tendency to factionalize is not overcome, a coordinated program of mass dissidence will be impossible. Instead, the protest will continue to be led on an idiosyncratic basis.

If the problems of ideology and leadership are overcome the chances for the successful exercise of mass dissidence will be multiplied. However, the ultimate success of the protest will not thereby be assured. The tactical rationale for such a campaign assumes that the disruption of orderly social process will eventually elicit an accommodation from the majority power structure, that given the inherent protections of the American legal system, repression will be impossible. While this assumption may be borne out in the long run, the immediate response of the threatened white majority to mass dissidence on the part of the Negroes might be devastating to such a movement. There are, unfortunately, enough current examples of repressive white resistance to the Negro's direct action protest to give even the most optimistic observer pause. Even in the so-called liberal cities of the North this has increasingly been the case. . . . Heightened Negro protest apparently activates the dormant fears and prejudices of many whites to the point where they react with uncontrolled violence. If the discipline of the protesters should break down so that they respond to their tormentors in kind, a situation might easily arise in which the power structure might feel justified in opting for the repressive alternative.

Any campaign of mass dissidence is likely to be faced with a threat of violent resistance, which, by virtue of its internal discipline, it must ignore. If it does not, formal repression may deal the movement a crippling, if not devastating, blow. That such discipline is possible is evident in the example of the Southern activists who have withstood intense pressure. Nevertheless, the probability of a breakdown in such discipline will be greater in a program of mass dissidence. Whereas the Southern activists have been selected cadres, the strategy of mass dissidence demands the widest range of participants. In the tinderbox situations which may be expected to arise if the strategy is initiated, one undisciplined response may destroy the movement's effectiveness.

Finally, even if mass dissidence should prove effective, even if a militant urban protest should ultimately wrest a meaningful accommodation from the majority power structure, unintended consequences would result. While the successful prosecution of mass dissidence would mean the lowering of formal barriers to full participation, it would also probably result in a major increment in the already existing interracial estrangement. The strategy implies the creative use of conflict—and conflict can be expected to intensify the personal antipathy of members of one side for the other, particularly when the conflict generates violence. Thus, although greater equity of opportunity may be achieved, true integration—a state in which race is irrelevant—would yet be unrealized.

Stan Steiner

Brown Power: The Cry from the Barrios

Across the southwest United States the barrios have taken on a new militancy. "Uncle Taco," the stereotype of the servile Mexican-American, has given way to the "sons of Zapata." Mexican-Americans, or Chicanos, the country's second-largest minority, have for generations felt the sting of poverty, high unemployment rates, diminished life expectancies, and violence. Stan Steiner focuses on the problem of cultural discrimination, especially as it has occurred in public schools, and describes one reaction in early 1968 when 15,000 students walked out of Los Angeles high schools in protest. Steiner is the author of *La Raza: The Mexican-Americans* and *The New Indians,* and has contributed to *The New Republic* and other journals.

The boy waves his hand bashfully, and the teacher tells him to come to her desk.

"Charles, what do you want?"

"I have to go," the boy whispers, in Spanish, "to the bathroom."

"Charles, speak English."

"I have to go," the boy whispers a little louder, in Spanish, "to the bathroom."

"English!" the teacher rebukes him, growing impatient. "We speak English in school, Carlos," she says in Spanish. "You ask in English, or sit down."

The boy, who is maybe ten, and small, looks up at the teacher with the awe and fear that schoolchildren of his age have for authority. He does not know what to say or do. Suddenly his eyes light up with a mischievous thought.

"If you don't let me go to the bathroom," the boy exclaims, in Spanish, "maybe I piss on your shoes."

Years later the grown man remembers the incident of his boyhood humiliation without smiling. In his village the schoolhouse was closed long ago, and the teacher is gone, but the conflict in the classroom is indelible in his memory.

"That teacher, she did not like us," he says. "She was a good teacher,

From pp. 208–15, 218–19, 225–29 in *La Raza: The Mexican-Americans,* by Stan Steiner. Copyright © 1969, 1970 by Stan Steiner. Reprinted by permission of Harper & Row, Publishers, Inc.

but for forty years she did not let children speak Spanish in her class-room. She made us shamed."

And the man of fifty is angry, still.

"Why did that teacher shame us? Spanish is a cultured language. It was here before English."

Children have been taught to forget the "foreign" ways of their fathers. Children have been cajoled, enticed, threatened, and punished for speaking Spanish. Children have been beaten.

In one school in South Texas the children are forced to kneel in the playground and beg forgiveness for uttering a Spanish word. Some teachers have pupils who talk the forbidden language kneel before the entire class. A popular punishment is to have the offender stand facing the blackboard. Cesar Chavez, the farm workers' leader, vividly recalls being forced to stand in a corner for defying the order, "No Spanish in the classroom." That teaching method is still practiced in the rural schools. "Spanish detention" is another widely used punishment for speaking the native language. A wispy, white-haired teacher in Tucson, Arizona, proudly tells how she teaches English. The child who answers in Spanish walks to her desk and "he drops a penny in a bowl, for every Spanish word." She boasts, "It works! They come from poor families, you know."

One Rio Grande Valley school goes further. The teachers assign students to be "Spanish monitors," who guard its corridors, writing down the names of their fellow students who are heard speaking Spanish. The culprits are reprimanded or beaten.

Not all the methods of de-educating the Chicanos to forget their native language are nonviolent. Some of the largest school systems in the Southwest still sanction the beating of recalcitrant children if they persist in being "Spanish-speaking."

Even now, the schoolchildren of Los Angeles may be "paddled" with the official approval of the Board of Education.

When the barrio students walked out of the high schools of East Los Angeles to protest what they called "racist education," one of their pleas was that, "corporal punishment, which is carried on in the East Los Angeles schools, should be abolished throughout the district." The Los Angeles *Times* commented casually: "Corporal punishment is mostly in the form of paddling. . . . Authorization of corporal punishment at the discretion of school personnel is the board's [Los Angeles Board of Education] policy." The offhanded defense of "paddling" the Chicano high school students, by the second-largest school system in the country, was offered in the spring of 1968!

"We are teaching these kids with psychological guns pointed at their heads," angrily observed Sal Castro, a Los Angeles high school teacher. "If a kid speaks in Spanish, he is criticized. If a kid has a Mexican accent, he is ridiculed. If a kid talks back in any language, he is arrested. If a kid wants to leave school, he is forced back. We have gun-point education. The school is a prison.

"Education in the barrio doesn't free the mind of the Chicano. It imprisons his mind," the teacher said.

One day that spring an honor student at the Sidney Lanier High School in San Antonio, Texas, was caught reciting his Spanish homework aloud, in the school cafeteria. He was taken to the principal's office and beaten with a paddle; there were several cases of young people being beaten for speaking Spanish. "Just a gentle whack or two does them good," a teacher said. When the students complained about the paddling, they were threatened with the loss of their college scholarships and suspended. In frustration there was talk of a school strike. A meeting was hastily held by the city's Human Rights Commission in the hall of a local Catholic church, where the young Chicanos cited dozens of incidents of intimidation because they dared to talk in their mother tongue.

Educators listened in silence. There were no denials; everyone knew that it had been this way for generations. Wasn't it everywhere? In Texas it is illegal, according to Section 288 of the State Penal Code, for a teacher, principal, or school superintendent to teach or conduct school business in any language but English. Textbooks have to be in English. By custom the language restriction has been stridently applied to the students as well.

The "son of Zapata" County Commissioner Albert Pena extravagantly praised the students: "Our generation didn't have the courage to speak out. You are brave," he told them.

In the San Antonio high schools there were months of turmoil, meetings, student strikes, firings of teachers and even priests, newspaper headlines, and charges of infiltration by "Castro-trained extremists" before the high school students won the right to talk openly in their mother tongue. Until that triumph they had to whisper the language of Cervantes in the secrecy of the girls' locker rooms and the boys' urinals.

It was so everywhere. Language is a vital teaching tool in the de-education process. The banning of Spanish in the classroom is not an arbitrary act of a callous teacher. In the metropolitan school systems and in the village schoolhouses the suppression of the Spanish language and the culture of La Raza reflects the de-education policy that has been dominant in the schools of the Southwest since the "conquest" of the region.

In the small town of San Luis in the high mountains of southern Colorado the people are mostly Spanish-speaking. Yet, there too the native language was prohibited inside the school gate.

"Until quite recently Spanish has been tacitly assumed to be an *inferior language* by nearly all of us," writes a village teacher in San Luis, Alan Davis. "Its use has been forbidden in our classrooms, and on our playgrounds, until this month [February, 1969]." Of course, the teacher adds, "we offered no courses in Spanish."

The native language of the Chicano child was treated with colonialist disdain. His voice was muted. "English is the national language of the United States, but it is not a native or indigenous language. It is one of the colonial languages," writes Dr. Vera John, in a comprehensive study
54

of bilingualism in the schools of the Southwest. In a conquered land the institutions of culture—theaters, books, libraries, academics—may be visibly suppressed. It is more difficult to eradicate the spoken word. Language then becomes the last resource of cultural survival. "If the language goes, the culture goes with it," writes a scholar of La Raza. And so, in the schools there are bitter skirmishes over the spoken word. The children have become combatants.

"They yell at our children in school, 'Do not speak Spanish!' You are a free man in the land of the free, but 'Do not speak Spanish!' English is the only language of freedom," Reies Tijerina, the prophet of cultural revival, tells a meeting in a village schoolhouse. "It's like the story of the man who took a bird from his cage, and set it free. But first he took the pair of scissors and clipped off its wings.

" 'Fly! Fly!' the man said.

"The blue-eyed cat, the Anglo, came and ate the poor, helpless bird," Tijerina says.

In the "migrant schools" proposed by the state of California's "master migrant plan," the process of de-education by which a Chicano child is stripped of his culture is bluntly outlined. The "sample migrant school curriculum" is explicit:

> Physical education—English cultural games and activities . . .
> Creative arts and crafts—Introduction to English culture, music and song . . .
> Arithmetic—Concrete objects, English concept of arithmetic . . .
> Social Studies—Developing knowledge of characteristics of English culture . . .

Nowhere in the curriculum is there a word on the Indian, Spanish, and Mexican cultures of the Southwest. In all the classes the emphasis is upon the de-education of the Chicano child.

He has to be de-educated before he can be re-educated—as "English"? The "English" cultural games he is taught may be the old Aztec sports of basketball and handball; the "English" music and song, Western style, may have originated in the vaquero music and song of the old West; and the "English" concept of arithmetic may be based on the sophisticated mathematics of the scholars of ancient Mexico. But none of these origins is mentioned in the textbooks or the curriculum. Education of the Chicano is de-education, first of all. The language and culture of the Southwest are seen by his teachers as a prime hindrance to his progress, not only in learning English, but in "becoming an American." In the better schools the ensuing conflict may be subtle, but in the poorer schools it is vulgar and cruel.

"Schools try to brainwash the Chicanos," says Maggie Alvarado, a student at St. Mary's University in San Antonio. "They try to make us forget our history, to be ashamed of being Mexicans, of speaking Spanish. They succeed in making us feel empty, and angry, inside."

De-education is a difficult process. The culture of La Raza and the Spanish language were native to the country for hundreds of years before the coming of the Anglo to the Southwest; they are not easy to uproot. Every generation the attempt at de-education has to begin anew, for the conflict of cultures in the schools of the Southwest is an unending conflict between the conquered and the conqueror. Colonialism has usurped the purposes of education. The schools have been one of the most effective instruments of the "conquest."

"It is safe to say that the school, more than barbed wire or the plowing up of the range, was responsible for the decline of the vaquero," writes the venerable old cowboy and settler of California, Arnold Rojas. The "Yankee schoolmarm" was a more efficient conqueror of La Raza than the United States Army, Rojas writes: "The children did not have a chance." . . .

The malaise of the de-educated child does not come entirely from the forbidding rules of the unfriendly school, where "English, a foreign language," mutes his voice. It comes from his home as well. Many of these children are hungry. They bring their hunger to school. They suffer from malnutrition and anemia that is so severe that a health survey of the Office of Education, in Washington, D.C., has estimated that as many as 15 percent may have their thought processes retarded due to lack of nutrition.

"They may need food, or medication, or warm clothes to be able to learn," reports a barrio classroom teacher, Hercella Toscano of San Antonio. "I do stress this need because I see it every day as I visit one class after another. I see children who are listless and restless. Some are in need of better clothes and some show signs of malnutrition.

"How can we expect these children to learn, especially if they are hungry?" asks the barrio teacher.

Poverty is not measured by the IQ tests. The hunger quotient is not registered, nor is the psychological effect of poor clothing, disease, and illness computed in the surveys of the lack of motivation, educational achievement, and rates of dropout. "Our kids don't drop out," says another barrio teacher, Froben Lozada, "they are pushed out by poverty."

The depressing effect of the de-education process upon the nearly two million Chicano youth of school age has been summarized by the sad statistics of the National Advisory Committee on Mexican-American Education of the U.S. Office of Education:

> . . . In the Southwest the average Chicano child has only a 7th grade education.
> . . . The drop-out, or push-out, rate in Texas for Chicano high school students is 89 percent, while in California 50 percent of Chicano high school students leave school between the 10th and 11th grade.
> . . . Along the Rio Grande Valley of Texas four out of five

Chicano children fall two years behind their Anglo classmates by the 5th grade. (The city manager of San Antonio estimates that 44.3 percent of the barrio residents are "functionally illiterate"; 20 percent never went to school "at all.")

... College enrollment is infinitesimal. In California, where 14 percent of public school students are Chicanos, less than ½ of one percent of college students at the seven campuses of the University of California are Chicanos.

Among the families of farm workers the process of de-education is most successful. The life on the road makes schooling difficult. The nature of the rural schools makes it worse. In the San Joaquin Valley of California, near Fresno, the results of a recent educational census show that the adult male Chicano has an average of 5.7 years of schooling.

The de-education of La Raza is indeed overachieved. Of all the children of the poor who go to school as though they go to battle to defend their cultural heritage, none come away with greater bitterness and frustration. In the barrios of the Southwest the Chicano child might echo the lament of a little Puerto Rican boy in the barrios of New York City, who told a social worker, "I am illiterate in two languages. I am an alien in two lands." ...

"We have to rediscover ourselves," says Luis Valdez, the director of El Teatro Campesino. "There are years and years of discoveries we have to make of our people.

"People ask me: What is Mexican history in the United States? There is no textbook of the history of La Raza. Yet the history of the Mexican in this country is four hundred years old. We know we predate the landing of the Pilgrims and the American Revolution. But beyond that? What really happened? No one can tell you. Our history has been lost. Lost!

"Our generation says: Wait! Stop! Let's consider our roots! Let's rediscover our history!" Valdez says.

Upon dusty shelves, frayed and forgotten, the books of this history may still be hidden. By word of mouth, from time to time, there is word of a lost literature, in reminiscences and folk memories. But the culture of La Raza has been effectively suppressed in the Southwest. The textbooks barely refer to it; the teachers are unfamiliar with it.

In the Faculty Forum of the Lincoln High School of East Los Angeles a teacher of Chicano youth, Richard C. Davis, dismisses that history: "Before the Spanish came, he [the Mexican] was an Indian grubbing in the soil, and after the Spanish came he was a slave." The teacher's ire is aroused by a fellow faculty member, Joe McKnight, who has the temerity to suggest that "Mexican and Mexican-American history should be a required course in all Eastside [Los Angeles] schools." Davis, who voices the "dominant view" of the faculty, disdainfully rejoins, "Mexican history is taught, what there is of it."

A few days after the teacher's contempt is publicized, two hundred parents picket the Lincoln High School with the inevitable signs of the times: "BRONZE IS BEAUTIFUL" and "WE ARE NOT INSECTS, DAVIS! WE ARE HUMAN BEINGS!" The *Chicano Student,* an underground campus newspaper in Los Angeles, complains of "teachers who at worst have contempt for our culture, and at best have no understanding of it." Chicanos are weary, they say, of "teachers who can't communicate, books in a strange language about blond, blue-eyed strangers named Dick and Jane."

In the beleaguered school a student is more explicit: "I am a prisoner of Lincoln High School," he writes, "where Richard Davis is allowed to preach racism; he should pack up and move out of our school."

Says a Chicano youth, in Texas: "The worst thing that happened to me in my life was when I went to a blasted high school which was mainly Anglo. I was taught how great the Anglo was. Never once did a teacher tell me, Oh yes, the Mexicans did great things in the Southwest. The only time they mention Mexicans in the schools is when they talk about the Mexican-American War. And then we are the bad guys, who lost.

"They teach white history and white education," the young man says. "You're white and you're great. So if you are Anglo you are given a superiority complex, and if you are not Anglo you are given a guilt complex. It's a racist way of teaching."

The children of La Raza, humiliated by the textbooks, tongue-tied by the teachers, de-educated by the schools, have had to hold onto what they can of their heritage by themselves. In the barrios they have created their own communal culture and have invented a language of their own beyond the pale of the Anglo schools. . . .

THE SHRUNKEN HEAD OF PANCHO VILLA

"Sorry, white man," wrote Ruben Gutierrez, a student at Woodrow Wilson High School in East Los Angeles. "La Raza has had enough." One mild day in March of 1968 some 15,000 Chicano students simply walked out of five Los Angeles high schools. By noon the strike had all but shut down classes throughout the barrio. The police invaded the classrooms and playgrounds. Swarms of sheriff's deputies blockaded the neighborhood, in an old-fashioned Western version of law and order. In an hour the arrests of students and teachers began.

The buoyant teen-agers called it a "blowout" and their hastily hand-drawn picket signs voiced their jubilant air—EDUCATION NOT CONTEMPT, EDUCATION NOT ERADICATION, TEACHERS, SI, BIGOTS, NO! QUE PASO? FREE SPEECH! WE ARE NOT 'DIRTY MEXICANS,' OUR KIDS DON'T HAVE BLUE EYES, BUT THEY DO GO OVERSEAS, SCHOOL NOT PRISON, and IS THIS A HOLIDAY?

Enthusiasm and admiration of the adults for the young Chicanos' boldness unified the entire barrio. "These kids are proudly saying, 'I'm a Mexican and I want to learn about my culture,' " said Philip Montez, a West Coast director of the U.S. Civil Rights Commission. "When I was a kid we used to play it pretty cool about the Mexican thing." In the old days, when he went to school, students did protest, said Julian Nava, the sole Chicano on the Board of Education, elected after a barrio-wide fight. Nava, who holds a doctorate in history from Harvard University, recalled that when he attended a barrio high school, "I was told to take auto shop. And I did. I did what I was told."

Students who led the "blowout" issued a long list of educational demands—thirty-eight in all—to the Board of Education. They ranged from "textbooks and curriculum should be revised to show Mexican contributions to our country" and "the transfer of teachers who show any form of prejudice to students," to the building of swimming pools in "all Eastside schools" and unlocked restrooms and "all campuses to be open and fences removed." Support for many of the Chicanos' proposals came from the Los Angeles Teachers Association and Local 1021 of the American Federation of Teachers. The abysmal conditions of the schools needed reform, the teachers' groups affirmed; especially did they support "more bilingual and bicultural training of school personnel, more Spanish-language library materials and textbooks," and "better cafeteria food."

But the city of Los Angeles replied by arresting the alleged thirteen leaders of the "blowout," including Sal Castro, a high school teacher. Those jailed were charged with "conspiracy" to disturb the educational process.

La Raza, the barrio newspaper, chortled that there were "thirteen Aztec gods," so the arrested ones were a select and prophetic number. It shows how "ignorant" the Board of Education is of our heritage, the editors wrote. "These are our people, the cream of the crop," declared the *Chicano Student;* and the youth did not really walk out of the schools, "they were pushed out!"

Hundreds of barrio groups came to the defense of the "conspirators." So did the Congress of Mexican American Unity, the Educational Issues Coordinating Council, the United Mexican American Students (UMAS), Cesar Chavez of the farm workers, the Council of Churches of Southern California, the Pacific Southwest Council of the Union of American Hebrew Congregations, the local American Federation of Teachers, the NAACP, and the Black Congress. Yet, when—after a year's delay, uproarious protests of thousands of barrio residents and students, and dozens of arrests—"the thirteen" were brought to trial, they were hurriedly convicted, fined, and placed on probation that forbade them to enter any barrio school, unless on official business. The probation was to last for three years.

The Los Angeles Board of Education voted to suspend the teacher, Sal Castro. In furious response the leaders of the barrios—students and parents—calmly walked into the board room of the Board of Education and staged a sit-in. For an entire week they occupied it. A young student, Paul Ruiz, was elected "temporary" Chairman of the Board; he presided over the exercise in community control. Every morning a priest offered mass, at the podium, using a tortilla as a holy wafer. He blessed the protesters, who spent the week discussing school reforms, singing Chicano songs to the music of guitars, and voting a new school system.

"Never was the Board of Education such a happy place," one of the Chicanos said.

"LIBERATED CHICANO BOARD OF EDUCATION," the barrio students and parents wrote on the blackboard. Then they went home.

The bemused members of the Board of Education returned to their silent chamber. Once seated they promptly voted to reinstate the barrio teacher, Sal Castro, whom they had suspended the week before. But in the barrio schools the rumblings have not ceased and the grievances have not changed.

"What, really, did the students benefit from the walkouts?" a Lincoln High School youth writes in the *Chicano Student*. "Not a damn thing! Why can't the white man see our side of the story? We Chicanos are damn sick and tired of talking. We want action, action now!"

"Our proposals have been made," the *Chicano Student* had editorialized earlier. "The big question is, will the School Board take positive action. If so, WHEN? IF NOT—BLOWOUTS, BABY, BLOWOUTS!"

Schools had become the no-man's-land of the cultural conflict. They are the most visible, best known, and most exposed institutions of the Anglo society in the barrios. On the inside they are the bastions where the language, philosophy, and goals of the conqueror are taught; but to those outside they are the bastions that the conquered can most easily besiege, with common cause, so that their children may be taught the language, philosophy, and goals of La Raza.

The "community control" of the schools, for the "better education of our children," is the social issue that has united the barrios more than any other. "Education is like a god to our people," says the barrio teacher Froben Lozada. But it is more than that.

Almost by mutual consent the schools have been chosen as the battlefield. The conflict in the classrooms may be fought, and won or lost, without threatening the sources of social power. The economic and political control of the barrios will not change, even if the Chicanos were to achieve new textbooks, a curriculum based on the heritage and needs of La Raza, and a wholly bicultural and bilingual teaching system. In a sense the schools are the safest places to continue the guerrilla warfare of the cultures that began with the "conquest" of the Southwest. They are safer battlefields than the streets or the voting booths, for both sides.

"Revolution" in the schools thus becomes a paradox that is supported by the Chicano activists and the Anglo establishment, at least federally, with equal fervor.

In the fall of 1969 the Chicano students declared a national "walkout" in celebration of Mexican Independence Day on September 17th. School officials in Denver, Colorado, acquiescing to the rebellious mood of the students, announced a special assembly in a high school where there had been a riot the previous spring, to permit "leaders of the walkout to present their views to the student body." Never before in the Southwest had school authorities given such recognition to the Chicano "revolution."

Everywhere, from rural Texas to metropolitan California, there are walkouts, "blowouts," and protest marches. The student activists demand community control of the barrio schools and an "educational revolution," based on a new curriculum that honors "the dignity of Chicano life," by teaching the language of the people and the "Mexican and Mexican-American cultural heritage."

In the barrios, where the classroom has become a battlefield, the "passive pupil" has found his voice. Schools are a common ground, most of all for the child. He sees that in the classroom he is not the minority; he is the majority. Growing up in two cultures may, at times, be precarious and absurd. But it demands agility of the Chicano. He develops survival skills in both worlds. He learns how to live "in the belly of the shark." He no longer feels he must suffer in silence or withdraw, as his father did. The Chicano is surer of himself. He is outspoken, once he starts to speak.

In *The Shrunken Head of Pancho Villa,* his play on de-education, Luis Valdez depicts a boy of the barrios who talks back, gets into trouble, and is sent to reform school. Joaquín, the Chicano antihero, returns home in the last act as a well-dressed, well-polished anglicized youth. But, he has no head! "He seems very reformed, rehabilitated," says his brother Mingo. "A clean-cut American boy." Lupe, his sister, is equally sardonic: "I think Joaquín, Jack, is gonna be okay, Ma. He can still find a job in the fields. A man doesn't need a head to work there."

All through the play the shrunken, stolen head of Pancho Villa is symbolically off-stage. When the headless, de-educated Chicano boy appears, the decapitated hero of the Mexican Revolution cries, "There's the body and here's the head. Let's get together!"

"It's time for a new Mexican revolution," Luis Valdez tells Chicano students at the University of California, in Los Angeles. "And which Chicanos are going to lead the next revolution? The ones in the belly of the shark! Nosotros! We! We're going to lead that revolution! We've got to stand up and talk straight to the *gabachos* [the Anglos] saying, 'Hell, no! I won't go!' to your whole lousy system."

Peter Collier

Indian Power: "Better Red Than Dead"

According to a fifth-grade supplementary reader in the 1960's, "Today the Indians go to school, join the army, live where they please. They are no longer the forgotten Americans. They are just like all citizens of the United States: Americans." Behind such an optimistic appraisal, however, is a grim reality: the life expectancy of America's 650,000 Indians is more than 25 years below the national average, their income per family is the lowest of any American group, their unemployment rate on reservations ranges from 20 percent to 80 percent, their average years of schooling is 5.5, and their tribal government has little real power because most day-to-day decisions rest with the Bureau of Indian Affairs. In the words of N. Scott Momaday, a member of the Kiowa tribe, Indians "constitute the most desperate and deprived minority in America." Peter Collier's essay provides insights into the experiences and anger that have galvanized a growing number of Indians to bid farewell to "Uncle Tom-Tom" and to join the movement for "Red Power." Collier is an editor of *Ramparts* magazine.

W hen fourteen Indian college students invaded Alcatraz on a cold, foggy morning in the first part of November [1969]—claiming ownership "by right of discovery," and citing an 1868 treaty allowing the Sioux possession of unused federal lands—they seemed in a light-hearted mood. After establishing their beachhead, they told the press that they had come there because Alcatraz already had all the necessary features of a reservation: dangerously uninhabitable buildings; no fresh water; inadequate sanitation; and the certainty of total unemployment. They said they were planning to make the five full-time caretakers wards of a Bureau of Caucasian Affairs, and offered to take this troublesome real estate off the white man's hands for twenty-four dollars, payment to be made in glass beads. The newspapers played it up big, calling the Indians a "raiding party." When, after a nineteen-hour stay, the Indians were persuaded to leave the island, everyone agreed that it had been a good publicity stunt.

If the Indians had ever been joking about Alcatraz, however, it was with the bitter irony that fills colonial subjects' discourse with the mother-country. When they returned to the mainland, they didn't fall back into the cigar-store stoicism that is supposedly the red man's prime virtue. In

From Peter Collier, "The Red Man's Burden," *Ramparts*, 8 (February, 1970), pp. 27–28, 30–31. © Ramparts Magazine, Inc., 1970. Reprinted by permission of the author.

fact, their first invasion ignited a series of meetings and strategy-sessions; two weeks later they returned to the rock, this time with a force of nearly a hundred persons, a supply network, and the clear intention of staying. What had begun as a way of drawing attention to the position of the contemporary Indian, developed into a plan for doing something about it. And when the government, acting through the General Services Administration, gave them a deadline for leaving, the Indians replied with demands of their own: Alcatraz was theirs, they said, and it would take U.S. marshals to remove them and their families; they planned to turn the island into a major cultural center and research facility; they would negotiate only the mechanics of deeding over the land, and that only with Interior Secretary Walter Hickel during a face-to-face meeting. The Secretary never showed up, but the government's deadlines were withdrawn.

> On this island, I saw not whether the people had
> personal property, for it seemed to me that whatever
> one had, they all took share of, especially
> of eatable things.
> CHRISTOPHER COLUMBUS

Alcatraz is Indian territory: The old warning to "Keep Off U.S. Property" now reads "Keep off Indian Property"; security guards with red armbands stand near the docks to make sure it is obeyed. Women tend fires beneath huge iron cauldrons filled with food, while their kids play frisbee in what was once a convicts' exercise yard. Some of the men work on the prison's wiring system or try to get more cellblocks cleared out for the Indian people who are arriving daily from all over the country; others sit fishing on the wharf with hand-lines, watching quietly as the riptides churn in the Bay. During the day, rock music plays over portable radios and a series of soap operas flit across a TV; at night, the prison is filled with the soft sounds of ceremonial drums and eerie songs in Sioux, Kiowa and Navajo.

In the few weeks of its occupation, Alcatraz has become a mecca, a sort of red man's Selma. Indian people come, stay a few days, and then leave, taking with them a sense of wonderment that it has happened. Middle-aged "establishment" Indians are there. They mix with younger insurgents like Lehman Brightman (the militant Sioux who heads a red power organization called the United Native Americans), Mad-Bear Anderson (the Iroquois traditionalist from upstate New York who fought to get the United Nations to stop the U.S. Army Corps of Engineers' flooding of precious Seneca Indian lands), Sid Mills (the young Yakima who demanded a discharge from the Army after returning from Vietnam so that he could fight his real war—against the state of Washington's denial of his people's fishing rights), and Al Bridges (one of the leaders of the first Washington fish-ins in 1964, who now faces a possible ten-year prison sentence for defying the state Fish and Game Commission). The composition of the *ad hoc* Indian community changes constantly, but the purpose remains the same: to make Alcatraz a powerful symbol of liberation springing out of the long American imprisonment.

The people enjoy themselves, spending a lot of time sitting around the campfire talking and gossiping. But there is a sense of urgency beneath the apparent lassitude. Richard Oakes, a 27-year-old Mohawk who worked in high steel construction before coming West to go to college, is one of the elected spokesmen. Sitting at a desk in the old warden's office, he talks about the hope of beginning a new organization, the Confederacy of American Indian Nations, to weld Indian groups all over the country into one body capable of taking power away from the white bureaucracy. He acknowledges that the pan-Indian movements which have sprung up before have always been crushed.

> But time is running out for us (he says). We have everything at stake. And if we don't make it now, then we'll get trapped at the bottom of that white world out there, and wind up as some kind of Jack Jones with a social security number and that's all. Not just on Alcatraz, but every place else, the Indian is in his last stand for cultural survival.

This sentiment is reflected in the slogans lettered on walls all over the prison, the red paint bleeding down onto the concrete. One of them declares: "Better Red than Dead."

I also heard of numerous instances in which our men
had cut out the private parts of females and wore
them in their hats while riding in the ranks.
A U.S. ARMY LIEUTENANT, TESTIFYING ABOUT THE
SAND CREEK MASSACRE OF 1864

The Alcatraz occupation is still popularly regarded as the engaging fun and games of Indian college kids. In its news coverage of the U.S. Coast Guard's feeble attempt to blockade ships running supplies to the island, one local television station found amusement in showing their films to the musical accompaniment of U.S. cavalry bugle calls. It was not so amusing to the occupiers, however. The California Indians now on the Rock know that their people were decimated from a population of 100,000 in 1850 when the gold rush settlers arrived, to about 15,000 thirty years later, and that whole tribes, languages and cultures were erased from the face of the earth. There are South Dakota Indians there whose grandparents were alive in 1890 when several hundred Sioux, mostly women and children leaving the reservation to find food, were caught at Wounded Knee, killed, and buried in a common grave—the old daguerreotypes still showing heavily-mustachioed soldiers standing stiffly over the frozen bodies like hunters with their trophies. Cowboys and Indians is not a pleasant game for the Alcatraz Indians and some must wonder whether, in another 150 years, German children will be gaily playing Nazis and Jews.

But the past is not really at issue. What is at stake today, as Richard Oakes says, is cultural survival. Some of the occupiers have known Indian culture all their lives; some have been partially assimilated away from it and are now trying to return. All understand that it is in jeopardy, and they want some assurance that Indian-ness will be available to their children. It sounds like a fair request, but fairness has never ruled the destiny of the Indian in America. In fighting for survival, the Indians of Alcatraz are challenging the lies perpetuated by anthropologists and bureaucrats alike, who insist that the red man is two things: an incompetent "ward" addicted to the paternalism of government, and an anachronism whose past is imprisoned in white history and whose only future is as an invisible swimmer in the American mainstream. The people on Alcatraz have entered a struggle on a large scale that parallels the smaller, individual struggles for survival that many of them have known themselves; it is the will to exist as individuals that brought them together in determination to exist as a people.

When Robert Kennedy came, that was the only
day they ever showed any respect for the
Indian, just on that one day, and after
that, they could care less.
    A Freshman Student at Blackfoot,
    Idaho, High School

One of the original fourteen on Alcatraz was a pretty twenty-two year-old Shoshone-Bannock girl named La Nada Means. Her hair is long and reddish-black; her nose arches slightly and prominent cheekbones square out her face. Her walk is slightly pigeon-toed, the result of a childhood disease for which she never received treatment. If you tell her that she looks very Indian, she will thank you, but with a searching look that suggests she has heard the same comment before, and not as a compliment.

> When I was little (she says), I remember my family as being very poor. There were twelve of us kids, and we were always hungry. I remember sometimes getting to the point where I'd eat anything I could get my hands on—leaves, small pieces of wood, anything. The other thing I remember is the meanness of the small towns around the reservation. Blackfoot, Pocatello—they all had signs in the store windows to keep Indians out. One of them I'll never forget; it said, 'No Indians or Dogs Allowed.' There were Indian stalls in the public bathrooms; Indians weren't served in a lot of the restaurants; and we just naturally all sat in the balcony of the theaters. You learn early what all that means. It becomes part of the way you look at yourself.

She grew up on the Fort Hall reservation in southern Idaho. The Jim Crow atmosphere of the surrounding small towns has lessened somewhat with the passage of time and the coming of the civil-rights bills, but it is still very much present in the attitude of white townsfolk towards Indians. And while there are no longer the small outbreaks of famine that occurred on the reservation when La Nada was growing up in the '50s, Fort Hall is still one of the bleakest areas in the country, and the people there are among the poorest.

Like most Indian children of her generation (and like a great many today), La Nada Means was sent away to school. Her youth became a series of separations from home and family, each more traumatic than the one before. The first school she attended was St. Mary's School for Indian Girls in Springfield, South Dakota. She remembers:

> I took a lot of classes in subjects like 'Laundry,' where the classwork was washing the headmaster's clothes. All Indian people are supposed to be good with their hands, you know, and also hard workers, so we didn't do too much regular schoolwork at St. Mary's. They also had what they called a Summer Home Program where you're sent out during the summer break to live with a white family. It was supposed to teach you white etiquette and things like that, and make you forget your savage Indian ways. When I was thirteen, I was sent up to Minnesota where I became a sort of housekeeper for the summer. I don't remember too much about it, except that the wages I got, about $5 a week, were sent back to St. Mary's and I never saw them. After being at that school a little while, I got all upset. They said I was 'too outspoken,' and expelled me. After I got back to Fort Hall, I had my first breakdown.

For awhile she attended public school in Blackfoot, the small town bordering the reservation. She was suspended because she objected to the racial slurs against Indians which were built into the curriculum. She was fifteen when the Bureau of Indian Affairs (BIA) sent her to its boarding school in Chilocco, Oklahoma. On her first day there, the matrons ordered her to lower the hems on the two dresses she owned. She refused and was immediately classified as a troublemaker. "At Chilocco you're either a 'good girl' or a 'bad girl,' " she says.

> They put me in the bad girls' dormitory right away with Indians mainly from the Northwest. The Oklahoma Indians were in the good girls' dorm, and the matrons constantly tried to keep us agitated by setting the tribes to fighting with each other. Everything was like the Army. There were bells, drills and set hours for everything. The food was called 'GI Chow.' There was a lot of brutality, but it was used mainly on the boys, who lived in another wing. Occasionally they'd let the boys and girls get together. You all stood in this big square; you could hold hands, but if the matrons saw you getting too close,

they'd blow a whistle and then you'd have to march back to the dorm.

La Nada made the honor roll, but was expelled from Chilocco after a two-month stay for being involved in a fight.

> The matrons just had it in for me, I guess. They got about a hundred other Indian girls against me and a few other 'bad girls." They put us in a small room and when the fight was ready to begin, they turned out the lights and walked out, locking the doors behind them. We had a "riot," and I got beat up. The next day, the head of the school called me into his office and said that I didn't fit in.

She was sent off with one dollar, a sack lunch, and a one-way bus ticket from Chilocco back to Idaho. She lived with her family for a few months, helping her father collect data about conditions at Fort Hall, and then was sent by the BIA to another of its boarding schools, Stewart Institute, in Carson City, Nevada. Her reputation as a "difficult Indian" followed her, and she was again sent home after being at Stewart for less than a day. The BIA threatened to send her to "reform" school; then it forgot about her.

> I stayed around the reservation for awhile, and when I got to be seventeen, I took GED [high school equivalent] exams. I only had about nine real years of schooling, but I scored pretty well and got into Idaho State College. I lasted there for a semester, and then quit. I didn't really know what to do. At Fort Hall, you either work in some kind of menial job with the BIA agency there, or you go off the reservation to find a job in one of the towns. If you choose the BIA, you know that they'll try to drill a subservient mentality into you; and in the towns, the discrimination is pretty bad.

La Nada again spent time working with her father, a former tribal chairman. They sent out letters to congressmen and senators describing conditions on the reservations, and tried to get the Bureau of Indian Affairs office to respond. As a result, her father was harassed by local law enforcement officials. La Nada drifted for a time and then asked the BIA for "relocation" off the reservation. Many of the Fort Hall Indians have taken this route and 80 percent of them return to the reservation, because, as La Nada says, "things in the slums where you wind up are even worse than on the reservation, and you don't have your people to support you."

The BIA gave her a one-way ticket to San Francisco, one of eight major relocation centers in the country. When she first arrived, she sat in the local BIA office from 8 to 5 for a few days, waiting for them to help her find a job. They didn't, and she found a series of temporary clerk jobs by herself. As soon as she found work, the BIA cut off her $140 a month relocation payment. She wound up spending a lot of time in the "Indian bars" which are found in San Francisco and every other relocation town.

She worked as a housekeeper in the private home for Indian girls where the BIA had first sent her, and as a barmaid in a beer parlor. She was "drunk most of the time," and she became pregnant. She was seventeen years old.

> After I had the baby, my mother came out from the reservation and got him. She said they'd take care of him back home until I got on my feet. I really didn't know what to do. The only programs the BIA has are vocational training for menial jobs, and I didn't especially want to be a beautician. Actually, I wanted to try college again, but when I told this to a BIA counselor, he said they didn't have any money for that and told me I was being 'irrational and unrealistic.'
>
> All types of problems develop when you're on relocation. The Indian who has come to the city is like a man without a country. Whose jurisdiction are you under, the BIA's or the state's? You go to a county hospital when you're sick and they say, 'Aren't you taken care of by the Indian Affairs people?' It's very confusing. You hang around with other Indians, but they are as bad off as you are. Anyway, I started sinking lower and lower. I married this Sioux and lived with his family awhile. I got pregnant again. But things didn't work out in the marriage, and I left. After I had the baby, I ended up in the San Francisco General psychiatric ward for a few weeks. I was at the bottom, really at the bottom. Indian people get to this point all the time, especially when they're relocated into the big city and are living in the slums. At this point, you've got two choices: either kill yourself and get it all over with—a lot of Indians do this —or try to go all the way up, and this is almost impossible.

As she looks at it now, La Nada feels she was "lucky." She tried to get admitted to the local colleges, but was refused because of her school record. Finally, because the University of California "needed a token Indian in its Economic Opportunity Program for minority students," she was admitted in the fall of 1968. She did well in her classes and became increasingly active, helping to found the United Native Americans organization and working to get more Indian students admitted into the EOP program. "After my first year there," she says, "everything was going along all right. I liked school and everything, and I felt I was doing some good. But I felt myself getting swallowed up by something that was bigger than me. The thing was that I didn't want to stop being an Indian, and there were all these pressures, very hidden ones, that were trying to make me white." At the summer break she went back to the reservation and spent some time with her family. The next quarter she became involved in the Third World Liberation Front strike at Berkeley, fighting for a school of Ethnic Studies, including a Native American program. She was suspended by the University.

La Nada's experiences, far from being extreme cases, are like those of most young Indians. If she is unique at all, it is because she learned the value of fighting back.

We need fewer and fewer 'experts' on Indians. What
we need is a cultural leave-us-alone agreement, in
spirit and in fact.
 VINE ·DELORIA, JR.

Each generation of Americans rediscovers for itself what is fashionably called the "plight" of the Indian. The American Indian today has a life expectancy of approximately forty-four years, more than twenty-five years below the national average. He has the highest infant mortality rate in the country (among the more than 50,000 Alaskan natives, one of every four babies dies before reaching his first birthday). He suffers from epidemics of diseases which were supposed to have disappeared from America long ago.

A recent Department of Public Health report states that among California Indians, "water from contaminated sources is used in 38 to 42 percent of the homes, and water must be hauled under unsanitary conditions by 40 to 50 percent of all Indian families." Conditions are similar in other states. A high proportion of reservation housing throughout the country is officially classified as "substandard," an antiseptic term which fails to conjure up a tiny, two-room log cabin holding a family of thirteen at Fort Hall; a crumbling Navajo hogan surrounded by broken plumbing fixtures hauled in to serve as woodbins; or a gutted automobile body in which a Pine Ridge Sioux family huddles against the South Dakota winter.

On most reservations, a 50 percent unemployment rate is not considered high. Income per family among Indian people is just over $1500 per year—the lowest of any group in the country. But this, like the other figures, is deceptive. It does not suggest, for instance, the quality of the daily life of families on the Navajo reservation who live on $600 per year (exchanging sheep's wool and hand-woven rugs with white traders for beans and flour), who never have real money and who are perpetually sinking a little further into credit debt.

To most Americans, the conditions under which the Indian is forced to live are a perennial revelation. On one level, the symptoms are always being tinkered with half-heartedly and the causes ignored; on another level, the whole thrust of the government's Indian policy appears calculated to perpetuate the Indians' "plight." This is why La Nada Means and the other Indians have joined what Janet McCloud, a leader of the Washington fishing protests, calls "the last, continuing Indian War."

Connie Brown
and Jane Seitz

Woman Power: "You've Come A Long Way, Baby"

As the newly crowned Miss America walks across the stage to the words "There she goes, my ideal," a growing number of women have retorted, "not mine!" Miss America has become a cliche—like "dumb broad," "nice chick," and Playboy bunnies—symbolic of woman as an object in a male-dominated world. Women have suffered not only income disparities and limited jobs, but also the psychological and social discrimination inherent in second-class citizenship. Two participants in the Women's Liberation Movement, Connie Brown and Jane Seitz, provide both a cry for independence and an assessment of some of the weaknesses inherent in the earlier women's rights movements, especially the tendency to mistake "emancipation" (the terms of which are defined by men) for "liberation," or the right of self-determination. Connie Brown served for a time as an organizer for an SDS community project. Jane Seitz was an editor at Random House.

The difficulty of learning about the history of women in America is that, for the most part, it is an unwritten history of millions of private lives, whose voices, those that were recorded at all, are scattered and buried in journals and letters. It isn't hard to find out what men thought of us—their ideas about women are accessible through the laws they passed and maintained, denying or restricting women's civil and property rights, through the religions they organized and practiced, through their literature. Women did write novels, essays, poems, magazine articles, but most of these are long out of print, and the task of digging up those old sources is still ahead of us.

There is the exception, of course, of the women's rights movement, which belongs to recorded history. Although, like the history of black people, it has long been suppressed, its documents—letters, speeches, newspapers, tracts—are available in various libraries and collections, and allow us a direct contact with the lives and the ideas of the nineteenth-century feminists. Because those women stepped out of private life into the public arena where recorded events take place, they created for us a brief "history," recognized by men in their books. (The Beards' *Basic History of the United States* has almost ten pages on the women's rights movement!)

But that movement is only a small part of our history. We need to know much more—about the women on plantations, on the lonely farms, in factories, schools, labor unions—in order to reclaim our past from obscurity, to rediscover our heroines, to understand our present. Our historical introduction to this anthology is necessarily superficial. It is written for other women as an introduction to the idea that we *have* a history.

> Man and wife are one person, but understand in what manner. When a small brooke or little river incorporateth with Rhodanus or the Thames, the poor rivulet looseth its name, it is carried and recarried with the new associate, it beareth no sway, it possesseth nothing during coverture ... To a married woman, her new self is her superior, her companion, her master.

This poetic description of the status of married women comes from seventeenth-century British Common Law. The law itself, and the view of women it implied, defined the legal position of women in America from the arrival of the first settlers until well into the second half of the nineteenth century. Woman's intellectual and physical inferiority to man was taken for granted. God and nature had clearly ordained her social inferiority. . . .

The trend toward increased democratization in the first half of the nineteenth century, the expanding frontier and the migration of country people to cities which accompanied industrialization, combined to produce a crisis of identity among statesmen, writers, clergymen, professionals—those who saw themselves as the inheritors and interpreters of the new republic. What were to be the limitations on individual enterprise? What were to be the civilizing influences on the wild frontier? What was to be the rationalization for the blood-sucking plantation system now expanding into Missouri, Arkansas, Texas? The stern Puritan had been transformed into the rapacious Yankee businessman, while the aristocratic Virginia gentleman was declining into effete libertinism. If the mercenary and self-aggrandizing impulse which was behind the rapid expansion of the country and its economy were to go unchecked—what then would become of the high principles on which the country claimed its legitimacy?

An answer of sorts, if not a satisfactory one, was found in Woman. In novels, in sermons, in political speeches, in popular magazines such as Sarah Hale's *Godey's Lady's Book,* woman was seen as the source of all those virtues which could hold within bounds the necessary but dangerous instincts of acquisitiveness in men. In a circular way, woman in her sanctified family domain became not only the restraining moral force on men's greed, but the justification of and excuse for that impulse. Some women, perhaps most, accepted this glorification, unprecedented in American history, and accepted the confined and tedious existence it implied. But some did not.

If Woman, as guardian of the hearth, carrier of tradition, influencer of morality, became a salve for men's consciences and a symbol of stability in a turbulent time, the same social turbulence had the effect of raising questions, in the minds of some women, about that image. In the 1830's, a period of expanding democratic rights for white men, the women's rights movement had its beginning.

Even in this atmosphere of questioning, however, the women's rights movement did not emerge at first as a self-conscious, independent movement. It had its immediate origins in another search for human rights—abolitionism. Excluded from the anti-slavery societies which were proliferating in the 1830's in the towns of New England, in New York, and in Philadelphia, women formed their own societies, and thus had their first experience in organizing and public speaking. Although the role that countless women played in the operation of the underground railway, harboring and transporting runaway slaves, required courage and ingenuity, their entrance into public affairs called for a defiance of prejudices deeply entrenched in themselves, as well as in the society, that was perhaps more taxing to them than physical danger. Women simply did not speak in public. With the exception of the Quakers, who allowed women to speak freely in Meeting, and ordained them as ministers, churches continued to practice the rule of St. Paul: "Let the women learn in silence with all subjection . . . I suffer not a woman to teach, nor to usurp authority over men, but to be in silence." However glorified by preachers and politicians in their "proper sphere," women were scolded, ridiculed and stoned when they attempted to transcend it by speaking against slavery. . . .

The women's rights movement had its official beginning in 1848, when several hundred women and sympathetic men met at Seneca Falls in upstate New York for a convention called by two active abolitionists, Elizabeth Cady Stanton and Lucretia Mott. The Seneca Falls Declaration of Rights and Sentiments remained for years the single most important document for the women's movement, and still speaks eloquently more than a century later:

> The history of mankind is a history of repeated injuries and usurpations on the part of men toward women, having in direct object the establishment of an absolute tyranny over her. To prove this, let facts be submitted to a candid world.
>
> He has never permitted her to exercise her inalienable right to the elective franchise.
>
> He has compelled her to submit to laws, in the formation of which she has no voice . . .
>
> Having deprived her of this first right of a citizen, the elective

franchise, thereby leaving her without representation in the halls of legislation, he has oppressed her on all sides.

He has made her, if married, in the eye of the law, civilly dead.

He has taken from her all right in property, even to the wages she earns.

... In the covenant of marriage, she is compelled to promise obedience to her husband, he becoming, to all intents and purposes, her master—the law giving him power to deprive her of her liberty, and to administer chastisement.

... He has monopolized nearly all the profitable employments, and from those she is permitted to follow, she receives but a scanty remuneration. He closes against her all the avenues to wealth and distinction which he considers most honorable to himself. As a teacher of theology, medicine, or law, she is not known.

... He has created a false public sentiment by giving to the world a different code of morals for men and women, by which moral delinquencies which exclude women from society, are not only tolerated, but deemed of little account in men.

He has usurped the prerogative of Jehovah himself, claiming it as his right to assign to her a sphere of action, when that belongs to her conscience and to her God ...

He has endeavored, in every way he could, to destroy her confidence in her own powers, to lessen her self-respect, and to make her willing to lead an abject and dependent life.

The Seneca Falls Declaration is couched in the typical enlightenment terms of basic and inalienable human rights. Its language is that of the Declaration of Independence, on which it was modeled. It gives a clear picture of women's civil status at the time it was written, and at the same time protests the psychological subjugation of women by men. Its program is an attack on the laws and customs that deny full citizenship and equal economic opportunity to women. Although it conveys a vivid sense of the depth, pervasiveness, and subtlety of women's oppression, as well as of its legal manifestations, it conspicuously avoids an analysis of the family, and of the connection between women's primary responsibilities there, and her exclusion from public life. To question the sacred rightness of the family, and women's place in it, would have brought upon these women a storm of outrage far beyond what they actually suffered. Feminist imagination, which envisaged radically new forms of dress, rebelled at the traditional marriage ceremony and the surrender of the maiden name, attacked established religion and male dominance of education and the professions—the fearless feminist imagination balked at an attack on the family. Although the early feminists cannot be accused of the mistake of the later ones in concentrating solely on the ballot as the key to equality, they dared only to insist on sharing public life with men—not to insist on men's sharing the burdens of home and family. ...

Until the outbreak of the Civil War, the women's movement continued to draw strength from the abolitionist movement, and to be closely associated with it spiritually and organizationally. During the war itself, most feminist agitation ceased while the women worked for victory for the North. However, if the feminists temporarily lent their energies to what they felt was a "larger cause," the ground was being prepared for a new growth of feminism after the war.

The most prominent organizations devoted to women's rights—the militant National Women's Suffrage Association (NWSA), headed by Elizabeth Cady Stanton and Susan B. Anthony, and the more respectable American Woman Suffrage Association (AWSA)—both concentrated their energies on the question of the franchise. The lack of the vote was a symptom of women's exclusion from the society and not its cause; yet it was such a powerful symbol that the suffragists expected, and the anti-suffragists feared, liberating results out of all proportion to what finally came about when women were granted the vote. . . .

As the women's movement concentrated more on the vote, it lost sight of the simple, forceful argument for equality based on the idea of natural rights as expounded by the Declaration of Independence, an argument that had been reinforced by the fight against slavery. The NWSA and AWSA, long split over methods and goals, were reunited on the basis of a surrender on the part of the more militant NWSA. The number of women in the suffrage organizations increased toward the end of the century, but the movement continued to recruit only middle-class women, who shared their husbands' fears that the huge numbers of poor immigrants—Irish, Italian, and Eastern European—would weaken the political power of the established classes. The women turned to a narrow and vicious, but persuasive, argument of expedience: that it was insulting to them, educated and true Americans, that ignorant, low-born foreigners should be able to vote while they could not; that if they were given the vote, the number of true Americans would be doubled and the forces of law and order strengthened. . . .

Although there was an obvious link between women's rights and unionism, few American suffrage leaders recognized it. British leaders, unlike their American sisters, recognized the common issues and embraced them. From its inception in 1903, the Women's Social and Political Union (WSPU), the strongest women's organization in England, included many working-class women.

Led by Emmeline (already well-known as a social reformer) and Christabel Pankhurst, organization began in Lancashire and Yorkshire. One of the early recruits, Anne Kinney, described the double oppression of working women:

> I grew up in the midst of women and girls in the works and I saw the
> hard lives of women and children about me. I noticed the great dif-

ference made in the treatment of men and women in the factory, difference in conditions, difference in wages, difference in status. I realized this difference not only in the factory but also in the home. I saw men and women and boys and girls all working hard during the day in the same hot stifling factories. Then when work was over, I noticed that it was the mothers who hurried home; who fetched the child who had been put out to nurse, prepared the tea for the husband, did the cleaning, baking, washing, sewing, and nursing. I noticed that when the husband ran home, his day's work was over, he took his tea and then went to join his friends in the club or in the public houses, or in the cricket or football field, and I used to ask myself why this was so. Why was the mother the drudge of the family, and not the complement and equal.[1]

The WSPU was militant from the start and increased its militancy with each confrontation. The first such confrontation took place in 1905 at a Liberal Party meeting when Anne Kinney and several others were attacked, thrown out of the hall, and finally arrested. Three days later, upon their release from jail, there was a large demonstration for suffrage.

A pattern of disrupting meetings, arrests, and rallies continued throughout 1906–07. "Rise Up Women" had become a familiar cry to the English. Tactics were expanded to include working in the countryside to defeat the Liberal Party which had refused to take a parliamentary stand in favor of the vote for women, as well as marches on Parliament. The confrontations between the militant women and the police at these marches were violent. Line after line of women was attacked by mounted police. Sixty-five women and two men were arrested during one of the first marches. "One thing is certain," said Christabel Pankhurst, "there can be no going back for us, and more will happen if we do not get justice."

In 1908, the Third Women's Parliament met and again decided to march on Parliament to demand that the members recognize the women's question. Some attempted to sneak into the building by jumping into a truck that drove close to the Parliament's doors; others came up the river in boats, shouting their complaints to onlookers. Fifty women were arrested that day, but there was no response from Parliament. Public opinion, however, was aroused in favor of the women, in favor, at least initially, of their spirit.

The cycle of action and punishment continued, and punishment grew more severe. A series of hunger strikes by the imprisoned women led to forced-feeding, and the great public outcry at this cruelty helped to hasten the final favorable vote in Parliament to grant women suffrage. After this victory, the English movement, which had been organized around this single issue, was absorbed into general reform movements.

[1] E. Sylvia Pankhurst, *The Suffragette* (London: Gay and Hancock, 1911), p. 74.

In 1907, Harriet Stanton Blatch, a daughter of Elizabeth Cady Stanton, returned from a twenty-year stay in England, where she had worked with the Pankhursts. She judged it impossible to revitalize the NAWSA and formed her own group which initiated the famous women's suffrage parades in New York, the first outdoor meetings, and attempted to interest trade-union women and suffragists in each other. If the mass meetings were somewhat effective, the attempt to unite the two classes of women was largely unsuccessful. Few middle-class women were objective enough or politically acute enough to recognize the necessity of abandoning the class prejudices of their men. It is hard to imagine working-class women, whose main interest was in survival, sympathizing with the singular importance placed on the vote, which must have seemed to be a middle-class luxury, a paper victory. Unlike English women, American women did not have an ideological framework for social change, a framework which would have shown the necessity of a connection between the poor working conditions and low wages of the working women and the lack of political power of all women.

It was not until factory women acted to improve their conditions that substantial support emerged among middle-class suffragists. The organizing of women workers progressed slowly until two International Ladies Garment Workers Union (ILGWU) shops in New York and Philadelphia struck in September of 1909. Thirty thousand workers, ten times the number expected by the organization, joined the strike, 75 percent of them women between the ages of sixteen and thirty. Throughout a cold winter these women picketed, held mass meetings, and built their union, sometimes at a rate of one thousand new members in a day. The picket lines were attacked by police and there were dozens of arrests. The courts were not sympathetic: one judge informed a striker: "You are on strike against God and Nature, whose prime law it is that man shall earn his bread in the sweat of his brow. You are on strike against God."

A link between the strike and the suffrage movement was provided by the Women's Trade Union League (WTUL), a group comprised of women union leaders and middle-class reformers (all of them also suffragists). The WTUL saw to publicity and raised thousands of dollars for strike funds.

Although some contact had been made between the two classes, the ILGWU strike was seen principally as a workers' struggle, only secondarily as a women's struggle.

No alliance of working-class women and middle-class women survived the enfranchisement of women. Neither side was fully aware of the importance and the potential of a united women's force.

The support for the trade-union movement by prominent suffragists did not, then, represent any great broadening of either movement. It did reflect a growing interest among the suffragist leadership in various reforming causes. A change also came about in the tactics of the suffragists. A group of younger women split from the NAWSA and formed the Congressional Suffrage Union (CSU). Learning from their British sisters, the

CSU held vigils at the White House, picketed, went to jail, went on hunger strikes, and were force-fed, bringing new publicity and new spirit to their cause. When five thousand women marched in Washington, D.C., in 1913, an angry mob attacked them, and a National Guard regiment was called out to protect the women.

This activity helped to revive interest in the women's suffrage amendment, an interest which had been languishing for over a decade. Meanwhile, the old NAWSA pulled itself together and in 1916 launched a four-year campaign on federal, state, and local levels to get the federal amendment passed by Congress and ratified by the state legislatures. It took an enormous effort on the part of hundreds of thousands of women. This was the last stage of a battle which had already been won in the minds of most Americans. . . .

Today the American woman can vote, get an education, and own property. The feminist movement accomplished this much. Of course, working-class women, black women, Mexican and Indian women have seen few changes in their long history of poverty, limited options, and humiliating dependence on an alien and greedy economy. Women have found that their subjugation goes far beyond the formal denial of civil rights. Women have obtained one limited objective after another, discovering again and again that liberation still lay ahead. The achievements of each successive movement have served to advance their status somewhat, to raise their ambitions, and to re-enlighten them each time about the nature of their struggle.

After World War I came the "emancipation of women" of which being able to vote was one aspect. Now all women could do what only "bad" women had done: show their legs, drink, smoke, go about with men without a chaperone. In intellectual and bohemian circles it was permissible to sleep with a man to whom one wasn't married. It became the rule, rather than the exception, for upper-middle-class women to go to college, and more women received Ph.D.'s in 1930 than ever before—or since. Getting married ceased to mean the end of social life for women. The figure of the young matron disappeared from American life, and the race to stay young began.

Difficult as it is to sort out and weigh the benefits and burdens of our "emancipation," one thing is clear. Somehow, what occurred was a terrible, cynical undercutting and buying off of the concepts of sexual, political, and economic liberation, and their replacement by new, more versatile forms of servitude. Isadora Duncan dreamed of, and practiced, a beautiful freedom of the body in dance and sex. Margaret Sanger tried to put into every woman's hands the power to choose whether and when to bear children.

The record numbers of female college graduates notwithstanding, economic independence and a career and a life of her own were still out of reach for the average woman, and, as a result, the new sexual freedom was used as "feminine attractions" have always been used, to purchase security from men.

In the Victorian era, before "sexual emancipation," the Virtuous Woman and the Prostitute were distinct and separate. The good, asexual wife may have felt bitterly deprived at the thought of her husband in the arms of a prostitute, but she was wrong if she envied the prostitute. The body's pleasure cannot be used to purchase security, either by a wife or by the prostitute who, notoriously, fakes pleasure to please her customer and earn more money. The Victorian wife who stifled her sexuality to buy her security at least was spared the hypocrisy of pretended pleasure.

Liberation would obviously dispense with the cruel dichotomy of sex and virtue, but instead after "emancipation" the roles were maintained, even combined. Now a woman must, to hold her man, act *both* the prostitute and the homebody, mistress and mother. The image of this good/bad woman has varied over the years—from flapper to the Playboy bunny who looks like the girl next door, or the housewife-sex kitten of TV commercials. A good girl, whose grandmother would have refused to kiss her fiance until the engagement was sealed, now has to decide "how far to go" on each date to keep her reputation poised between prudish and loose. The decision has to be based on the need to keep a man's respect while maintaining his sexual interest—her own needs and feelings must come second. Our pleasure and our womanhood are still defined by what men want from us.

There are, of course, practical reasons for this state of affairs. We would not need to distort and disguise ourselves and our sex if we did not still need to purchase from men what should be ours by right—equal opportunity for making money, for doing work we like, and equal responsibility on the part of individual men, and from the society, for taking care of the children. Sex and love have been so contaminated for women by economic dependence that the package deal of love and marriage looks like a con and a shill. We will not be able to sort out what we do want from men and what we want to give them until we know that our own physical and psychological survival—at home and at work—does not depend on men. Like all oppressed peoples, we need, first of all, *self-determination*.

Suzannah Lessard

"Gay Power" and the Homosexuals

The growing militancy of homosexuals —who number from three to four million Americans according to the National Institute of Mental Health— should have come as no surprise. In government service and private industry, for example, homosexuality has long been considered grounds for refusal to hire, and, in the 1950's, homosexuals were prime targets of Senator Joseph McCarthy's crusade to save America from "pinkos and perverts." Although recent court decisions have begun to overturn some discriminatory laws, homosexuals are still subject to the daily abuses of a society that views them as social pariahs and mental cases. Suzannah Lessard's essay describes specific examples of gay protest (e.g., the Christopher Street riot of 1969 and the "gay-in" demonstration of perhaps 15,000 homosexuals in June, 1970), distinguishes between prominent factions within the gay movement, and describes the movement's relationship to other protests such as that of women's liberation. She is an associate editor of *The Washington Monthly*.

O h no, not the fairies too!" said a woman watching the Gay Liberation movement march up Sixth Avenue last June, with a quizzical, good-humored expression on her face, as though they were so many puppies. "I'm from Ohio. I think it's funny," said a tourist. "I'd like to kick the shit out of them," said a clean, tense young man turning on his heel. No one quite knew how to react. Few grasped the implications or viewed it as more than either a circus or an abomination. But the marchers were confident. They had taken the trick out of the trick mirror; the invisible homosexual was now massively visible. With what seemed hardly more than a flick of the wrist they had upturned a whole new complex of bigotry and exclusion into broad sunlight, and the astonished prejudices could do little more than blink.

And once again, with the emergence of the gay movement, the old image of society as a vertical structure with one group holding another in subjugation was transformed into something more like a many-leveled house of cards, suits straining against each other, queens standing on knaves, one-eyed jacks trumping queens, the ceiling of one set forming the floor of another, with only one simple element in the complex of relationships—the position in the throne room of the white, male, heterosexual king.

The movement was born one night in August, 1969, when the New York police raided the Stonewall Inn, a gay bar on Christopher Street. It was by no means the first time—few of the many gay bars in the Village vicinity were immune to the arbitrary raids which usually ended in several arrests and many more bruises and broken heads. But this time, to the amazement of the Sixth Precinct, the homosexuals refused to take their punishment passively. The sissies fought back. Word of the brawl traveled, the gay community turned out in force, and the battle spread from the bar into what came to be known as the Christopher Street riot, a free-for-all in which cars were overturned, fires lit, and police sent to the hospital. After that the image of the homosexual in the eyes of the world, and, more important, in his own eyes as well, was irrevocably altered.

Prior to Christopher Street, the two major homosexual organizations, the Mattachine Society and the Daughters of Bilitis, were small and necessarily timid. Though Mattachine did make statements to the effect that homosexuality was neither pathological nor depraved, its objectives were in fact limited to helping the homosexual adjust within the society, providing social activities and legal and medical help, and backing conservative campaigns to change the more flagrant anti-homosexual laws. They were limited because their members were limited: homosexuals tended to be isolated and inhibited, having taken the one course they could really afford, which was to pass for heterosexual in order to pursue careers and life within the society, both of which would likely be destroyed were their homosexuality exposed. So their endeavor was not to battle the dragon but to sneak around it, to "get by" with a minimum of pain.

Furthermore, most people view the homosexual as a criminal and a pervert, an attitude deeply embedded in the culture; and it would take rare assurance for a homosexual not to let this attitude pervade his own image of himself and further deter his drive to challenge it.

OUT OF THE CLOSET INTO THE STREET

Out of Christopher Street the Gay Liberation Front was formed. In New York and subsequently in every major city in the country, the Front recruited, held workshops, and started newspapers. Many of the members were also part of the New Left, and, like the women, they started by confronting prejudice among their peers, educating them to the oppressiveness of their attitudes and the problems of the homosexual. After ten months they had grown big enough and become inwardly confident enough to organize a mass march up Sixth Avenue in New York. It was touch and go down to the wire, however. No one knew until the last minute whether more than a handful would actually show up, and few thought the march would reach its destination in Central Park without a violent confrontation with bystanders or the police.

But thousands and thousands turned out for the first big holiday from the closet. The festive mood was intoxicating. People in their Sunday best, their hippie best, lots of work-shirt and jeans types, a few fantastic costumes—they looked more like a peace march to whom the President had just capitulated than *homosexuals*. They just didn't *look* queer, and that fact registered everything from horror to discomfort to plain surprise on the faces of people on the sidelines. As one marcher put it, "So much has been accomplished in terms of who we are. We are people." And not only were they people, but they were evidently quite happy. The happy homosexual was supposed to be an impossibility. These together struck a solid blow at the assumption that homosexuality is in itself distorting, sad, and sick. Rather, it becomes clear that the conditions under which society forces it to exist are the causes of all those traits—deviousness, self-deprecation, unstable relationships—that we have been accustomed to linking inextricably with that way of life.

This seemed to have been a discovery for the marchers as well. After lives of secrecy and guilt, coming out into the open with the assertion "gay is good" gave them a healthy sense of self many hadn't known for years. "Coming out has been a delight," a woman recently told me. "It's difficult to imagine what it was like before. We are conditioned not to remember pain."

The briefest glance uncovers the depth of prejudice which the movement hopes to vanquish. The psychoanalytic tradition describes homosexuality entirely in terms of sickness, arrested development, unhealthy parental relationships, etc. Upon learning that a friend is homosexual, most of us, however sympathetic, have a tendency to conjure up an image of his mother. We assume that something has gone wrong, that the person has become homosexual for negative reasons, because he was unable to deal with some problem, and hence his choice represents a failure of sorts. The masculinity cult in America colors all our attitudes. Qualities like courage, effectiveness, and leadership are considered superior and are associated with virility, and conversely, the "feminine virtues" of tenderness, docility, and patience are considered of lesser importance. Men are expected to embody virility, and women maternity. Deviates from these roles are thought to be "half a man" or "half a woman"—and inferior in areas which have nothing whatever to do with sexuality. To most straight people, it is simply self-evident that a heterosexual is "better" than a homosexual. The notion that it's not a misfortune to have a child become a homosexual is as strange as the suggestion of one member of the movement that when a child discovers he is homosexual, the parents, not the child, should go to a psychiatrist to try to overcome their hang-ups about homosexuality.

The legal tradition is even harsher. In all states but one (Illinois), sodomy is a crime with sentences running as high as ten years' minimum and referred to in such phrases as "infamous crime against nature." Under this legal umbrella, discriminatory hiring practices exist unchallenged. For instance, the Civil Service Commission handbook on personnel states flatly that a homosexual is not suitable for service because his condition would automatically impair his efficiency as well as "inhibiting" those who were forced to work with him. This policy was recently overturned in a District of Columbia Court of Appeals, but the decision applies only to hiring within the D.C. circuit. Further, because many homosexuals are reluctant to expose themselves to publicity, Civil Service has been able to pursue its old policy within the district with few challenges.

The armed forces also have policies to the effect that homosexuality is an incapacitating condition which undermines discipline and makes the individual incapable of leading a constructive life. These policies have led to the dishonorable discharge of many men as well as Wacs and Waves. The women's services are one of the few areas where intense job discrimination against lesbians exists. In most cases lesbians, who can in any event hide their homosexuality more easily than men, are discriminated against primarily as women.

Beyond these formalities, antihomosexuality permeates the popular culture. "Faggot" is a universal term of derision. Wherever homosexuals are portrayed in movies they are ridiculous or desperate or disgusting. The old man in *Midnight Cowboy* was revolting, and Joe Buck responded "naturally" when he hit him. The host in *Boys in the Band* was pathetic. Both lesbians in *Five Easy Pieces* looked ugly in a movie full of pretty people. These versions of the homosexual generally go unquestioned. They fulfill our preconceived notions and affirm heterosexual superiority.

It seems clear that this overall attitude is irrational, that there is no necessary connection between worthiness and sexuality, and that whether or not one considers homosexuality a sickness these policies and attitudes are a barbarous response. It would seem that attitudes towards homosexuality are far more unacceptable, far more degrading to those who hold them—as well as those who endure them—than homosexuality itself could ever be.

SISTERS

Bonds between gay lib and women's lib grew early. It was a natural affiliation; they both were rebelling against roles predetermined by sex and felt oppressed by the chauvinistic heterosexual male. Both worked to develop a sense of self-worth against the long-accepted condition of second-class citizenship. The women were also struggling with the influence of the psychoanalytic tradition which, as Kate Millett put it in speaking of Freud, "assumed that to be born female was to be born castrated," and therefore innately inferior to the potent male. It was not a smooth affiliation, however. Straight women found they had to struggle with sex chauvinism in dealing with the gay men and were, in turn, guilty of resisting the lesbian within their own ranks for fear the movement, which was already being ridiculed as "a bunch of dykes," would be discredited. However, despite the resistance they encountered in women's lib groups, the larger percentage of activist lesbians has chosen women's liberation as their primary point of identification and gay liberation second, thus bringing the gay struggle into the heart of the women's movement. . . .

So, though the relationship has been trouble-fraught (in some places they're not speaking to each other), gay lib and women's lib have played crucial roles in each other's development. Together they expose the underbelly of society in a more extensive, penetrating way than either could alone, uncovering the depth and extent to which predetermined masculine/feminine roles have governed social dynamics, not only allowing but often forcing one group of people to exploit another.

HO-HO-HOMOSEXUAL

A sector of gay lib has extended its horizons beyond women's lib. A strong element in the Gay Liberation Front of New York brought radical politics explicitly into the Gay platform, ultimately causing a split within the New York group. A break-off group, the Gay Activists Alliance (GAA) was then formed. The GAA limits its activities to gay liberation *per se* and works, though militantly, within the system, while the GLF men consider themselves revolutionaries first. Though groups in other cities haven't split, the same elements exist in all, the more militant factions resolving their position within the whole by forming radical caucuses. GLF women in general identify primarily with the women's lib movement; the more revolutionary lesbians having formed their own group, Radicalesbians, which like the GLF/New York men identifies primarily with political revolution. These groups are by no means mutually exclusive.

The revolution-oriented gay men and women explain their fusion of the two causes thus (their arguments being greatly reduced here): the basic unit of sex role structure is the family in which the woman performs menial chores for the man, who is thus freed to pursue more lofty ambitions. The family is also the basic consumer unit of the capitalist system, which stresses the connection between worthiness (you can read power here) and the acquisition of objects. This is directly related to the sex role nature of the family, in that among the objects a man accumulates is his wife (this is a version of the thesis that men treat women primarily as sex objects), hopefully beautiful, efficient, and at the service of his pleasure. This relationship between the acquisition of goods and power over women is emphasized unequivocally in advertising, the lubricant of capitalism in its function of engendering greed. Capitalism, then, is based on the assumption that people are greedy for goods—and the power that goods bring. It assumes that these basic facts cannot be changed, that social planning can only be corrective within the system, not redirective. The result of this power-acquisitive urge has been racism, imperialism, and sexism. Revolution says these "facts of nature" can be changed, but to do so you have to raze the system which nourishes them. In other words, to achieve true gay liberation you have to do away with capitalism which, in its present form, is deeply intertwined with sexism—just as in order to achieve black liberation you must dissolve the system, because in the same power-oriented manner it induces people of one race to beat up on another. And this is why the causes of the nigger, the dyke, the bitch, and the faggot are one and the same and why these Causes Incorporated must be geared to the overthrow of capitalism.

It is easy to punch holes in this argument, to call it simplistic, metaphorical, in parts fanciful, but that would be, I think, a dodge to avoid recognizing a certain genius at work in it. The genius is in great need of refinement, granted, but it is there. My reaction to the argument at this point is that somehow it doesn't manage to produce its own kernel. And while I'm no great defender of capitalism it seems clear that sexism, racism, and imperialism have occurred under every system, Marxism included, and that by doing away with capitalism you will by no means insure yourself against these evils. The revolutionary gays will agree with me there, but counter that while oppression can certainly exist without capitalism, the particular form of capitalism which has actually evolved is so deeply rooted in oppression that it would be impossible to purge the system without in effect destroying it. . . .

THE SPOILS OF KINGSHIP

And the culprit, the white male heterosexual king who sits in the throne room guarding his birthright, the recipient of all this wrath, what of him? Isn't the throne room as vicious a dungeon of his humanity as those in which he keeps his underlings?

The faces of men commuting on trains between affluent suburbs and their high-level work in the big-time world of the city are blank and worn beyond their years. They don't seem like people in the flush of fulfillment, the inheritors of the earth, or for that matter like cruel, arrogant nobles gripped with the excitement of power. They sit on the train between battlefields wrapped in their newspapers, for a spell excused from guarding their titles, and they seem in this rare unselfconscious moment a tired, dreary lot. It would seem that rather than the possessors they themselves are the spoils of kingship. Their wives, however bored and discontented with their role, have observed intimately the price their husbands have had to pay, and with the thought of that cost can turn to their laundry with a fleeting perhaps, but distinct, sense of reprieve.

Just as the black militants for a long time seemed to be aspiring to the bourgeois ideals of the white society they challenged, women's lib groups for a time emphasized their desire to live like those men who they felt oppressed them. Those early days, again like those of the first black militants, were marked by simplistic rhetoric, humorlessness, and inflexibility. But as the movement developed, confidence was gained, and discussions began to probe more deeply, the realization evolved that the roles assigned to men were not enviable, but in ways as pernicious to the men themselves as to women. Men have been the most rigorously programmed of all. From childhood it is impressed on them that they must be dominant, the strong authoritative guardians of weaker human beings—and to the extent that they are, they are "real men." To the extent they fail in this role, to the extent they betray "feminine" traits of docility, repugnance to violence, and tenderness and also unsureness, a need for comfort, and timidity—to that extent they are "womanly." And in the eyes of society, the womanly man is a pathetic thing indeed. Since a major tenet of both women's lib and gay lib is that the division of "traits" between the sexes is for the most part arbitrary and without foundation in reality, it follows that men are as arbitrarily conditioned as women. A less vituperative look at that sex—and not just those stodgy commuters—reveals that the same behavior which women find oppressive is in many instances evidence of the strain their predetermined role has put on their humanity. Why do so many men compulsively talk louder than women, interrupt them, and make it difficult for them to contribute their side of a conversation? Why do they constantly have to make it clear that they are "important" and that they speak with authority, the more so in instances where they don't have any particular authority? Why do they find it so painful to be found wrong, especially by a woman, sometimes insisting that they are right despite overwhelming evidence to the contrary? These very common ways, rather than suggesting that men are naturally overbearing, suggest more that they are insecure, fearful of insignificance, not strong and right, unable to dominate. . . .

The king will be liberated when the whole pack of role cards falls—when he is not restricted by the king-male role. Much of the physical violence that wracks the country is committed by males between fifteen and twenty-five—the period in which traditionally a boy proves his manhood. The masculinity curse also drives the less gory but more common psychological violence, which pervades business meetings, dinner parties, and the home—as people pierce, jab, and scrape to wrest some form of triumph and have it saluted. It's the crying of uncle that's at stake in the worst cases, psychological submission, and the king-male must abhor that most of all. He strains to make sure someone is below and knows it.

The masculinity complex lives in our national throne room. The last three Presidents have been nearly obsessed with proving their toughness; Presidents have bled the nation white to keep from backing down in Vietnam—to keep from looking chicken in backbone warfare.

But when more men feel that they no longer *need* to be the king-male —or share his compulsive desire to be crowned, to reign virile and proud and appreciated—maybe there will be fewer bloodied people, fewer good things ravaged, and maybe even fewer wars.

Utopias have an air of death about them. Fortunately, they never come true. They are deathly because they omit the basic mystery of life and reduce existence to a smooth-running machine. Utopias are humorless. But life, death, beauty, ugliness, good, and evil are here to stay and will insure us against all utopias, so one can look at the vision projected by all these new developments without fear for the future.

The vision of these sexual freedoms is not a very full one, a kind of comprehensive liberation in which all oppressed groups unbind each other for a hazy new purpose. Reasonable as the idea is, it seems to exist in a thin, improbable future.

It also seems to include the seeds of disasters, such as large numbers of people, having no role assigned to them, going out of their minds for lack of identity—like a lot of bureaucrats without their bureaucracy. But as things change, the vision firms up and even becomes a little part of reality —like the Panthers' trying to accept the gay liberation people. A large part of it all lies in just getting used to separate ideas, such as that homosexuals are just as good as heterosexuals. America seems to be on the brink of a Dark Age which will tolerate none of these new ways. But on the other hand, as a man marching up Sixth Avenue on that bright euphoric Sunday said to me, "There's a lot of people in this."

"Keeping up with the literature" regarding many social, ethnic and racial groups was for years little problem at all. But recently there has been a veritable explosion of popular and scholarly treatments of groups who have not been part of the traditional centers of privilege and advantage. In fiction, for example, writers outside the predominant Anglo-Saxon Protestant orbit of earlier American novelists have had a profound impact, both in rendering to a larger public the conditions and thoughts of long-ignored people and in providing a key source of self-discovery for such people. Unquestionably, such novels as Ralph Ellison's *Invisible Man* (which focuses on the struggles of a Negro), Scott Momaday's *House Made of Dawn* (whose protagonist is an American Indian), and Piri Thomas's *Down These Mean Streets* (a searing portrait of Spanish Harlem) provide superb insights into the lives and viewpoints of victims of discrimination.

Several excellent anthologies of black protest are available. August Meier and Elliott Rudwick (eds.), *Black Protest in the Sixties* (Chicago, 1970), is a selection of interpretative essays from *The New York Times Magazine* since 1945; Richard B. Young (ed.), *Roots of Rebellion: The Evolution of Black Politics and Protest Since World War II* (New York, 1970), is an exceptionally fine collection of scholarly essays; and Floyd B. Barbour (ed.), *The Black Power Revolt* (Boston, 1968), combines historical selections with recent interpretative articles. Two very useful collections of documents are Francis L. Broderick and August Meier (eds.), *Negro Protest Thought in the Twentieth Century* (Indianapolis, 1965), and Broderick, Meier, and John H. Bracey, Jr. (eds.), *Black Nationalism in America* (Indianapolis, 1969).

THE PROTEST OF DISCRIMINATION

Among the leading studies of black power and black nationalism are Arna Bontemps and Jack Conroy, *Anyplace but Here* (New York, 1966); E.V. Essien-Udom, *Black Nationalism: A Search for Identity in America* (Chicago, 1962), which focuses on the Nation of Islam; C. Eric Lincoln, *The Black Muslims in America* (Boston, 1961), the standard work on the subject; Lewis M. Killian, *The Impossible Revolution: Black Power and the American Dream* (New York, 1968), a historical and social analysis; Robert L. Allen, *Black Awakening in Capitalist America* (New York, 1969), which puts its subject in the context of an anticolonial revolt of black Americans who are part of an "oppressed nation" and a "semicolony"; Nathan Wright, Jr., *Black Power and Urban Unrest* (New York, 1967), an explanation and defense of the idea of black power by an urban sociologist who was a freedom rider and a field secretary for CORE; and Theodore Draper, *The Rediscovery of Black Nationalism* (New York, 1969), which sees the concept of black nationalism in America as mainly fantasy. For an interesting review of Draper's book, as well as a perceptive analysis of black nationalism, see Eric Foner, "In Search of Black History," *The New York Review of Books* (October 22, 1970).

Important biographies of leading representatives of twentieth-century black protest are Francis Broderick, *W.E.B. DuBois: Negro Leader in a Time of Crisis* (Palo Alto, Calif., 1959); E. David Cronon, *Black Moses:*

II *Suggestions for further reading*

The Story of Marcus Garvey and the Universal Negro Improvement Association (Madison, Wisc., 1955), and Stephen R. Fox, *The Guardian of Boston: William Monroe Trotter* (New York, 1970). Unquestionably one of the most important of all books on black protest is Malcolm X's *Autobiography* (New York, 1965).

Among the classic calls for black self-determination are Stokely Carmichael and Charles V. Hamilton, *Black Power: The Politics of Liberation in America* (New York, 1967), and Julius Lester, *Look Out Whitey! Black Power's Gon' Get Your Mama!* (New York, 1968). Basic studies of specific movements include Herbert Garfinkel, *When Negroes March* (New York, 1959), on the March on Washington Movement, and Howard Zinn, *SNCC: The New Abolitionists* (Boston, 1965).

There are a number of books on the urban riots of the 1960's—such as Robert Conot, *Rivers of Blood, Years of Darkness* (New York, 1967)—on Watts—but for superior analyses which place the events in a large context see Robert Fogelson, *Violence as Protest; A Study of Riots and Ghettos* (New York, 1971), and Joseph A. Boskin, "The Revolt of the Urban Ghettos, 1964–1967," *Annals of the American Academy of Political and Social Science,* 381 (March, 1969), 1–14.

Robin Morgan (ed.), *Sisterhood is Powerful: An Anthology of Writings from the Women's Liberation Movement* (New York, 1970), contains a highly diversified selection of writings and a long bibliographical list of books, articles and films concerning women's liberation. Another excellent anthology is Elsie Adams and Mary Louise Briscoe (eds.), *Up Against the Wall, Mother . . .* (Beverly Hills, 1971), which includes readings reflecting traditional

views of women and modern rebuttals. Leslie B. Tanner (ed.), *Voices from Women's Liberation* (New York, 1970), combines past and present statements of protest from American women. *Women: A Journal of Liberation* is a recently founded quarterly which includes summons to the movement along with scholarly appraisals of it; the Spring, 1970 issue on "Women in History: A Recreation of Our Past," featured short biographical sketches of such women as the Grimké sisters, Harriet Tubman, Emma Goldman and Margaret Sanger. Robert J. Lifton (ed.), *The Woman in America* (Boston, 1965), is a fine collection of essays, most of which originally appeared in *Daedalus* (Spring, 1964); included is Carl Degler's insightful "Revolution Without Ideology: The Changing Place of Women in America."

The most recent and extensive treatment of feminism is William L. O'Neill, *Everyone Was Brave: The Rise and Fall of Feminism in America* (Chicago, 1969). O'Neill's *The Woman Movement: Feminism in the United States and England* is a comparative analysis combined with historical documents. Eleanor Flexner, *A Century of Struggle* (Cambridge, Mass., 1959), is a good survey of the women's rights movement, while Aileen S. Kraditor skillfully dissects *The Ideas of the Woman Suffrage Movement, 1890–1920* (New York, 1965). A very readable, although less interpretative, account of the history of the woman's rights movement is Andrew Sinclair, *The Better Half: The Emancipation of the American Woman* (New York, 1965). Much more insightful are Christopher Lasch's superb analyses, "Woman As Alien," in *The New Radicalism in America, 1889–1963* (New York, 1965), and "Emancipated

Women," *The New York Review of Books* (July 13, 1967). For a critical profile of "The Liberated Woman," see Midge Dector's article in *Commentary* (October, 1970); and for a spectacular contrast, see the angry and militant *I, B.I.T.C.H.*, by Caroline Hennessey (New York, 1970). A superior overview of the recent women's movement is the highly informative and comprehensive *Rebirth of Feminism* (New York, 1971), by Judith Hole and Ellen Levine.

Stan Steiner's eloquent *La Raza: The Mexican Americans* (New York, 1969) is a moving account and includes a useful bibliographical essay. Peter Nabokov, *Tijerina and the Courthouse Raid* (Albuquerque, 1969), is a powerful rendering of the dramatic events of June 5, 1967, in Tierra Amarilla, New Mexico; Nabokov's book and Richard Gardner's *Grito! Reies Tijerina and the New Mexico Land Grant War of 1967* (New York, 1970) provide significant insights into the Alianza protest. For an excellent overview of several Mexican-American organizations— including the Alianza, the Brown Berets, and the United Mexican-American Students—and for a succinct statement of the conditions to which they object, see Gilbert W. Merkx and Richard J. Griego, "Crisis in New Mexico," in Norman R. Yetman and C. Hoy Steele (eds.), *Majority and Minority: The Dynamics of Racial and Ethnic Relations* (Boston, 1971). Also useful are Nancie L. Gonzalez, *The Spanish-Americans of New Mexico, A Heritage of Pride* (Albuquerque, 1969), especially chapters 5 and 8; Joseph P. Love, "La Raza: Mexican Americans in Rebellion," *Trans-Action,* 6 (February, 1969), 35–41; and Julian Samora (ed.), *La Raza: Forgotten Americans* (South Bend, Ind., 1968).

Joan London and Henry Anderson, *So Shall Ye Reap: The Story of Cesar Chavez and the Farm Workers' Movement* (New York, 1970), is a sympathetic study by two participant-observers, while John Gregory Dunne, "To Die Standing: Cesar Chavez and the Chicanos," *The Atlantic* (June, 1971), stresses Chavez's role in awakening pride among the Chicanos. A provocative essay on the contemporary plight of Mexican-Americans is Edgar Z. Friedenberg, "Outcasts," *The New York Review of Books* (December 18, 1969). Ed Ludwig and James Santibanez (eds.), *The Chicanos, Mexican American Voices* (New York, 1971), is a collection of articles (on such subjects as the Delano grape strike), poems and fiction.

Stan Steiner's *The New Indians* (New York, 1968) is an outstanding treatment of its subject. Also of special importance are Vine Deloria, Jr., *Custer Died for Your Sins* (New York, 1969) and *We Talk, You Listen: New Tribes, New Turf* (New York, 1970); N. Scott Momaday, "Bringing on the Indians," *The New York Review of Books* (April 18, 1971); and Alvin M. Josephy, Jr., *Red Power: The American Indians' Fight for Freedom* (New York, 1971).

A pioneering work on homosexuality is psychiatrist Martin Hoffman's *The Gay World* (New York, 1968), which examines its subject in a large social setting. On homosexuals and the path to self-discovery, see Merle Miller, *On Being Different* (New York, 1971), John Murphy, *Homosexual Liberation, A Personal View* (New York, 1971), and Allen Young, "Out of the Closet: A Gay Manifesto," *Ramparts,* 10 (November, 1971). Other recent books are Don Teal, *The Gay Militants* (New

York, 1971), and Colin J. Williams and Martin S. Weinberg, *Homosexuals and the Military, A Study of Less Than Honorable Discharge* (New York, 1971).

Trans-Action, 6 (February, 1969), devoted an entire issue to "The American Underclass: Red, White and Black." Other noteworthy essays on the themes of self-discovery and protest among groups are Michael Novak, "White Ethnic," *Harper's Magazine,* 243 (September, 1971), which focuses on descendants of non-English-speaking immigrants; Jerry Farber, *The Student as Nigger* (North Hollywood, 1969); and Tom Wolfe, "The New Yellow Peril," *Esquire,* 73 (December, 1969).

THE PROTEST
OF POLITICS AND PEACE:
SOCIALISTS, STUDENTS,
AND PEACE ADVOCATES

In 1912, Eugene V. Debs, the Socialist party candidate for president, won 6 percent of the total vote, a proportion never again obtained by that party's standard bearer; at the same time, Socialists held some 1200 public offices, including 79 mayoralties. At varying points during the twentieth century, Socialist administrations controlled Milwaukee, Wisconsin, Reading, Pennsylvania, and Bridgeport, Connecticut. Yet the fact remains that socialism as a political force in the United States never approached the strength that it achieved in many European nations; as a political protest movement against the capitalist system, it attained little success.

Reasons assigned by historians, seeking to explain this failure, fall into four main categories. Some contend that when Socialists did assume power, they were always too reformist and never true revolutionaries; others maintain that socialism as a political philosophy was too radical and thus alien to the customs and traditions of the United States. (Although seemingly contradictory, some observers have adhered to both of these explanations in the same interpretation.) A third view points to the internal factionalism within the American left as the reason for its impotency. Finally, some students of political socialism contend that it succeeded only too well in its role as a third party; it contributed ideas to one of the two major parties and hence eliminated the need for its own existence.

During the Great Depression of the Thirties, a time that might have seemed fertile for the growth of socialism in America, it made little impact. On the national level, Norman Thomas received 187,342 votes in 1936 as against 884,781 in 1932; the 1936 vote represented the lowest Socialist total since 1900. For Thomas, the reason for the failure was simple; in a word, it was "Roosevelt." Franklin D. Roosevelt's New Deal with its reform, relief and recovery legislation had co-opted the Socialist program; the New Deal's introduction of the welfare state to America seemed to contemporaries to obviate the need for a Socialist party. In light of some historians' recent criticism of the New Deal as limited in its approach to America's problems and

91

overlooking, or sometimes even hurting, rather than helping many of the undergroups in American society,[1] it is ironic that a leading Socialist would accuse the Democrats of stealing his party's program. If that were the case, and if the critics of the New Deal are correct, then the fourth explanation of Socialist failure reinforces the first—American socialism has been too reformist. Whether the satisfaction of immediate Socialist demands is tantamount to saying that the basic Socialist ideals had been accepted, needs still to be considered, however. As D. H. Leon has recently noted, "Nationalization of the means of production and distribution, democratic planning and production for use rather than profit have not been accepted, and one could effectively argue that the old socialist ideals remain unfulfilled."[2]

Moreover, even if the depression years represented the final opportunity for the triumph of political socialism and its time of greatest failure, most observers agree that some earlier time between 1912 and 1925 witnessed the beginning of its actual decline. Its vitality had certainly been sapped by the crash in 1929, but a dozen years earlier party approval of the St. Louis Manifesto of 1917 denouncing America's entrance into World War I hurt the Socialists in some areas of the country, causing internal factionalism and leading to wartime repression. However, in places like New York City peace advocates rallied to the Socialist banner; Socialist antiwar candidate for mayor, Morris Hillquit, won almost 22 percent of the vote, a nearly fivefold increase over the usual Socialist proportion.

Nevertheless, channels of communication between Socialist and non-Socialist that existed before the war began to close, with the exception of the Intercollegiate Socialist Society, founded in 1905 to "promote an intelligent interest in Socialism among college men and women." The ISS was in the vanguard of early student activism and endlessly debated America's entrance into WWI; the debate shattered the organization's unity. Two decades later while the Socialists advocated neutrality before America's entrance into World War II, after Pearl Harbor the majority of Party members gave the war "critical support." The Party, itself, never adopted a clear statement on the war, merely making, in Norman Thomas' phrase, a "general condemnation of wickedness."

While socialist objections to war have frequently been premised on the belief that all wars are capitalist adventures, prior to the twentieth century antiwar dissent for other reasons had not been uncommon in American history. Loyalists opposed the American Revolution; New England Federalists objected to the

---

[1] For example, see Paul Conkin, *The New Deal* (New York: Crowell, 1967).
[2] "Whatever Happened to an American Socialist Party?" *American Quarterly,* 23 (May, 1971), p. 258.

War of 1812; there was vigorous opposition to President Polk's policies during the Mexican War, leading Abraham Lincoln, then a Whig Congressman, to point out that the President tried "to argue every silent vote given to supplies into an endorsement of the justice and wisdom of his conduct." During the Civil War, Copperheads like C. L. Vallandigham battled the war policies of the very same Abraham Lincoln, no longer antiwar dissenter but leading proponent of the war to save the Union. And at the turn of the twentieth century, America witnessed opposition to the Spanish-American War and especially to the annexation of the Philippines and the consequent insurrection there which resulted in savage guerrilla warfare that took 10,000 American and nearly 250,000 Filipino lives. Thus, although the more recent dissent associated with the Vietnam War does not stand alone in American history, it is for the reader to determine whether its intensity, quality and effect are very different from the past.

The first two essays in this section by Shannon and Weinstein relate to the question of why political socialism failed in America, while the third by Altbach and Peterson chronicles the history of student activism in the twentieth century, beginning with the formation of the ISS. The reader should consider which reasons are the soundest explanations for the decline of American socialism—those dealing with internal factors or those concerned with the uniqueness of the American environment. Is socialism permanently dead as a major force in our society or will it rise up like the phoenix and take on new life? If the latter, under what circumstances will this rebirth take place? Will student activism mirror adult movements, or has American society so changed that older people will reflect campus trends? Will the eighteen-year-old vote permit students to have the voice they always sought in politics or will it simply co-opt student protest?

In our own time, this type of protest has been closely tied to the Vietnam War. In the fourth selection, Robert Beisner compares the anti-Vietnam doves of 1968 with the critics of Philippine annexation. Does this type of comparison encourage valid analysis? In what way is the Vietnam conflict different from the situation of 1898? In what way is it similar? Finally, Lawrence Wittner discusses the organized peace movement during the era of Senator Joseph McCarthy and concentrates on pacifist organizations which cannot condone any war. Wittner's essay raises the question of whether the repressive tendencies in American society can dampen the enthusiasm of committed pacifists. Is opposing war subversive?

David A. Shannon

The Predestined Death of American Socialism

Studying American political socialism, David A. Shannon finds both internal and external reasons for its failure to protest effectively against the capitalist system and gain greater acceptance during the twentieth century. The internal factors relate to the organizational failures of the Socialist party in the United States;

the external reasons, more significant in his view, concern the uniqueness of the American environment, with traditions and conditions that militated against a strong Socialist heritage. The latter view, stressing consensus within American society, reflects the thinking of liberal historians who wrote during the 1950's. Do Shannon's conclusions seem as convincing in the 1970's as they might have seemed to the American public during the 1950's? Professor Shannon, in addition to writing *The Socialist Party of America,* is the author of *The Decline of American Communism, Twentieth Century America,* and other works dealing with recent American history.

Elsewhere in Western civilization Socialists of various kinds have retained their strength or become stronger as American Socialism deteriorated to almost nothing. The British Labor party at mid-century is at its strongest. There are vigorous social democratic movements in Australia, New Zealand, and western Canada. Socialists are a major political force in western Germany and in the Scandinavian nations. In almost all the democratic nations of the Western world Socialists of some variety are a significant political force, but in the United States, the most powerful of the Western democracies, there is no Socialist political movement.

The decline and death of American Socialism has occurred despite the fact that the course of recent American history has demonstrated the validity of much of the Socialist analysis and criticism of capitalism. As Socialists predicted, economic power has become increasingly concentrated. As Socialists predicted, capitalism has not provided the American nation with a confidently stable economy. What economic stability and health there has been in the nation's economy since 1940 has been largely attributable to past, present, or possible future war. As Socialists predicted, American businessmen have become increasingly interested in and dependent upon foreign markets. There are, of course, very important aspects of the Socialist analysis and prediction that time has shown to be in error. The lot of the worker in the American economy has improved, contrary to Socialist predictions. Real wages have risen. And the Socialist doctrine of the inevitability of socialism, although not susceptible of proof or disproof, certainly does not seem to be validated by recent American history. But if some Socialist predictions have turned out to be mistaken, others were quite acute. Yet in America at mid-century there is no Socialist political movement. It is the purpose of the balance of this book to seek an explanation of why this is true.

At the outset it must be made clear that this discussion is concerned only with Socialism as a political movement. As an intellectual movement an autopsy is not in order, for intellectually Socialism is far from dead. Many historians, economists, and sociologists employ at times what originally were Socialist concepts, and the extent to which Socialism has forced an examination of the assumptions of capitalism is probably great. Undoubtedly there are some major-party voters who adhere to some Socialist principles. But here we are concerned with Socialist politics, not Socialist theory.

There are two categories of factors to be considered in dealing with the question of why the American Socialist party died. There are, first, weaknesses, inadequacies, failures, errors of commission and omission on the part of the Socialist party. Besides these internal factors there are external factors, basic conditions in American society that militated against Socialist success and were largely beyond the power of the Socialists to change. This book, concerned primarily as it is with the Socialist party's internal history, comes nearer offering insights into the internal factors than into the external ones. The external factors of Socialist failure, however, are probably the more important. A full investigation of these external factors requires much more than a history of the Socialist party; it requires an investigation into all of American history.

One of the most serious errors of the Socialist party was its failure to behave the way political parties in the United States must in order to be successful. The Socialist party never fully decided whether it was a political party, a political pressure group, a revolutionary sect, or a political forum. It tried to play all these roles at the same time. One of the first rules of American politics is to build strong local and state organizations. Outside of a few places, notably Milwaukee and Oklahoma, the Socialists failed to establish political machines. Indeed, they usually did not even try to build them. The Socialist party time and again committed itself to political action, rejecting first the "direct action" of the syndicalists and later the revolution of the Communists, but it usually made little attempt to organize political machines at the local level. . . .

Despite all the shortcomings of the Socialist party, its failure was not primarily its own fault; the failure of the Socialists was due less to their errors than to basic traditions and conditions in American society which the Socialists could do little or nothing to change. Socialist parties in Great Britain, Europe, and elsewhere have also made mistakes, perhaps greater mistakes than their American comrades made. The American Socialists, for example, never suffered a blow like the defection of Ramsay MacDonald. Yet the United States is one of the few important Western democracies not to have at mid-century a significant Socialist movement. One can only conclude that Old World conditions were more conducive to the growth of Socialism than conditions were in the United States. Properly and fully to describe and analyze the American traditions and conditions that impeded and killed American Socialism would be a major task, and it must suffice here only to indicate some of these basic American conditions.

In the first place, there are many features of the American political system that hamper the development of any third party, whether Socialist or not. The two-party system in the United States is so strong that no genuine third party has ever succeeded in becoming one of the major parties. The election laws of most of the states make it difficult for third parties to get on the ballot and stay on. The large amounts of money necessary to finance an election campaign handicap third parties. The major parties tend to "steal the thunder" of minor parties when that thunder seems popular. The two-party system is very deeply ingrained in American voting habits. Time and again it has seemed to political observers that a third party would amass a significant minority of the popular vote, but the actual returns have seldom borne out the expectation. If all the people who subscribed to the *Appeal to Reason* to read [Eugene V.] Debs . . . , and who paid their money to hear Debs speak, had voted for Debs as they cheered for Debs, his percentage of the popular vote would have been considerably higher than it ever was. The same is true of Norman Thomas, whose measure of respect among the American people is considerably higher than the vote they gave him. But many voters are reluctant to vote for a candidate who does not have a good chance of winning, reluctant to "throw away" their votes. The emphasis in American politics upon the presidential campaign is another disadvantage to the development of a national third party. Citing the difficulties of third parties, however, falls far short of explaining why American Socialism failed. Socialists never did as well as many other third parties; Socialism failed to attract more than a relatively small part of the American people.

The primary reason that American Socialists never developed the strength of their comrades in other countries was that in America there is considerably less class-consciousness than there is in other Western nations. The Socialists directed their efforts to "the working class," "the proletariat," "the workers," but generally the members of this class failed to realize their class status. When Debs during his war trial said, "While there is a lower class I am in it; while there is a criminal element, I am of

96

it; while there is a soul in prison, I am not free," he expressed a noble sentiment, but relatively few Americans recognized the statement as an expression of solidarity with themselves. This is not to say that there are no social classes in America nor that there have been none, nor even that there has been no recognition of social class. It is to say that in the United States class-consciousness and solidarity have been considerably weaker than in Great Britain or western Europe.

Late in the Great Depression, when millions were still unemployed, Elmo Roper made a study of public opinion about social class. His conclusions were discouraging for Socialists. When asked, "What word would you use to name the class in America you belong to?" 27.5 percent of those polled replied they did not know, indicating, if the sample were a fair one, that about one-fourth of the American people were very little if at all aware of social class. The answers to his questions were such that Roper concluded that 79.2 percent of the population believed itself middle class. Of those whose incomes were so small that Roper considered them "poor," 70.3 percent thought they were middle class. Only 7.9 percent of the total considered themselves of the "lower" class. Of the factory workers polled only about one-third thought their interests and those of their employers essentially opposed. Surely in a society with such disregard of social class as this a political movement based primarily upon class appeal will have a difficult time.

But to point out that Americans have relatively little class-consciousness or regard themselves as members of a class that has no quarrel with capitalism is not to push back very far the original questions: Why did the Socialist party die? Why was it never stronger than it was? We must go behind the American attitudes toward social class and seek to explain these attitudes.

The lack of a feudal tradition in America, the result largely of a new civilization on a continent with a vast amount of inexpensive land, is undoubtedly a major factor in the American people's failure to develop a class-consciousness comparable to that of European peoples. When a modern capitalistic system of production developed in the United States, it did not displace a large and settled class of craftsmen, as happened in the Old World. From these displaced artisans in Great Britain, for example, came many of the Luddites and Chartists, and these movements tended to create a sense of class solidarity among British workers. The absence of a need for unpropertied Americans to battle for the franchise and political representation in anything like the way the Chartists had to fight for these rights likewise tended to blur class lines. It was difficult for British and European workmen not to conclude that their states were for the advancement and protection of the propertied classes when they had to struggle so long and arduously with these classes for the right to participate in politics. The American workman, on the other hand, received the franchise relatively early and with comparative ease, leaving only social and economic lines between him and men of property, lines less definite than the political line had been.

Similarly, since there has never been a firmly established aristocracy based upon birth in America, the middle class has never had a great struggle to assert its superiority. The United States has had nothing comparable to the Puritan Revolution, the agitation for the Reform Bill in 1832, or the French Revolution. This is significant because where there has been sharp conflict between an aristocracy and a middle class, radical and class-conscious ideas have gained circulation among the working class. But in America there has been no middle-class revolt to call forth a Gerrard Winstanley or a Babeuf.

The lack of a feudal heritage, however, has perhaps not been as important a factor in the development of class attitudes in America as has the relative success of American capitalism. The United States' exceptionally rich natural resources, its technical ingenuity, and its tremendous domestic market have combined to produce a huge gross national product. The distribution of the product has been something less than equitable, but the total product has been so great that the United States has enjoyed a better standard of living than have most European nations. The American economy has also, except during a few periods of hard times, been an expanding economy, and this fact has many implications for the question under consideration.

One effect of the tremendous expansion of the American economy has been that as the rich became richer the poor did not, in the long run, become poorer. Industrial capitalism undoubtedly widened the gap between the wealthiest families of the nation and the poorest, but the poor have generally been able, except during economic depressions, to look back upon their fathers' and grandfathers' status and conclude that their own material comfort is greater. And the widespread assumption that the future holds even greater material comforts reflects an optimism that is not conducive to the development of class solidarity.

The growth of the American economy has also made possible a relatively high degree of class mobility. It has been possible for many able and ambitious young men of working-class origins to escape from their class. Many of their sisters have through marriage similarly risen on the social ladder. Free public schools have played no small part in the process of class circulation. And besides the *actual* degree of class fluidity there is a considerable amount of myth. A firm belief in the story of rags to riches is a part of American folklore. Horatio Alger's manly young heroes are a real part of American beliefs, whether or not they actually exist. The actuality and the dream have combined to produce an optimism about one's chances to better his position in the social order, an optimism that has militated against the development of class consciousness. Americans have generally believed it easier and more desirable to rise *from* their class rather than *with* their class. For many the belief proved justified. It is a matter of pure speculation what might have happened had the American class structure been static, but it seems reasonable that there would have been considerably more class-consciousness and conflict. It is probable the working class would have had better leadership. It is not inconceivable that the Andrew Carnegies would have been, under different circumstances, leaders of labor.

Still another factor in American history that tended to hamper the development of class consciousness is the ethnic heterogeneity of American workers. The American working class has been composed of many races and nations, and there has been a tendency for American workers to identify themselves with their racial or nationality group rather than with their class. The steady stream of immigrants to the United States made organization of American workers more than usually difficult. Many American workers were not so aware of class antagonisms as they were of religious, ethnic, and racial tensions. The aspirations of immigrants and Negroes to become assimilated presented a special problem for the Socialist party. For the Negro it was enough of a burden to be black without also being red. The immigrant who wanted to become an "American" realized that being a Socialist would be a handicap to his assimilation. It was no accident that Debs was the idol of many of the immigrants who did become Socialists; Debs was a living demonstration that it was possible to be both Socialist and American.

Although a major factor, the relative lack of class-consciousness of Americans was only one of several basic conditions of American life that hampered Socialists. Perhaps because of the Socialists' inadequate explanation of their philosophy most Americans felt that Socialism would submerge their individualism. Certainly Americans have confused Socialism with communism and have recoiled from the monolithic Soviet state. The Russian Revolution and the subsequent strained relations between the Soviet Union and the United States were undoubtedly a factor in the decline of the Socialist party even though Socialists were among the earliest of anticommunists.

Another American condition that has militated against Socialist success is the widely held pragmatic view of life that demands visible and practical results, and the quicker the better. Much of Socialism was not attractive to those who held such views. Just as American labor rejected the reformism of the Knights of Labor for the "practical" business unionism of the AFL, it rejected the promises of Socialism for the more immediate results of progressives. Victor Berger was fond of saying: "Socialism is coming all the time. It may be another century or two before it is fully established." In the meantime, one might have concluded, there was little to do but make the best of it and wait for the new day. Surely this vague promise of the millennium was not as attractive as the prospect of achieving less, but achieving it soon, through trade unions and the major parties. To most people half a loaf in the hand, or even a few slices, was preferable to the hope of the whole loaf. The IWW song, "The Preacher and the Slave," might well have had another verse about this millenarian aspect of Socialism, to be followed by the song's refrain, "You'll get pie in the sky when you die."

These, then, are some of the basic conditions and traditions of American society that prevented the success of the Socialist party of America. There were undoubtedly other obstacles in the way of Socialist growth, and the author is not prepared to defend these few pages as definitive. In a manner of speaking, it was American history that defeated the Socialists. Thus ends the post mortem examination of the Socialist party.

Is there a possibility of the Socialist party's rebirth? Might it revive and embarrass the conductor of the autopsy? In these days of rapid change, when a nation's enemies become its friends and its friends become its enemies within a decade, almost anything seems possible. But today it does not seem at all probable that the Socialist party shall arise from its grave. Today it seems more likely that the Know-Nothing party might arise from a century's sleep than that the Socialists might revive. The ideals of social democracy will remain part of the American tradition as long as American soil produces rebels, and there may develop some day, under the impact of fundamental social change, another social democratic political movement of significance. But should there again be a vigorous political organization with democratic and socialist principles in the United States, it is most unlikely that the party of Debs, [Morris] Hillquit, and Thomas will provide its impetus.

James Weinstein

For James Weinstein, the American experience elaborated upon by Shannon had less effect on the decline of Socialism than the internal disputes of the nation's political left. Pointing out that, despite its antiwar stand, the Socialist party actually thrived during World War I years, Weinstein finds that the factionalism arising after the Russian Revolution and the concomitant development of an American Communist party were responsible for the weakening of this form of political protest. Moreover, he contends that because Soviet developments rather than events in the United States shaped Socialist

The Self-Inflicted Death of American Socialism

and Communist attitudes in this country, these parties were of little relevance to America's workers and farmers. James Weinstein has edited the periodical *Studies on the Left* and has written *The Corporate Ideal in the Liberal State,* as well as *The Decline of Socialism in America, 1912–1925.*

The rapid growth in the early 1960's of radical social movements on several university campuses, in the South and in a few Northern ghettoes, has led many to speak of a "New Left" in the United States. In part this new radicalism is located in movements organized in direct response to particular social problems—the continuing second-class status of Negroes both North and South, poverty among whites and Negroes, United States intervention against anticolonial revolutions, particularly in Vietnam. At the same time, most of the activists in these movements, the great majority of whom are students from middle-income families, are infused with a general quality of estrangement from the dominant values in American society and from the nature of our social existence. Although the explicit political content of the programs of such groups as the Student Nonviolent Coordinating Committee, or the Free Speech Movement, or the Economic Research and Action Project of the Students for a Democratic Society seldom goes beyond the standard demands of traditional liberal pressure groups, there is an underlying belief among young radicals that their purpose is to change the character, possibly even the structure, of American society.

But the New Left lacks an ideological or strategic unity that might enable it seriously to challenge the power of those institutions in American

From James Weinstein, *The Decline of Socialism in America, 1912–1925,* pp. vii–xi, 326–339. Reprinted by permission of Monthly Review Press. Copyright © 1967 by James Weinstein. Footnotes have been renumbered.

society to which it objects most strongly. It has rejected the "Old Left" of the 1930's and 1940's as irrelevant, both because of the debilitating entanglement of communists and socialists of various parties in the ideological disputes of the European movement in the 1920's and 1930's, and because of the rigidly bureaucratic and authoritarian concepts of state and party organization that have characterized those parties that style themselves "Leninist." In other words, the young activists of the New Left have been unable to relate to the existing socialist parties or to identify any meaningful tradition for themselves in the experience of these parties. This is true largely for ideological reasons, but also because there is no surviving popular knowledge of what was once a broadly based, deeply rooted, self-conscious movement for socialism in the United States.

Everybody recognizes the United States as the only industrial nation in the world with no significant socialist movement. Since World War II most Americans have come to assume that this has always been so, for not only in the affluent postwar years but even during the Great Depression (when American capitalism had collapsed and could revive itself only with the start of arms production for another world war) the idea of socialism remained the property of small and isolated groups of radicals. Liberal historians and political scientists rarely tire of telling all who will listen of America's standard of living, of the impact of free land and unique class mobility, of the speed and ease with which sophisticated progressives, starting with Theodore Roosevelt, have been able to appropriate enough radical demands to capture a good part of a potential socialist following. They also explain that the United States, being an immigrant nation, has been as sharply divided along lines of national origin as along those of class. Occasionally, we even hear of the effect of suppression of radicals' right to speak, of the removal of socialist publications from the mails, of the harassment of socialist organizations and the prosecution of their leaders by federal, state, and local governments.

Unquestionably, the success of American capitalism has been outstanding. Yet the reasons for the absence of a meaningful socialist movement in the United States for the past forty-odd years cannot wholly be understood by the celebration of entrepreneurial vigor and nature's largesse. In large part, the failure of American socialism has been internal.

This internal failure has contributed to the prevailing myth that there is no indigenous tradition of American socialism, for it has been as much in the interest of most socialists as in that of most liberals to deny such a tradition. The nature of the old Socialist party has led almost all socialists to acquiesce in the myth of original impotence, even if some have not actively promulgated it. Those who have identified with the Communist movement have downgraded the old Socialist party because to do so was to reduce the proportions of their own failure. Those who identify with the Socialist party and its policies since World War II have gone along with this deprecation because of their changed attitudes toward the Soviet Union and their abandonment of the perspective of building a revolution-

102

ary movement. The liberals, on the other hand, have adopted the view that since the advent of Wilsonian progressivism, or later the New Deal, a political movement for socialism has been irrelevant.

Yet a broadly based movement for socialism did exist in the United States before and during the First World War. Like the "New Left," it grew out of American experience; but unlike the new radicalism, it was conscious of its traditions and was ideologically unified by a commitment to a socialist reorganization of society as the solution to the inequalities and corrupting social values it believed were inherent in American capitalism. Before 1920, the old Socialist party had mass support at the polls, a widespread and vital press, a large following in the trade union movement, and a profound influence on the reformers and the reforms of the day. Furthermore, the prewar Socialists overcame the very obstacles that have allegedly explained their impotence. The Party united those of old American stock with newly arrived immigrants, developed major strength among the small farmers of the most recently closed frontiers, flourished in a period of general prosperity, and garnered its greatest presidential vote in 1912, the year that Theodore Roosevelt took over substantial sections of its platform.

Standard interpretations of American socialism, by academic historians such as Ira Kipnis, Daniel Bell, and David A. Shannon, and also by Communist historians, such as William Z. Foster, have agreed that the American Socialist party started on an irreversible decline in 1912, and that it was finally destroyed during World War I. The liberal historians take the position that this occurred because of the success of Wilsonian liberalism, and the unpopularity of the Party's antiwar views. The Communist historians (with whom Kipnis should be aligned) take the view that the decline was the result of the betrayal of socialist principles by the Party, and by its vacillation on the war. Both groups are incorrect. There was no serious decline after 1912; the Party grew in strength and popularity during the war. . . .

Until 1919 the movement for socialism in the United States was drawn to and revolved around one party. After 1919, contrary to what little has been written on the subject and to popular belief, a general movement of a socialist character continued to exist, even briefly to flourish, but it lost its organizational cohesion and a sense of direction. . . .

The history of American socialism, then, can be treated as Party history until 1919, but from 1919 to 1925 (during which time the idea of socialism still had mass appeal) the movement must be traced through many parties, some coexisting, others appearing and disappearing serially, some explicitly socialist (or communist), others calling themselves labor or farmer-labor parties. Until 1925 this movement had theoretical and organizational links with the earlier socialist politics. In a sense it was a culmination of the early experience. After 1925, as the old Socialist party disintegrated and the farmer-labor movement collapsed, the Communist party emerged as the central force of American radicalism. At that stage, and also because the character of that Party changed then, the movement for socialism assumed most of the characteristics it has had continuously for the pasty forty years; that is, it became narrow, sectarian and dominated by the theoretical and ideological disputes (in the Marxist sense of ideology as false consciousness) inherent in what Isaac Deutscher calls the problem of primitive socialist accumulation in Russia. . . .

* * *

For the Socialist party, 1924 ended all hope either of becoming a major national movement in its own right or of being an essential participant in a coalition on the left. After two dozen years of activity, the Socialist party had returned to the beginning, except that its initiative, youth, and identification with the international revolutionary movement had passed to the Communists. Debs's death in 1926 symbolized the fate of the Party. For another two decades the Socialists would continue to go through the motions, but they would never regain their position as the political center of American radicalism.

The Party had reached the peak of its strength just halfway to 1924. As we have seen, its decline was not a simple or steady process of disintegration. From 1912 until the United States entered the war, the Socialist party remained a vital radical force in America, despite the widespread disillusionment with the world Socialist movement that followed the failure of the European Socialists to prevent, or even to oppose, the war in 1914. While it lost support and strength in some areas in these years, it gained adherents and influence in others. During the war the Party sustained serious losses. Many of its best-known intellectuals and trade unionists quit it to support the war. Socialist newspapers and magazines were banned from the mails and hundreds of locals were disrupted or destroyed. In addition, the federal government prosecuted hundreds of Socialists under the Espionage Acts of 1917 and 1918, while local and state vigilante groups denied halls to Socialists and broke up their meetings in thousands of small towns and cities throughout the country. To make the world safe for democracy, the Wilson Administration sponsored a reign of terror far worse than any conducted in Europe, either among the Allied Powers or within the German Empire.

Nevertheless, despite these unprecedented denials of even the most elementary democratic rights, the Party grew in size and prestige during the war. As the only national political organization in opposition to the Administration's war policies, the Socialists won support from substantial numbers of Americans. In addition, after the Russian Revolution in November 1917, thousands of immigrants flocked into the Party. By 1919, Party membership had climbed back to 109,000, only a few thousand below its 1912 total. There were, however, many differences between the postwar and prewar parties. First, the geographical distribution of Party membership and strength had shifted heavily eastward and into the

104

large cities. States like Oklahoma, Texas, Nevada, Montana, Idaho, and Minnesota no longer led in relative numbers of Socialists, whereas New York City, Milwaukee, Buffalo, Cleveland, and Chicago did. New York, for example, had contributed only 7.6 percent to the total Socialist vote in 1916, but it accounted for 22 percent of Debs's vote in 1920.

Second, as a concomitant of the first, the percentage of foreign born in the Party increased sharply during the war years, from 20 percent before the war to 53 percent just before the split.

Third, under the impact of the Russian Revolution and the expulsion of pro-war Socialists, the Party as a whole had shifted decisively to the left. This movement was accelerated by a conviction, even among such "right-wingers" as the Milwaukee Socialists, that the AFL had proven to be hopelessly corrupt, and that it had acted as the "tail of capitalism." All factions in the Party actively supported the Russian Revolution, fought for recognition and trade, and opposed the American invasion of Siberia.

When the war ended, Socialists of every tendency looked to the future with optimism. They did so not only because of the revolutionary wave that seemed to be sweeping Europe but because their criticisms of the war were daily being vindicated. As the details of the postwar settlement became public, it was clear to all that the war had not been one for democracy, that it had not ended colonialism, that secret diplomacy had not been repudiated, that the people of the world had not won the right of self-determination. In other words, Wilson's Fourteen Points had been proven a sham. Furthermore, within the United States, workers and farmers were finding that their wartime gains had been only temporary, and that those who pressed for fulfillment of wartime promises were branded as Bolsheviks. Given a period in which it could rebuild its organization and press, prospects looked bright to the Socialists in 1919.

The Party was, of course, not to have that opportunity. Instead, it faced further organizational disintegration as a result of the Bolshevik insistence that the Russian Revolution was only the first step in the imminent overthrow of world capitalism. The Russians, as we have seen, not only desired revolution in the West but believed their own survival was impossible without it. For three years following their revolution, they called on all Socialists to rise and seize power without delay and looked upon those who refused to do so as traitors to the working class. This policy led to a series of splits in the European Socialist parties, although in countries such as Germany, Britain, and France it was partly obscured by the earlier splits which had resulted from the support given the war by the Socialist leaders. In Germany, the Socialists had not only joined the wartime government but had also participated in the attacks on the Bolsheviks after the revolution. In Europe, in other words, the basis for splitting with the pro-war Socialists was real, even though the Bolshevik demands for immediate revolution had been inappropriate in some countries.

Whatever political justification existed for the splits in Europe, there was none in the United States. The so-called right wing of the American Socialist party had opposed the war with at least as much vigor as the left. But immediate revolution was out of the question in the United States, and those Socialists who recognized this pushed for unity and reorganization, rather than for splits and insurrectionary tactics. Only a small group of English-speaking Socialists took up the cry for revolution in 1919, supported—or rather pushed—by the vast majority of newly recruited Eastern Europeans in the Party foreign language federations. One of the reasons the left moved so easily toward its mistaken position was that many of its most effective and respected leaders were revolutionaries from Europe or Asia who had sought sanctuary in the United States during the war. In the early organizational activity of the new left wing, Trotsky, Bukharin, V. Volodorsky, Grigorii Chudnovsky, and Mme. Kollantai were both active and prominent. So was Sen Katayama, who returned to the United States from his native Japan in 1916, and followed the Russians to Moscow after the split. Even among the English-speaking Socialists who organized the Communist Labor party, foreigners were prominent. The Irish Socialists, James Larkin, Eadmonn MacAlpine, one of the original editors of *The Revolutionary Age* in 1918, and Jack Carney, editor of the Duluth left-wing paper *Truth,* were heavily influenced by European syndicalism. Larkin came to the United States when war broke out in 1914 and recognized his limited understanding of conditions in the United States, but still helped lead the movement toward a Communist party.

Most of the Americans who joined the left wing and helped form the Communist Labor party (the majority of the Party in such states as California and Washington) had no concept of what later came to be called the Leninist party. Quite the contrary, they had traditionally opposed Hillquit and Berger as bureaucrats, and had advocated greater decentralization and autonomy. In 1914, Robert F. Hoxie, a political economist at the University of Chicago, confided to Ralph Easley that "the chief trouble with the Socialist party is lack of discipline. When a majority decision is reached (especially if the minority is ultra-radical, red, IWW-ish) the minority gets up on its hind legs and yells 'boss rule,' 'steam roller.' " Hoxie's conclusion was that the Socialist situation indicated "the impossibility of attempting to combine democracy and efficiency"; but we know now that this seemingly inefficient, yet open and diverse Party, was much more viable than the highly centralized and disciplined Communist parties of the 1920's and 1930's. The native left-wingers who went Communist did so out of romantic identification with the Russian Revolution, and because of the panicked, bureaucratic action of the Old Guard in expelling the foreign-language federations in the spring of 1919. But few of them could remain for long in a Party that boasted, as Alexander Bittelman did in 1924, of its ability to change its line in twenty-four hours at the behest of the International, despite the fact that the policy changed was that of an overwhelming majority and had been followed successfully for six months.

106

Had the Party still been 70 percent native born, substantial unity might have been preserved. But almost to a man the Eastern European federations sided with the position of the Third International. Together with some 15 percent of the English-speaking Socialists—whose ranks were increased by the unprincipled maneuvers of the Old Guard—they split off to form the several new Communist parties.

After the split the Socialist party was in an anomalous position. Friendly to Soviet Russia, it was unceasingly and bitterly attacked by the Third International and the American Communist parties. Actually, by expelling seven language federations and the state organizations of Michigan and Massachusetts, the right had effectuated the split. But it was the left that had pursued the policies that made the split inevitable. Under the impact of these attacks, and with a growing belief that the example of the British Labour party was more relevant to American conditions than the Russian experience, the Socialists moved gradually away from close identification with the Bolsheviks. By 1925, the Party convention was openly and sharply critical of the Russians. Increasingly, the Party leadership took this position, although for the next decade many leaders—James H. Maurer and Norman Thomas, for example—remained defenders of the Soviets.

But the Socialist position, theoretically sound, was politically untenable. As the Party moved away from identification with the world revolutionary movement it suffered a steady stream of defections to the Workers' party. At the same time, as it espoused a British-style labor party it experienced continuous losses to the various Farmer-Labor party movements. At first the Socialists reacted to the Labor party by jealously guarding their own leadership. Later, when it had become clear that their Party was disintegrating, they tied their hopes so closely to the [Conference for Progressive Political Action] that they were unwilling to cooperate with the Chicago or Minnesota Farmer-Laborites. In 1924 they finally won admission to a major coalition of labor and the left, but when the trade unions abandoned independent political action after the La Follette campaign, the Socialists were stranded and isolated. From then on the Party declined steadily until the crash of 1929 revived it and gave it brief renewed growth in the 1930's.

*   *   *

Unlike the Socialists, the Communists were not to have their major impact on American political life until the middle 1930's. Even so, the events of 1924 established the pattern of their work and revealed their insurmountable weaknesses, marking them as essentially irrelevant and as a divisive political force among radicals. Ironically, the Communists' primary source of strength and appeal also made success as a mass political movement impossible. Their relationship with the Third International attracted radicals and others who sought identification with the world revolutionary movement, but their attempts to duplicate the Russian experi-

107

ence and form of party organization alienated the Communists from American radicals, from labor, and from the farmers. The very formation of the Communist parties had been a mistake, both from the point of view of the best interests of the Socialist movement in the United States and the national interests of Soviet Russia. At a time when the Soviets desperately needed support, the Communists had split the pro-Soviet radicals in the United States into a myriad of warring sects. Nor had they merely debilitated the Socialists. So far out of touch with American life were they that in less than two years their original combined membership of almost 70,000 had faded away to less than 10,000.

At the end of these two years, after it had become clear that the revolutionary wave in Europe had receded, the American Communists were rescued from permanent obscurity by the insistence of the Third International that they give up their illegal status, begin to work in the trade unions, and adopt a program of immediate demands so as to appeal to the masses of American workers and farmers. In effect, the Communists had returned to the policies and assumptions of the Socialists in 1919, even though they still harbored illusions about securing positions of influence so that when the right moment came their small, tightly disciplined Party would be ready to seize power. . . .

They counterposed the tight discipline of the Third International to the situation in the Second International which had allowed most of the European Socialist parties to betray their prewar pledges and to support the war. In compensating for the weaknesses of the Second International, however, the Communists did not attempt to develop a firmer adherence to socialist principles among the masses. Instead, they relied upon organizational means to guarantee ideological hegemony. It did not work; the establishment of a highly centralized "Leninist" party in the United States led to a procession of crises and splits and contributed to a continuous process of fragmentation of the broader radical movements. The Communists were not entirely to blame for the latter. As we have seen, their presence in the Minnesota movement was used as a pretext to attack the Farmer-Laborites by those opposed to a third party.

But the Communists certainly helped the enemies of radicalism, both by their concept of organization and their strategy. In the 1920's they openly proclaimed their intention to isolate the leaders of any organization with which they worked from the membership. In the 1930's and 40's, they acted in a similar manner, even though denying an intention to do so. At least until 1956, the Communists saw themselves as the only true socialists, and the Russian example as a model for American Socialism. Thus, in Foster's campaign speeches in 1932 he would devote a sentence or two to attacking Roosevelt and Hoover, and spend the bulk of his energies fulminating against the Socialists—as if the Socialist party were the main barrier to revolution in the United States. Similarly, in reporting the vote in 1930, the *Daily Worker* listed the Socialists along with the Democrats and Republicans as a "capitalist" party.

By the 1930's the Communists, not without a degree of Socialist acquiescence, had erected an entire mythology about the origins of their movement. In 1936, for example, Joseph Freeman described a meeting that had taken place in 1925 sponsored by the International Political Prisoners' Committee. Among the scheduled speakers was Charney Vladeck, business manager of the anti-Soviet *Jewish Daily Forward,* by then a right-wing Socialist paper. Vladeck was to speak on political prisoners in Russia, following Carleton Beal's address on political prisoners in Latin America. When he began to speak the entire gallery "lumbered to its feet" and commenced to sing the "International," breaking up the meeting. This disturbed Freeman, and the next day he commented to a Communist organizer that it was too bad Communists and Socialists had to fight each other. The organizer replied,

> It's too bad, but whose fault is it? They split the labor movement when they supported the war, when they threw the left out of the Socialist party. They're splitting it now by kicking us out of the unions, by attacking the Soviet Union. We are with the socialist workers, and if they have anything against us it's because of the lies they are told by their misleaders.[1]

Similarly, John Gates, in a passage describing his conversion to Communism while attending City College, reveals the manner in which this myth complemented the Communists' basic appeal. Gates asks,

> Had not the Communists brought into being the first successful socialist country, the Soviet Union? And wasn't this accomplished over the opposition of the Socialists? Was not the Soviet Union moving forward with its Five Year plans, was it not planning production and abolishing unemployment when the richest country in the world, the United States, was in the throes of terrible depression?[2]

*   *   *

By the late 1920's both Socialist and Communist ideological positions concerning the Soviet Union had hardened and were central to the development of their political movements. Neither was able to view Russian Communism essentially within the context of Russian history. The Communists were committed to the view that the Soviets represented utopia, and that all of Russia's internal problems and experience had universal application. For their part, the Socialists tended to accept the Communist view that every policy forced upon the Soviets had general relevance and to see this as proof that the Russian experience was not a specific combination of Marxism and Russian history, but a new form of political theory. Insisting on evaluating the Soviets in terms of conditions in the United States, even those Socialists most friendly to the Russians adopted

[1] Joseph Freeman, *American Testament* (New York: Farrar, 1936), pp. 349–351.
[2] John Gates, *The Story of an American Communist* (New York: Nelson, 1958), p. 17.

the position expressed by James H. Maurer in 1927. If, Maurer wrote, the Soviets were really anxious for the workers of the world to throw off the yoke of capitalism, they should "turn the old Russia of poverty, suffering, despair, and official corruption into a workers' paradise and then invite suffering humanity to look them over—in other words, demonstrate to the world their fitness as a proletarian government and the crumbling system of capitalism would pass into history."

To the extent that Maurer and his comrades followed through on the implications of this statement, they were abdicating their responsibility as American Socialists. But this was not the main weakness of the multiform socialist parties in the 1920's and 1930's. Rather, it was the extent to which Soviet developments, for the most part irrelevant in so far as American workers and farmers were concerned, were so close to the center of Communist and Socialist attention. The major events in the United States did not shape basic Communist and Socialist attitudes in this period. The crash of 1929, the New Deal of the NRA and AAA, the policy of "neutrality" during the Spanish Civil War, the organizing drives of the CIO, and the process by which the United States became involved in World War II, loom large in Socialist and Communist histories of the late 1920's and 1930's; but the expulsion of Trotsky from the Russian Party in 1929, the adoption of the popular front policy in 1934, the Soviet treason trials in 1936, and the Nazi-Soviet pact in 1939 emerge as equally important milestones.

From 1929 to 1934 the Socialist party did experience a resurgence under the leadership of Norman Thomas. Party membership increased and the number of locals multiplied to 1,600 (compared to 5,000 in 1917). In 1932, Thomas received 885,000 votes, and many leading intellectuals endorsed him. But the membership had a different character from that of the old Socialist party. Farmers were virtually absent, strength among industrial workers and in the trade unions (except for the needle trades) was slight. The difference was symbolized by the contrast between Debs and Thomas. Debs came to socialism through his experience as a trade unionist and as a railroad worker; Thomas was converted during World War [I] as a pacifist Presbyterian minister. A Princeton graduate, he appealed to and brought into the Party many intellectuals and urban middle-class voters, but he did this more on the basis of a thoroughgoing program of reform than on the basis of an ideological commitment to social transformation. And, within the Socialist party, those who fought to re-establish a revolutionary strategy were attacked by the Old Guard as Communist. By 1934, a statement of the militant majority within the Socialist party on war and on social transformation, although more mild than Hillquit's own writing before and during World War [I], was condemned by the Old Guard as "anarchist, illegal and communist." Two years later, when the Old Guard was gone, the debate was over the individual's relationship to the Party, with the newly allied Trotskyists insisting on the "Leninist" concept of total discipline. The

110

merits of either debate are not of concern here. The point is that both the Communists and the Socialists had been hopelessly caught up in conflict over forms of organization, attitudes toward fellow Socialists, and concepts of strategy and tactics that did not grow out of American experience or the problems of transforming American society. The legacy of 1919 was the alienation of American socialism.

Philip G. Altbach and Patti Peterson

Before Berkeley: Historical Perspectives on American Student Activism

In their study of student political activism during the first six decades of the twentieth century, the authors find that it has often been linked to the issues and organizations discussed in the earlier selections by Shannon and Weinstein. While rarely centered on the university itself, the student movement focused on such matters as socialism, war and peace, and civil liberties. In general, it followed political trends in society and in the adult radical movement. The authors' investigation indicates that student protest is not a new phenomenon, although its methods, goals, and orientation may have changed during recent years. Professor Altbach has written and edited several books which deal with student activism, including *Student Politics in Bombay*. Patti McGill Peterson is engaged in research on the relationship of the student pacifist movement to radical student politics. This selection is part of a larger study investigating the historical origins of American student activism.

$\mathbf{A}$merican student activism has a long history, although it was only in the Sixties that it received national attention and serious analysis. In 1823, half the Harvard senior class was expelled shortly before graduation for participating in disruptive activity, and students were involved in anti-conscription campaigns during the Civil War. Student activism before 1960, however, had no major impact on national policy, and prior to 1900, no organized student activist groups emerged. Yet there is a tradition of student involvement in politics in the United States, and many of the concerns of the activists of the Sixties are reflected in the past.

This essay provides a broad historical picture of American student activism from 1900 to 1960. We have concentrated on organizations and movements, and have omitted a more detailed sociological analysis. Although religious student movements, pacifist groups, and conservative organizations are important during this period, it was liberal and radical

From Philip G. Altbach and Patti Peterson, "Before Berkeley: Historical Perspectives on American Student Activism," *The Annals of the American Academy of Political and Social Science*, 395 (May 1971), pp. 2–14. Reprinted by permission of the authors and The American Academy of Political and Social Science. Footnotes are omitted.

student activity which exerted greater impact on the campus—hence our emphasis.

The American student movement prior to 1960 closely followed political trends in society. Members of the Intercollegiate Socialist Society (ISS), founded in 1905, were a vanguard among university students. But until major political crises mobilized large numbers of students, such groups remained small. The student movements which flourished prior to 1960 were generally linked closely with adult movements and no "generation gap" is readily discernible among activists. In fact, the independence of the current student movement might well be one of its strengths, since it is not necessarily bound by the organizational or ideological limitations of adult movements.

The student activism which developed in the early twentieth century took place in a context different from that of the modern American university. The colleges were much less in the mainstream of American life and the academic community was much smaller than at present. In 1912, for example, there were approximately 400,000 students in American universities. Activism, even of the moderate type reported here, was confined to a very small proportion of the student community and to a relatively few institutions. Yet, the student "movement," if it can be called that, set the political tone of a basically apathetic campus community and influenced a small number of students who later played important roles in American public life. The foundations for student political activity on the campus were formed in the early years of this century.

EARLY ACTIVIST GROUPS

As the earliest major leftist student political organization, the ISS included among its early active members Upton Sinclair, Morris Hillquit, Jack London, Charlotte Perkins Gilman, Clarence Darrow, Walter Lippmann, and others later prominent in reformist and radical movements. Interestingly, most of the ISS founders were not students. From the beginning, the ISS was an educational organization, formed to "promote an intelligent interest in socialism among college men and women." While the major strength of the ISS was in the prestige colleges of the eastern seaboard, from 1910 until the outbreak of World War I it spread across the country, and by 1917 claimed sixty chapters with 2,200 members.

The major thrust of ISS activity was educational. The organization's journal, the *Intercollegiate Socialist,* published regularly from 1913 until 1919 and featured articles on aspects of Socialist thought as well as on university-related issues and public affairs. ISS affiliates sponsored radical speakers on campus and often caused local crises over free speech. These speakers were the main educational thrust of ISS activity.

A number of themes emerged from ISS campus activities in the early 1900's, and also in its national conventions and summer conferences. The debate over American rearmament and entry into World War I caused substantial disagreement among members, and was a constant topic of discussion. Other popular topics were free speech on campus, immigration, a World Court, and various aspects of socialism. In this period, there was relatively little attention paid to foreign affairs and, surprisingly, only slight emphasis given to internal university problems and academic reform. The ISS convention of 1916, however, voted to oppose the introduction of military training on campus.

The society did not take the complexities of ideological politics very seriously. In 1913, a questionnaire of 450 ISS members indicated that a third of the membership was non-Socialist, and a few members were even anti-Socialist. If the *Intercollegiate Socialist* is any indication, the factional disputes over Socialist doctrine which characterized the 1930's and later periods were rare in the ISS.

As the Intercollegiate Socialist Society became more concerned with the creation of a broader movement, it began to shift its emphasis from the campus. In 1919, it changed its name to the League for Industrial Democracy, and its journal became the *Socialist Review*. Although this was done to broaden the movement, the organization remained more intellectual than activist and most of its strength stayed on the campus.

Another organization which attempted to build a broad-based youth movement but which had some strength on campus was the Young People's Socialist League (YPSL). Organized in 1907 as the youth affiliate of the Socialist party, the YPSL claimed 4,200 members in 112 chapters by 1913. Much of YPSL's membership was, however, off the campus. The YPSL tended to engage in more direct political campaigns, usually in support of Socialist candidates and other struggles, although it also carried on an active educational program.

Less obviously political than the ISS or the YPSL, the Student Christian Volunteer Movement (SCVM) played an active and important role on the campuses. Founded in 1886, the SCVM was a federation of various Protestant religious youth organizations, among which the YMCA's and YWCA's were perhaps the most active. The SCVM exhibited a strong sense of social concern, although prior to 1920 its main emphasis was on foreign missionary work. The SCVM's journal, the *North American Student,* was concerned with foreign missionary activity but also featured articles on problems at home. Some of the earliest articles supporting educational reform and women's liberation appeared in the *North American Student*. During both the pre-World War I period and the Twenties, religious student organizations played a key role in bringing social concerns to the campuses and particularly to those colleges somewhat out of the mainstream of academic life, in which religious groups were the only source of social concern.

World War I and the post-war Red Scare of 1918–1919 inhibited the student movement as it did the adult radical movement. Many liberal and radical intellectuals were perplexed by the war issue, and this question split the radical movement. The ISS did not support the war, but maintained a position which neither condoned nor condemned it and in the process lost much of its membership. The YPSL, which strongly opposed the war, was also decimated during the war.

THE MOVEMENT IN THE TWENTIES

The issues. The Twenties were a curious period in the history of the student movement, as they were for American society generally. The period was characterized by political apathy on and off campus, but at the same time exhibited some significant political and social currents. For example, the student movement strongly criticized the universities for the first time, and devoted itself to some extent to educational issues. A study conducted in 1926 showed that a majority of the 1,026 students responding opposed ROTC. In addition, college students were involved in a minor "cultural revolution." It can be argued that the "new" cultural patterns of the Twenties which were stimulated largely by youth were in a sense similar to the hippie and other countercultural developments of the 1960's and 1970's. While the data are somewhat rudimentary, they seem to indicate that college students of the Twenties were substantially freer in their sexual and religious attitudes and were in general more tolerant than their elders. Articles in student journals as well as commentary in intellectual magazines indicate that many socially conscious students felt that adult society was hypocritical, base, and anti-intellectual. Indeed, many of the charges sound very similar to those made at present by radical students.

The organized student movement of the previous decade was destroyed by the war and repression, and never regained its strength in the Twenties. Much of the student activity which took place had no organizational roots and little continuity. The *New Student,* a journal founded in 1922, reported extensively on student events and tried to provide a communications link between disparate local groups. Despite the lack of organization, there was a good deal of ferment taking place during the Twenties. The period was characterized by substantial repression; students with radical inclinations were often expelled from colleges, student newspapers were censored, and administrators often acted in a heavy-handed manner. Much of the thrust of student activism was aimed at establishing and protecting free speech on the campus. Campus newspaper editors protested censorship, and student groups attempted to bring radical speakers on campus.

Students criticized "giganticism" in universities, and many of their criticisms have a very modern ring to them. Students complained that professors were boring and that there was too little contact with them, that academic bureaucracy was overwhelming the campus, and that they generally were alienated from their colleges. Articles reprinted in the *New Student* from college newspapers indicate that these kinds of criticisms were very strong. The Twenties were a period of rapid expansion of higher education—the proportion of youth attending college rose from 4 percent in 1900 to 12 percent at the end of the Twenties. This period was also one of rapid social change, and college curricula did not often keep up with currents in society.

The groups. A number of student groups emerged in the 1920's which have been generally ignored because of the more dramatic events of the following decade. Strong student sentiment in favor of the League of Nations and for disarmament sparked the organization of the National Student Committee for the Limitation of Armaments. This group sent antiwar speakers to college campuses. In 1922, it merged with the Intercollegiate Liberal League to form the National Student Forum (NSF), and the new group claimed a thousand student members and several hundred graduate and faculty members. The NSF avoided general social reform issues, and its leadership tried to prevent it from getting a "radical" image. The *New Student* was the official organ of the NSF, and both the organization and the journal saw their image as stimulating thought and social concern among American college students.

The National Student Forum was not the only group to emerge during the Twenties. Organizations such as the National Student Federation of America (NSFA), the Student League for Industrial Democracy (SLID), and various Christian groups were attempting to unite students on social and, to some extent, political issues. The SCVM convention of 1923 considered a number of social action issues, and a number of radical speakers pressed for social change. Many Christian youth organizations passed strong antiwar statements at their meetings and, in 1924, a group of 700 Christian students at an SCVM convention took a strong pacifist stand under the leadership of the Fellowship of Youth for Peace, an affiliate of the Fellowship of Reconciliation, a prominent pacifist organization.

The SLID claimed seventy-five student chapters and about 2,000 student members in 1927. Its major activities included campaigns against ROTC on campus, organizing student committees to defend Sacco and Vanzetti, and campaigning against American intervention in Nicaragua and Mexico. Among the SLID's active members in the late 1920's were Walter Reuther, Sidney Hook, and Max Lerner. Indeed, one observer in the 1950's stated that one of the SLID's main functions in the Twenties was to train leaders for the labor, Socialist, and other reform movements.

A forerunner of the present-day National Student Association, the NSFA was founded in 1925. The NSFA was a loose federation of student governments, and was interested mainly in international cooperation and understanding among student groups. Other efforts at student involvement in the Twenties were issue-oriented.

Single-issue conferences were common. For example, students gathered at Bear Mountain, New York, in 1924 to discuss "Youth's Standard of Living." Among the sponsors of this meeting—foreshadowing the coalitions of student groups in the 1930's—were the YPSL, YM and YWCA's, Young Workers' League (the youth group of the Communist party), Rand Students League (Socialist), and the Ethical Culture Society. In

1927, the first conference of the American Federation of Youth, representing fifty youth organizations, met and went on record favoring a nationwide campaign against compulsory military training, militarism, imperialism, and child labor. Conventions of religious students were addressed by SLID speakers, and often took radical or reformist stands.

THE THIRTIES

The 1930's saw the growth of the first mass student movement in American history. The most important campus issue was the antiwar question; thousands of students were involved in many American colleges. For the first time, the student movement engaged in a political campaign which, although ultimately unsuccessful, aroused substantial public support on and off the campus. Despite its size—the American Student Union claimed 20,000 members in 1938, and several hundred thousand students participated in peace strikes during the decade—the impact of the student movement should not be overestimated. For the most part, the activities of radical students were a reflection of other, more significant, social movements and organizations.

The generation gap, so much a part of the political rhetoric of the Sixties, was absent during the Thirties. Politically active students were generally affiliated with adult political groups and usually took their cues from the adult movement. Even the antiwar movement was stimulated as much by conservative isolationists as by radical students. Finally, the activism of the Thirties was mainly confined to metropolitan centers, most notably New York City, and to the more cosmopolitan campuses. The majority of colleges was unaffected by the political ferment taking place. Despite these limitations, the student movement of the Thirties was one of the most significant in American history, and in terms of proportions of students involved in activism, perhaps more significant than the New Left of the 1960's.

The student movement of the Thirties had a number of key foci. It was not generally interested in issues of academic reform. In fact, the continuing criticisms of the educational system which were made in the Twenties generally stopped in the Thirties. Students fought battles over ROTC and over free speech on campus, and occasionally defended academic freedom, but in general their concerns were more political. The antiwar issue was the most volatile campus question of the Thirties despite the Depression and other domestic crises, perhaps reflecting the overwhelmingly middle-class student population. The more ideologically sophisticated students were also involved in labor organizing, and in the internal politics of the significant left-wing movements of the period.

The radical trend. The early Thirties saw the radicalizing of existing student groups and the formation of new leftist organizations. The Student League for Industrial Democracy, perhaps the most important left-wing campus group with an historical tradition, moved substantially to the left although it maintained its social democratic orientation. The Socialist and

Communist parties, which had been unenthusiastic about campus organizing in the early Thirties, became active in the universities by 1933. In 1931, the National Student League was organized with Communist support and eventual domination. While the NSL was more radical than SLID—its program included an effort to "promote student participation in the revolutionary movement against capitalism"—it tried to appeal to a range of student opinion. NSL received national publicity when its members went to Harlan County, Kentucky in 1932 to support striking coal miners. SLID and NSL did work together, however, in organizing "united front" antiwar campaigns on campus in 1931 and 1932 and in the American Student Union.

The Thirties also radicalized the Christian student movement. The Council of Christian Associations, the organization uniting the YM and YWCA's, published a pamphlet in 1931 entitled "Toward a New Economic Society" in which collective ownership of natural resources and public utilities was advocated. Older national leaders of the Y's became disturbed at the council's publication and disavowed its Socialist position. The SCVM placed less stress on overseas missionary work and paid more attention to domestic problems. Resolutions passed at the first National Assembly of Student Christian Groups in 1938 indicated religious students had become more radical. One resolution, passed by a substantial majority, stated that capitalism and fascism were unacceptable and that the goals of the cooperative movement and of Marxian socialism were preferred.

The peace issue. The most dramatic campus issue of the period was peace and disarmament. A poll conducted by the Intercollegiate Disarmament Council in 1931 indicated that 39 percent of the 22,627 students polled at seventy colleges would not participate in any war and 33 percent stated that they would fight only if the United States were invaded. The Brown University *Daily Herald* polled approximately 22,000 students in sixty-five colleges; and of the 15,636 students who responded, around 50 percent stated they would bear arms only in case of an invasion of the United States. Students also fought over civil liberties and academic freedom, and with somewhat more success than they had had in the Twenties. The most dramatic case involved the editor of the Columbia University *Spectator,* who was expelled from the university in 1932 for publishing "misrepresentations." One of the first successful campus student strikes took place over this issue.

Events in Europe and a continuing domestic crisis greatly increased the constituency for radical student activism in the United States. By 1935, the most active student groups were the SLID (Social Democratic), the National Student League (Communist), religious pacifist groups such as the Fellowship of Reconciliation, social-action-minded religious groups like the Y's, and the National Student Federation of America (Liberal). Attempts at unity among progressive students were made during the early Thirties, such as the National Conference of Students in Politics in 1933, but the major united-front student group was the American Student Union (ASU), which functioned from 1935 to 1939.

Like many of the other campus trends of the period, the formation of the ASU reflected broader events in society. The Communist International's stress on the formation of "united fronts" provided the major impetus for the ASU and other similar groups among other constituencies. The ASU was basically a union of the Communist NSL, the Socialist SLID, and various unaffiliated liberals. From 1935 until 1937, there was an effective sharing of power between Socialists and Communists, due in part to liberal support of the Socialist position. By 1937, however, the Communists were able to take control of the ASU and from that time until the ASU's demise it slavishly followed the turns of Communist policy.

The Oxford Pledge was a center of controversy in the ASU, and a key issue in the student movement as a whole. In 1933, the Oxford Union adopted a resolution that stated that under no circumstances should one fight for "King and Country." The ASU adopted an American version of the pledge in 1936 and it became the center of campus organizing by both the ASU and various liberal and pacifist groups. National student peace strikes were organized from 1935 until 1939, and these attracted great public attention. Among the most successful strikes, one took place in April, 1935 which involved more than 150,000 students and had the support of a number of liberal college presidents, and another in 1938 involved more than 500,000 students. On many campuses these "strikes" involved only a one-hour work stoppage, however. The campus peace movement lost support as groups like the ASU closely followed Communist policy in supporting collective security, and as war in Europe looked increasingly possible.

Despite the fact that in 1938 the ASU claimed 20,000 members in 150 colleges and 100 high schools, all was not well with the organization. ASU's reversal of its antiwar stand and its increasingly clear Communist domination disillusioned many students. Vocal Socialist and pacifist groups also took away some ASU supporters. The final blow to the organization came when collective security was abandoned by the ASU at the time Stalin signed the Nazi-Soviet nonaggression pact. ASU membership dropped to 2,000 in 1940, and the organization soon went out of existence.

The "active left." At the same time that mass "united front" student groups were functioning, the political parties and sects of the left were also active on the campuses. The Young Communist League, clearly the largest of the political groups, claimed 22,000 members in 1939, both student and non-student. The Young People's Socialist League continued to function during this period, and although it took more of an interest in students than it previously did, its effectiveness was limited by internecine factional disputes. Smaller political student groups affiliated with Trotskyist, pacifist, and other tendencies on the left also existed, although it is unlikely that their combined membership was more than 3,000 nationally, with a major segment concentrated in New York City. One of the political trends of the Thirties, on the campus as well as more broadly, was a splintering of the radical movement. Student groups spent much of their time fighting each other. The major thrust of the student movement was leftist during the 1930's, but there are indications that not all politically conscious students were radicals. The liberal National Student Federation of America continued to function throughout this period. Furthermore, students were involved in a number of antistrike activities in the Thirties, indicating that conservative activism also existed. Right-wing Berkeley students helped to break the San Francisco general strike, and some radical students were thrown into the lake at the University of Wisconsin in 1937. There are no indications of a major right-wing organizational thrust on the campus at this period, but sentiment did exist.

The student movement of the 1930's involved large numbers of students in impressive demonstrations and in large organizations. But in the last analysis it failed to build a viable movement. Its lack of interest in campus issues and its deep involvement in the factional politics of the left cut it off from many students. The adult movement allowed the students little autonomy, and when political difficulties emerged on the adult level, the student movement immediately collapsed. Yet, the student movement of the Thirties involved impressive numbers of individuals, many of whom received their political education in the movement and many are the parents of today's generation of activists.

THE FORTIES

The contrast between the Thirties and the following two decades is dramatic. With the onset of World War II, the American student movement simply collapsed. Radicals who opposed the war were disillusioned and confused by the splits in the adult radical movement concerning the war and related foreign policy issues. Other radicals and liberals threw themselves behind moves for collective security and supported the Allied cause. And with American involvement in 1941, many students volunteered or were drafted into the armed forces and campus activism came to an end. The most active groups on campus were such organizations as the Student Defenders of Democracy.

The immediate postwar period saw a number of efforts to revive the student movement, but none of these was very successful. The first postwar convention of SLID, held in 1946, was attended by only forty delegates from twelve schools. Communist activists organized the American Youth for Democracy (AYD) in 1943, which sought to combine campus-oriented issues with opposition to the beginning of the Cold War. While AYD had a respectable membership, it did not inspire major student support, nor was it a force on the campus. Perhaps the most successful postwar student groups were those related directly to the desire for a durable peace; among these students, many were returning veterans anxious to complete their studies and settle down to a job. The United World Fed-

120

eralists had a short period of support on the campus, and engaged in various kinds of educational programs aimed at convincing Americans to give up their national sovereignty and join in a world government.

The liberal movement also was reflected in a number of student groups which were formed around 1948. These organizations reflected in part a growing anti-communism, both on and off the campus, and a desire to counter groups like the AYD, as well as large numbers of students who supported Henry Wallace's presidential campaign in 1948. The Students for Democratic Action (SDA), founded in 1947, was an affiliate of the liberal, anti-Communist Americans for Democratic Action. It attracted substantial support on the campus but did not engage in major campus-oriented campaigns. There was a brief upsurge of student political activism during the 1948 presidential election campaign. The Young Progressives of America, formed largely with AYD initiative, provided strong campus support for Wallace's election campaign, and involved thousands of students under Communist direction. When the Wallace forces were roundly defeated, many of those who were active became disillusioned and left the political scene altogether.

Efforts at reviving the student movement in the late 1940's faced substantial odds. The mood of the campus, as of the country at large, was decidedly apolitical. As previously mentioned, many veterans returned to their studies and were anxious to finish their academic work quickly. The student movement itself was unable to shift its attention to campus issues, such as overcrowding in universities, poor housing conditions, and other problems created by the returning veterans. The adult left was in substantial disarray and could provide no guidance, and no independent student groups existed which could strike out on their own. But perhaps the major reason was the general political climate in the country, which was confused in the immediate postwar period, and increasingly anti-Communist and conservative during the 1950's. The Korean War, the development of the Cold War, the Communist coup in Czechoslovakia, and the increasingly anti-Communist foreign and domestic stance of the American government, combined to make radical or even liberal student organizing difficult.

THE FIFTIES

The one major national student organization founded in the late 1940's reflected many of the trends which have been noted. The U.S. National Student Association was founded in 1948 in the flush of international student unity and coöperation. It was not long before the NSA became involved in the Cold War, and its stand became strongly anti-Communist. The NSA's early support was impressive—some 1,000 student leaders representing 1,100,000 students and more than twenty national student organizations attended the founding convention of the NSA—but the organization never achieved major active support on the campus. It was from the outset a federation of student governments without grass-roots support. Although there was a small minority of Communists in NSA, and a rather substantial minority of conservative Catholics, the NSA's policies were from the outset "mainline liberal." Recent disclosures of the CIA's involvement in NSA's financial affairs are not so surprising, considering the political climate in the early 1950's and the strong anti-Communist position of NSA's liberal leadership during this period. Although clearly the largest and probably externally the most influential student organization of the 1950's, the National Student Association made very little impact on its more than one million student "members."

The 1950's were also a period of direct political repression and general apathy. Investigations by Senator Joseph McCarthy and various congressional committees instilled fear in many liberals and radicals. Faculty members were forced from their jobs in some cases because of their political views, and loyalty oaths became common. Journals like *The Nation* and *The New Republic* chronicled the silent generation, and the liberal press decried the apathy of the young. Right-wing student groups gained some prominence on the campuses for the first time in years. The pro-McCarthy Students for America, founded in 1951, had a short period of strength in the early 1950's; and other conservative groups were founded, often with substantial outside financial support, later in the decade. The Students for America was a blatant arm of McCarthyism with a national security division that maintained direct liaison with antisubversive government agencies. The Intercollegiate Society for Individualists, founded in 1957, reflected an intellectual concern for right-wing libertarianism, while the Young Americans for Freedom (YAF), founded in 1960, is a more activist-oriented, conservative student organization.

It is a curious paradox that although antiwar feelings among students in the 1930's and the 1960's helped to sustain active radical student movements, similar tendencies among students in the 1950's had no organizational effect. The Korean War was never very popular on the campuses. A poll taken in 1953 indicated that 26 percent of those responding were strongly opposed to the war while 36 percent had strong reservations. No groups emerged to mobilize this feeling, and as a result the campus was virtually silent on the subject of the Korean conflict.

Despite pervading apathy and repression, left-wing student groups did survive the 1950's, providing some organizational continuity which kept radical thought alive in the United States during a rather difficult period. The Communists changed the name of their student group from American Youth for Democracy to Labor Youth League, to reflect shifts in party policy. The LYL maintained a small number of chapters during the Fifties, mainly in New York and a few major campus centers, and it was subjected to substantial repression by campus authorities and others. The pacifist Fellowship of Reconciliation maintained a presence on the campus and was especially active among seminarians. The Young People's Socialist League and the SLID both continued to function, although with memberships varying around two hundred each. As in the Twenties, religious student organizations kept the spark of social reform and political concern alive on many of the less politically active campuses. Groups like the YM-YWCA were especially active in this area, and they provided a forum of radical speakers, and engaged in some mild social action campaigns.

THE SIXTIES AND THE "NEW LEFT"

The end of this narrative brings us to the beginnings of the New Left. The late 1950's saw a rebirth of student activism in the United States and the emergence of some of these organizations and political concerns which contributed to the student movement of the 1960's. A number of crucial developments was taking place outside the campus which had a major impact on the student movement. The end of the Korean War and a period of somewhat greater tolerance in the United States made political activism a bit easier. The "beatniks" indicated the first stirrings of a major counterculture. The 1954 Supreme Court decision on segregation and the beginning of an active and militant civil rights movement focused the attention of students on a key issue in American society for perhaps the first time. The growing consciousness of the dangers of nuclear war stimulated the resurgence of a peace movement. It is significant that the student movements of the postwar period placed little emphasis on university-related issues. This lack of concern with the environment of the student continued until the early 1960's, when questions of educational reform and of the university generally became important issues.

The student movement of the late 1950's had strong intellectual concerns. It was interested in moving beyond the stale ideologies of the "old left" sects and in breaking new ground. Substantial disillusionment with the Communist party was evident after Khrushchev's speech denouncing Stalin, and especially after the Soviet invasion of Hungary in 1956. Several new journals were founded which reflected a searching for fresh ideological currents. *Studies on the Left,* founded by graduate students at the University of Wisconsin in 1959, *New University Thought,* from the University of Chicago, and several other journals began to establish the ideological and tactical basis for a new radical movement.

The new concerns. Several new student organizations and campaigns emerged at the end of the 1950's which reflected new concerns of politically conscious American students. The Students for a Democratic Society (SDS), perhaps the most publicized organization of the New Left, emerged from the Social-Democratic Student League for Industrial Democracy. While SLID changed its name to SDS in 1959, ties were maintained with the adult League for Industrial Democracy until 1963, and SDS received a financial subsidy during this period. The ideological and tactical development of the SDS, while beyond the scope of this essay, reflects some of the changing emphases of the student movement. As the

SDS became more radical it broke its ties with the LID, indicating a trend away from student involvement in the adult "old left" political organizations.

The three main threads of student activism in the late 1950's were civil liberties, peace, and civil rights, in chronological order. *Ad hoc* civil liberties groups such as the Committee to Abolish the House Committee on Un-American Activities aroused interest in issues of academic freedom and civil liberties. These efforts culminated in violent demonstrations in San Francisco in 1960. The peace movement emerged from two major trends—the traditional pacifist organizations such as the Fellowship of Reconciliation, and newer, liberal groups such as the National Committee for a Sane Nuclear Policy (SANE). The student affiliate of SANE was founded in 1958 and, although it included many left-wing students, it generally followed SANE's liberal policies. Its major focus was on ending nuclear testing. The other major student peace organization, the Student Peace Union (SPU), was founded in 1959 by a combination of pacifists and moderate radicals. The SPU was for a period the largest radical student group in the United States, with a membership of about 5,000 in some 100 campus groups. The civil rights movement is perhaps the most important stimulus for the recent upsurge in student activism. While the major successes of the campus civil rights movement took place in the early 1960's, many of the roots were established in the Fifties. Many students supported groups like CORE and the NAACP, and small civil rights demonstrations occasionally took place. In the days before black power, it was easier for white middle-class college students to involve themselves in campaigns for equality and integration, and the plight of the Negro caught the attention and sympathy of the campus.

While the 1950's saw a re-establishment of radical and social action organizations on campus, the major mood of the campus remained, in the words of *The Nation,* silent and apathetic. Only a tiny proportion of the student population was involved in any of the new organizations, and most campuses remained placid. Yet, groups like SDS, SPU, and the newly formed Student Nonviolent Coordinating Committee (SNCC) caught the attention of some students and indicated a trend away from reliance on adult guidance. New student journals helped to lay the ideological foundations for the new movement. The period can, in the words of one radical journal, be characterized as one of hope in the midst of apathy.

CONCLUSION

Easy generalizations concerning student activism in America are impossible. While there is a clear historical tradition of student activism, each period is marked by distinctive factors. The American student movement in the period under consideration was never a direct threat to the established order nor did it play a leading role in any of the social movements of the period. Nevertheless, American students in the 1920's were among the most socially conscious elements of the population. Students were influential in at least one political struggle, the antiwar movement of the Thirties. Throughout the period under consideration, the majority of the American student community was never involved in a major way in politics. Even during the 1930's, most of the campuses were untouched by activism, and in the less active 1920's and 1950's only a tiny minority of the student population was involved in politics.

Perhaps more important than the number involved, however, was the fact that the student political movement—mostly of a radical nature—helped to shape the political and intellectual climate of the campus and particularly of the prestigious universities. The impact of the university on student activism has hardly been mentioned in this essay, although it is of importance. During this period, the numbers of students on American campuses increased from 355,000 in 1910 to 3,580,000 in 1960. The university was transformed from an important yet somewhat "ivory tower" institution into the "multiversity" at the center of economic and political life. Higher education was transformed from a preserve of the upper middle classes to a much broader phenomenon.

Despite substantial differences between periods and among organizations, there are a number of generalizations that can be made with regard to the period between 1900 and 1960.

1) There is little evidence of generational conflict in the organized student movement. There was discontent with adult cultural forms in the Twenties and some conflicts between youth and adults in groups ranging from the YMCA to the YPSL, but few direct attacks on adult institutions. Throughout this period, student activists worked closely with and generally took direction from the adult political movement.

2) The student movement generally limited its tactics to educational campaigns and nonviolent and legal direct action. This generalization seems to hold regardless of political ideology throughout the period.

3) The thrust of the student movement was in general directed at broad social issues and not basically concerned with the university itself. Although there was some concern with academic issues in the Twenties, most activists were more interested in political questions.

4) The organized student movement was not part of any kind of a "counterculture" or other similar effort. The radical political groups felt that the basic necessity was a change in power relationships in society and social reform.

5) Student activism involved not only radical (or conservative) organizations, but religious and other groups. For several periods, groups like the YM-YWCA were in the forefront of student social action programs.

6) With the exception of the late 1950's, the student movement followed political trends in society and in the adult radical movement.

A comparative analysis of the student movement of the pre- and post-1960 period is beyond our present scope. It is clear that while there are some similarities, there are also important differences. Quick comparisons will probably result in errors, as student activism has been shaped by the different circumstances of varying historical periods. If there is any lesson from this consideration, it is perhaps that student activism is very much tied to events in society and on the campus. Although the movement on a number of occasions acted as a conscience for its generation, or at least kept radical traditions alive, it never exhibited the potential for revolution.

Robert L. Be

1898 and 1968: Anti-Imperialists and Doves

While the political left discussed in the first three readings in this section took antiwar stands, the opposition to the Spanish-American and Vietnam wars was not necessarily of the political left. The dissenters discussed by Robert Beisner were often traditional politicians who accepted the American system of liberal capitalism and opposed these wars because of the damage they did to this system and its inherent values. Successfully employing the comparative method, Beisner demonstrates the similarities and differences between the anti-imperialists of 1898 and the doves of 1968. He is the author of *Twelve Against Empire: The Anti-Imperialists, 1898–1900.*

In comparing the doves with the anti-imperialists of seventy years ago, three distinct problems arise: those of definition, contemporaneity, and generalization.

To speak of definition first. How was an "anti-imperialist" defined in 1898 and how was a "dove" defined in 1968? Both terms cover a broad range of sentiments and proposals, but their general meaning is clear enough to preclude much confusion in using them. Theodore Roosevelt was not an anti-imperialist; Lyndon Johnson was not a dove. Carl Schurz was obviously no imperialist, and Senator Fulbright can hardly be mistaken for a hawk.

The term "anti-imperialist," as it was employed seventy years ago and as it will be used here, describes a person who opposed the acquisition of a colonial empire in the wake of the Spanish-American War. The all-out anti-imperialists dissented from the decision to go to war with Spain in the first place, denounced the annexation of Puerto Rico, the Philippines, and Hawaii, and opposed the imposition of a protectorate over Cuba. Other anti-imperialists were less adamant, but nearly all fought the acquisition of the Philippines. Though they did not always agree among themselves, they were in no sense difficult to distinguish from their expansionist opponents.

Doves, too, have adopted various positions on the war in Vietnam, but in this essay "dove" will be used to describe those critics who favor deescalation over escalation, urge a compromise peace, and base their recommendations on the conviction that American intervention was ill-conceived and has been poorly executed. As this is written, such attitudes

Reprinted with permission from the *Political Science Quarterly,* 85 (June 1970), pp. 187–207, 216. Footnotes have been renumbered.

are held by perhaps a majority of the American people; the doves discussed here, however, are those who emerged early as critics of official policy, not the millions who subsequently came to accept their arguments or who merely tired of the war. Some hawks and doves have refused to wear the plumage assigned to them by the headline-writers. Before John P. Roche took on the job of defending White House policies against the attacks of other intellectuals, for instance, he had insisted that he was "neither a hawk nor a dove" but "a slightly frightened robin who wants to avoid a war with China. . . ."[1] Senator George McGovern, claiming that the antiwar dissenters have been more "tough-minded" than those "who have dreamed about exporting American freedom to the jungles in B-52's," proposed that the inhabitants of the American aviary were not really hawks and doves after all, but ostriches and owls. Here we shall confine ourselves to the conventional usage. . . .

The most obvious difference between the two movements is their contexts. The international situation in 1968 was radically dissimilar to that of 1898, when powers competed for Asian empire but no one worried about an international communist movement, when the United States had only begun to emerge as a world power, and—most importantly—when no one lost sleep over the possibility of a local war sliding uncontrollably into a world nuclear holocaust. The stakes in 1968 were as high as they could get, and the harrowing fears of the doves have been worse than any the anti-imperialists could imagine.

The recent debate has been fundamentally more complex than the controversy of 1898–1900, which was innocent of the Byzantine arguments about the viability of a containment policy in Asia, counter-guerrilla military strategy, Vietnamese religious politics, and the relationship among the N.L.F., Hanoi, and Peking. To the anti-imperialists of 1898, however, the questions arising from the Spanish-American War seemed formidable enough. "Mr. Dooley," Chicago's favorite tavern-keeper, remarked that

> Wan iv the worst things about this here war is th' way it's makin' puzzles f'r our poor, tired heads. Whin I wint into it, I thought all I'd have to do was to set up here behind th' bar with a good tin-cint seegar in me teeth, an' toss dinnymite bombs into th' hated city iv Havana. But look at me now. Th' war is still goin' on; an' ivry night, whin I'm countin' up the cash, I'm askin' mesilf will I annex Cubia or lave it to the Cubians? Will I take Porther Ricky or put it by? An' what shud I do with the Ph'lippeens? Oh, what shud I do with thim? I can't annex thim because I don't know where they ar're. I can't let go iv them because some wan else'll take thim if I do. They are eight

[1] Bernard B. Fall, Richard N. Goodwin, George McGovern, and John P. Roche, "Containing China: A Round-Table Discussion," *Commentary*, 41 (1966), p. 27.

thousan' iv thim islands, with a popylation iv wan hundherd millyon naked savages; an' me bedroom's crowded now with me an' th' bed. How can I take thim in, an' how on earth am I goin' to cover th' nakedness iv thim savages with me wan shoot iv clothes? An' yet 'twud break me heart to think iv givin' people I niver see or heered tell iv back to other people I don't know. An', if I don't take thim, Schwartzmeister down th' street, that has half me thrade already, will grab thim sure.[2]

The doves of 1968 were protesting a war; in 1898, for the most part, it was the aftermath of a war and the formal annexation of new territories. Most commentators who have considered the 1898/1968 parallel insist that nothing remotely resembling the imperialism of 1898 has been involved in Vietnam. Some war critics, however, have not agreed with this confident assumption and maintain that something like old-fashioned imperialism *is* involved. Doctrinaire Communists and certain representatives of the New Left harbor no doubts about the issue of imperialism, seeing evidence of it wherever the American flag flies abroad, including Vietnam. More provocative, however, is a contention like John McDermott's that America's well-intended aid and modernization programs, in those areas where they have "succeeded," have produced "a loss of national independence, erratic and imbalanced economic development and growing social chaos." He believes the United States has become imperialistic, by aspiring to be not the world's policeman, but the "world's social worker." In more conventional terms Noam Chomsky, Christopher Lasch, William Pfaff, John K. Fairbank, Mary McCarthy, Walter Lippmann, and Senator J. William Fulbright have all described the United States presence in Vietnam as imperialistic. In language that strongly echoes that of the anti-imperialists of 1898, Fulbright has stated that the underlying cause for dissent today is

> a feeling that America has betrayed its own past and its own promise . . . most of all, the promise of the American Revolution, of free men building a society that would be an example for the world. Now the world sees that heritage being betrayed; it sees a nation that seemed to represent something new and hopeful reverting to the vanity of past empires, each of which struggled for supremacy, each of which won and held it for a while, each of which finally faded or fell into historical oblivion.[3]

---

[2] [Finley Peter Dunne], *Mr. Dooley in Peace and in War* (Boston: 1905), pp. 44–45.
[3] J. William Fulbright, "For a New Order of Priorities at Home and Abroad," *Playboy* (July 1968), pp. 116, 152, 157; Noam Chomsky, "On Resistance," *New York Review of Books* (Dec. 7, 1967), p. 12; Christopher Lasch, "Same Old New Class," *ibid.* (Sept. 28, 1967), p. 12; William Pfaff, "No Victory in Vietnam," *Commonweal* (Apr. 23, 1965), p. 136; John K. Fairbank, "Perspective on Vietnam," *New Republic* (Jan. 20, 1968), p. 17; Mary McCarthy, "Report from Vietnam II: The Problems of Success," *New York Review of Books* (May 4, 1967), p. 8; Walter Lippmann, "The White Man's Burden," Washington *Post* (Apr. 28, 1966).

How many and what kind of people became anti-imperialists? Who are the doves? What does the membership of the two movements reveal about their characters and goals? It is impossible to say what percentage of the public was sympathetic to the anti-imperialists, but there is little evidence that they ever represented as great a proportion as the doves have or that nearly as many of them were as deeply involved—emotionally, intellectually, politically—in their protest as the doves have been. It is true that the Democratic Party was basically anti-imperialist in 1898 and 1900, but largely out of ritualistic partisanship. Few prominent leaders of the anti-imperialist movement were Democrats. This statement will not pass without objection from some other students of the period who insist that Democrats were very important to the movement and who base their argument on votes in Congress, especially on the Treaty of Paris in February of 1899, and on some of William Jennings Bryan's speeches in the 1900 presidential campaign. But the heart of the anti-imperialist movement did not usually reside within the halls of Congress, and Democrats played a distinctly limited role in the verbal and printed agitation on the issue as well as in the sustained organizational activity. . . .

A listing of the leadership of the movement—the chief officers of the anti-imperialist leagues, the senators who mounted the opposition to ratification of the Treaty of Paris, those persons who most frequently attacked American imperialism in speeches and articles—reveals a fairly clear pattern. Although their ranks included a few Democrats, most of the leaders were either dissident Republicans or "Mugwumps," the one-time Republicans who for fifteen or twenty years had played a rigorously independent role in politics. They were concentrated in the northeastern part of the United States, particularly in the Boston and New York areas. They were men of education and means. Though numbering a few remarkable immigrants among them (such as Schurz, Carnegie, and Godkin), most were of established British stock; in 1896, when several of them affixed their names to an antiwar petition, the New York *Herald* was prompted to remark, "They read like a roll call from Bunker Hill." They were members of the old upper-middle and upper classes, conservative in social outlook and frequently aristocratic in demeanor. They took for granted that they could speak for the American conscience. Politicians of the old school, businessmen, editors, lawyers, and intellectuals, they were also elderly men with clear memories of gentler times and with little taste for the tone of modern America.

The leaders of the doves have not been such a homogeneous flock. *Ramparts* and the *New York Times* both have been "leaders" in the criticism of American policy in Vietnam. Norman Mailer and Hans Morgenthau, Cassius Clay and Dr. Spock all did their part. American policy has been attacked by some of the most impeccable representatives of the "establishment," side by side with some of the most scorned and rebellious elements in American society. Still, the doves were not a formless mass, and it is possible to make certain generalizations about them. While

130

conservatives dominated the anti-imperialist movement, few such have been doves. Unlike the old men who guided the dissent against McKinley, the under-thirty set (nonexistent, in a political sense, in 1898) were among the most vociferous, outspoken, and uncompromising critics of President Johnson. Negro leaders added their force to the doves; they did not count, except as objects of discrimination, in the days of Cuba Libré. Professional men and intellectuals have been prominent in both protest movements. In contrast to the anti-imperialists, however, doves have not been easily identifiable by class, region, or ethnic background. The "Stanford Poll" taken in February and March of 1966 found that religious beliefs had no bearing on attitudes toward the war, though a Boston survey of college professors concluded that Jews and the religiously uncommitted have been far more dovish than Protestants, who in turn have been more dovish than Catholics. Some polls of the general public seemed to indicate that working-class and poorly educated groups in America have been relatively hawkish, but the Stanford pollsters were of the not entirely convincing opinion that "variables of social status—occupation, income, or education—do not relate to policy preferences on the Vietnamese War."[4]

Doves are not only younger and much less conservative in their politics than the anti-imperialists were, but, as has been stated, they form a more heterogeneous group. This difference is interesting because it suggests that far more Americans today are politically alert and aggressive than in 1898. It also suggests that far more was at stake in 1968. Seventy years ago a relatively small group of people dominated by intellectuals and idealists were alarmed by imperialism because they believed it violated American principles. A much wider range of people have been alarmed by the Vietnam war, not only on principle, but also because the war has appeared to be a failure and has seemed to be actually contrary to the interests of the United States. The tensions caused by the current war have cut across class, regional, political, and generational lines as the acquisition of a tropical empire never did.

In what ways have the critics of these two eras made their protests? The anti-imperialists limited themselves almost exclusively to voting, speechmaking, and writing pamphlets and letters. Anti-imperialist members of Congress tried unsuccessfully to block ratification of the Treaty of Paris and to defeat Hawaiian annexation. Speaker Thomas Reed slowed House action on Hawaii and delayed passage of appropriation bills on the grounds that the money was "needed to pay for the Malays." The dissenters' most remarkable organizational accomplishment was the creation of anti-imperialist leagues, which sprang up in Boston, New York, Washington, Cleveland, Los Angeles, and half a dozen other major cities. The parent Anti-Imperialist League, which in 1899 claimed 30,000

---

[4] Sidney Verba *et al.*, "Public Opinion and the War in Vietnam," *The American Political Science Review*, 41 (1967), pp. 324–25, 331; David J. Armor *et al.*, "Professors' Attitudes Toward the Vietnam War," *Public Opinion Quarterly*, 31 (1967), p. 170.

members and over 500,000 "contributors," mailed out hundreds of thousands of anti-imperialist pamphlets and other propaganda items. The most generous subsidizer of this paper flood was Andrew Carnegie, who also offered to buy the independence of the Philippines with a personal check for twenty million dollars, a proposition predictably denounced as "wicked" by the New York *Times*. The most energetic organizer in the movement was Edward Atkinson, a Boston businessman and indefatigable polemicist. Shortly after the Anti-Imperialist League was founded in his office on November 19, 1898, Atkinson furiously set about writing broadsides with such titles as "The Hell of War and Its Penalties" and an anti-imperialist periodical, all of which he distributed to those "influentials" he thought could most affect the government's imperialist policies—congressmen, clergymen, mayors, state government officials, and officers of commercial, agricultural, and labor organizations. Working from an ingeniously compiled mailing list of about 23,000 names, Atkinson spread the anti-imperialist message throughout the nation. The government seized some of his pamphlets in 1899 when he attempted to mail them to American servicemen, officers, civilian officials, and newspapermen in the Philippines. Legal prosecution was rather idly threatened; Atkinson was made something of a martyr, and the circulation of his manifestoes jumped sharply.

The methods of protest employed by the more conventional and "respectable" doves have been essentially the same as those of 1898. Some of the doves' less inhibited allies, however, have added tactics to the arsenal of dissent that would never have been dreamed of (except in nightmares) by their predecessors of three-quarters of a century ago, including teach-ins, picketing, speech walk-outs, civil disobedience, military insubordination, draft resistance, marches on the Pentagon, medical aid to the enemy, "lie-ins" in front of troop trains, refusal to pay taxes, and even self-immolation.

The tone of both campaigns has often been impassioned and sometimes bitter, but the doves have produced more vulgarity. No anti-imperialist ever wrote an anthem like the Fugs' "Kill for Peace," which contains the line "Strafe them creeps in the rice paddy, daddy." . . . Rather more discreet, Arthur Schlesinger, Jr., insisted in a 1966 "talk-in" that the President did not want a large Asian war and quoted him as saying, "I don't want to save my face, I just want to save my—," only to have Elizabeth Hardwick respond, "I can't, being a lady, use that word, but does he conceive of that portion of himself as extending all the way to Southeast Asia?"

Anti-imperialists were less coarse in their language but, if anything, more accomplished masters of invective, which, in its developed form, is almost a lost art. William James called the McKinley administration's suppression of the Filipino rebellion "the most incredible, unbelievable, piece of sneak-thief turpitude that any nation ever practised." E. L. Godkin charged the McKinley administration with substituting "keen

132

effective slaughter for Spanish old-fashioned, clumsy slaughter." To an expansionist friend, Carnegie wrote: "It is a matter of congratulation . . . that you have about finished your work of civilizing the Fillipinos [*sic*]. It is thought that about 8000 of them have been completely civilized and sent to Heaven. I hope you like it." And in a little-known volume of malevolence called *The New Flag,* Henry Blake Fuller threw some doggerel at Mark Hanna:

> Grinning, coarsely fleshed and gross
> Following a mighty cross,
> Nailed upon whose either side
> Hangs a Malay crucified—
> Which some Christians, over-civil
> Carry to oblige the Devil.

and at McKinley:

> Hail! stalwart son and Canton Hero!
> Thou Xerxes up to date, or Nero! . . .
> Who for a coral bead or rattle
> 'Gainst unarmed babes doth march to battle!

Some of this rhetoric was aimed at influencing the outcome of the elections of 1900 and 1968. In both years critics were largely dissatisfied with the choice of candidates available to them, although Bryan gladdened more dissenters than either Richard Nixon or Hubert Humphrey were able to do. In both years the intrusion of other issues—trusts, radicalism, urban problems, race, crime—made it impossible to produce a referendum on the issues of war and imperialism. McKinley's re-election did not prove that American imperialism had been endorsed by the public, only that it had not been repudiated. The 1968 election campaign provided just as ambiguous a measure of the national mood on the Vietnam war. The manner in which doves searched for a way to express their views—pre-convention struggles for Eugene McCarthy, Robert Kennedy, Nelson Rockefeller, and George McGovern; fourth-party tactics; write-in votes—resembled the distracted maneuvers of the anti-imperialists in 1900. Some of the latter voted happily for Bryan, others for McKinley; some worked to nominate a third-party candidate—one possibility mentioned was Lew (*Ben Hur*) Wallace—while others preferred a quasi-independent candidate to serve as a stalking-horse for Bryan; some voted for Bryan but also for Republican congressmen who could prevent him from taking any maniacal action in domestic affairs; others voted for McKinley and Democratic congressmen who could vote down funds for any more of his imperialist adventures. Others simply sulked in their tents on election day.

One major difference in the two election years deserves notice. Early in 1968 the campaigns of Eugene McCarthy and Robert Kennedy, Senator J. William Fulbright's continuing hearings, and the Communists' "Tet" offensive effectively unseated a president of the United States and left his heir with a desperately divided party. Neither the anti-imperialists nor the Filipinos ever accomplished as much in 1900.

Both anti-imperialists and doves opposed their government's policies for varying and often conflicting reasons. Though they sometimes overlapped and merged, these motives can be separated from one another for purposes of analysis. I should like to discuss them, first with regard to the anti-imperialists and then with regard to the doves, beginning with the least and proceeding to the most significant motivation, a ranking which of necessity will be suggestive rather than definitive.

Personal grudges and narrowly conceived political partisanship had surprisingly little bearing on the actions of the most prominent spokesmen for the anti-imperialists. Had war with Spain begun during a Democratic administration, the anti-imperialist ranks might not have included either Bryan or Cleveland. Had such Republicans as Reed, John Sherman, and Benjamin Harrison had warmer personal feelings toward William McKinley, they too might have felt differently in 1898. But most anti-imperialist leaders (and, again, it should be mentioned that few Democrats are included in this group of "leaders") did not stand to gain politically by opposing the government. Senator George Hoar loved both the Republican party and McKinley but made a glorious fight against their Philippine policy. Conservative independents who called Bryan a "communist" in 1896 voted for him in 1900.

Economic considerations carried a little more weight with anti-imperialists than did hopes of political advantage. A few, including Thomas Reed, emphasized the need to complete the internal development of the United States before plunging into faraway enterprises. A larger number of anti-imperialists believed that the United States, on the contrary, did need increased foreign markets but that colonialism was a poor and unnecessary way to get them. President David Starr Jordan of Stanford University, who held that more trade would enter the open door than follow the imperial flag, pointed to America's "peaceful conquest of Mexico" as "a legitimate form of expansion." The United States, he stated, "could fill all tropical countries with consular agents and commercial agents, men trained to stand for good order and to work for American interests, for less than it costs to subdue a single tropical island." Most anti-imperialists, however, either ignored economic issues altogether or treated them as low-priority concerns.

Third in ascending importance was the there-are-problems-enough-at-home argument, implicit in the remark of Charles Francis Adams in 1898 that a "Roman-candle foreign policy" was inappropriate as long as "popular discontent" was widespread, cities were misgoverned, and Bryan and other malcontents were on the loose. Whether concerned with race relations, civic corruption, the currency, or trusts, these anti-imperialists held that such problems disqualified the United States from initiating adventures overseas.

Constitutional questions were even more important. McKinley was frequently charged with sending troops to seize the Philippines without constitutional authority and ignoring an alleged constitutional ban on the acquisition of non-contiguous territory. Heard more often was the charge that the Constitution forbade acquisition of colonies not destined to be made states and the closely related contention—rejected by the Supreme Court in the Insular Cases—that a colony could not be treated by Congress as though it were a separate and inferior part of the American constitutional system. The anti-imperialists argued that the breaching of these rules would endanger all American principles.

Diplomatic issues were equally important to the anti-imperialists. They deplored the violence done by imperialism to the traditional isolationism and self-sufficiency of America. They condemned imperialism for breaking the nation's ocean belt of security and placing the flag in regions vulnerable to intimidation or attack by others. They held that expansion in the Far East was particularly ill-advised because, first of all, it would throw the United States into the thick of a dangerous contest for empire with European powers. Secondly, it would encourage fresh European encroachments in the Caribbean by undermining the Monroe Doctrine pledge that the United States would stay out of the affairs of the Old World in return for European restraint in the New. And thirdly, it would involve the United States too closely with British interests, with the result that America would almost certainly get burned raking English chestnuts out of Asian fires.

Next on the list were those considerations that might charitably be called cultural but, more accurately, should be called racial. Most anti-imperialist leaders believed that any mixing of "Anglo-Saxon" America with the unwashed coloreds of the tropics would lead to racial decadence and contamination. E. L. Godkin complained in *The Nation* that the annexation of Hawaii would admit "alien, inferior, and mongrel races to our nationality," and Carl Schurz proclaimed it impossible for the United States to absorb "Spanish-Americans, with all the mixture of Indian and Negro blood, and Malays and other unspeakable Asiatics, by the tens of millions!" It was a rare anti-imperialist, like George Hoar or Moorfield Storey, who would bracket America's suppression of Filipino rebels with her everyday treatment of Negroes and condemn both.

Nearly all anti-imperialists had moral objections to American imperialism. They believed it was simply *wrong* for one people to impose its will on another, especially when it was clear that many Filipinos were prepared to resist American authority. As late as 1902 William James wrote, "God damn the U.S. for its vile conduct in the Philippine Isles!" George Hoar was perhaps most eloquent of all in his moral outrage:

We converted a war of glory to a war of shame. We vulgarized the American flag. We introduced perfidy into the practice of war. We inflicted torture on unarmed men to extort confession. We put children to death. We established reconcentrado camps. We devastated provinces. We baffled the aspirations of a people for liberty.

The two most important anti-imperialist arguments, the political and what might be called the historical arguments, are very closely related, the first being the foundation and the second the inner core of the anti-imperialist protest. The foundation was built of solid political principles. The anti-imperialists, nurtured on American ideals and convinced of the truth and universal applicability of abstract political principles, asserted in 1898 that a republican government could not also be an imperial government, that the right of self-rule could not be abrogated in faraway territories, and that all men deserved to enjoy the blessings of freedom, whatever their capabilities or limitations.

The historical core of the anti-imperialist message was essentially that imperialism was a denial of the "American Mission," which was to establish a just and free nation whose people would be at peace with each other and the rest of the world. During the Eighties and Nineties this image was being tarnished in anti-imperialist eyes by new waves of immigration, growing urban problems, agrarian radicalism, severe depressions, and disputes between capital and labor. Then, in 1898, when the United States began to assume the appearance of a land-grabbing European state, the anti-imperialists lashed out in anger, taking the opportunity to attack all the ills of American life at the same time. . . .

As might be expected, such a ranking of the motives and impulses of the doves reveals both similarities and differences. Economic considerations have been of even less significance today than they were at the turn of the century. Occasionally the more dovish business press (as well as the more hawkish for that matter) has worried about inflation and the distortions in the economy caused by the war, but almost no doves have echoed the anti-imperialists' interest in the issue of foreign trade and investments.

Nor have the doves echoed the racism of 1898, a sign of the twentieth-century transformation of elite views on race. The nearest thing today to the racism of the 1890's is a not uncommon disdain for Asian peoples, a feeling they are not worth the trouble Americans have given themselves on their account. Surely a touch of the old Godkinesque scorn for lesser breeds is evident in John Kenneth Galbraith's comment that were it not for American intervention in Southeast Asia, "all of that part of the world would be enjoying the obscurity that it richly deserves."

Third on the list of motivations is partisanship, a bit stronger now than seventy years ago, though still not very significant. Dovishness was a potentially useful political tool to Robert Kennedy, George Romney, and Nelson Rockefeller. Most Republicans, however, were slow to criticize

President Johnson's policy in Vietnam. When they did, they usually favored stiffening it—there have been few Republicans in the dovecote. And most Democratic politicians, originally at least, found it as painful to attack the President as it was for George Hoar to attack McKinley. This was clearly the case with Senator Fulbright, who remarked on the similarity of his dilemma to Hoar's.

Despite years of exposure to the Hamiltonian-Rooseveltian view of the Constitution, the doves have charged President Johnson with usurping the power of Congress to declare war. Senator Fulbright used the Senate Foreign Relations Committee to reassert the constitutional prerogatives of the Senate in foreign affairs, and George Kennan criticized Rusk's "commitments" in part on the grounds that they were not sanctioned by appropriate "constitutional processes." Constitutionalism is clearly not yet a dead issue.

Far more important, however, has been the question of international legality, virtually absent from the anti-imperialist campaign. Opponents of the war have accused the United States of violating the United Nations Charter and other international treaties, the rulings of the Nuremberg Trials, and the general principles of international law. They have consistently maintained that the SEATO treaty does not provide justification for American intervention. The Lawyers' Committee on American Policy Toward Vietnam spoke for most doves in accusing the United States government of breaking the Geneva Accords of 1954, and Quincy Wright, along with others, charged that the United States was violating the basic right of any society to undergo internal revolution.

Next in ascending priority has been concern about the immediate consequences of the war upon American society and democracy. This has taken two different forms, charges that the war is producing serious neglect of pressing social problems and that the war itself is having a disintegrative impact on American society. The war critics have repudiated the "guns *and* butter" formulation of the Johnson administration and, like the anti-imperialists, have questioned how Americans could be expected to reorder a far-off society when they apparently can not reform their own. They have charged that while billions of dollars have been spent in Vietnam, the issues of poverty, racial tensions, urban decay, crime, water and air pollution, and general physical ugliness are tragically short-changed in money and attention. According to Senator Fulbright, the war diverts America "from the sources of its strength, which are in its domestic life." . . .

Because the circumstances of 1898 and 1968 differed so markedly—in 1898, for instance, Americans were mopping up after a clearly victorious war while recently they have been trying to extricate themselves from what no one could call a victory—there is little point in comparing the detailed proposals of each group of dissenters for settling the issues in question. Suffice it to say that the anti-imperialists suggested many programs, few of which were persuasive. Their primary accomplishment was to lodge a moral protest, reassert traditional ideals, and, as I have written elsewhere, "warn a nation of optimists that America could not escape the consequences of its own conduct." The doves have played a similar role. Their enclave strategy suffered as great a setback from the Tet offensive of 1968 as did the administration's policies, and many of their proposals for negotiation were frustrated by a lack of amiability from Hanoi as often as by a lack of receptiveness in Washington. But despite these discouragements, the doves have served the American people as a conscience and, more than any critics of the past, as a voice of diplomatic reason. And their effect—witness the events of 1968 and 1969—has been historic.

Lawrence S. Wittner

The Organized Peace Movement During the McCarthy Era

The anti-imperialists and doves studied by Robert Beisner objected to specific wars; a more constant voice against war is America's permanent and organized peace movement composed of pacifist organizations such as the War Resisters' League and the Fellowship of Reconciliation. Lawrence S. Wittner considers the plight of these and similar groups during the era of Senator Joseph McCarthy in the early 1950's. A casualty of the Cold War mentality of the period, the "movement consisted of little more than a small band of isolated pacifists"; nevertheless, it offered a viable intellectual alternative to American foreign policy of the time. Pacificism as a social movement was revived during the next decade. In light of the earlier readings in this section, one should note the pacifists' attitude toward Socialist Party foreign policy as expressed by Norman Thomas. Professor Wittner is the author of *Rebels Against War: The American Peace Movement, 1941–1960.*

Reduced to insignificant proportions by the Cold War, the peace movement had only begun its time of troubles. As the very forces it sought to restrain grew stronger and bolder, they subjected the peace movement to a withering attack that left it barely clinging to existence. In a strange half-life, the remnants of the historic movement continued their struggle against war, formulating radical alternatives to American military policies and serving as prophets in the Cold War wilderness. Yet rarely had the prospect seemed so bleak and their witness so hopeless.

The loyalty-security mania of the early Fifties has attracted considerable attention among scholars, who have concentrated upon sociological or psychological explanations of its development. But they have often failed to stress the obvious: that McCarthyism was the domestic counterpart of American foreign policy. Indeed the unique genius of the junior Senator from Wisconsin lay in tying his relatively insignificant concern with a few individuals who may once have had some connection to the American Communist party to the great drama of world conflict. After describing "a conspiracy on a scale so immense as to dwarf any previous such venture in the history of man," McCarthy asked: "What is the ob-

From Lawrence S. Wittner, *Rebels Against War: The American Peace Movement, 1941–1960* (New York: Columbia University Press, 1969), pp. 213–228, 239. Reprinted by permission of publisher. Some footnotes have been omitted.

jective of the conspiracy?" He answered grandly: "To diminish the United States in world affairs, to weaken us militarily, to confuse our spirit with talk of surrender." To what end, he asked, pressing his Cold War advantage. "To the end that we shall be contained and frustrated and finally fall victim to Soviet intrigue from within and Russian military might from without."

Few Americans concerned with "subversion" doubted that unity was essential to the anti-Communist crusade. Polling public opinion in 1950, 1952, and 1954, Samuel Lubell was struck by the support which voters frustrated by the Korean War gave to McCarthy. "Why don't we clean up these Commies at home with our boys dying in Korea?" they demanded. Police Commissioner Eugene ("Bull") Connor of Birmingham, Alabama, vowed to "put the exterminator" to local "Reds." The opening prayer of the United States Senate in February, 1952, led by the Reverend Billy Graham, contained a two-pronged reference to "barbarians beating at our gates from without and moral termites from within." Operating on a similar theory, the government of the United States maintained six "detention camps" under the authority of the McCarran Internal Security Act. The *New York Times* observed that "in the climate of a national emergency hundreds, perhaps thousands, could be sequestered in security camps who were not actual, or even potential spies or saboteurs." . . .

The loyalty investigations churned up an atmosphere of fear and suspicion extremely inhospitable to peace action. "In the United States," wrote Lewis Mumford, "reason is cowed by governmental purges" and "criticism and dissent . . . are identified as treason." Monogram Studios abandoned plans for a feature-length film on the life of Hiawatha, the Onondaga Indian chief immortalized by Longfellow, because of its fear that Hiawatha's peace efforts among the Five Nations might serve the cause of Communist propaganda. *Time* magazine remarked: "The academic motto for 1953 is fast becoming: Don't say, don't write, don't go." . . .

Self-styled loyalty experts frequently organized attacks upon pacifists. In a pamphlet entitled "How Red is the Federal Council of Churches?" the American Council of Christian Laymen listed the FOR [Fellowship of Reconciliation] as a "radical-pacifist group using Christian terms to spread Communist propaganda," and the WRL [War Resisters' League] as the co-sponsor of "numerous Communist-controlled movements." Actor Robert Montgomery charged on his radio and television program in 1951 that members of the Philadelphia Peace Caravan, sponsored by the FOR, were stooges of the Communist Party and that the FOR itself was Communist. An excerpt from the files of the House Committee on Un-American Activities called the FOR "allegedly a strictly pacifist organization" which maintained "that class war is necessary." Insinuations could be as devastating as direct accusations of subversion. In November, 1954, Herbert Philbrick's column, "The Red Underground," carried in the *New York Herald Tribune* and sixteen other newspapers, announced that "highly trained and skilled underground Communist party agents"

140

would infiltrate a FOR anniversary dinner scheduled in Boston. The organization had "many" members who were "loyal and sincere," Philbrick added in a dubious compliment, but now stood in danger of serving as a "transmission belt" for Communist propaganda. Pacifist heroes, tried posthumously, fared poorly. When E. B. White wrote a satire for the *New Yorker,* maintaining that if McCarthy knew of Thoreau he would damn him as a security risk, William F. Buckley, Jr., came back with the claim that "Thoreau *was.*"

The inflammatory accusations of the Anti-Communist Crusade often led to action against the pacifist heretics. A FOR member was removed from her job as city librarian of Bartlesville, Oklahoma, a post she had held for thirty-five years. A local Citizens Committee, composed of members of the American Legion, the D.A.R., and the United Daughters of the Confederacy, had complained of her to the city commissioners, who thereupon questioned the pacifist librarian on "subversive" literature in the library (the *Nation,* the *New Republic,* and *Soviet Russia Today*), about her race relations activities (she had organized a local CORE group), and as to whether or not she was a Communist (she was not). An hour after the interview, the city manager telephoned to announce that her employment had been terminated "forthwith." In New York two Legionnaires attacked a pacifist distributing leaflets during a Loyalty Day parade. Goaded on by bystanders, they knocked him to the pavement and commenced beating him, yelling "dirty Communist" from time to time until the police arrived. In Baltimore three members of the Society of Friends and of the FOR lost their jobs when they refused to sign a loyalty oath required of all state and municipal employees by Maryland's Ober Law. An FOR member lost his teaching position at a New Jersey college for failure to sign that state's loyalty oath.

The tactics of persecution took their toll of pacifist strength. "The mass hysteria . . . has now reached a climax that is making our work difficult and presenting us with new problems," noted the W.I.L.P.F.'s [Women's International League for Peace & Freedom] administrative secretary. WRL members distributing leaflets in Times Square found people afraid to accept their mimeographed circulars; sometimes they waited twenty minutes before a passerby took one. Pacifist ministers told A. J. Muste that they could not talk about peace to their congregations because they would be labeled as Communists. *Fellowship* observed in late 1950: "Anti-Communist feeling and hysteria make it far more difficult to get a hearing for the pacifist position now than at any time during World War II." Membership in pacifist organizations melted away. The WRL dwindled to a tiny hard core, while the FOR lost three thousand members —about one quarter of its total. "Is Peace a bad word?" asked an FOR pronouncement. "Because the Communists misuse the word, are Americans going to agree that they prefer war?"

Quasi-pacifist organizations such as CORE experienced serious difficulties in the early Fifties because of the "subversive" onus attached to social action. One local Woolworth's manager, for example, questioned on his employment practices, fired back: "Do you have anything on you to show that you are 100 percent American, and not on the list of the Justice Department?" A typical incident occurred during July, 1951, when nine CORE members held a sit-in at a Whelan's drugstore counter in Washington, D.C. Met with belligerent refusal of service and a horde of children chanting "Communist" for several hours, the demonstrators turned wearily to leave only to be followed by the juvenile gang. According to a CORE account, the latter "were voluble with their charges of 'Communist' and 'Go Back to Russia!' Although we tried to reason with them, they were too excited to listen, and followed down the street throwing stones, firecrackers, and miniature torpedoes." In such an atmosphere, CORE led only a tenuous existence.

Public fears of atomic spies and espionage made the atomic scientists a focal point of public concern. In the early Fifties the hapless scientists were subjected to constant political pressures, epitomized by the Oppenheimer hearings of 1954, which labeled the prominent physicist a "security risk" and denied him reinstatement to his post in the Atomic Energy Commission. The proceedings in the Oppenheimer case enraged the scientific community. Dr. Vannevar Bush told the loyalty panel: "No board should ever sit on a question in this country of whether a man [served] his country or not because he expressed strong opinions. If you want to try that case, you can try me." Others fled from government service rather than commit themselves to the new security regulations. Postmaster General Arthur Summerfield boasted proudly of Republican "progress in rooting out the eggheads." In late 1954 Albert Einstein remarked:

> If I would be a young man again and I had to decide how to make my living, I would not try to become a scientist or scholar or teacher. I would rather choose to be a plumber or a peddler in the hope to find that modest degree of independence still available under present circumstances.[1]

The advocates of world government, or, as Senator McCarthy often referred to them, the "one-worlders," provided a favorite target for professional patriots. "World Government Means Communism" read a headline in the Bridgeport (Conn.) *Telegram* during late 1952. . . .

Ironically, the loyalty hunt tore through the American peace movement at a time when it had already largely ceased to pose any effective opposition to the American military. In the Fifties the United World Federalists adopted increasingly conservative policy positions until they became virtually indistinguishable from those of the American government. Norman Cousins, U.W.F. vice-president, told a radio audience in 1952 that "America represents the hope of men everywhere." Moreover, as the Cold War settled into a seemingly permanent pattern of East-West

---

[1] Albert Einstein, Letter to the Editor, *Reporter*, 11 (November 18, 1954).

hostility, world government appeared chimerical. "Realists" turned their attention to less grandiose projects. "Seven years ago, when world law was mentioned, people said it was too soon," complained Cousins in late 1952. "Now, when it is mentioned, they say it is too late."

Socialists and others on the democratic left reluctantly backed American defense policies with only minor reservations well into the 1950's. Responding to a plea by A. J. Muste for America to take a "unilateral initiative" in disarmament, Norman Thomas replied: "Repeatedly men have been forced to use clumsy and self-defeating tools in their struggles for a larger measure of freedom and justice. I desperately want to avoid war," he wrote, "but for America to avoid war simply by surrender to communism would in no way avoid the ultimate violence" of "Stalin's imperialist communism." Muste responded that Thomas and other radicals failed "to make a real effort to determine whether non-violent resistance would not be at least as effective and much less costly" than nuclear war. In addition, the pacifist leader remarked, "you now have to condone the use of more and more destructive and diabolical weapons," as well as "get involved in a situation where unwillingly you seem to . . . play the game of the reactionary interests in the United States and elsewhere." Thomas sadly answered: "The dilemma which you describe is very real."

Like the more traditional pacifists, radical pacifists continued their activities in a greatly reduced form. Non-registration for the draft persisted as the favored approach to conscription for a few young men of radical libertarian ideas. An issue of *Alternative,* the pacifist-anarchist periodical banned from the mails during the Korean War by the New York postmaster for "advocating or urging treason, insurrection or forcible resistance to . . . [the] law of the United States," told the reader to "become an open nonviolent resister"; "REFUSE TO BE DRAFTED!" its editors proclaimed. Abandoning the policy it had pursued during World War II, the A.F.S.C. [American Friends Service Committee] declined to serve as an "approved" employer of C.O.'s in the early Fifties. On the other hand, despite the official shift in Quaker policy, most pacifists continued to accept alternative service. . . .

A pacifist report on political action in 1952 asked "whether U.S. foreign policy is not essentially bipartisan, the differences among major party candidates purely technical, each such candidate really a 'war' candidate, so that the vote is a Tweedle-dee or Tweedle-dum." As "the military viewpoint" appeared "very weighty, if not dominant, in *both* parties," the position paper urged the pacifist not to "stultify himself by voting for either." The Socialist party, virtually nonexistent as a political force, excited little interest. "It is questionable, apart from questions of terminology and general 'ultimate aims,' whether there is a decisive difference between Norman Thomas' position on war and peace and Truman-Eisenhower, or Kefauver, Paul Douglas, etc." observed the pacifist report. "The actual number and the percentage of pacifists who . . . look hopefully toward the Socialist Party . . . has markedly declined." Independent political action appeared hopeless. The FOR contended that "because the nation is involved in a power struggle to which most of the people of the United States are committed . . . a small minority . . . will not be effective." Consequently, while most Americans concerned with ending the Korean War probably voted for Eisenhower, those involved in long-term peace action probably sat out the election. . . .

From 1950 to 1956, then, the peace movement consisted of little more than a small band of isolated pacifists. "Americans . . . had few organizations to help them act to keep the nation's foreign policy from courting war," remarked an *ad hoc* Chicago committee. Even the remaining faithful were disheartened by the course of events. "For three hundred years we have professed a way of life which does away with the occasion for war," wrote Clarence Pickett of the A.F.S.C. "Have we been mistaken in believing that a world without war is possible?" Pacifism was "marking time," A. J. Muste told the readers of *Fellowship*. "The movement . . . is in a stalemate."

Yet while the Cold War had relegated pacifism as a social movement to insignificance, it had not broken its intellectual vitality. In the dark days of the early 1950's the best of the pacifist thinkers subjected America's role in the international power struggle to a critical re-examination and, finding it wanting, sought to develop a viable political alternative. The result was an incisive critique of American foreign policy and a revolutionary call to nonviolent action. . . .

*   *   *

Yet despite its best efforts at intellectual innovation and a sudden flurry of activity in 1955 and 1956, the tiny American peace movement was not able to reestablish itself as a social force between 1950 and 1956. All too often it seemed to be talking to itself; only in Montgomery did a social movement flare up for a moment around a pacifist ideal. Politicians continued to pledge their unswerving fealty to the Cold War against the Communist Menace, while the nation girded itself for thermonuclear war with relative apathy. Ravaged by McCarthyism and rejected by many of its closest allies, the barely surviving peace movement failed to stir a ripple in public complacency.

Writings on American socialism grow more and more voluminous with the passing of each year. In 1952, Donald Drew Egbert and Stow Persons edited a two-volume study, *Socialism and American Life* (Princeton University Press), the first volume containing a series of essays and the second an extensive bibliography on the topic of socialism to that time. One of the essays, an especially long and important one by Daniel Bell, "Marxian Socialism in the United States," has been reprinted as a paperback book (Princeton, 1967); it contends that the failure of socialism can be attributed to the fact that "the American Socialist Party, though often called reformist or right wing, was actually too much of a Marxist Party." It was, Bell argues, borrowing Martin Luther's phrase describing the church, "in the world, but not of it."

In the same year that essay first appeared, Ira Kipnis in *The American Socialist Movement, 1897–1912* (New York, 1952) saw the Socialist Party as a reformist movement and claimed that the Socialists "repeatedly diluted their party's program until by 1912 it could be described as the left wing of the progressive movement." David A. Shannon in *The Socialist Party of America* (New York, 1955) agreed, but noted, pointing to the conditions and traditions of American life, that "in a manner of speaking it was American society that defeated the Socialists." While this became a generally accepted consensus view, a dozen years later it was challenged by James Weinstein's *The Decline of Socialism in America, 1912–1925* (New York, 1967), which argued that the Socialist Party did not disintegrate as a result of the uniqueness of the American environment, but because of internal party conflicts occurring

THE PROTEST
OF POLITICS
AND PEACE

after 1919. Using Weinstein's work as a starting point, Christopher Lasch shows the consequences of the destruction of socialism for American radicalism in his essay "The Collapse of Socialism and the Isolation of the Intellectuals" in *The Agony of the American Left* (New York, 1969). For a general review of the debate over the fate of American socialism, see: D. H. Leon, "Whatever Happened to an American Socialist Party?: A Critical Survey of the Spectrum of Interpretations," *American Quarterly, 23* (May 1971), 236–258, Bryan Strong, "Historians and American Socialism, 1900–1920," *Science and Society, 34* (Winter 1970), 387–397, and Leonard B. Rosenberg, "The 'Failure' of the Socialist Party of America," *The Review of Politics, 31* (July 1969), 329–352. A worldwide perspective on the fate of radicalism during the 1930's is presented by John A. Garraty, "Radicalism in the Great Depression," in Jerome L. Rodnitzky, et al., *Essays on Radicalism in Contemporary America* (Austin, Tex., 1972).

The effect of the Socialists' antiwar stand is discussed in Sally M. Miller, "Socialist Party Decline and World War I: Bibliography and Interpretation," *Science and Society, 34* (Winter 1970), 398–411. Samuel Eliot Morison, Frederick Merk, and Frank Freidel investigate opposition to the War of 1812, the Mexican War and the Spanish-American War in *Dissent in Three American Wars* (Cambridge, Mass., 1970). Opposition to expansionism and the aftermath of the Spanish-American War is considered in Robert L. Beisner, *Twelve Against Empire: The Anti-Imperialists, 1898–1900* (New York, 1968). Attention is paid to the permanent peace movement in two volumes by Merle Curti, *The American Peace Crusade, 1815–1860* (Durham, N.C., 1929) and *Peace or War: The American Struggle, 1636–1936* (New York, 1936). A more recent survey is Peter Brock, *Pacifism In the United States: From Colonial Era to World War I* (Princeton, 1968). The period hitherto left uncovered is discussed by Charles Chatfield, *For Peace and Justice: Pacifism In America 1914–1941* (Knoxville, Tennessee, 1971) and Lawrence S. Wittner, *Rebels Against War: The American Peace Movement, 1941–1960*. In 1971, Random House issued a forty-four-book facsimile collection, *The Peace Movement In America,* in which many significant works dealing with that topic were reprinted.

For excellent bibliographies on student activism, both past and present, see: Philip G. Altbach, *A Select Bibliography on Students, Politics, and Higher Education,* revised edition (Cambridge, Mass., 1970), and *Student Politics and Higher Education in the United States: A Select Bibliography* (Cambridge, Mass., 1968). Student protest during the 1930's is highlighted in firsthand accounts by James Wechsler, *Revolt on the Campus* (New York, 1935) and Joseph Lash, *The Campus Strikes Against War* (New York, 1935); a retrospective view is provided by Hal Draper, "The Student Movement of the Thirties: A Political History," in Rita J. Simon (ed.), *As We Saw the Thirties* (Urbana, Illinois, 1967), 151–189. Two useful anthologies which consider worldwide student protest are: Philip G. Altbach and Robert S. Laufer (eds.), *The New Pilgrims: Youth Protest in Transition* (New York, 1972), and Alexander DeConde (ed.), *Student Activism: Town and Gown in Historical Perspective* (New York, 1971).

THE PROTEST
OF ECONOMICS:
LABOR AND AGRICULTURE

For many years the philosophy of American labor has been molded by the thoughts and policies of Samuel Gompers, a founder of the American Federation of Labor (AFofL), and president from its beginnings in 1886 until the time of his death in 1924. Gompers worked within the capitalist system and hoped to use trade unionism to reap capitalism's bounty for the worker. In short, his "pure and simple" unionism looked not to a workers' revolution to change the system, but to better wages, hours and working conditions within it. Even after the formation of the Congress of Industrial Organizations (CIO), which abandoned Gompers' narrow, skilled worker-craft union formula for a more broadly based industrial unionism, the goals of American workers have remained essentially the same; organized labor became a leading component of the liberal corporate state and a force for the maintenance of the status quo in American society.

There are exceptions to this image of labor unions in the United States and the Industrial Workers of the World is the most prominent. Founded in 1905, the Wobblies, as they were called, aimed at organizing the dispossessed of the American working class. Although it later led several strikes in the east, the IWW began by working with migratory and itinerant workers who came to the frontier west; they arrived just as it was quickly being transformed into an urban and industrial environment by the large and impersonal corporations engaged in mining, lumbering, construction and railroad building. Samuel Gompers' style of unionism neglected, perhaps even shunned, these workers; on the other hand, IWW leader William "Big Bill" Haywood saw his organization's industrial unionism as leading them to power, for Haywood maintained that he who held power ruled society.

Taking to the streets proved the most effective way to organize such workers, and many a Wobbly received a busted head while involved in one of the numerous free speech campaigns to win the right to recruit openly. The IWW's desire for the overthrow of capitalism by means of a general strike did not endear the union to those in authority, nor did its militant direct action tactics of passive resistance (which should not be confused with pacifism). Wobbly organizing and strikes in industries deemed vital to the World War I war effort gave the federal government the excuse to crack down on the union; in 1917 the Justice Department proscribed the IWW and raided Wobbly headquarters throughout the nation. These raids resulted in the arrest of many of the union's important leaders.

For some, the IWW legend has been passed down through the songs—conveniently assembled for later generations in the *Little Red Songbook*—that the Wobblies sang while demonstrating in and outside of prison. For others, the legendary Joe Hill summed up Wobbly bravado when, while standing before a firing squad in Utah, he proclaimed, "Don't mourn for me. Organize." In an attempt to shed light on the meaning of the IWW's contribution to the history of American protest, Melvyn Dubofsky in the first article in this section discusses the Wobbly legacy to our own time and the reasons for the IWW's failure to bring about the downfall of capitalism.

Although the Industrial Workers of the World was probably the most radical union in American history, the campaigns during the 1930's of later labor organizing groups appeared equally radical to some observers. In 1933, Section 7a of the National Industrial Recovery Act guaranteed the right of collective bargaining to workers. After the Supreme Court declared that legislation unconstitutional in 1935, the National Labor Relations Act (Wagner-Connery Act) made the same guarantee, but strengthened it by prohibiting "unfair labor practices" such as the establishing of employer-dominated company unions or the discharging of workers for membership in noncompany unions. Several large employers had engaged in such practices after the passage of Section 7a. Subsequent to 1935, the unions took full advantage of federal support and began organizing among the rubber, steel and automobile industries. Drawing upon earlier American precedent and recent events in Europe, the workers seized upon the sit-down tactic when employers proved reluctant to deal with them.

The major sit-down strike occurred against the General Motors Corporation in 1936–37; the triumph of the United Auto Workers, and, shortly afterward, the Steel Workers Organizing Committee in the steel industry, marked a turning point in American labor history. As historian Sidney Fine has noted:

> The successful outcome of the strike helped to determine that decision-making power in large segments of American industry where the voice of labor had been little more than a whisper, if that, would henceforth have to be shared in some measure with the unions in these industries, and the trade-union movement as a whole would enjoy a higher status in American life than it ever had before.[1]

---

[1] Sidney Fine, *Sit-Down: The General Motors Strike of 1936–1937* (Ann Arbor, Mich.: U. of Michigan Press, 1969), p. 338.

In short, the unions were accepted as an equal member of the liberal corporate state, indicating that, if successful, protest against the system by those outside is usually a means of gaining entrance into it.

Joel Seidman's article in this section presents a contemporary analysis of the sit-downs, and may indicate why it seemed such a radical tactic for workers to sit down in a factory and prevent it from operating. To some Americans, the procedure flouted highly prized property rights; for the workers, on the other hand, it was an assertion of what they considered their human rights. Traditionally, when the two views have conflicted, protest follows.

Such has been the case not only in industrial America, but in the nation's rural areas as well, where agricultural discontent has often erupted. From Shays's Rebellion in 1786 to the farm strikes of the early 1960's, farmers have protested independently and through organizations such as the Grange, the Farmers Alliance, the Populist Party, the Nonpartisan League, and the Farmers' Holiday Association. Frequently believing themselves to be victims of bankers who foreclosed mortgages or charged high interest rates, of shippers who charged what the traffic would bear, and of middlemen and processors who siphoned off their profits, the farmers used violent as well as peaceful means.

Moreover, as American society developed through the twentieth century, the small farmer quickly felt the squeeze of agricultural commercialism; by 1970 there were only 2 million small farms left. Between 1950 and 1970, more than 2.7 million farmers, nearly all small operators, abandoned farming or sold out to larger competitors; the total number of farm residents declined from 23 million to 9.7 million people during that period. Moreover, during the same years, average farm size changed from 215 to 387 acres and the nation's 40,000 largest farms—less than one percent of all farms—accounted for at least one-third of all production. This squeeze, felt by the small farmer, came long before 1950, however, and the Cornbelt Rebellion described by John L. Shover explains how farmers facing this problem manifested their discontent during the Great Depression; following that selection is one by A. William Hoglund which compares the farm strikes of 1932 and 1962.

Finally, while the small farmer has suffered as a result of agricultural consolidation and the government's farm policy, which from its beginning in 1933 with the Agricultural Adjustment Act aided the large farmer most, the sharecropper and tenant farmer, often black, have suffered even more. In 1970, hired farm workers earned $887 in cash wages annually for an average of 80 days of farm work; about 2.5 million persons were engaged in such work and many of these were migrant workers, like the followers of Cesar Chavez.

IV *The protest of economics*

Just as in recent years the United Farm Workers Organizing Committee has worked to better the lot of these hired workers, during the Depression the Southern Tenant Farmers' Union was formed for a similar purpose. In the final selection, Jerold S. Auerbach describes that union's activity and its criticism of New Deal agricultural policies.

While reading the essays in this section, one should consider the parallels between Wobbly and sit-down strike tactics and the methods of recent "radicals," especially students who occupied university buildings. Do you think the sit-downers in the auto industry had common ground with the Wobblies or were they a different breed entirely? Were the sit-downs an example of what Arthur Waskow calls "creative disorder"? That is, were they engaged in a politics of disorder

> invented by people who are 'outside' a particular system of political order, and want to bring change about so that they can enter. In doing so, they tend to use new techniques that make sense to themselves out of their own experience, but that look disorderly to people who are thinking and acting inside the system.[2]

Were the sit-downers invading the property rights of others?

The same question would apply to the farmers engaged in attempts to prevent mortgage foreclosures. If a debt is not paid does the banker have the right to seize what he contends has become his property? Do extenuating circumstances legitimatize the acts of the farmers engaged in the Cornbelt Rebellion? Were the planters justified in the violent action they took against the southern tenant farmers? What would account for the ultimate failure of the tenant farmers' union and the Wobblies, while the sit-down strikers succeeded in winning their demands? Whose protest was more effective and on what basis do you make your judgment?

[2] Arthur I. Waskow, *From Race Riot to Sit-In: 1919 and the 1960s* (Garden City, N.Y.: Doubleday & Company, 1967), p. 278. Reprinted by permission of publisher.

Melvyn Dubofsky

If ever an American labor union was committed to ultimate revolution, the Industrial Workers of the World must be considered that union. However, as Melvyn Dubofsky explains, the leaders' desire for revolution often confronted the rank and file Wobblies' desire for immediate gains. As more and more of these gains came to fruition, the IWW radicalism diminished; reform, rather than repression (of which the IWW leadership was often the target), weakened the organization's appeal. Nevertheless, in terms of methods, organization, and goals, the Wobbly legacy to the radicalism of the 1960's and the early 1970's appears great, even if its own

The IWW: Legacy of Labor Radicalism

immediate labor radicalism ultimately failed. Professor Dubofsky is author of *When Workers Organize: New York City in the Progressive Era* and *We Shall Be All: A History of the IWW*. The latter title is taken from the IWW's favorite revolutionary hymn, the *Internationale,* which proclaims, "we have been naught—WE SHALL BE ALL!"

In their analyses of the IWW's [Industrial Workers of the World] eventful history, several scholars have concluded that had it not been for America's entry into World War I and the repression of the organization that ensued, the IWW might well have usurped the CIO's subsequent role in organizing mass-production workers. These scholars believe that the base established by the IWW among harvesters, loggers, and copper miners would have become sufficiently stable, had war not intervened, for the Wobblies later to have penetrated other unorganized sectors of the economy. This rendering of history leads one to conclude that the IWW's ultimate failure was more a result of external repression than of internal inadequacies.

Nothing, of course, need be inevitable. Yet given the internal deficiencies of the IWW, the aspirations of most of its members during the organization's heyday, and the dynamics of American capitalism—what might better be called the "American system"—the Wobblies' attempt to transform American workers into a revolutionary vanguard was doomed to failure. Wobbly doctrine taught workers how to gain short-range goals indistinguishable from those sought by ordinary, non-revolutionary trade unions. Able to rally exploited workers behind crusades to abolish specific grievances, the IWW failed to transform its followers' concrete grievances into a higher consciousness of class, ultimate. purpose, and necessary revolution; to create, in short, a revolutionary working class in the Marxist sense. This was so because the IWW never explained precisely how it would achieve its new society —apart from vague allusions to the social general strike and to "building the new society within the shell of the old"—or how, once established, it would be governed. Wobblies simply suggested that the state, at least as most Americans knew it, would disappear. Hence, at their best, IWW ideologues offered only warmed-over versions of St.-Simon's technocratic society, with gleanings from Edward Bellamy's *Looking Backward*—scarcely a workable prescription for revolution in the modern world. In their imprecise ideology and vague doctrine, the Wobblies too often substituted romantic anarcho-utopianism for hard analysis of social and economic realities.

Even had the IWW had a more palatable prescription for revolution, it is far from likely that its followers would have taken it. In fact, IWW members had limited revolutionary potential. At the IWW's founding convention [William "Big Bill"] Haywood had alluded to lifting impoverished Americans up from the gutter. But those lying in Haywood's metaphorical gutters thought only of rising to the sidewalk, and once there of entering the house. Individuals locked in the subculture of poverty share narrow perspectives on life and society; as Oscar Lewis has observed, the main blight of the "culture of poverty is the poverty of its culture."[1] Struggling just to maintain body, such men lacked the time or comfort to worry much about their souls; they could think only of the moment, not the future, only of a better job or more food, not of a distant utopian society.

This placed the IWW in an impossible dilemma. On the one hand, it was committed to ultimate revolution; on the other, it sought immediate improvements for its members. Like all men who truly care about humanity, the Wobblies always accepted betterment for their members today at the expense of achieving utopia tomorrow. This had been true at Lawrence, McKees Rocks, and Paterson, among other places, where the IWW allowed workers to fight for immediate improvements, a result which, if achieved, inevitably diminished their discontent and hence their revolutionary potential. Even at Paterson, where IWW-led strikers failed to win concessions, some Wobblies discerned the dilemma of their position—the leaders' desire for revolution coming up against their members' desire for palpable gains.

Internally, the Wobblies never made up their minds about precisely what kind of structure their organization should adopt. By far the most

---

[1] Oscar Lewis, *La Vida* (New York: Random House, 1966), p. 1.

capable IWW leaders favored an industrial union structure under which largely independent, though not entirely autonomous, affiliates organized by specific industry would cooperate closely with each other under the supervision of an active general executive board. But many lesser leaders, and more among the rank and file, were captivated with the concept of the One Big Union (the mythical OBU) in which workers, regardless of skill, industry, nationality, or color, would be amalgamated into a single unit. Incapable of negotiating union-management agreements owing to its protean character, the OBU would be solely the vessel of revolution. Considering the inherent difficulties involved in organizing unskilled workers on a stable basis, organizational form and structure was an issue of the utmost importance. Yet it remained a problem that the Wobblies never resolved satisfactorily.

This was not the only issue the IWW failed to resolve. Operating in industries traditionally hostile to unionism, Wobblies aggravated hard-core employer prejudices. To employers who rejected negotiations with AFL affiliates that offered to sign and to respect binding legal contracts, the IWW offered unremitting industrial war, for it refused to sign time agreements reached through collective bargaining, and declined to respect labor-management contracts. Hesitant to recognize unions on any basis, management thus had less reason to acknowledge the IWW. If the IWW had had the raw economic power to win concessions without time agreements and written contracts, its policies might have made some sense. But time and again it challenged powerful employers from behind union fortifications erected on sand.

Its mythology concerning rank-and-file democracy—comprising what today is known as "participatory democracy"—further compounded the IWW's internal deficiencies. The IWW had been most successful when led by strong individuals like Haywood, who centralized general headquarters in 1916, or Walter Nef, who constructed a tightly knit and carefully administered Agricultural Workers' Organization. Too often, however, jealous and frustrated Wobblies, lacking the abilities of a Haywood or a Nef, but desiring their power and positions, used the concept of "participatory democracy" to snipe at the IWW's leaders on behalf of an idealized rank and file. And without firm leadership the organization drifted aimlessly.

Even had the IWW combined the necessary structure, the proper tactics, and experienced, capable leaders, as it did for a time from 1915 to 1917, its difficulties might still have proved insurmountable. There is no reason to believe that before the 1930's any of America's basic mass-production industries could have been organized. Not until World War II was the CIO, an organization with immense financial resources, millions of members, and federal encouragement, able to solidify its hold on the nation's mass-production industries. And even then the CIO made no headway among migratory workers or Southern mill hands. What reason, then, is there to think that the IWW could have succeeded in the 1920's or earlier, when it lacked funds, counted its members by the thousands, not the millions, and could scarcely expect government assistance? To ask the question is to answer it.

Yet had the IWW done everything its academic critics ask of it—established true industrial unions, accepted long-term officials and a permanent union bureaucracy, signed collective agreements with employers and agreed to respect them—done, in other words, what the CIO did, what would have remained of its original purpose? Had the founders of the IWW been interested in simply constructing industrial unions on the model of the CIO, the advice of their scholarly critics would be well taken. But the IWW was created by radicals eager to revolutionize American society, and to have asked them to deny their primary values and goals would have been to ask too much.

Whatever the IWW's internal dilemmas, the dynamics of American history unquestionably compounded them. Unlike radicals in other societies who contended with established orders unresponsive to lower-class discontent and impervious to change from within, the Wobblies struggled against flexible and sophisticated adversaries. The years of IWW growth and success coincided with the era when welfare capitalism spread among American businesses, when all levels of government began to exhibit solicitude for the workingman, and when the catalyst of reform altered all aspects of national society. This process became even more pronounced during World War I, when the federal government used its vast power and influence to hasten the growth of welfare capitalism and conservative unionism. Whatever success the Wobblies achieved only stimulated the reform process, for employers who were threatened by the IWW paid greater attention to labor relations, and government agencies, initially called upon to repress labor strife, encouraged employers to improve working conditions. While IWW leaders felt federal repression during World War I, their followers enjoyed eight-hour days, grievance boards, and company unions. Put more simply, reform finally proved a better method than repression for weakening the IWW's appeal to workers.

Although the IWW ultimately failed to achieve its major objectives, it nevertheless bequeathed Americans an invaluable legacy. Those young Americans who practice direct action, passive resistance, and civil disobedience, and who seek an authentic "radical tradition," should find much to ponder in the Wobblies' past. Those who distrust establishment politics, deride bureaucracies, favor community action, and preach "participatory democracy" would also do well to remember the history of the IWW. Indeed, all who prefer a society based upon community to one founded on coercion cannot afford to neglect the tragic history of the IWW.

In this history, two lessons stand out. The first underscores the harsh truth of Antonio Gramsci's comment, quoted earlier, that in advanced industrial nations revolutionaries should take as their slogan: "Pessimism

154

of the Intelligence; Optimism of the Will." The second lesson emphasizes the irony of the radical experience in America, and elsewhere
in the Western industrial world. As a result of their commitment to
ultimate revolution as well as to immediate improvements in the existence of the working class, radicals the world over quickened the
emergence of strong labor unions and acted as midwives at the birth of
the "welfare state." But success, instead of breeding more success, only
produced a new working class enthralled with a consumer society and
only too willing, even eager, to trade working-class consciousness for a
middle-class style of life. The ultimate tragedy, then, for all radicals,
the American Wobblies included, has been that the brighter they have
helped make life for the masses, the dimmer has grown the prospect
for revolution in the advanced societies.

Yet no better epitaph could be written for the American Wobbly than
A. S. Embree's comment from his prison cell in 1917: "The end in
view is well worth striving for, but in the struggle itself lies the happiness
of the fighter."

Joel Seidman

Sit-Down

Although the federal government never sanctioned and usually vehemently opposed unionization as espoused by the IWW, after 1935 and the passage of the Wagner Act, union organization found greater favor in Washington. It did not, however, win easy acceptance by the nation's largest corporations such as General Motors. The effort to gain recognition in the auto industry led to the GM sit-down strike of 1936–37, which one historian has called "the most significant American labor conflict in the twentieth century." In the selection that follows, Joel Seidman, a sympathetic and contemporary observer of the strike, discusses the history of the sit-down technique and its application during the 1930's; the similarity to civil rights sit-ins and campus sit-downs and take-overs of recent years should be apparent to the reader. Seidman's original study *Sit-Down,* a firsthand account, was published by the League for Industrial Democracy, which is discussed in the Altbach & Peterson selection on student protest in Section III.

A new strike technique has swept the country, arousing enthusiasm among workers, and bewilderment among employers. In industry after industry, in state after state, the workers remain at their posts but refuse to work. No longer is it possible to introduce strikebreakers, for the workers are in possession. Nor are the workers readily dispersed, for they can barricade themselves in a strong defensive position. If strikebreakers or police storm the factory gate, they are clearly responsible in the eyes of the public for whatever violence may occur. The employer cannot too easily afford to alienate public opinion, nor risk damage to his machinery. And so the workers remain in possession of the plant, in much more comfort and security than on the picket line.

Employers and their allies have been quick to attack sit-down strikes on the ground of illegality. It is precisely because such strikes seem to challenge the rights of property ownership that such controversy has been aroused over them. And yet it should be clear that sit-down strikers are not challenging the ownership of the plant, but merely the employer's right to dismiss them and operate with strikebreakers. That is admittedly legal, for otherwise the right to organize and bargain collectively could not be exercised. Nor should one be unduly disturbed if conservative judges at first hold sit-down strikes illegal, for virtually every weapon developed by labor has been held illegal in its early stages. Another charge leveled against the sit-down strike is that it permits

From Joel Seidman, *Sit-Down* (New York, 1937), pp. 9–36. Reprinted by permission of the League for Industrial Democracy.

a minority to coerce the majority. Unfortunately for its ability to convince, that argument is heard too much from the employers or from organizations sponsored by them, and not frequently enough from workers themselves. It is precisely those who seek absolute industrial power for themselves who are loudest in their defense of the liberty of the non-unionist. The truth of the matter is that a strike can only be maintained .and won by the solidarity of the great mass of workers. If they are indifferent or hostile the strike is doomed, whether it be of the sitdown or the walk-out variety. It should be remembered, moreover, that sometimes the strikers delegate a minority of their number to occupy the plant, to lessen the problems of sanitation, feeding, and organization. If those employers who so zealously protect the rights of non-unionists to remain unorganized would instead admit the principle of labor organization and engage in genuine collective bargaining, the number of strikes would be very few indeed.

Nor is the sit-down strike a revolutionary weapon, as some have proclaimed. It asserts, not the right to the factory, but the right to the job. It is scarcely more revolutionary to bar strikebreakers by remaining inside the plant than by maintaining a picket line outside. Nevertheless the sit-down should be regarded as a distinct forward step, for it exhibits a healthy disregard of the property rights held supreme under our present system of law. The sit-down strike should be sharply distinguished from the seizures of Italian factories by workers following the [First] World War, for there is no attempt to operate the plant. The sit-down is a challenge to constituted authority, but so is every picket line. Indeed, if our experience to date is typical, there is likely to be less violence and less destruction of property in a sit-down strike than in a walk-out. The sit-down has been compared by some to the Gandhi passive resistance movement in India. It has also been compared to the tactics of some workers' groups in Europe and the Industrial Workers of the World in the United States, who in certain cases stayed on the job but accomplished as little as possible.

The sit-down strike should be viewed, not as an isolated occurrence, but in the light of the complex social situation that gives rise to it. Those who wish to avoid it will make most progress, not by attacking the result, but by removing the cause. No worker for slight cause cuts off his income, even temporarily, and it is no comfort to sleep in a factory instead of a home. If workers strike, whether by remaining in or walking out of the factory, it is because they have suffered from grievances to the limit of their endurance, and because they have learned that only by striking will their complaints be adjusted. . . .

In November and December, 1936, the campaign of the United Automobile Workers of America to organize the General Motors Corporation workers was nearing a climax. The auto workers enjoyed the backing of the progressive unions of the Committee for Industrial Organization.

In the warfare between non-union mass production industry and the CIO, the General Motors strike was the first major battle. Realizing that much might depend upon the outcome, both sides unstintingly threw their resources into the struggle. . . .

On January 2 the struggle entered a new phase. Upon the company's petition, Judge Edward S. Black issued a sweeping injunction restraining the union from continuing to remain in the plant, from picketing, and from interfering in any manner with those who wished to enter the plant to work. To obey the injunction would be to concede the loss of the strike. The injunction exposed the hollowness of the company's complaint against possession of its plant, for a stay-out strike would have been crushed as surely as the sit-down, had the writ been obeyed. Later, in Cleveland, the corporation was to seek an injunction against strikers who had left the plant to form a picket line. Small wonder that when the sheriff read the injunction to the Flint strikers and asked them to leave voluntarily he was laughed out of the plant. Three days later it was discovered that the injunction judge owned stock in General Motors. The union charged that he owned 3,665 shares, worth $219,900 at the current market quotation, and the judge admitted ownership of 1,000 shares. The union thereupon petitioned the state legislature to impeach Judge Black, for his violation of the statute forbidding a judge from sitting in a case in which he has an interest. The company, sensing its weak position, did not apply for the writs of body attachment which would have required the sheriff to attempt to arrest the sit-down strikers for contempt of court.

Suddenly, on January 11, the company changed its tactics. Heat in the plant was shut off, and city police mobilized in the area. Company police attempted to starve out the sit-downers, attacking carriers of food and removing the ladders by means of which food had been brought in. The sit-downers, in return, captured the gates from the company police. The city police, who had cleared nearby streets in advance, then attacked in an effort to recapture the gates. Tear gas bombs were hurled against the sit-downers and their sympathizers outside. Strikers used the fire hoses within the plant to direct streams of water on the police and on the gas bombs. During the battle the sit-downers, who had until then occupied only the second floor of the plant, took possession of the entire building. For four hours the strikers fought the police, who used clubs, tear gas, and riot guns. Fourteen workers were wounded by the police gunfire, one of them seriously, and dozens were tear-gassed. Within the sound truck union organizers took turns at the microphone, shouting encouragement to the strikers, and giving direction to the battle. When the battle ended the strikers remained in victorious possession of the plants.

The county prosecuting attorney, who owned 61 shares of General Motors stock, jailed the wounded as they were released from the hospital, and obtained 1,200 John Doe warrants under which any strike sympathizer could be arrested. Seven of the Flint strike leaders were arrested, charged with unlawful assembly and malicious destruction of property. The union demand for the arrest of the police, company guards, and others who had been responsible for the attack was disregarded. In the meantime National Guardsmen were mobilized and sent to Flint.

At this point, the public was relieved to learn that a truce had been arranged. General Motors agreed to enter into negotiations with the union in an effort to settle the strike, and the union in return agreed to evacuate all plants held by it, whether in Flint or elsewhere. One of the most important matters to be considered in the negotiations was whether the United Automobile Workers should be recognized as the sole bargaining agency for the workers. Thirty minutes before the sit-downers were to march out of the Flint plants, and after other plants had already been evacuated, the union discovered that W. S. Knudsen, executive vice-president of the corporation, had agreed to bargain collectively with the Flint Alliance, a semi-company union, semi-vigilante strikebreaking organization inspired by the company. Regarding this as a violation of the truce, the union refused to evacuate the plants, and General Motors thereupon cancelled the scheduled conference. Several days later the corporation announced that 110,000 workers had signed petitions asking to be returned to work, but this number was exaggerated and the union showed that large numbers of the signatures had been obtained by intimidation.

On February 1 came the turning point in the strike. General Motors had taken the offensive, and the union had suffered defeats in Anderson, Indiana, and Saginaw, Michigan. Hearings on another application for an injunction were in progress, this time before Judge Gadola. The Flint Alliance was becoming dangerous, and there was some fear that the back-to-work movement inspired by the company might spread. Something had to be done to bolster morale. The union had again to take the offensive.

The Chevrolet plant in Flint, the scene of discrimination against union members, provided the opportunity. Of most strategic importance was plant No. 4, in which all Chevrolet motors are assembled. A hundred feet from this plant, however, was the personnel building, headquarters of company police and hired gunmen. The strategy decided upon was to make a sham attack upon plant No. 9, in the far corner of the tract. At 3:30 P.M. a sit-down started there, and the excitement brought the company police on the run. At 3:35 the union men in plant No. 6, starting to No. 9 to help, were instead directed by union leaders in the sound truck into No. 4, where a sit-down simultaneously began. The company police arrived too late, and the union was in control of the key plant, without which no production was possible. The Women's Emergency Brigade, made up of wives, mothers and sisters of the strikers, played a heroic and important part in the battle, both at No. 9 and No. 4. They smashed windows of the plant to keep the men from being suffocated by tear gas, and with locked arms barred the police attack upon the main gate of No. 4.

On the following day Judge Gadola issued the injunction requested by the company. Though not a stockholder, as Judge Black had been, he proved himself just as willing a servant. His injunction, similar in many ways to that issued by Judge Black a month before, was much more drastic. It ordered the union officers and the sit-downers, under penalty of $15 million, to evacuate the plants by 3 P.M. the following day, and to refrain from picketing and from interfering with the operation of the plants or the entry of strikebreakers. The sheriff was ordered to evacuate the plants within twenty-four hours. Again the strikers refused to budge, and the judge ordered them all arrested. Sheriff Wolcott, explaining that he lacked a sufficient number of deputies, refused to carry out the order unless Governor Murphy provided the aid of the National Guard.

Meanwhile sit-downers within Fisher Body plant No. 2 and Chevrolet No. 4 were in a virtual state of siege. National Guardsmen surrounded the plants, and refused to allow friends and relatives to speak to the men at the factory gates. A hunger siege at first imposed by the Guardsmen was lifted in less than a day. Reporters who tried to speak to the strikers at the gates were escorted out of the military zone at the point of bayonets. At Fisher No. 1, on the contrary, the strikers were able to receive visitors and come and go as they pleased, under no restrictions except those imposed by their own shop council.

The stumbling block to peaceful settlement of the strike remained the issue of recognition. The union, which first asked recognition as sole bargaining agent for all General Motors employees, later surrendered that claim and asked merely to be sole bargaining agent in 20 plants closed by the strike. The union proposed that, if this was agreed upon, all plants immediately resume operations, and all other points at issue be settled in conference. This the company likewise refused. Company spokesmen favored a plebiscite to determine the wishes of the men, but refused to recognize the union as sole bargaining agent in those plants where it might win a majority.

Finally, on February 11, an agreement was reached and the strike ended. Much of the credit for its settlement without further bloodshed belonged to Governor [Frank] Murphy, who proved a skillful and patient mediator. Under the agreement the United Automobile Workers was recognized as bargaining agent for its members, and the company agreed not to bargain on matters of general corporate policy with any other group from the 20 struck plants without the governor's sanction. There was to be no discrimination against union men, and all court proceedings were to be dropped. Collective bargaining negotiations were to begin on February 16. The union, on its part, was to evacuate the occupied plants, refrain from recruiting on company property, and exhaust every possibility of negotiating before calling any other strike. At the same time

160

the company announced an increase in the average wage rate of five cents an hour, swelling its normal annual wage bill by $25 million.

The strikers hailed the settlement as a signal victory for them. For the first time the giant General Motors Corporation had been fought to a standstill by its workers, and forced to engage in collective bargaining with them. After forty-four days the sit-downers marched out of the plant, heads and spirits high, singing "Solidarity Forever." Out they came, two by two, with a large American flag at the head of the procession, to the cheers of 2,000 sympathizers assembled at the plants. . . .

THE SIT-DOWN AS A UNION TACTIC

The sit-down strike has gained such popularity in a short time, not only because it is novel, but also because it possesses distinct advantages over the walk-out strike from the point of view of effective tactics. If a strike is to be won it is essential that the plant not be operated. Even if production is low or nonexistent, the appearance of operation has a disturbing effect upon the strikers' morale. How can workers make more certain that the plant will not operate than by remaining in physical possession?

In a walk-out strike a picket line is maintained to keep strikebreakers out of the plant. Often they succeed in entering, especially where police furnish assistance or the employer hires strong-arm men from a strike-breaking agency. Strikebreakers cannot enter a plant held by sit-downers, however, until the strikers are ejected. That is no easy matter, for they occupy a strong defensive position behind the factory walls. Out on the streets the police, with their armament and discipline, have obvious advantages. Mounted police may scatter a picket line in a single charge. Even tear gas may be ineffective against sit-downers, as the Fansteel Metallurgical Corporation workers proved. When deputies hurled tear gas bombs into their North Chicago plant, the strikers turned on the ventilating apparatus, and the spread of the gas was checked. It was the deputies themselves who were most affected by the gas.

If violence occurs in an attack on sit-downers, it is obviously the employer and his police allies who are directly responsible for it. Such attacks will affect public opinion, and may hurt the employer's standing with the buying public. It is of no value to the employer to eject the strikers if by so doing he loses public sympathy. If a fight occurs on the picket lines, on the other hand, it is easy for the employer to charge that attacks by pickets on strikebreakers were the cause. A bitter struggle within the plant, moreover, may result in damage to valuable machinery.

Morale is more easily maintained in a sit-down strike. The strikers acquire greater confidence in their own strength, and are more effectively welded into a militant and determined force. Outside influences that might have a weakening effect upon morale are excluded. . . .

Not all plants are so situated as to permit a successful sit-down strike.

Certain big steel mills, for example, are built on large tracts of company property, entirely surrounded by steel fences. The buildings may be located as far as a mile and a half from the gates. The sit-down is most apt to be successful in a plant with windows opening on a street. It is then possible for the strikers to receive food and messages from their friends outside, even though company or city police win control of the outside door or gates. In Flint, when the National Guard surrounded the plant and for a time barred the entry of food, the union threatened to drop provisions to the besieged men from a plane. If the plant is situated some distance from the street, the sit-downers may find themselves besieged, without means of communicating with the outside world or obtaining food. For this reason, among others, a sit-down strike is best reinforced with a strong picket line around the plant. Difficulties of feeding or sleeping or the lack of sanitary facilities, moreover, may make it inadvisable to keep all the strikers within the plant. Sometimes outside picketing cannot prevent the entry of strikebreakers, because a railroad runs directly into the company's plant. This was true in the case of the Electric Storage Battery Company of Philadelphia. In such cases the sit-down is the only effective form of strike, and the Electric Storage Battery workers were among the early users of that method.

The sit-down may be spontaneous or planned. If planned in advance, the exact time must be kept a secret until the moment of action, for otherwise the employer will learn of it, the plant will be shut, and the workers not allowed in. Many sit-downs have started directly after lunch. The workers may have suffered some grievance in the morning, and have had their first opportunity to consult with each other during the lunch period. Short, spontaneous sit-down strikes, to which the name of "quickies" has been attached, are especially important in fighting speed-up and building an organization.

Sit-down strikers merely wish to make certain that the plant will not operate during the strike, or that machinery will not be moved. Had General Motors promised this in Flint, the plants would have been evacuated at once. The refusal of the company to make the promise convinced the workers that plans for operation or removal had been made. In the Bendix strike in South Bend, the strikers evacuated on the company's agreement to negotiate, and within two days an agreement was reached.

In some instances the sit-down method may lead to abuse, with a handful of workers stopping a huge plant because of a petty grievance. This is not likely to happen where proper machinery for settling grievances is set up, and so operated that the workers acquire confidence in it. A few workers can stop production only where large numbers are ready to support them. Union members soon learn to act as disciplined unionists, utilizing machinery for the peaceful settlement of disputes, and resorting to strikes of any variety only after other methods have proven fruitless. . . .

Sit-downers have had a host of new problems to solve, not the least of

162

which have been living in factory buildings. Food, sleeping quarters, and sanitation are matters that must be properly attended to if morale is to be kept up and health maintained for long. The necessary work must be done, and facilities for recreation provided. In all of these respects our experience with sit-downs, brief though it has been, is illuminating.

With hundreds or perhaps several thousands of sit-downers in a plant, the problem of food becomes urgent. The union must assume responsibility for seeing that the workers receive three meals a day. This is a severe strain on the union treasury, but thus far adequate meals have been furnished. Indeed, in some strikes most of the sit-downers have gained weight. One of the most important committees in many sit-down strikes is the chiseling committee, which seeks donations from food merchants. It calls for resourcefulness when the committee is unable to obtain the food for the menu as planned, and the cook must prepare whatever is brought back. The Midland Steel Products Company sit-downers in Detroit were aided by a daily donation of 30 gallons of milk by the milk drivers' union. Often the meals furnished by the union are supplemented by food brought to individual strikers by their families or friends.

Usually the food is cooked in a nearby hall or restaurant, and brought in milk cans, kettles, or other large containers to the plant. In the case of the Wahl-Eversharp Pen Company of Chicago, police refused to allow friends of the strikers to bring food into the plant. The sit-downers then lowered a rope from an upper window to the roof of an adjoining bakery, and obtained food in this fashion. The menu of sit-downers is usually simple, but adequate. Barrels, kegs, and whatever else is suitable are used for chairs, and tables are likewise improvised. Newspapers sometimes serve as tablecloths. Liquor is strictly forbidden.

Usually the cooking is done by a committee of the strikers' wives. In large strikes, however, a professional cook may be obtained. The cook in the Flint strike, for example, was sent there to help by the Cooks' Union of Detroit. He had previously cooked for four other sit-down strikes. For the Flint strike the union installed new kitchen equipment worth more than $1,000.

"The food goes into the factories in twenty kettles of various sizes," the cook reported. "The amount of food the strikers use is immense. Five hundred pounds of meat, one thousand pounds of potatoes, three hundred loaves of bread, one hundred pounds of coffee, two hundred pounds of sugar, thirty gallons of fresh milk, four cases of evaporated milk!" . . .

Other important committees were the drivers' committee, which delivered the food, and the chiseling committee, which covered the city for donations of food or money. About two-thirds of the supplies were obtained in this fashion.

One of the important problems is to obtain comfortable sleeping quarters. Sit-down strikers in an automobile body or final assembly plant are fortunate in this regard, for they may sleep on the floor of the cars, removing the seats if necessary or arranging the seats between the conveyor lines. In the Midland steel plant some of the men tied burlap to machines, and so rigged up cots. Elsewhere tables have been made to serve. Sometimes cots have been brought to the plants by friends, and usually all have obtained blankets after the first night. Standard Cotton Products Company sit-downers in Flint built houses of cardboard packing boxes, and made beds of cotton padding designed for automobile seats. Their houses were in two rows, one labeled "Union Street" and the other "Cotton Street."

Most visitors to sit-down strikes have been impressed by the neatness of the men and the tidy appearance of the plants. One of the important jobs is to see that the factories are kept clean. The machinery is kept in good order, for the sit-downers wish to return to work as soon as possible after the strike ends. Often a former barber is found among the strikers, and he is made to resume his old trade. In the Kelsey-Hayes plant a wheelbarrow on a platform served as a barber chair. In one sit-down strike where there were women employees, a beauty parlor was opened for them by a former worker in such an establishment. Washing is often a problem, however, for in most plants only ordinary washbowls are available. One sit-down, in the Detroit plant of the Aluminum Company of America, had to be transformed into a walk-out because a number of the men became ill and lack of sufficient sanitary facilities made further stay in the plant hazardous to health.

Obeying the rules. A certain amount of work is required, for meals must be served, the place kept clean, a watch kept, and discipline maintained. For recreation the men play cards, listen to the radio, or provide their own entertainment program. There are dancers, singers, and musicians in every large group, and often an orchestra can be formed. Frequently the sit-downers write songs about their own strikes. A bowling alley was set up in one plant, and horseshoes pitched in others. Basketball courts have been improvised, hockey games played, and boxing and wrestling matches promoted. Where the company has provided a recreation room, with ping-pong tables and other games, these facilities are used to the utmost.

Those who are studiously inclined may prefer to read. The educational director of the United Automobile Workers has organized regular classes for the sit-downers, with parliamentary procedure, public speaking, and trade unionism among the popular subjects. Even where no formal classes are organized the sit-down has considerable educational value, for the workers must set up their own community government, and solve the many problems that arise. In some cases church services have been held regularly. Loud speaker systems are rigged up, so that announcements made at the gate or in the nearby union office may be heard by all. Pep speeches are made in the same manner, and entertainment is similarly broadcast. Often the sit-downers amuse themselves, at the very start of the strike, by hanging up the "No Help Wanted" sign.

Where both men and women are employed, the sit-downers must be extremely careful to avoid the charge of immorality. Usually the women have been sent home, partly for this reason and partly because the hardships were more difficult for them. Often the married women had to leave in any event, because of their family responsibilities. Where women have stayed in the plant, strict chaperonage rules have been established. In the Kelsey-Hayes strike the girls were not permitted to leave their dormitory after 11 p.m. The sit-downers asked that two of the regular plant matrons be placed in charge of the women's dormitory, and this request was complied with. The girls in this strike were not permitted to go through a dark tunnel that connected two buildings. Sit-down strikers of the Brownhill-Kramer Hosiery Company of Philadelphia included both men and women. The latter entered the factory each morning at 8 and stayed until 6 p.m., and only the men remained in the plant all night. Most sit-downers have not permitted women to enter the buildings at all. In several cases, however, the overwhelming majority of the sit-down strikers have been women. This was true, for example, in the cigar plant of Webster-Eisenlohr, Inc., of Detroit. "This is a woman's sit-down," said one of the strikers. "The men are just around—that's all."

Discipline and morale are of vital importance. Those who do not conform to the rules may be sentenced to extra clean-up duty for minor offenses, and ejected for serious violations. In the General Motors strike in Flint, court was held each morning, with bringing in liquor and circulating rumors the most frequent offenses. Elsewhere it may be overstaying leaves that is most frequently punished. In the Standard Cotton Products Company strike in Flint the judge himself was twice convicted of breaking the rules, and had to do extra dishwashing as the penalty. Sometimes foremen and other company officials are allowed to converse only with union officers, for fear that they may adversely affect the strikers' morale. In some instances subterfuges have been employed by strikers or their wives in order to get out of the plant. Serious illness has been reported at home, or a birth in the family. Where too many such cases seemed to be reported a check was made, and the member immediately dropped. In some cases foremen have visited wives of sit-downers, making false reports of illness or hardships within the plant, in order to break down morale.

Except when trouble is feared, sit-downers are usually permitted to leave the plant for short intervals, under rules that they decide upon. In most cases they are required to return by a specified hour, and a check is made as they go and come. If an outside picket line is maintained as well, the strikers take turns staying within the plant. In one case a sit-downer who belonged to the National Guard was released for strike duty with the Guard.

Visitors are admitted only after a careful check of their credentials. Usually a pass signed by a responsible union officer is required. In many plants everyone who enters must submit to a search for weapons, and a similar search is made of all who leave. A communications system calls to the gate those who have visitors. A post office is sometimes set up to handle the mail, which may be censored. Gates and doors are often barricaded against a surprise attack, with guards on duty at all times. In Flint, sentries in six-hour watches were on duty twenty-four hours a day, with an alarm system to warn quickly of impending danger. Sometimes metal strips are welded across doorways and windows, to make police entry more difficult, and to provide protection from gas bombs and bullets. In some plants pickets assigned to make the rounds have had to punch the time clock as they went on or off duty.

Heat, light, and water are important to the health and comfort of the strikers. Usually the companies have permitted these services to be maintained. The cutting off of these facilities has precipitated some of the most bitter battles yet fought by sit-downers. In some instances the employer has alternately turned the heat off and on.

Race relations may be another problem faced by sit-downers. In the Midland plant in Detroit both whites and Negroes were employed. Workers of both races occupied the plant, and worked together in harmony throughout the strike.

In Flint an amusing episode occurred while the sit-downers were in possession of the plants. Chevrolet plant No. 4 had just been seized and considerable disorder had occurred. Following the seizure everything was peaceful, and the many camera men on the scene had little to do. They therefore engaged in a baseball game, with the still camera men playing the movie camera operators. The umpires were several hundred sit-downers on the roof of plant No. 4, and the spectators were the National Guardsmen on duty. One team, displeased with a decision, sat down on the ball field, and promptly won a reversal, amid cheers, from the union umpires. Several innings later the other team was similarly dissatisfied. Its tactics were to sing "Solidarity Forever"; and the umpires, after joining in the song, again reversed the decision.

Marching out of a plant when the strike has been won or a truce arranged offers opportunity for a colorful demonstration, as in Flint. The Bendix strikers marched out in military order, headed by their own drum and bugle corps, and paraded to the union hall. After the settlement proposals had been adopted, the strikers paraded through the business section of South Bend, headed by the effigy of the Bendix company union hanging on a long pole.

A typical set of rules. Sit-downers must govern their community, and solve each problem as it arises. Fundamentally these problems are similar, though new situations will arise in each plant. The rules adopted by the sit-down strikers in the Standard Cotton Products Company in Flint, Michigan, may be taken as fairly typical. With fewer than a hundred strikers, they were able to transact business in a full meeting held at ten o'clock each morning, without the more complex and elaborate organization that a large plant would require. A strike committee of five members was placed in charge. Other officers included a chairman, a secretary, a

166

judge, a press agent, and three clerks. There was a patrol committee of two, a food committee of two, a clean-up committee of three, and an entertainment committee of one.

Posted on the wall of the mess hall were the following rules, which were added to from time to time by majority vote:

RULES AND REGULATIONS

Rule No. 1. Any man who disturbs anyone while sleeping without good reason will have to wash the dishes and mop floor for one day.

Rule No. 2. Any man found drinking or looking for arguments will wash dishes and mop floor for one day—1st offense.

Rule No. 3. Every man who leaves must get a pass from the committee and check with the clerk. Passes must be shown to the doorman when going in and out, and on returning must check with the clerk. The doorman must obey these rules very strictly.

Rule No. 4. Doorman answers the phone and if call is important he calls a committee man. No long-distance calls shall be made. All local calls are allowed. No profane language used over phone.

Rule No. 5. When photographers or outsiders come in no one speaks to them but a committee man.

Rule No. 6. Everyone must line up single file before meals are served. Dishwashers will be appointed before each meal by the clean-up committee. Every man must serve his turn.

Rule No. 7. Anyone eating between meals must wash his own dishes.

Rule No. 8. Every man must attend meetings.

Rule No. 9. No standing on tables.

Rule No. 10. No passes will be issued after 12:00 P.M.—except emergency calls.

Rule No. 11. Judge's decision on all broken rules will be regarded as final.

Rule No. 12. No conversation about the strike to the management. Any information concerning the strike will be furnished by the committee.

Rule No. 13. No more than a two-hour grace period allowed on passes. No grace period on a 20-minute leave.

Rule No. 14. No women allowed in the plant at any time.

Rule No. 15. No passes issued during meals and not until the dishes are done unless it is business.

Rule No. 16. All committees must attend meetings and report their activities.

Rule No. 17. No card playing or walking around or any disturbance during meetings.

John L. Shover

Cornbelt Rebellion

Rural protest, which had been ever present in American history, reached a peak of intensity during the depression of the 1930's. Finding themselves at the mercy of the adverse economic conditions of the day, and confronted by the steamroller of agricultural consolidation, farmers organized groups such as the Farmers' Holiday Association, led by Milo Reno, to protest the demise of the family farm. Engaging in farm strikes, battling mortgage foreclosures, and advocating a legislative program, these militant agrarians, according to John L. Shover, ultimately surrendered to the immediate gains offered by the New Deal's benefit payments and price supports; farm protest, following a traditional pattern, faded with the promise of better times, if not necessarily with its realization. Professor Shover is the author of *Cornbelt Rebellion: The Farmers' Holiday Association* and co-author of *Political Change in California: Critical Elections and Social Movements, 1890–1966.*

F arm prices began a downward spiral in April, 1931 that was unchecked until June, 1932 when across the board a farmer's income had dwindled to half that of the preceding year. Hogs sold for 3 cents a pound, cattle for 5 cents, and corn for 10 cents a bushel. Within this interval the first direct action movement appeared in Cedar County, Iowa and by the summer of 1932 a plan for organized withholding of produce from market was taking shape in Iowa.

State veterinarians attempting to enforce Iowa's law for compulsory inoculation of dairy cattle against tuberculosis were assaulted in Cedar County in the spring and summer of 1931 and a thousand farmers from the area converged on the state capitol to demand repeal of the law. This county, where the President of the United States, Herbert Hoover, had been born in 1874, was in the midst of a prosperous farming region. The value of land per acre was the highest of any county in the state and as a corollary, average mortgage debt was the greatest in Iowa. Farmers were faced not only with the perennial problems of debt and falling prices, but the wave of bank failures that had spread across Iowa had taken a heavy toll in the county. The very day the first farmer protest meeting was held, the Cedar County Bank at the county seat, Tipton, closed its doors. The compulsory tuberculin test was salt that stung the wound of economic

From John L. Shover, *Cornbelt Rebellion: The Farmers' Holiday Association* (Urbana: University of Illinois Press, 1965), pp. 28–33, 77–81, 114–118, 124–125; 166–167, 215–216. Reprinted by permission of the publisher. Footnotes are omitted.

discontent. A cow condemned as a reactor had to be committed to slaughter and even with partial compensation by the state and federal governments, the owner lost an average of $130 on each animal. The veterinarians were scapegoats for deeper frustrations, but the history of social movements is replete with examples of irrational protests that have distorted facts and attacked those who were neither real problems nor real enemies. . . .

As it was, in the depression year of 1931, when state veterinarians, strangers in Cedar County, appeared on farms to conduct a test in which farmers had no confidence and which could result in a loss of several hundred dollars a farmer could ill afford, the interlopers were greeted with sticks, stones, and mob resistance. . . .

The Cow War was an isolated event, but it was a harbinger of the rebellious spirit depression had set astir in the countryside. If the trouble in Cedar County gave any indication of what form future unrest might take, it was a revolt of traditionalism against modernism and change. It was initiated by farmers more prosperous than most of their fellows, but beset by critical economic conditions. It was irrational in form and chose scapegoats as enemies; it displayed little internal discipline and was easily roused to violence. It collapsed quickly when force was brought into play. The Farmers' Protective Association, like the later Holiday Association, was an independent adjunct of the Farmers' Union. . . .

*   *   *

The withholding of produce and the picketing of highways were not the major manifestations of depression discontent in the farm belt; the most important and most consequential activity of the Farmers' Holiday was the movement to restrain foreclosures of farm mortgages. The antiforeclosure movement came to a climax in January and February of 1933 when at least seventy-six penny auctions or Sears-Roebuck sales took place in fifteen farm states. These months also marked the crest of rural insurgency. More men were involved in antiforeclosure activity than any other single manifestation of protest. Crowds of obstructionist farmers at auctions ranged from about 100 to the crowd of 2,000 that appeared at Pilger, Nebraska in January. The nucleus of activity remained northwest Iowa, but unlike the farm strike, the location of demonstrations against foreclosures dot the map of the entire farmbelt. Added to the general unrest in these months was the strike of dairy farmers in Wisconsin, where the Cooperative Milk Pool, an organization independent of the Farmers' Holiday, dumped milk and blockaded highways in an attempt to force price increases.

That farmer protest should take its most militant form in the drive to resist mortgage foreclosures was a predictable outgrowth of depression conditions. Foreclosure was a countryside tragedy: ". . . the most discouraging, disheartening experiences of my legal life have occurred," wrote a small town attorney in Iowa, "when men of middle age, with families, go out of bankruptcy court with furniture, team of horses, a wagon and a little stock as all that is left from twenty-five years of work." Casper West-field of Madison, Minnesota was a seventy-five-year-old pioneer and on January 30, 1,500 Minnesota Holiday members saved for him a farm he had worked for forty-three years. Louis Larson of Niobrara, Nebraska was not so fortunate. He was a graying man of sixty, weighing at least 300 pounds, who hitchhiked across Nebraska addressing meetings of the Madison County Plan. This hulking man often burst into tears describing how he had lost the farm that he had homesteaded. Max Cichon of Sugar Creek, Wisconsin refused to vacate his foreclosed farm and a small army of deputies armed with machine guns, rifles, and tear gas attacked the farm the evening of December 5, 1932, routed the family, and bore Cichon off to jail. Monthly figures on foreclosure sales are not available, but circumstantial evidence indicates that farmer resistance was most frequent at the time when farm foreclosures were more numerous than any period in the twentieth century. Nineteen thirty-three was the peak year for involuntary sales; there were almost eight for every one hundred Iowa farms compared to only five in 1932. Along with the increment in foreclosures, the climax of farmer protest followed another unfailing barometer of discontent: the price index. The index of Iowa farm prices, forty on the 100-point scale in January and forty-two in February, was at the low point in the depression period.

Like the farm strike, the antiforeclosure movement was spontaneous, unguided by any leaders or organization. The first sale, probably, was one in Wright County, Iowa in October, 1931, even before the Farmers' Holiday Association came into being. Unbeknownst to the participants, the method of the penny auctions followed that of squatters' "claim clubs" fifty years before which contrived to prevent sale of land homesteaded without benefit of title. Of the initial twenty-three sales held in 1932, most were inspired by the United Farmers' League or the Madison County Plan, the groups linked to the Communist party agrarian offensive. The United Farmers' League picketed a sale in Frederick, South Dakota in late September and attempted to halt a sale in Baraga County, Michigan in November. The Madison County Plan Farmers' Holiday Association followed up its success at Elgin, October 7 by halting another chattel sale at Petersburg just one week later and preventing a tax sale at Madison, Nebraska on November 1. Nevertheless, there would have been a penny auction movement even had there been no Communist-front farm organizations. Participants in the sales at Elgin, at Chili, Wisconsin on November 11 and at Granite Falls, Minnesota, January 28 all believed that their penny auctions were the first.

Whether in Iowa, Michigan, or Ohio, the methods of a penny auction were the same. Sometimes, as at the Cecil Kestner farm near Deshler, Ohio, the presence of a hostile crowd was indicated by a noose which dangled from a tree or haymow. Often, as at Elgin, Nebraska, no bidders but friends and neighbors were present and by arrangement with the

170

auctioneer, only one bid was accepted. A prospective bidder, not party to the scheme, might find himself surrounded by a cluster of hefty farmers and if he spoke, might feel a heavy hand on his shoulder and someone would mutter, "Plenty high, ain't it?" In the end the final sum realized might be like the $1.90 on the $800 mortgage on the Walter Crozier farm at Haskins, Ohio or the $5.35 at Elgin, Nebraska. Farmer "bidders" would pay up and the property returned to the original owner. The Supreme Court of Nebraska held that inadequacy of bids could not justify a court in refusing confirmation of a sale.

The antiforeclosure movement was most intense in the old farm strike areas of northwest Iowa, bearing out [Milo] Reno's admonition to one of the participants, "In every part of the United States, from California to Maine, the Sioux City territory is known . . . it is a fact that you boys have did more to put the Farmers' Holiday on the map and fix it there for the future than any other group in the United States." On January 4, a thousand Plymouth County farmers, led by C. J. Schultz, county Holiday Association chairman, gathered at the courthouse in Lemars when the farm of John Johnson was offered for sale. Johnson was willing to sacrifice his farm for the $33,000 mortgage if he could avoid a deficiency judgment. Mr. Herbert Martin, attorney for the mortgagor, the New York Life Insurance Company, offered the only bid, one of $30,000. When he stated he had no authority to change the amount he was rushed by the crowd and dragged down the courthouse steps. Sheriff Ralph Rippey, who raced to Martin's aid, was rudely slapped and locked in among the crowd. On threat of his life, Martin was compelled to telegraph the company for permission to bid the entire amount. The company complied. The melee over, the mob converged on the office of Common Pleas Judge C. W. Pitts, refusing to allow him to leave until he promised to sign no more foreclosure decrees. The judge contended he was powerless but agreed to write an immediate letter to Governor Clyde Herring. . . .

Outside the old disturbed areas, Minnesota farmers successfully halted three sales on a single day, January 28. President Bosch of the Minnesota Holiday addressed the 2,000 farmers present at Madison, the largest sale of the day. Disorder was less in Minnesota than in Iowa, but there was a fist fight on the courthouse steps at Fairmount where farmers tried without avail to prevent a sale on February 17. A week later the sheriff of Martin County outwitted 150 protesters by holding a sale inside the courthouse while the disrupters waited outside. Governor William L. Langer of North Dakota, however, crowned proceedings by ordering the state militia to *prevent* county sheriffs from conducting foreclosure sales. . . .

*   *   *

On the afternoon of April 27, Charles C. Bradley, senior judge of the 21st Iowa district, sixty years old and a bachelor, was hearing a foreclosure case initiated by a group of banks and insurance companies to test the constitutionality of the Iowa moratorium law. The hearing was in progress when about one hundred farmers entered the courtroom. Although the group was orderly, Bradley was disturbed and ordered them to take off their hats and stop smoking. "This is my courtroom," he called to them. For the farmers, some of whom were still smarting from wounds received . . . [elsewhere] a few hours earlier, this was too much. Seized by a vengeful spirit of mob anger, they surged to the front of the courtroom, some slipped bandanas over their faces, and Bradley was pulled off the bench. Slapped and shaken by the mob, the helpless judge was borne out of the courthouse and thrust into the bed of a farm truck. Carried to a crossroads a mile outside of Lemars, his trousers were removed and he was threatened with mutilation. A rope was thrown across a roadside sign and pulled tight around the judge's neck as the mob demanded that he swear to authorize no more foreclosures. "I will do the fair thing to all men to the best of my knowledge," was all the judge would promise. Perhaps the dignity and bravery of Judge Bradley, perhaps the realization it was murder they were bent upon, perhaps the pleas of R. F. Starzl, editor of the *Lemars Globe-Post* ("Even some of those who were actively handling the judge seemed strange, moving like automatons, or like self-conscious actors who knew many eyes were upon them. Their eyes sought approval . . . ," he later wrote), checked the insane passion of the mob. A hubcap full of grease was dumped on the judge's head, his trousers, filled with gravel, were thrown into a ditch and the mob departed, leaving the judge besmirched and nearly unconscious in the road.

This was as much a lynch mob as any pack of angry men that ever disturbed the peace of a southern town. There was a hidden factor behind the assault upon Bradley—he had long been the victim of some vicious gossip that passed in Plymouth County. Rumor had it that Bradley, an unmarried man, was living in sin in Lemars. Whether this is true is not important; the farmers who attacked him believed it was true. Had another of the district judges, like C. W. Pitts, been presiding at Lemars that day it is doubtful the attempted lynching would have occurred. . . .

The men who mobbed Judge Bradley may have been members of the Farmers' Holiday Association, but they operated beyond the control and sanction of the leaders. Milo Reno hastened to make a public statement condemning the incident as "deplorable, in fact, revolutionary" but adding that the farmers of the community were God-fearing, law-abiding citizens who had been driven to law violation "due to some intolerable wrong under which the people have been suffering." Such declarations availed little to protect the Holiday Association from the avalanche of adverse criticism heaped upon it. Attorney General O'Connor charged that racketeering methods had been used to force farmers to join. Not 20 percent of the members in northwest Iowa had joined of their free will, he contended. Recruiters had threatened farmers that if they did not pay their dues they might find their haystacks burning some night. In the wake of the disorder, right-wing extremists moved into northwest Iowa. Dr. Harry Jung, honorary general manager of the American Vigilante Intelligence Federation, told an audience at Sheldon, Iowa, "Farmers who participate in open defiance of law and order are playing into the hands of the Communist International. . . ." The Holiday Association, he declared, was a subsidiary of the Communist United Farmers' League, and wherever there were milk riots, farm strikes, and labor disorders, investigation always revealed the sinister presence of Communists in the background. "Mother Ballou [sic] had been involved," he charged, in the recent outrages in Plymouth County. He urged farmers to support the American Farm Bureau Federation. A few weeks later, G. Simon Carter of the Vigilante Federation linked Milo Reno, Wallace Short, Lester Barlow, international Jews, the IWW, Socialists, and Communists in a common conspiracy. Governor Herring told an audience at the University of Iowa, "Iowa has not gone bolshevik, and the leaders in the unfortunate occurrence in Plymouth and Crawford county were not farmers." In a private letter he advised a Farmers' Union officer not to listen to "a few mercenary [sic] leaders who are trying to line their pockets at the expense of the distressed farmers." In a barely printable letter, Milo Reno replied, "I am wondering just how a man, who occupies the exalted position of Governor of the State of Iowa can adopt the methods of the ordinary cheap shyster. . . ." Barbed words could not eliminate an unavoidable truth: if the Farmers' Holiday Association professed to be the spokesman for protesting farmers, it had to bear, more than any other single organization, the responsibility for their acts of violence. . . .

* * *

Two elements made up the Farmers' Holiday protest. The first was the formal organization consisting of the core who paid dues and were firmly committed to a cost of production and inflationary agricultural program. The second was a spontaneous movement element that in its farm strikes and penny auctions gave the Association what driving force it had. Reno erred in believing that those who blocked highways or interfered with foreclosures necessarily did so because they believed in the Holiday legislative program. The most important feature of the direct action movement was its singular focus on immediate and tangible economic benefits—better prices tomorrow or saving a neighbor's home today. All Milo Reno had to offer in November was continued struggle and sacrifice—small remuneration in contrast to the generous loans and benefit payments offered by the Agricultural Adjustment Administration.

The New Deal agricultural program sapped the strength of the rural protest movement. Yet its successes no more indicate farmers' support for its basic philosophy than picketing of highways implied commitment to cost of production. The AAA won support because it promised farmers the immediate economic assistance they so gravely needed. Evidence is convincing that more farmers favored cost of production than domestic allotment—but why press demands when the mail carrier was delivering government checks? A random poll of Iowa farmers in November, 1933 revealed only 17 percent favorable to the NRA; 37 percent favorable to the hog reduction program; and 57 percent in favor of corn loans (the program that promised money for farmers soonest). However, when asked if they were "in general" favorable to the President, 72 percent replied they were. In sum, farm protest waned when there appeared a hope that economic conditions would improve, regardless of the methods by which this would be achieved.

In its focus on immediate economic goals and lack of ideology, the farm protest of the Thirties parallels earlier farm movements. The Granger movement, the Farmers' Alliance, and the Populist party all waned as farm income rose. Farm protest has been a transitory phenomenon, spurred by immediate economic crisis; the promise alone of a return of better times has been sufficient to assuage it.

*   *   *

Milo Reno was the last ideological radical to fight the farmers' battle with the old Populist principles of economic individualism and unqualified opposition to elitism in the form either of monopoly or bureaucracy. Looking to the past, not to the future, he was defending not just an economic system, but a way of life. Reno spoke for a day that had been; the radicals of the Popular Front spoke for a day that never came. The New Deal was the catalytic agent of time and change that defeated both of them. The agricultural program removed the rural discontent which provided Reno's ideology with the only driving force that could sustain it; benefit payments and price supports rendered the steady force of social and technological change that absorbs and destroys the family farmer far more painless than the radical left could have imagined possible.

A. William Hoglund

A Comment on the Farm Strikes of 1932 and 1962

America witnessed another farm strike three decades after the eclipse of the farmers' movement discussed by John Shover in the previous selection. The latter strike might very well have been the final gasp of the small farmers who continued to diminish in number until in 1962 only 10 to 15 percent of total U.S. agricultural products originated from such small units. As corporate farming expanded rapidly and young people left rural areas in increasing numbers, the concept of the family farm seemed doomed. A. William Hoglund, commenting on Shover's work on the Thirties and another scholar's investigation of the early Sixties, affords insight into the comparison between the two eras. In light of the discussion herein of

Shover's attribution of ideological purpose to strike leaders—but not to rank and file—the role that ideology plays in protest movements as motivation for both leadership and its mass following should be considered. Professor Hoglund is the author of *Finnish Immigrants in America, 1880–1920* and is working on a study of the movement of people away from the farms in New York State between 1860 and 1960.

Like other brain workers, historians share the intellectual fads and moods of their day. With the vogue for psychology after World War II, for instance, the facetious might say that historical study had merely become a substitute for psychoanalysis. Much postwar psychological interpretation has belabored the idea that man is basically irrational. One could not, therefore, expect to understand man by an examination of his formal statements, for they all hide the true reality—the troubled psyche. Those historians who take a dark view of the consequences of this notion of human nature attribute the past and present shortcomings of our world to the warped makeup of the average man. They make heroes of Brooks and Henry Adams, whose works blame civilization's ills on mass man's unthinking participation in the conduct of the social order. American reform movements are explained in terms of the neuroses of the individuals involved. Such agrarian movements as Populism are seen as seedbeds of bigotry. Settlers are described as men driven by the same greedy impulse to ravage the public domain as speculators. Other historians, however, take a somewhat brighter view. They regard the pragmatic experience of the American as the saving virtue that set the New World apart from the

From A. William Hoglund, "A Comment on the Farm Strikes of 1932 and 1962," *Agricultural History*, 39 (October 1965), pp. 213–216. Reprinted by permission of the Agricultural History Society and the author.

Old, and they celebrate the supposed "end of ideology" in the 1950's as completing America's liberation from Europe. These historians are not sure whether the unthinking American had blundered nobly or ignobly into the chaos of the twentieth century.

In the past five years or so, historians like other intellectuals have been rudely reminded that the so-called average man still exists—ignored, baited, or manipulated by what is now termed the Establishment. Politicians have been pressured by ethnic groups and civil libertarians. Agricultural organizations have been challenged by farm strikers. Even college administrators have been harassed by students who until very recently were regarded as silent. Although the nature of the new assertiveness is not fully clear, it is probable that the average man cannot be dismissed as simply irrational and selfish. If given the chance to rise above his limitations, he may after all have the only real human perspective on what is worthwhile and rational while men of the Establishment pursue goals which have alienated them from the rest of mankind. . . .

The[se] two papers [compared here] represent case studies on the farm movements of 1932 and 1962 in the Midwest, particularly in the corn-hog, dairy, and cattle regions of Iowa. They are focused primarily on four points: the kind of farmers who became strikers, the economic conditions that created the strike movements, the ideological nature of those movements, and the impact the strikers made. . . .

Both authors agree that the strikers were not the poorest "down and out" farmers. Each, of course, recognizes that the economic status of the strikers has to be defined in order to analyze the nature of their movements. But the evidence is not entirely convincing, or, at least, it is not satisfactorily developed. Because their conclusions challenge the simplistic "have-not versus have" interpretation of agrarian conflict, it should be better defended.

Mr. Shover explains that the Iowa strikers in 1932 came from "the most prosperous farming counties in the livestock and dairy belts." Most strike action took place in counties where the gross income per farm was well above the state average. Least strike activity, moreover, occurred in counties with the lowest gross income, the highest tenancy, and the fewest home conveniences. Before his thesis is conclusive, it must be shown that the dairy strikers did not represent the economically depressed farmers of their counties. For instance, how does their burden of mortgage debt compare with that of other dairy farmers? Did the striking dairymen have market experiences which differed from those who did not strike? Were the Iowa dairy strikers different from those in other dairy states? (In Wisconsin and New York, the striking dairymen were largely those who sold their milk for non-fluid uses, such as ice cream and butter making, which brought lower returns than when milk was sold direct to consumers for fluid use. Wisconsin milk strikers, moreover, in 1932 had smaller herds than the nonstrikers.) Because all farmers in the Iowa counties with the highest incidence of strikes did not participate, the economic position of the strikers must be defined carefully.

The 1962 strikers, according to Mr. Schlebecker, did not represent the marginal farmers. Those at the bottom were leaving agriculture and thereby could not have been around to strike. Moreover, he seems to assume that only those at the bottom leave, forgetting that relatively prosperous farms have been withdrawn from operation when owners retire or heirs refuse to run them. Second, he argues that the bottom half of Iowa's farmers could not account for the amount of livestock withheld from the market which he says represented a one-third drop in deliveries. The conclusion is not fully demonstrated. The "one-third drop" is based on what is termed "common report." Why is common report adequate to show the drop in livestock sales when nearly unanimous critiques made after the strike are regarded as inadequate proof on the kind of farmers who became strikers? On the other hand, the 1959 agricultural census figures suggest that the bottom half of the farmers might have withheld one-half the swine but not the cattle. Even if the bottom half could have withheld all the cattle that were kept off the market, it still would not mean that the bottom farmers were the only ones who withheld. Many farmers at the bottom were outside the sphere of agricultural organizations and their influence. Only with more direct evidence on income distribution and the size of farm operations can one determine conclusively whether or not the NFO [National Farmers' Organization] represented principally the bottom, middle, or top rank of farmers.

Next, the two writers agree that low farm price levels moved farmers to strike. The 1932 strike, according to Mr. Shover, was prompted by the spirit of frustration that overwhelmed "individuals whose level of expectation had been conditioned by better times and some immediate crisis, in this instance, foreclosure or drought, [that] threatened to deprive them of property or accustomed income." In Mr. Schlebecker's view, "most agrarian uprisings in the past have taken place during fairly bad times, which appeared, nevertheless, to be getting better. Hope of greater prosperity seemed to motivate farmers to protest, although farmers tend to remain fairly quiet if all is well, or if all is perfectly terrible. In general, in the United States in the summer of 1962," the writer continues, "farmers were in trouble, but not much. What seems to have initiated the great discontent was the farmers' realization that they were steadily falling behind the rest of the population in economic well-being. They resented this relative decline, especially since they had only recently known prosperity." Of course, no one will doubt that the strikers were frustrated by low prices. But the same could be said of most nonstrikers. Therefore, it would seem necessary to determine whether or not there was anything unique in the individual striker's experience or outlook that had moved him to strike.

That experience included a struggle with the cost-price squeeze resulting from tremendous technological and market changes. To remain on the farm required expansion of output through investment in new equipment and services. Expansion required additional capital that might be obtained by reducing household expenses, borrowing, cutting farm expenses, or selling more products. But it is difficult to make ends meet in periods of low prices and even more so when those periods also demanded costly expansion. The 1950's was such a period of low prices and tremendous change in agricultural technology, particularly in the livestock and dairy fields. Frequent references were made by newspaper reporters to the members of the NFO who complained about the burden of keeping up with the purchase of new equipment and machinery needed for most efficient production. In the 1920's dairy farmers also experienced changes in farm practice, arising partly from the increased use of the tractor. Iowa dairy and cattle farmers, according to the 1930 census, had achieved a significantly greater investment in machinery and equipment than other specialized farmers. Is it possible that the increased pressure to expand at a time of low prices made dairymen and cattlemen more inclined to strike than other farmers? Because farmers at all income levels tried in varying degrees to keep up with the demands of technology and marketing, it is no surprise that the strikers included farmers from all income groups. But the cost-price squeeze may not of itself be enough to explain why some farmers struck and others did not.

The writers, as their third major concern, discuss or suggest the catalytic impact of self-conscious ideological aims. Neither discusses, however, to any extent the class features of the anti-middleman tradition in agrarian thought. Certainly in 1933 the striking dairymen in Wisconsin and New York employed the anti-middleman argument extensively, causing state officials to make studies of the milk price spread between the farmers and consumers. Mr. Shover's reference to the relationship between the farm cooperative and the J. R. Roberts Dairy Company suggests that Iowa farmers had anti-middleman sympathies. By the 1960's, there was less reason to expect as much of the anti-middleman tradition because, by then, the Farm Bureau and business cooperatives had muted it somewhat. Mr. Schlebecker does show that the NFO directed its attack against the processors, believing that organized business and labor had made more gains than agriculture. By 1962, perhaps, the NFO had developed a "live and let live" attitude willing to tolerate other economic groups if organized agriculture's claims were properly recognized.

Mr. Shover categorically denies that the 1932 strike was ideological in character, attributing ideological purpose only to the Holiday leaders who formulated "cost-of-production" schemes. He insists that the rank-and-file strikers created a spontaneous and irrational uprising that looked for immediate remedies to relieve their economic frustrations. The ideological leaders thus did not express the rank-and-file point of view and could not

178

control them. Milo Reno undoubtedly failed to control the strikers but this does not exclude the possibility that the strikers might have had an ideological commitment that Reno failed to appreciate. Views hostile to the middleman, the belief that the dealer expropriated the farmers' product unjustly, and conclusions that the businessman had to be put in his place—these surely are strongly ideological in character. Because they did not develop fully their ideological analysis and because their leaders did not fully help them to shape it, the strikers may thereby have succumbed to the bait of the New Deal and lost that momentary group identity and power which came from an erstwhile ideological commitment.

Mr. Schlebecker, on the other hand, does not see any real gulf between the leaders and the rank-and-file members in the NFO, nor does he question the ideological tone of the withholding movement. Through a series of meetings, he points out, the leaders did their best to act in accord with rank-and-file sentiment towards the holding action. He concludes that the 1962 strike was "not a protest, but a carefully planned long-range effort to change the economic power structure." In particular, that effort was designed to compel the processors to bargain with the farmers and to establish satisfactory prices for farm products. But there is no elaboration in depth of the case made for the strike beyond the explanation that the strikers felt left behind other economic groups in sharing prosperity.

Only the future can tell whether the strikes of the 1960's are the last major ones evocative of the spirit of earlier agrarian movements. In the next few decades, farmers may be so reduced in numbers and so completely identified as businessmen that agricultural historians may have to think of joining the business historians. If the future should see no more agrarian rebellions, agricultural historians have urgent reason to study the last strikes, to interview the participants, and to pursue the other evidence. Because average rank-and-file farmers are less apt to write than farm leaders, recapturing their thought is difficult, and doubly so if historians make strong assumptions regarding human nature. Historians should appreciate the effort to meet the challenge made by the writers of the papers on the strikes of 1932 and 1962. Their efforts give reason to believe that the study of agriculture can still contribute significantly to the social history of mass behavior.

Jerold S. Auerbach

Southern Tenant Farmers: Socialist Critics of the New Deal

While the farmers engaged in the Cornbelt rebellion and the strikers of the early Sixties were landowners, the sharecroppers and tenant farmers discussed by Jerold S. Auerbach comprised rural America's landless poor. Either victims of, or neglected for the most part by the New Deal's early agricultural program, they banded into the Southern Tenant Farmers' Union. This Socialist-inspired organization, although a failure in the long run as a union, propagated radical alternatives to New Deal agricultural policy. As an instrument of labor organizing, the union brought the strike to the rural South; it is noteworthy that the violence accompanying these strikes was solely a reaction on the part of the planters, rather than a tactic of the strikers. Professor Auerbach is the author of *Labor and Liberty: The La Follette Committee and the New Deal.*

In 1927 Harry L. Mitchell, the son of a Tennessee tenant farmer, moved to Tyronza, a tiny Arkansas town thirty-five miles west of Memphis. Mitchell hoped to make a crop there, as he had done earlier in Tennessee and in Mississippi. Local sharecroppers fared so poorly, however, that he decided to purchase a small dry-cleaning establishment instead. The Depression left Mitchell with unexpected leisure; he used it to read Upton Sinclair and to follow the progress of Huey Long's "Share Our Wealth" program. One day he wandered into the gas station operated by his neighbor, Henry Clay East. After listening to East expound his political theories Mitchell told him that he sounded like a socialist. Before long, both men were exploring socialist solutions to capitalism's mounting ills. During the 1932 presidential campaign they drove to Memphis for inspiration from Norman Thomas, the Socialist party's nominee. Thomas' speech struck a responsive chord; Mitchell and East returned to Tyronza and decided, "We should organize."

Mitchell became state secretary of the Socialist party. He and East organized Socialist locals and led vigorous protests against planter control over administration of New Deal relief and public works programs. Increasingly, however, their attention turned to the desperate plight of thou-

From Jerold S. Auerbach, "Southern Tenant Farmers: Socialist Critics of the New Deal," *Labor History*, 7 (Winter 1966), pp. 3–18. Reprinted by permission of *Labor History*. Footnotes are omitted.

sands of sharecroppers and tenant farmers, who constituted "a kingdom of neglect and want. . . ."

The rich delta bottom lands of northeastern Arkansas, which thirty years earlier had supported a prosperous lumbering industry, no longer seemed capable of sustaining their human inhabitants. Sharecroppers tilled the cotton fields "from can to can't," but entire families rarely received as much as two hundred dollars for a year's work. Their diet consisted of cornbread, molasses, and fatback, and their decrepit hovels could hardly be called homes. Many tenants, it was said, "could study astronomy through the openings in the roof and geology through holes in the floor. . . ." Scantily clothed children attended school primarily to keep warm; malaria and pellagra took a constant toll. Sharecroppers owned nothing but their own labor. An archaic credit system, which left them without cash and at their planters' mercy, also contributed to an impoverished and degrading rural society.

The Agricultural Adjustment Act of 1933, the New Deal's initial response to the rural ravages of the Depression, only exacerbated the sharecroppers' distress. Congress paid scant attention to the croppers when it considered this legislation. They were not parties to AAA contracts between landlords and the Secretary of Agriculture. Nor did sharecroppers participate in local administration of the act; county committees were invariably dominated by the planters. AAA provisions for acreage reduction often meant tenant displacement. From the sharecroppers' perspective, however, the act's most deplorable feature was the disproportionate allocation of benefit payments to landlords, because of their greater equity in the crops produced. Initially, when payments went directly to landlords, croppers complained that they rarely received their share. Subsequently, when payments to croppers were required, landlords altered their status to wage hands to disqualify them. AAA policy thus tended to drive sharecroppers and tenant farmers from the land, to lower their status still further, or to reinforce their subservience to their landlords. The purpose of the act, AAA director Chester Davis reminded his district agents, was to meet the agricultural emergency, not to solve a "deep-seated social problem." However justifiable New Deal policy appeared to officials in Washington, it enraged the sharecroppers, who hoped for so much and, as always, received so little.

Friction between landlords and tenants in the Arkansas delta, fanned by AAA, threatened to ignite a social conflagration. Delta plantations—new, large, and highly commercialized—attracted thousands of tenants, whose distress absentee planters rarely gauged. Displacement resulting from government policies, which coincided with rapidly increasing mechanization, confronted the sharecroppers with a dismal future. Disenchanted with the New Deal, and disgruntled over their squalid existence, they grew receptive to alternatives. The Socialist party, which spawned vigorous locals in the delta, eagerly became the catalyst for their discontent.

In northeast Arkansas, a Party organizer told Norman Thomas late in 1933, "you will find the true proletariat ... moving irresistibly toward revolution and no less." Communists, Thomas was warned, might "sweep these bottom-lands like wildfire"; therefore, "We *must* have a Socialist program for sharecroppers." Heartened by the news that H. L. Mitchell had "pepped up things" in the delta, Thomas decided to personally encourage his southern disciples.

In mid-February 1934, Thomas visited Tyronza and addressed gatherings of socialists and sharecroppers. During lunch at Clay East's house, Mitchell and East related their recent futile attempt to run for local office on the Socialist party ticket. Thomas conceded that political activity was a risky venture for Arkansas socialists but, he suggested, why not organize a sharecroppers' union. The idea appealed to Mitchell and East, both of whom pledged their cooperation. Within six weeks Mitchell was predicting that nearly every sharecropper would join; in fact, he told Thomas, with ample time and sufficient funds all the croppers might be brought into the Socialist party as well. "No other organization or persons," Mitchell observed, "have dared to challenge the landlords' supremacy."

While Mitchell and East extended their network of Socialist locals, Thomas launched a vigorous verbal assault against the New Deal's agricultural program. "Never in America," he told Secretary of Agriculture Henry Wallace, "have I seen more hopeless poverty" than among the Arkansas sharecroppers. "My criticism is not of a section," he insisted, "but of a nation and of an economic program." The political overtones of Thomas' and Mitchell's activities did not escape notice. Tyronza's town council passed a resolution deploring the Socialist party's "frenzied efforts to organize and send forth propaganda intended to discredit the Democratic party. . . ." And the chief of AAA's cotton section noted the development of "a well-defined and very widespread political attack upon our entire agricultural adjustment program. . . ."

Mitchell's tireless efforts soon registered impressive results. By July he could count on three full-time organizers and more than a dozen communities with Party locals. Mitchell even hoped to swallow up Huey Long's Share Our Wealth clubs. "We can fix things," he promised Thomas, "so that it won't look as tho' these things are direct party activities." Mitchell was particularly successful in the Tyronza area where, two years earlier, absentee landlord Hiram Norcross had earned the sharecroppers' enmity by evicting fifty of them from his plantation. Subsequently Norcross, his sharecroppers alleged, cheated them out of their AAA benefit payments. During the spring of 1934 Mitchell organized Norcross' croppers into a branch of Tyronza's Socialist party local. When Norcross insisted that they sign a contract which they considered highly unjust, they verged on rebellion. Mitchell parlayed their discontent into the sharecroppers' union suggested by Thomas.

On a sultry July evening a small group of white and Negro croppers, encouraged by Mitchell and East, gathered in a rickety schoolhouse on

182

the Norcross plantation to organize the first local of the Southern Tenant Farmers' Union. Several had been members of a Negro union wiped out in the Elaine massacre fifteen years earlier; some of the whites were former Ku Klux Klan members. For the moment, however, they put racial animosities aside and elected a white sharecropper as chairman and a Negro minister as vice-chairman. Mitchell and East arrived during a heated debate on the merits of the union becoming a legal organization; they supported the proposition. On July 26 the union was incorporated. Its declaration of principles spoke of two agricultural classes: exploiters, and "actual tillers of the soil who have been ground down to dire poverty. . . ." The union dedicated itself to the abolition of tenancy. "We seek," it stated, "to establish a co-operative order of society by legal and peaceable methods."

The very existence of the union posed a direct and radical challenge to the established order in Arkansas. Militantly class conscious and avowedly interracial, it ran roughshod over local prejudices. Borrowing some of the tactics of trade unions and the fervor of religious revivals, it quickly became the sharecroppers' advocate, teacher, preacher, and lobbyist. But the salient characteristic of the Southern Tenant Farmers' Union was its role as Socialist critic of New Deal agricultural policy. Its organizing drive illustrated its agitational character; the attendant nationwide publicity never ceased to be a Socialist thorn in the New Deal's side. Perhaps in no other area did Socialists mount such an effective counterthrust to the Roosevelt administration. . . .

Planters translated their political and economic power into persistent anti-union violence. They padlocked church doors and packed schoolhouses with bales of hay to deter union rallies. Their riding bosses flogged sympathetic croppers and drove them from their plantations. The Harahan bridge, spanning the Mississippi at Memphis, became the gateway to safety for union organizers. Two days after the formation of a Crittenden County local, its organizer, a Negro minister, was beaten and jailed. His arrest posed a grave challenge to the union: failure to defend a Negro member might split it asunder. Mitchell and East approached a Memphis attorney but he told them: "I'm one Jew who isn't going over to Crittenden County to get a Negro out of jail because he is charged with organizing a union." The lawyer claimed to have left his courage in the Argonne Forest and ushered them out of his office with a copy of *Progress and Poverty* as a gift. But an attorney from Marked Tree, accompanied by fifty white sharecroppers, marched to the local jail and secured the organizer's release.

During the winter of 1934–35 the union, confronted by unremitting violence, sought redress from Washington. When the Department of Agriculture failed to respond with sufficient vigor, union demands upon the Roosevelt administration grew more strident and union criticisms of the New Deal became increasingly vitriolic. The union despaired of government action, yet it never tired of seeking federal assistance. Alleged federal indifference served as a perpetual union rallying cry; union leaders vented their local frustrations in attacks against a remote target which, unlike the planters, could not retaliate. Furthermore, union publicity was grist for the Socialist party's mill. As one Party official wrote, during a well-publicized union fracas: "This is our chance to make a real splash in the country, because we are right there in the heart of the business." . . .

Early in 1935 two incidents focused national attention on the union, winning it many new converts and underscoring the New Deal's failure to alleviate sharecropper distress. At a union rally in Marked Tree, called to celebrate the return of a delegation from Washington, Methodist preacher Ward Rodgers told the assembled sharecroppers that if necessary, in the absence of relief, he "would lead a group that would lynch every planter in Poinsett County. . . ." Rodgers was arrested as he left the speakers' platform and charged with anarchy, blasphemy, and attempted overthrow of the government. A jury of planters, meeting in an impromptu court session held in a local store, convicted him of anarchy. Shortly thereafter, Marked Tree adopted an ordinance prohibiting public speeches without the prior consent of town officials.

The Rodgers incident had predictable consequences. It enraged the planters, some of whom had heard Rodgers' remarks; it attracted hundreds of new union members, who responded to Rodgers' foolhardy courage; and it made the union a pawn in efforts by Socialists and Communists to capitalize upon the incident. Socialists in New York worked diligently to thwart attempts by the International Labor Defense, legal arm of the Communist party, to assume responsibility for Rodgers' defense. A trusted Socialist was sent to work with the union and Norman Thomas decided to return to Arkansas.

In mid-March Thomas arrived in the delta. Union leaders hoped that his visit would expedite the transfer of their following to the Socialist party. Rodgers expected Thomas' appearance to spur "a terrific organizational campaign for the Socialist party of Arkansas. . . ." Mitchell told the Party's executive secretary that Thomas' trip "would mean that the entire section would go for us." Thomas' visit was, however, abruptly interrupted. Speaking in Birdsong, he was surrounded by a crowd of angry planters and deputies. Thomas, demanding to know by whose authority he was being restrained from speaking, was told that "no Gawd-Damn Yankee Bastard" was welcome in Arkansas. Thomas was driven from the platform and pursued to the county line; he returned to New York and described a "reign of terror" to a nationwide radio audience. Eastern Arkansas, he told a friend, "is more cruel and barbarous than any place I've ever seen."

The Rodgers and Thomas debacles marked the onset of a critical period for the Southern Tenant Farmers' Union. Arkansas planters and officials, observed a *New York Times* correspondent, had become firmly

184

convinced that only drastic steps would forestall the overthrow of "white supremacy, Christianity, the American flag and the sanctity of home and family ties. . . ." They banned union meetings and arrested members on the slightest pretext. Sharecroppers were evicted, their churches were burned, and vigilantes patrolled the highways. Mitchell and other union officers fled to Memphis to establish new headquarters. Night riders tried to assassinate the union attorney and vice-president; Clay East was escorted from Mississippi County; and the body of a union member was found floating down the Coldwater River. Planters in Marked Tree sponsored a company union, placed a loyal minister in charge, and tried to lure union members with promises of immediate employment. "We are on the edge of bloodshed," Mitchell told the Department of Agriculture. "When that blood flows it will drip down over your Department, from the Secretary at the top to [the] Cotton section at the bottom." . . .

Seeking ways to strengthen the union and unify the sharecroppers, Mitchell proposed a strike. Union members enthusiastically endorsed his suggestion; in September nearly five thousand cotton pickers struck for higher wages. After ten days the union claimed a resounding victory, though it doubtlessly exaggerated its success in securing wage increases. As a tactic to solidify the union and to expand membership, however, the strike was indisputably successful. Throughout the delta it boosted the morale of union members. Union headquarters were flooded with applications for new charters. Even the American Federation of Labor offered assistance. Early in October Mitchell told Norman Thomas: "We are in a strong position that will not be easy for the planters to overcome."

By the time of its second annual convention, three months later, the union boasted 25,000 members in two hundred locals scattered through six states. Its strategy was now clear: to combine relentless pressure on the New Deal with trade union tactics. During its first eighteen months both had served the union well, although neither weakened the foundations of the plantation system. Political pressure made the Roosevelt administration, and the nation, sharecropper conscious. The purge of liberals from AAA early in 1935 had marked a defeat for the sharecroppers but establishment of the Resettlement Administration and numerous government investigations testified to the union's impact. New cotton contracts also reflected union pressure; payments to sharecroppers increased by 10 percent over their 1935 levels. Trade union tactics brought fewer successes as landlords displayed far more stubbornness than did New Dealers. Yet union leaders did not relinquish the strike as a weapon and they never minimized its impact upon the sharecroppers. As the union newspaper advised, "Raise plenty of Hell and you will get somewhere."

In many respects 1935 had tested the union's capacity for survival. Nineteen thirty-six began with a test of durability and ended with the union apparently a permanent southern institution. A wave of evictions during the worst weeks of the winter ushered in the new year. More than one hundred sharecroppers camped in snow drifts in below freezing weather, without food, adequate clothing, shelter, or firewood. To publicize their distress, and hopefully to alleviate it, union officials pressed for a congressional investigation. A signal consequence of their efforts was Senate authorization for a civil liberties inquiry. In the spring of 1936 the La Follette Civil Liberties Committee launched the most extensive investigation of infractions of the Bill of Rights in American history.

The union could not, however, afford to wait for congressional action. Throughout the winter and spring its fortunes ebbed. Arkansas Governor J. Marion Futrell, called "Old Futile" by the union, dismissed its protests as "much ado about something which amounts to very little." H. L. Mitchell complained bitterly: "We need men and money and we don't have either." Once again a strike call seemed the only alternative to disaster.

In May, after planters had refused to meet union wage demands, cotton choppers in Cross, Crittenden, and St. Francis counties refused to work. Union members marched hundreds abreast across the cotton fields to gather additional recruits. Instead, they incensed planters and politicians. Memphis police broke picket lines at the Harahan bridge; striking croppers were arrested and leased to planters to work off their fines and court costs; and a Crittenden County landlord built and filled a small concentration camp. On the fourth day of the strike Governor Futrell sent in National Guardsmen and State Rangers and the union quietly surrendered. "We didn't make one dent," Mitchell conceded.

During these troubled months Mitchell found many New Dealers "very sympathetic" to the union, but he concluded that "their hands are tied by the southern bourbon politicians. . . ." The union's nemesis, Arkansas Senator Joe Robinson, had dismissed the union organizing drive as the work of "professional agitators, representatives of communistic and socialistic organizations. . . ." Roosevelt's disinclination to embarrass Robinson, who faced a campaign for reelection in 1936, deterred a federal investigation of Arkansas terror.

Roosevelt aroused the union's wrath when he spoke in Little Rock shortly after the cotton choppers' strike, without mentioning the sharecroppers. Norman Thomas had admonished him in advance for participating in the centenary celebration of a state "which has not yet abolished slavery in [its] cotton fields," but to no avail. A delegation of union members tried to present a petition to the President or to his secretary, but without success. This rebuff marked the high-water mark of official indifference to the sharecroppers. As the union persisted, and as the 1936 election grew near, its actions brought party, state, and federal reactions.

At the Democratic convention Mitchell won Robinson's consent to platform planks protecting the sharecroppers' civil liberties and their right to organize. Before the summer ended Governor Futrell announced that he would appoint a farm-tenancy commission; Futrell also called a conference of southern governors to discuss the problem. At the federal level the Department of Justice indicted Paul Peacher, town marshal of Earle, for peonage; during the cotton choppers' strike Peacher had arrested thirteen croppers on vagrancy charges, secured their convictions, and forced them to work out their sentences on his farm. President Roosevelt also responded. During the campaign he urged Senator Hollis Bankhead (D.-Ala.) and Representative Marvin Jones (D.-Tex.) to formulate plans for a federal program to reduce tenancy. Soon after his reelection Roosevelt appointed the President's Committee on Farm Tenancy; its efforts laid the groundwork for the Bankhead-Jones Farm Tenancy Act of 1937 and for establishment of the Farm Security Administration.

The appointment of a union representative to the President's Committee, the union claimed, "is a recognition that the union is a power in the movement to end the condition of tenancy and that its point of view must be heard by the Government." The New Deal's cautious responses to the problems of tenancy hardly detracted from the magnitude of union achievements. By the end of 1936 it had enrolled nearly 31,000 members in seven states. Anti-union violence had subsided and Democratic administrations in Little Rock and in Washington were committed to redressing the sharecroppers' grievances. New crises awaited the union, but its right to exist and its ability to be heard were no longer in doubt.

Viewed from the perspective of traditional trade unionism, the organizing drive of the Southern Tenant Farmers' Union seemed an anomaly. Its most effective weapons were agitation and publicity, not strikes or collective bargaining. The union's Socialist antecedents, leadership, and sources of support dictated a strategy based on jeremiads against the New Deal. During these early years the union's organizing drive always had twin objectives: recruitment of new members and propagation of radical alternatives to New Deal agricultural policy. The Southern Tenant Farmers' Union sought to organize a protest movement no less than to organize the sharecroppers.

Shrill pronouncements from the union, which served both of these ends, often made it seem more unique than it really was. It probably encountered no more violent resistance to its organizing drive than did new and militant unions elsewhere in the country during the 1930's. Norman Thomas' laments to the contrary, the Southern Tenant Farmers' Union did not suffer disproportionately. Furthermore, although the union unfurled the banner of interracial justice, it was not integrated at the local level. Socialist ideology, and the previous failures of segregated unions in the South, may have encouraged integration but local mores exerted a powerful pull in the opposite direction. While Negroes and whites were welcome, an overwhelming percentage of union locals contained members of one race only. "Separate but equal" governed race relations within the union.

The distinctiveness of the Southern Tenant Farmers' Union was a product of its hostility to capitalism and its vision of the future. A member once predicted that the union "will speed up the day when the rope spun by God will be used to hang the planters." His prophecy proved to be inaccurate: plantations outlived the union, which barely survived a disasterous two-year affiliation with the CIO's United Cannery, Agricultural, Packing and Allied Workers of America and virtually ceased to function by 1941, when H. L. Mitchell declared that no basis existed for trade unionism in southern agriculture. The STFU seemed like a dismal union failure. Yet as an outspoken but effective critic of the New Deal the Southern Tenant Farmers' Union was unsurpassed.

The history of American labor has been surveyed in Henry Pelling, *American Labor* (Chicago, 1960), Philip Taft, *Organized Labor in American History* (New York, 1964) and Joseph G. Rayback, *A History of American Labor* (New York, 1966). For a New Left point of view concerning American labor ideology, see: Ronald Radosh, "The Corporate Ideology of American Labor Leaders from Gompers to Hillman," *Studies on the Left*, 6 (November–December 1966), 66–88; *Radical America*, 3 (March–April 1969) includes a bibliographical survey of working-class history and culture. Robert H. Zieger, "Workers and Scholars: Recent Trends in Labor Historiography," *Labor History*, 13 (Spring 1972), 245-266, provides both an overview of recent literature and a discussion of New Left interpretations.

Two books concerning nineteenth-century labor violence are Robert V. Bruce, *1877: Year of Violence* (Indianapolis, 1959) and Wayne G. Broehl, Jr., *The Molly Maguires* (Cambridge, Mass., 1964). Philip Taft and Philip Ross deal with the subject generally in their long essay, "American Labor Violence: Its Causes, Character, and Outcome," in Hugh Davis Graham and Ted Robert Gurr (eds.), *Violence in America* (New York, 1969); they find that industrial violence was greatest when employers tried to break existing unions or deny recognition to new ones. "No major labor organization in American history ever advocated violence as a policy, even though the labor organizations recognized that it might be a fact of industrial life."

The Wobblies certainly recognized violence as a fact of industrial life and their colorful history has been chronicled by Melvyn Dubofsky, in

We Shall be All: A History of the IWW (Chicago, 1969), excerpted herein. Other studies of the Wobblies are: Joseph R. Conlin, *Big Bill Haywood and the Radical Union Movement* (Syracuse, N.Y., 1969); Patrick Renshaw, *The Wobblies* (New York, 1967); Robert L. Tyler, *Rebels of the Woods: The IWW in the Pacific Northwest* (Eugene, Oregon, 1967); and the fourth volume of Philip S. Foner's *History of Labor in the United States, The Industrial Workers of the World, 1905–1917* (New York, 1964). The autobiography of "Big Bill" Haywood, *Bill Haywood's Book: The Autobiography of William D. Haywood* (New York, 1929) helped to build many of the Wobbly myths.

The sit-down strikes receive attention in historian Sidney Fine's *Sit-Down: The General Motors Strike of 1936–1937* (Ann Arbor, Michigan, 1969) and in Joel Seidman's first hand account, *"Sit-Down"* (New York, 1937). Irving Bernstein is concerned with the development of widespread unionism and collective bargaining during the 1930's in the second volume of his *A History of the American Worker, Turbulent Years: 1933–1941* (Boston, 1970).

Farmers' responses to twentieth-century agricultural problems are discussed in Theodore Saloutos and John D. Hicks, *Agricultural Discontent in the Middle West, 1900–1939* (Madison, Wisconsin, 1951), reprinted as *Twentieth-Century Populism* (Lincoln, Nebraska, 1964); Robert L. Morlan, *Political Prairie Fire, The*

Nonpartisan League, 1915–1922 (Minneapolis, 1955); James H. Shideler, *Farm Crisis, 1919–1923* (Berkeley, 1957); and John L. Shover, *Cornbelt Rebellion: The Farmers' Holiday Association* (Urbana, Illinois, 1965), excerpted herein.

While the preceding works deal with landowning farmers who were able to organize politically, agricultural undergroups such as sharecroppers and tenant farmers, who lacked resources, faced a much more difficult task of organization. In addition to the article by Jerold S. Auerbach reprinted in this section, which deals with such an attempt in the South during the Great Depression, see M. S. Venkataramani, "Norman Thomas, Arkansas Sharecroppers, and the Roosevelt Agricultural Policies, 1933–1937," *Mississippi Valley Historical Review,* 47 (September 1960), 225–246. The first full-scale account of the STFU is Donald H. Grubbs's *Cry from the Cotton: The Southern Tenant Farmers' Union and the New Deal* (Chapel Hill, North Carolina, 1971) which contends that the union drew on Socialist support only in its infancy, relying instead on native Southern fundamentalism and Populist traditions until its demise during the mid-forties. David Conrad takes a broader view of sharecroppers in his monograph, *The Forgotten Farmer: The Story of Sharecroppers and the New Deal* (Urbana, Illinois, 1965). An account of one specific sharecropper protest can be found in Louis Cantor, *Prologue to the Protest Movement:* The *Missouri Sharecropper Roadside Demonstration of 1939* (Durham, N.C., 1969); also see his article of the same title in *Journal of American History,* 55 (March 1969), 804–822. Still one of the most moving accounts of the plight of the sharecropper during the Depression is John Steinbeck's classic portrayal of the Joad family, *The Grapes of Wrath* (New York, 1939). The reader interested in investigating for himself whether there has been much change in the sharecropper's lot over the past three-and-a-half decades should see: *Farm Tenancy: Report of the President's Committee* (Washington, 1937) and James M. Pierce, *The Condition of Farm Workers and Small Farmers in 1970: Report to the National Board of National Sharecroppers Fund* (New York, 1970).

Finally, Bernard Sternsher's *Hitting Home: The Great Depression in Town and Country* (Chicago, 1970), contains an excellent introduction and several articles in which farm protest is discussed. Gilbert C. Fite's *American Agriculture and Farm Policy Since 1900* (Publication Number 59 in the American Historical Association's Service Center for Teachers of History series) provides historiographical insight into and bibliographical references for study of that topic.

THE PROTEST
OF
VALUES
AND STATUS

At noon, May 8, 1970, several thousand construction workers suddenly and angrily left their jobs and surged into the midst of an antiwar rally outside New York's City Hall. For several violent minutes they hurled epithets and punches, beating up some seventy antiwar demonstrators and bystanders. The issue was not just the war but—in a very real sense—a way of life. The grim events that day were part of the scenario for a larger cultural struggle which involved life styles, status, traditions, values and morals. To the construction workers, the issue went beyond Vietnam; it was also a matter of "long-hairs" and "hippies," of young people who had lost respect for nation and common decency, of a countercultural movement that rejected traditional ideals of hard work, private property, family, and law and order. Hence the statement several days later of one ironworker in lower Manhattan: "This is our country and we ain't gonna let anyone tear it down."

Throughout the nation's history, the theme of "our country" has quite often been as divisive as it has been unifying. While it has evoked feelings of camaraderie, unity and shared goals, it has also time and again tended toward exclusiveness and intolerance. This motif has been a source of security and identity, but has also encouraged a siege complex in which individuals feel anxious, defensive, endangered. The incredible pace of social and economic change in America has often resulted in volatile mixtures that include, at once, the exhilaration of "coming of age," and feelings that range from quiet uneasiness to the hurts and fears of uprootedness and displacement. The individual's reactions to the ferment around him have been very much influenced by his social position and world view. Invariably the stakes have seemed high, ranging far beyond dollars and cents to a person's place in his society and the very ends and purposes of his life. One man's life style can easily be another man's living hell. Only this can account for the deep passion behind such slogans as "Better dead than red," or the statement in 1970 by a woman from Minneapolis that "we should clear out all the ultra-radicals from Congress, and clear out the State Department of all homosexuals and liberals. And get back to patriotism and put God first."

v The protest of values and status

Due in large part to its rapid development, American history has been full of clashes over issues involving status and culture. Examples range from the seventeenth-century Pilgrims' raid on Merry Mount, with its licentious life style and wicked maypoles, to battles in the late 1960's over People's Park in Berkeley. Puritans, invoking God's authority, hanged Quakers, who believed just as passionately they were serving God's cause. Spokesmen for the Enlightenment engaged in a bitter ideological struggle with the enthusiasts of evangelical religion concerning the roles of reason and emotion as guides to proper conduct and authority. Federalists and Jeffersonians were locked in deadly partisan battle during the intensely anxious 1790's over questions that, presumably, vitally affected the very existence of the new republic. In the rapid expansion and material growth of the Jacksonian era some groups perceived unprecedented opportunities to reconstruct and purify society; the result was an outburst of communitarian experiments, abolitionism and a wave of religious revivals. At the same time, these very movements helped to confirm fears that ugly forces were at work to destroy time-honored certainties and values; consequently, Know-Nothings and others sallied forth to halt alleged subversion. In the late nineteenth century, the influx of new immigrants evoked sometimes violent opposition to "long-haired, wild-eyed, bad-smelling, atheistic, reckless foreign wretches," who were supposedly threatening the nation with mongrelization, alien religions, and anarchy.

The technological breakthroughs and social upheavals of the twentieth century continued to send cultural shock waves across the country. Divisions over such cultural issues as Prohibition and immigration restriction ultimately helped shatter the pre-World War I progressive consensus. The Red Scare of 1919–1920 was, as historian Stanley Coben has shown, largely an effort "to end the apparent erosion of American values and the disintegration of American culture."[1] In this context, Kenneth Jackson's study of the rebirth of the Ku Klux Klan is especially pertinent. The chapter included here from Jackson's book argues that the KKK was in major ways the product of urban, lower-middle-class, blue-collar groups who feared that the world was passing them by. If a patriotic call to save the Republic lured thousands into the Klan in the Twenties, so at mid-century did it summon those who joined the "radical right." Ira S. Rohter, in his analysis of "The Righteous Rightists," concludes that anxieties about social status galvanized them into active protest against a ubiquitous Communist conspiracy.

Undoubtedly the other examples of protest treated in this volume have also been replete with cultural implications. To opponents of the IWW or the sit-downs of the Thirties, organized labor loomed as an anarchistic movement

---

[1] Stanley Coben, "A Study in Nativism: The American Red Scare of 1919–1920," *Political Science Quarterly*, 79 (March 1964), p. 69.

that threatened to destroy, among other things, traditional respect for authority and rights of property. To some worried and angry groups, the civil rights movement undermined long-standing moral values (hence, perhaps, the rumor that white women participants in the movement did not wear panties). Similarly, skeptics of the New Woman have tended for decades to view her as a threat to home and family. Theodore Roosevelt, for example, feared that the liberated woman would have less time for childbearing and would thus doom the nation to race suicide. Hiram Johnson, another leading Progressive politician, stated in 1921 that he preferred "the womanhood of old to the non-child-bearing, smoking, drinking, and neurotic creature" who now stalked triumphant throughout the land.

Such views have received encouragement, moreover, from those advocates of protest who believe that meaningful social change cannot occur without a genuine revolution in values. Black militant Eldridge Cleaver, for example, argued in *Soul on Ice* that black culture *does* have strong sexual implications— implications, however, which are desirable and which, by breaking down the artificial distinction in white culture between mind and body, can save the self from fragmentation and reaffirm man's faith in his own biology. Some advocates of women's liberation have seen their cause as a necessary assault on the long-dominant "masculine mystique"—a deeply engrained set of cultural attitudes that tend toward violence, exploitation, and the recognition of manhood, but not humanity. The purpose of women's liberation from this view is, indeed, to change the fundamental character of a society heretofore obsessed with toughness and artificially imposed sexual roles. For similar reasons Suzannah Lessard has said that "Gay is Good for Us All."

The essays in this section by Christopher Lasch, Sheldon Wolin and John Schaar, and Philip Slater focus on several groups or subcultures that have embraced social change: intellectuals, campus radicals of the 1960's, and recent advocates of the counterculture. Members of these subcultures have been relatively free from the sense of loss that characterized the KKK and the radical right. They have for the most part been the sons and daughters of privilege who have rejected the world of their parents with deliberation and fervor; in their eyes the dominant middle-class, technologically centered culture is vacuous and destructive. Samuel P. Hays's analysis of reactions to the Columbia University demonstrations of 1968 lends credence to Wolin's and Schaar's interpretation that campus confrontations reflect deep-seated cultural problems and extend far beyond specific issues such as Vietnam. Whereas the right tended to see the events at Columbia as yet another threat to the imperiled republic, the left assumed that the republic was not worth saving and interpreted the campus upheaval as only an important battle in the larger war to reconstruct society.

Most advocates of the counterculture have argued that major social change
in the nation will occur peacefully through a revolution in consciousness.
Philip Slater, who believes that America is in the midst of such a revolution,
discusses in this section some of the causes, meanings, and manifestations of
this shift in life styles. Skeptics of the counterculture have replied that it is
in reality a substitute for genuine social transformation because it confuses
changes in fashion with wide-ranging revolution. In the past, as historian
James Hitchcock has pointed out, political revolution has preceded cultural
change and revolutionary leaders such as Cromwell and Lenin have been cultural
reactionaries. Hitchcock and others have described the counterculture as the
joy of Madison Avenue—buying new clothes, music and drugs—thereby giving
new strength to the existing capitalistic, consumer culture.

Similarly, there are charges that the musical harbingers of the counterculture
(for example, the Beatles, the Rolling Stones, Janis Joplin, and Bob Dylan)
have been successful entrepreneurs engaged in a kind of "hip capitalism,"
lining their pockets but hardly uprooting the existing social system. The selection
included here by R. Serge Denisoff casts doubt upon the effectiveness of music
as a countercultural weapon, but for different reasons. Denisoff concludes
that popular songs of protest probably do little more than confirm the views of
those already in agreement with what they hear. For those who might reply
that the number of people predisposed to agree will grow as the new culture
enlarges its constituency, the essay "The Blueing of America" is especially
relevant. Peter and Brigitte Berger believe that the counterculture unquestionably
will affect the life styles of a few "beautiful people," but they doubt that it will
succeed in reducing the larger technologically and consumer-oriented portion
of society; instead, as bluebloods "drop out," blue collars, long relegated to
lesser positions, will rush to fill the vacancies.

The reader will undoubtedly have a number of questions regarding specific
essays. Are there, for example, analogies between the KKK that Jackson
describes and the supporters of Alabama's George Wallace? Do anxieties and
insecurities about social status encourage aggressive posturing and conspiratorial
fantasies? Assuming the emerging intellectual subculture was, in Lasch's
words, "predisposed to rebellion," is this still generally true? If intellectuals
tend to be critical of their society, what does this suggest about the relationship
of intellectuals to their society? If Schaar and Wolin are correct that campus
protests reflect a prevailing sense of powerlessness in a technological society,
how can one account for the suddenly quiet academic year of 1970–71 following
the turbulent upheavals that culminated in the bloody events of Spring 1970?
Were the observers of both the right and the left during the Columbia
demonstrations reading too much importance into the power and influence of
the university in American life? If, as Slater points out, the attitudes and
priorities of the counterculture are in large part products of an economy of

abundance, what will be the future of that culture in a tightening job market? (Peter Drucker's essay, the last in this volume, is most provocative regarding this.) Is Denisoff generalizing too much upon a small sampling? Does the new music indeed help to effect a change in consciousness which can ultimately reshape society? What about charges that the counterculture is primarily an example of "hip capitalism"? If the Bergers are correct, is the story of the counterculture a part of the larger theme of "the passing of the aristocracy"?

Yet, beneath specific questions relating to the essays, there are broad, general problems that concern the protest of values and status. Since matters of values and social status directly affect the individual's sense of purpose and worth, they are terribly complex to deal with. Moreover, since they, like beauty, rest in the eye of the beholder, protest that involves them may be most difficult to understand. The obsession of a radical rightist with Communist conspiracies may strike the critical observer as an example of paranoia. But, as historian William W. Freehling has emphasized, the crucial question is whether "irrational-sounding rhetoric offers clues to real social conflict." If the radical rightist is mouthing "irrational-sounding rhetoric," the tendency may be to dismiss him as a crank and turn his problem over to the psychiatrist. But if the observer attempts really to understand the rightist's fears he may discover that, again in Freehling's words, "monstrous fears feed on monstrous realities."[2]

This does not necessarily mean that the observer will himself come to believe that Moscow-manipulated groups are overwhelming the country. But it may make him more sensitive to the possibility that the values and perceived social status of the rightist are indeed very much in jeopardy. No Communist plot may be involved at all; but the process of social change (which in the rightist's eye may be proof of Communism) may very well be undermining a life style. Put differently, the rightist's analysis of the threat may be absurd; but his fear of the threat may have basis in reality. Similarly, the black man who sees a well-defined and conscious plot on the part of "whitey" to destroy black culture may fear a conspiracy that does not exist; but he may be quite correct in fearing for the safety and integrity of black culture.

The point is not merely academic. It may get at the foundation of much of America's discontent. During mid-century there was much confidence in an American consensus—a consensus of goals, ideals, purposes. Economic grievances hardly seemed insoluble in a nation of unprecedented affluence. Matters of discrimination did not seem insurmountable in a country that agreed fundamentally upon the ideal of equality of opportunity. But a rising gross national product and the early confidence of the civil rights movement did not

[2] William W. Freehling, "Paranoia and American History," *The New York Review of Books* (Sept. 23, 1971), pp. 36–38.

bring an end to discontent. A political "backlash" and anxieties about the loss of community only seemed to increase. By the 1970's, some Americans were beginning to wonder if the nature of their discontent perhaps had deeper roots than many had thought. All the talk about a deeply divided society and "pulling us together again" suggested that there were—and probably always had been—some very severe fissures running through the national consensus: fissures that ran along lines of values and social status and that may have widened with the pressures of twentieth-century social change.

During the conspiracy trial of the Chicago 7, prosecuting attorney Thomas Foran burst out in frustration that America had lost its children to "a freaking fag revolution." Such a statement may, of course, have been sheer hyperbole; but it may also have reflected anxieties that went deep down, anxieties that made Foran sincerely fear for the future of his life style (with all that it meant for his sense of personal worth and security) in a world of Abbie Hoffmans and Jerry Rubins. Is it really paranoia that worries parents who plead for universities not to put "dangerous" questions and ideas in the minds of their sons and daughters? Can it be that those questions and ideas—which the university would justifiably defend as vital to the very process of education— really make "all the difference in the world"? Is it paranoia among intellectuals that feeds their suspicions that "the life of the mind" is really superfluous (and generally ineffectual) in a market society concerned with "delivering the goods"? Is it the result of paranoia that the protagonists of the counter-cultural film, *Easy Rider,* were shown as victims of violence at the hands of "straight" society?

"This is my country," goes a popular tune. But the crucial question has been: Who is making that claim and who believes him?

Kenneth T. Jackson

Investigating the Ku Klux Klan of the 1920's, Kenneth T. Jackson, unlike other interpreters who located the Klan in rural America, discovers that much of its membership and leadership was to be found in the city. Bewildered by rapid technological change that seemed to be eroding old value systems, the urban Klansman was more bewildered by, and even fearful of, the new immigrants and in-migrant Negroes who came in increasing numbers to America's cities. Thus, the lower-middle-class American, feeling threatened primarily by ethnic change, protested by exchanging his white or more likely blue collar for a white sheet and hood. The reader

The Urban Klansman and the Fear of Change

should consider whether the Klansman of the Twenties is the spiritual ancestor of the "forgotten American" of the late Sixties and early Seventies. Professor Jackson is the author of *The Ku Klux Klan in the City, 1915– 1930* and co-editor of *American Vistas* and *Cities in American History*.

Among the questions hardest to answer about the urban Klan are those which concern the character of its membership and the nature of its appeal. Who was the urban Klansman? Why did he turn to the "Invisible Empire"? The questions defy simple answers but must be analyzed if the movement is to be understood. It will not suffice to call Klan members cowards and scoundrels or to dismiss the secret order as a simple manifestation of ignorance and bigotry. Most members were not innately depraved or anxious to subvert American institutions. Rather they regarded their initiation as a patriotic gesture and believed the tenets of "one hundred percent Americanism" to be both moral and Christian. As sociologist Frank Tannenbaum has observed: "Sincerity is a common virtue, and must not be denied in an analysis of group behavior."

There is general agreement among students of the Invisible Empire that the typical Klansman was decent, hard-working, and patriotic, if narrowminded. But very little specific research has been done on the socioeconomic status of the average member. Most observers have placed the responsibility for nativist resurgence on the "common man" rather than upon either social extreme. . . .

This study has sought to reopen the inquiry into the socioeconomic

From *The Ku Klux Klan in the City: 1915–1930* by Kenneth T. Jackson, pp. 238, 239–245. Copyright © 1967 by Oxford University Press, Inc. Reprinted by permission. Footnotes have been omitted.

character of the Ku Klux Klan. The evidence indicates that in the city the secret order was a lower-middle-class movement. Few men of wealth, education, or professional position affiliated with the Invisible Empire; the exceptions, such as Dr. John Galen Locke in Denver and Vice President Edwin Debarr of the University of Oklahoma, usually served in high Klan office. White-collar workers in general provided a substantial minority of Klan membership and included primarily struggling independent businessmen, advertising dentists, lawyers, and chiropractors, ambitious and unprincipled politicians and salesmen, and poorly paid clerks. The greatest source of Klan support came from rank-and-file nonunion, blue-collar employees of large businesses and factories. Miserably paid, they rarely boasted of as much as a high school education and more commonly possessed only a grammar or "free school" background. Their religious loyalty was to conservative, nonritualistic Protestant denominations such as the Baptist, Methodist, or Christian churches.

Although evidence regarding the geographical background of the membership is meager, there was a statistically significant correlation between Klan success and population growth. For example, the secret order was active and strong in such cities as Detroit, Memphis, Dayton, Youngstown, Dallas, and Houston, all of which claimed high growth rates between 1910 and 1930. Conversely, it was weak in comparatively stable Boston, St. Louis, New Orleans, Providence, and Louisville. But Klansmen were not necessarily urban newcomers. On the contrary, in the only city for which statistics are available (Knoxville), one-third of the members were lifelong residents and the remainder had lived in the community for an average of more than nine years. These figures suggest that urban newcomers were the cause rather than the source of Klan strength.

The appeal of "one hundred percent Americanism" to urban, lower-middle-class fundamentalists was undoubtedly complex. It was not, however, related to a suppressed penchant for violence. The notion must be dispelled that Klansmen were essentially sadists reveling in murder and torture. Scores of floggings, tar and featherings, and other forms of physical abuse were reported in the South between 1920 and 1925, and no fewer than six murders were directly attributable to the secret order. But lawlessness had a long tradition in the region, and not all violations of justice could be charged to the Klan account. This basic fact was recognized by both the American Civil Liberties Union and *New Republic,* which declared in 1927: "Some hoodlums signed up in order to participate in night-riding, but it is safe to say that 90 percent of the total membership never indulged in such practices." Outside the South only a very small number of members participated in any form of violence. In fact, in many parts of the country (such as Perth Amboy, New Jersey; Niles, Ohio; and Carnegie, Pennsylvania), Klansmen were more often the victims than the instigators of foul play.

Fear of change, not vindictiveness or cruelty, was the basic motivation of the urban Klansman. He was disillusioned by the Great War and its aftermath, by the Senate rejection of the League of Nations, and by the economic recession which came in the summer and fall of 1920. He was aware of the Red Scare and of reports of "petting parties," "wild dancing," and other indications of a revolution in morals. Sensing that the traditional values, religion, and way of life of an older America were in danger, he donated ten dollars to a hypocritical secret society in a vague attempt to halt the forces of time. Ordinarily, the decade of the Twenties is thought of as an era of "normalcy." Actually, it was a period of rapid, almost bewildering, change; the Model T, the telephone, the radio, the airplane, and the motion picture were transforming American life. But the changes of greatest concern to the urban Knight were ethnic and racial, not technological.

Two far-reaching, distinct migration patterns provided the basis for the phenomenal career of the Ku Klux Klan. The first was a shift in the sources of European immigration, particularly noticeable after 1890, from the English, Irish, Scandinavians, and Germans of earlier years to the peasantry of southern and eastern Europe—Hungarians, Italians, Slovaks, Czechs, and Poles. The predominantly Catholic and Jewish newcomers frightened nativists by clinging tenaciously to Old World customs and celebrations, by establishing hundreds of foreign-language newspapers, and by voting for the supposedly corrupt and inefficient urban political machines. Spurred by Lothrop Stoddard's *The Rising Tide of Color* and Madison Grant's *Passing of the Great Race,* older Americans made excited appeals for immigration restriction. Their basic fear was that if the immigration flow were not shut off or drastically reduced, then white, Anglo-Saxon Protestants would become a minority in the land of their fathers, and the nation would be ethnically transformed.

The second major migration pattern of concern was that of American Negroes from farm to city and from South to North. First noticeable about 1910, the trend was accelerated by World War I, which restricted the supply of foreign labor, increased the demands of industry, and encouraged many industries to experiment with Negro labor. An additional factor was the boll weevil, which ravaged hundreds of thousands of acres of fertile cotton fields and forced white farmers temporarily to abandon their custom of advancing money to field hands. The traditional Negro dependence upon southern agriculture was weakened; between 1910 and 1920 the Negro rural population fell by 239,000 while the urban total increased by 874,000. Almost 400,000 Negroes moved to southern cities in the decade, and an even larger number trekked to the urban North. During the Twenties the black stream became a flood and an additional 600,000 Negroes crossed the Mason-Dixon line. The impact was startling, particularly in the Midwest. In the twenty years between 1910 and 1930, the nonwhite population of Chicago increased from 44,000 to 160,000, that of Detroit from 6,000 to 125,000, and that of Indianapolis from 22,000 to 44,000.

Ultimately, both migration patterns posed a threat to white Protestants throughout the United States, but the immediate impact was primarily upon urban residential stability. By both choice and necessity the immigrants and Negroes crowded into ghettos, often located near the center of the city. White Protestants, on the other hand, were more likely to reside nearer the edge of a community. Thus divided geographically as well as religiously, socially, economically, and politically, the inner core and the residential fringe were consistent opponents and created an intra-urban environment favorable for the growth of the Ku Klux Klan.

Neighborhood transition has been a neglected but omnipresent dimension of American urban history for at least the last one hundred years, but its rapidity and extent increased markedly in the first quarter of the twentieth century as immigrants and Negroes crowded into burgeoning cities. Some physical expansion of the bulging racial and ethnic ghettos was inevitable; but equally threatening to the tranquillity of the older (i.e. white Protestant) residents was the desire of ambitious second-generation immigrants and successful Negroes to escape completely from the old neighborhoods and to buy or rent in the "zone of emergence," the broad belt separating the core of the city from its outer residential fringe. The "zone of emergence" was usually made up of working-class neighborhoods of modest homes and apartments, and it was here, among white laborers, that the Invisible Empire thrived. Unable to afford a fine home far removed from minority problems, the potential Klansman could not live along Chicago's Lake Shore Drive or Indianapolis's Fall Creek Parkway, or in Memphis's Hein Park or Atlanta's Druid Hills. Rather, he was forced by economic necessity to live in older transitional areas close to his place of employment. He was bewildered by the rapid pace of life and frustrated by his inability to slow the changes which seemed so constant and so oppressive. He perhaps remembered an earlier neighborhood transition and was frightened at the prospect of a Negro or a Pole coming into his block and causing him to sell his house at a low price. Unable to escape and hesitant to act alone, the threatened citizen welcomed the security and respectability of a large group. Seeking to stabilize his world and maintain a neighborhood status quo, he turned to the promise of the Klan. Not a reaction against the rise of the city to dominance in American life, the Invisible Empire was rather a reaction against the aspirations of certain elements within the city.

The problems of the potential Klansman were complicated by his economic condition. Whether a struggling cafe proprietor in Indianapolis, a lumber mill worker in Knoxville, a milkman in Chicago, or a cotton oil company employee in Memphis, he had obviously been left at the post in an economic race he perhaps only inadequately understood. His wages were below average, his tasks often menial, his responsibilities slight, and his opportunity for advancement remote. Yet this was an age heavily influenced by the Horatio Alger notion that hard work would be rewarded and that all Americans had ample opportunity in the competition for

200

prestige and economic advantage. Having fought his way above the lowest rungs of the financial ladder, the potential Klansman remained something less than a success. Life seemed to offer him little dignity or personal significance. Moreover, he was faced with increasing competition from Catholics and from a new kind of Negro, who seemed anxious to take his job and live in his neighborhood. What was he to do?

Ira S. Rohter

The Righteous Rightists

Do members of America's "radical right" assume that political stance because they are victims of status frustration? Ira S. Rohter conducted a study involving 169 individuals classified as rightists and 167 as non-rightists to test that theory. Drawing upon newspaper articles listing members of the John Birch Society and the Liberty Amendment Committee in a northwestern city, "letters to the editor," and contribution and sub-scription lists to another radical right organization and publication, Rohter formulated his sample of rightists; the non-rightist sample was compiled from content analysis of other "letters to the editor" and from referenda petitions. Thus, Rohter lends empirical strength to the status theories explaining the proliferation during the 1950's and 1960's of such organizations as Robert Welch's John Birch Society, Rev. Carl McIntyre's Twentieth Century Reformation, Dr. Fred Schwarz's Christian Anti-Communist Crusade and Rev. Billy James Hargis' Christian Crusade. Is there a relationship between the Klansmen described by Jackson in the previous selection and Rohter's righteous rightists? A more complete report on the study, "Social and Psychological Determinants of Radical Rightism," appears in Robert A. Schoen-berger (ed.), *The American Right Wing: Readings on Political Behavior.*

The Watts riots have been traced directly to plans laid down by Lenin in Moscow. (The Los Angeles Communists, who organized the riots, cleverly blew up their own headquarters in order to appear as innocent martyrs.)

Progressive education (a term including most modern educational methods) was inaugurated by a Columbia University professor on his return from Moscow; it is a deliberate design to expedite the Red take-over by turning our children into un-Christian, un-American, mindless, and will-less robots. For proof of success, we have only to look at Berkeley.

The two stories above—much more heavily elaborated and "documented"—are typical of the items that appear in radical right publications. They illustrate well the characteristic that distinguishes radical rightists from other Americans.

From Ira S. Rohter, "The Righteous Rightists," *Trans-Action,* 4 (May 1967), pp. 27–35. Copyright © May, 1967 by Transaction, Inc., New Brunswick, New Jersey. Reprinted with permission of publisher and author.

Radical rightists are not merely conservatives or even arch-conservatives. What occupies them full time, what gives them their unique voltage and drive, is not their reverence for old-fashioned fiscal policies and morals, but what Richard Hofstadter calls their "paranoid style"—the overriding and galvanizing belief in a gigantic, insidious Communist conspiracy that has infiltrated and infected all levels of American government and most of its social institutions. The calm conservative who would merely like to see a balanced budget and less welfare is not really a rightist, and they both know it.

Another distinct characteristic by which the rightist (I shall call him that for brevity) may be known is his dedication to *action*. When the enemy is already within the gates attacking all that we hold dear, the true patriot does not sit idly by discussing the income tax or civil rights—he mounts the counterattack.

For the purposes of this study, therefore, (and because membership lists and other identifications are often secret) I have used these two characteristics—belief in Communist conspiracy and in direct action—to define and describe rightists, and I have drawn my samples accordingly.

WHO'S RIGHT?

How do people get to be rightists? A major thesis of this article is that rightists are the victims of *status frustration*. That is, for some reason they are dissatisfied or insecure about their places in society and feel that others do not esteem them sufficiently; further, they express their frustration, and compensate for it, by political and social acts which give them emotional identity and support as well as real influence.

Many psychologists regard the striving for self-regard as an essential social and psychological need. To a large extent self-regard must depend on how others regard us. Nobody can really tolerate feeling downgraded or ignored; he must make some defense. The rightist chooses the path of radical right ideology and action, which pinpoints and personifies his enemy as a horrendous evil (and the rightist, therefore, as a kind of St. George) and gives him a means to combat it—not merely for himself but as a champion for all decent mankind.

The rightist becomes loudly superpatriotic—which makes anyone disagreeing suspect of un-Americanism. Those who are higher or richer than he (as the Communist-infiltrated world sees them) or who possess different values can be pulled down to their true levels—below the rightist on the scale of virtue—by being exposed as "Communist."

DUEL WITH THE DEVIL

Of course, such an orientation—and such action—depend heavily on a highly charged emotionalism and a closed system of paranoid-like logic that is impervious to objective facts that happen to differ. For instance, Communism cannot be considered primarily a political, social, and economic movement and system of thought capable of objective study. Such an idea horrifies the rightist. Communism is Satan personified; it can be faced only in a fight to the death, and only by those properly armed and inoculated.

People who undergo status frustration generally fall into three categories: the *decliners,* the *new arrivals,* and the *value keepers.*

The decliners. These are the people in our modern, changing society who are going down in the social scale—undeservedly, as they see it.

Modern technology and modern organizations increasingly require new skills, new orientations, more education. Those trained under different and outmoded disciplines (small farmers, for instance) and those with insufficient or outdated educations must feel their positions becoming more and more insecure.

Also threatened are the old professional and entrepreneur classes, especially from the smaller communities: the small-town general practitioner in medicine, the small home builder, gas station owner, neighborhood grocer—in fact most independent operators trying to survive in the shadows of the great corporations, large labor unions, and big government agencies. The well-educated professionals and corporate executives are taking over the small businessman's role in the community. He is being shoved aside; the hard work and independence on which he had built his self-esteem and his concept of the good and righteous life become increasingly worthless and irrelevant. He begins to ask *why?* Who is doing this to me?

A similar process affects workers, both white and blue collar, displaced by new methods and machinery. They find themselves useless, and their self-regard wavers. The elderly without funds are in an even worse situation—our society no longer respects age, especially when it pulls no economic weight.

As these groups decline, their consciousness of rejection is made even more acute by the rise of those formerly considered low-class or rejected. An Irish Catholic, grandson of an immigrant, is elected President; a Negro "agitator" receives many honors and confers frequently at the White House. Jews are everywhere in prominent places. Again the decliner—often of old white stock—asks *why?*

The new arrivals. Status frustration occurs not only on the way down, but on the way up. There is almost always a lag between the time the gauche new arrival achieves success and the time those who got there first accept him as an equal. Like the decliner he can easily feel that he has come into a closed and unfriendly society that will not recognize virtue. He is especially upset since he earned it himself in the good old American way instead of being handed prestige on a silver platter.

To the newly arrived, radical rightism can be a potent weapon to destroy their mighty enemies—those who had the opportunity to be better educated, better mannered, more cosmopolitan, and, obviously, more prone to liberal ideas and "bohemian" behavior and immoralities. The charge of "Communism" is a great leveler, and the newly rich can often be counted upon to be twice as narrowly patriotic as anybody.

The value keepers. Those moving up or down the ladder of success are bound to find themselves, temporarily at least, among aliens who know not the Lord, but so should those who merely stand still long enough in a society that changes as fast as ours.

A person of any conviction or integrity has social and moral values and beliefs that help determine his behavior, his self-definition, and his place in the community. But let the community begin to re-examine those values critically or displace them with others, and the foundation of his whole universe begins to turn to sand.

For the great majority of us, many of the traditional rural or small town ways or virtues are no longer useful or true. Modern society needs education and expertise more than hard work and self-denial; an expanding economy rather than thrift; organized community welfare programs rather than primary reliance on savings, personal charity, relatives, and contemplation of the sufferings of Job.

Moreover, the preponderance of political and economic power, for good or ill, has definitely shifted from the country with its white settlers to the metropolis with its combinations of minority populations. Those whose beliefs and behavior were shaped by older traditions—who, as they see it, settled and built this country—now find themselves, in effect, increasingly disinherited.

Even more important than the objective loss of power and prestige are the *subjective* feelings of loss, of being displaced and discredited. God and the devil, good and evil, are absolutes and do not change; therefore, the change that discredits and displaces the old morality must be evil triumphing over good. Only by such rationalization can true believers retain their orientation and self-regard.

The values defended include hard work, saving, prudent investment, and self-discipline—the Protestant ethic. As the name implies, these values are not only economic but moral, with deep psychological meaning. They are supposed to result in independence and individualism, as the rightist sees them. An apparent attack on them—such as increased government control or taxes—becomes not only an economic change but an immorality and must be answered.

Therefore, as experience demonstrates daily, those most closely identified with older traditional values reduce and discuss almost all social problems to moralistic terms: If the wayward society or individual would only cease transgression and return to the old tried-and-true paths of religion, decency, and family virtue, all would in time be well.

This accounts for much of the intense and emotional opposition to social change by rightists—the counterattack, often blind, to government controls, integration, religious secularism, welfare, the United Nations, foreign aid, Supreme Court decisions, modern education, and even such apparently non-controversial scientific and health advances as fluoridation and mental health programs.

Fundamentalism is an important source of rightist fervor. In fact, from their titles and rhetoric, it is hard to distinguish between a rightist political rally and an evangelistic campaign—note the Rev. Carl McIntire's "Twentieth Century Reformation" and Dr. Fred Schwarz's "Christian Anti-Communist Crusade." Communism, a twentieth-century abomination, becomes the catchall for everything that seems evil and unacceptable in the easygoing, affluent, sophisticated, urban twentieth century.

These then are the theses advanced about the rightist which I tested in this study:

Rightists are people undergoing status frustration. They feel they do not have the prestige and power they should have if the world were just—and their enemies have too much. They are on the move as far as status is concerned—either they are going down in a changing world (which should be true of most of them), they are standing still as the world passes them by, or they are rising more rapidly in economic position than in social recognition.

They identify themselves with the older, traditional (Protestant ethic) values of work, religion, and morality, so that their fight for status recognition also becomes a crusade for truth, justice, decency, God, and America.

They believe that their troubles—and therefore also the attack against Christianity and America—are caused by an all-pervasive conspiracy, wholly evil and implacable, called Communism.

They relieve their anxieties and feelings of resentment and inadequacy by radical right belief and activity. This gives them an effective explanation and compensation for their difficulties, a means of bringing their enemies down, and a method of gaining power, prestige, and mutual support.

Do these hypotheses survive empirical examination?

To start with objective findings first: Are the rightists of our sample actually undergoing status mobility and frustration?

The data show that there are only 10 percent of rightists in the highest occupations, such as executives and professionals, compared to 24 percent of non-rightists; and that rightists are overrepresented among the lower-middle class (such as clerical and salesworkers)—15 to 4 percent.

Further, nearly twice as many rightists as others are retired—removed, for most practical purposes, from economic importance to society altogether. Rightists also tend to be older (median age 54 compared to 45) and are more often self-employed (although at lower levels)—if businessmen, they tend to run smaller businesses; if professionals, their standing is lower.

In profile, therefore, the radical rightist is older, less secure financially, and less often an important part of a major modern industrial enterprise; he more often has a low-prestige, white-collar job or is thrown on his own resources—retired or operator of a marginal "independent" business. Such a picture is quite consistent with the status-frustration hypothesis; such a person, especially if he identifies with an older tradition that was once dominant, could hardly help feeling frustrated.

Occupation alone, however, is not enough to measure social standing. What of education? In our increasingly sophisticated society, education is not only a necessity but a mark of prestige, especially in the middle and upper classes. But even in these occupational strata the rightists have less education than their non-rightist equivalents. In the highest levels (high executives, proprietors, major professionals, etc.) almost twice as many non-rightists as rightists have graduate degrees (64 percent to 33 percent), while three times as many rightists (12 percent to 4 percent) never went beyond high school. In the middle levels over twice as many non-rightists got college degrees (27 percent to 12 percent) while over twice as many rightists (54 percent to 24) never went beyond high school.

What about mobility? Comparing a male rightist's (or a female rightist's husband's) occupation and education with those of his father (this is called "inter-generational status mobility"), we found, as hypothesized, that the rightist did undergo much more status mobility than non-rightists, most often downward. . . .

THAT OLD-TIME RELIGION

Are rightists to any significant extent fundamentalists? Belief in traditional values, along with many rightist attitudes, was earlier related to religious fundamentalism. Empirically, this is true. Rightists very much subscribe to fundamentalist tenets and belong to these churches; nearly half the rightists (44 percent compared to 17 percent of the non-rightists) are affiliated with fundamentalist denominations. Rightists were also more often raised in rural areas or small towns, environments most likely to produce traditionalism and hostility toward modernity.

So much for objective factors. How do the people themselves view their plights?

Fewer rightists than non-rightists actually belong to the upper class; but more of them *rated themselves* "upper class." When asked, "How hard do you think it is for people today to move upward from one social class to another?" their answers revealed a view of society as essentially closed, dominated by personalities, controlled by the wrong kinds of people:

> Not much opportunity anymore; it's getting harder; depends on having money, knowing the right people.

The views of the non-rightists were much more objective and impersonal:

> Depends on education; must work hard and have abilities to get it; special skills; hard to change direction of early life. . . .

We asked, "Do you think that people . . . influential in this community are, in *general,* friendly . . . or cliquish?" Rightists answered "cliquish and unfriendly" more often than non-rightists. When those answering "cliquish" were asked to give reasons, rightists more often indicated belief in a closed structure run by a small group:

> Old residents tend to look on new people as outsiders; certain families run things here; segregated groups want their own way; all have common political views.

The rightist, then, more often sees himself as the outsider, discriminated against in a closed society run by an elite.

What about the predicted concern with the Protestant ethic? We asked, "Are there any differences between what you believe should be the American way of life, and the way things are done in the country nowadays?" "In what way are things different?" Typically, from the rightists:

> Morality and standards are going bad; the American way of life is deteriorating because of a suppression of morality; we need a moral and spiritual revival among our leaders; we need to follow the Ten Commandments more.

RUGGED INDIVIDUALISTS

What about individual initiative, self-reliance, respect for authority?

> I am worried about the drift of the country; the amount of crime and disrespect for authority shows things are going the other way; we must instill more emphasis on respect, integrity, and individual responsibility; parents aren't teaching their children the right things anymore.

Traditional morality and values dominate many rightists' perception of everything. No matter what the topic—what things they worried about, what community concerns they had, what qualities they admired, what things Communists actually believed in, whatever—sooner or later they indicated that if we would only return to the old morality every problem would be solved.

Our findings are clear: The rightists are more dissatisfied with the values of contemporary American society; they adhere to the "old truths" and believe everyone else should "return" to them. They suffer severe frustration because of this, a frustration heavily reinforced by a religious righteousness expressed in absolute and positive terms.

"In your own case . . . do you think that *everyone* gives you as much respect as *you feel you* deserve?" This question was deliberately worded to emphasize extremes—yet rightists answered "no" more frequently than non-rightists. This is true both of rightists who are on the way up and those on the way down; but the decliners say "no" *twice* as often as those on the rise—emphasizing that it is the losers who are most impelled to

208

seek radical rightism. (Presumably, once those on the rise secure recognition, they will cease attacking high-status people and changing times.)

Rightists felt more unaccepted than non-rightists, and rightists on the decline more unaccepted than anybody.

Does joining radical right organizations and causes help the rightist combat his anxieties successfully? By being more patriotic and anti-Communist than anybody else, the rightist seems to wrap himself in greatness and goodness, in importance, righteousness, and self-satisfaction. He is a savior carrying out a holy crusade. As the *John Birch Society Bulletin* (November, 1964) points out, if you join their society ". . . you feel a tremendous satisfaction . . . to save for our children and their children the glorious country and humane civilization which we ourselves inherited."

We asked them to select "two great Americans" and describe what is admirable about them. Later, we asked them to describe "the typical member of an anti-Communist group"—that is, in effect, an idealized version of themselves. Their great people, they said, were "true" Americans and "very" patriotic; 75 percent found the same things true of themselves (compared to 22 percent of non-rightists, who tended to use less extravagant terms). Courage, strength, and "guts" were likewise qualities they shared with the great, as was deep Christian faith and high moral standards. And 50 percent further saw the great to be honest, truthful, and sincere—like themselves.

Non-rightists, however, viewed rightists very differently—"dishonest," "hypocrites," "no integrity," "use character assassination."

This tactic of rightists to acquire status and importance by associating themselves closely with the great and the good is perhaps best illustrated by their emphasis on "self-education." They are, in fact, less well-educated than the non-rightists. But the world of radical rightism is full of parades of quasi-experts, study groups, monographs, footnotes, and bibliographies—almost all with no standing among scholars. But the rightists study them avidly, mention intelligence and education highly among those things they admire in the great, and give themselves strong ratings as "intellectuals, very brilliant," "well informed," "people with sound judgment, good reasoning," and "lots of sense." Needless to add, non-rightists hold almost precisely the opposite view of them.

THE RIGHTIST PERSONALITY

The need to relieve status anxiety and to attack values that do not conform to their beliefs are not enough to explain why some people become radical rightists and others, in like circumstances, do not. The rightist tends also to have certain personality characteristics—to be, in effect, a particular kind of human being.

Simplism. Psychologists say that a basic need of man is his desire for meaning, to understand what is happening to him. In an important sense the rightist, a traditionalist in changing times, is adrift in frightening darkness—he needs landmarks, he needs simple guidelines, before he loses direction altogether. Radical rightism gives him this "understanding"— and this security. All becomes clear and very simple. It is all a conspiracy. Nothing is really changed—God is still in His heaven; but He needs help.

Extremely simple explanations have great attractions for the confused. They are a necessity for those personalities who have what psychologists call "simplistic cognitive structure"—who have a strong need for simple, firm, stereotyped views of people and events, with no place for ambivalence and ambiguity. Such persons reject unbelievers, need external authorities, and, for emotional reasons, hold their beliefs so tightly that compromise is intolerable.

Testing for this rigidity of belief, using statements on Communism and Russia ("Communism is a total evil." "The Soviet Union is 'mellowing.' "), on intolerance of ambiguity ("There is usually only one right way to do anything."), on anti-compromise and closed-minded stances ("The compromise of principles leads to nothing but destruction." "A group which tolerates too much difference of opinion cannot exist for long."), we found the rightist to fit this description. He is intolerant of ambiguity, opposed to compromise, and closed-minded.

Extra-punitiveness. It is difficult not to be struck by the strident negativism and combativeness of rightist writings, thought, and speech. Terrible things exist all about, the future is steeped in gloom; everything is in strong blacks and whites—the forces of light are locked in mortal combat with the forces of darkness. It is not only necessary, therefore, but moral and virtuous to be resentful, discontented, belligerent, and full of hate. While the rightist justifies his behavior in the name of Americanism and anti-Communism, the actual thrust of his attacks are against the political, social, and intellectual leaders of the community—those who have the respect and influence he does not.

This vehement scapegoating is characteristic of a psychological defense mechanism called "extra-punitiveness." The extra-punitive have a great deal of free-floating hate and aggression they project outward, blaming others or the world for their personal or social failures. Their view of the world is paranoid.

We tested for extra-punitiveness by asking what measures they would take against "Communists" and, in later questions, against other "safe" scapegoats (those with few defenders, such as delinquents, sex deviates, homosexuals, and "disrespectful persons"). Rightists were more in favor of strong measures against Communists (sample statement with high response: "Take them out and hang them"); but their *generalized* hostility showed up even more clearly in their attitudes toward nonpolitical deviants. (Sample statements: "There is hardly anything lower than a person who does not feel a great love, gratitude, and respect for his parents." "Homosexuals are hardly better than criminals and ought to be severely punished.")

Rightists not only condemn Communists but define them so differently that it is sometimes hard to believe they are talking about real people. There is a heavy emphasis on religion and black-or-white morality: To believe that we can live with Communism is to be a dupe or worse. Communism is the anti-Christ, it is evil incarnate. This allows for convenient projection of personal hatreds. Rightists often find the highly educated—including professors—to be Communists. "From what racial or religious groups are Communists most likely to come?" Rightists frequently mentioned "atheists," "Jews," "Methodists," "Unitarians," and "modernistic religious groups." (Non-rightists denied more frequently and more vigorously that race or religion was involved.)

Powerlessness. It is a basic tenet of rightism that individual freedom—as they define it—is being lost and that the ordinary citizen (meaning themselves) is being ignored. Is "the federal government . . . extending too much . . . power into . . . everyday life?" Nearly 70 percent of the rightists "agreed very much." "Are there any groups . . . that you think have too much power or influence?" "Yes," the rightists said, significantly more often than non-rightists, and listed labor (and its leaders), Communists, big government, and such groups as the ADA, ACLU, and Council on Foreign Relations. Who has *too little* power? They mentioned twice as many groups as the non-rightists, most often the two surrogates for themselves: the individual "common man" and "conservative" organizations.

Do rightists, as hypothesized, feel maligned and persecuted? They pointed out with considerable heat that their idealized "great men," with whom they identify, were mistreated: "Got a raw deal; treated badly by others, his country; a victim of injustice."

Alienation. We found our rightists to be significantly more alienated politically than the non-rightists, to feel that their elected public officials do not actually represent them, that local officials avoid or ignore them, responding only to special interests. On referenda on community issues—such as new bond issues or taxes—they more consistently than others vote "no."

Do they trust other people? (A person who feels lost, who has little sense of personal competence, often lives in a jungle of suspicion and distrust.) We found a significant association between radical rightism and low trust in others. Generally, the rightists in our sample were less often involved in social and community organizations.

Finally, the rightist *feels* that by joining other rightists he can overcome his own powerlessness and estrangement.

Extra-punitiveness, a paranoid view of society, a great deal of free-floating hostility and aggression, desire for direct action, a rigid devotion to absolutes in religion and morality and to black-or-white standards—all these characteristics describe particular kinds of closed-minded, insecure, authoritarian persons undergoing particular kinds of status crises. And that is who the radical rightists are.

Christopher Lasch

Intellectuals and "The New Radicalism"

When Herman Melville described himself as "an exile here," he articulated the feelings of isolation that came to dominate the views of American intellectuals as a group. Historian Christopher Lasch emphasizes that this process of alienation was a result of the fragmentation of industrial society and the failure of the nation to define the role of the intellectual. The intellectual's growing sense of estrangement from the mainstream of his society had a profound effect in shaping a "new radicalism," that went far beyond conventional politics and attacked the middle-class culture itself. Professor Lasch has explored the nature of American radicalism in *The New Radicalism in America, American Liberals and the Russian Revolution, The Agony of the American Left,* and in essays in *The Nation, The New York Review of Books* and other journals.

$\mathbf{M}$y main argument . . . is that modern radicalism or liberalism can best be understood as a phase of the social history of the intellectuals. In the United States, to which this study is confined, the connection is particularly clear. There, the rise of the new radicalism coincided with the emergence of the intellectual as a distinctive social type.

The intellectual may be defined, broadly, as a person for whom thinking fulfills at once the function of work and play; more specifically, as a person whose relationship to society is defined, both in his eyes and in the eyes of the society, principally by his presumed capacity to comment upon it with greater detachment than those more directly caught up in the practical business of production and power. Because his vocation is to be a critic of society, in the most general sense, and because the value of his criticism is presumed to rest on a measure of detachment from the current scene, the intellectual's relation to the rest of society is never entirely comfortable; but it has not always been as uncomfortable as it is today in the United States. "Anti-intellectualism" offers only a partial explanation of the present tension between intellectuals and American society. The rest of the explanation lies in the increased sensitivity of intellectuals to attacks on themselves as a group. It lies in the intellectuals' own sense of

From *The New Radicalism in America 1889–1963,* by Christopher Lasch, pp. ix–xv, 147–49, 254–56. Copyright © 1965 by Christopher Lasch. Reprinted by permission of Alfred A. Knopf, Inc.

themselves, not simply as individuals involved in a common undertaking, the somewhat hazardous business of criticism, but as members of a beleaguered minority. The tension is a function, in other words, of the class-consciousness of the intellectuals themselves.

Intellectuals have existed in all literate societies, but they have only recently come to constitute a kind of subculture. In fact, the word "intellectual" does not seem to have found its way into American usage much before the turn of the century. Before that, most intellectuals belonged to the middle class, and though they may sometimes have felt themselves at odds with the rest of the community, they did not yet conceive of themselves as a class apart. The modern intellectual, even when he chooses to throw himself into the service of his country or attempts to embrace the common life about him, gives himself away by the very self-consciousness of his gestures. He agonizes endlessly over the "role of the intellectuals." A hundred years ago these discussions, and the passion with which they are conducted, would have been incomprehensible.

The growth of a class (or more accurately, a "status group") of intellectuals[1] is part of a much more general development: the decline of the sense of community, the tendency of the mass society to break down into its component parts, each having its own autonomous culture and maintaining only the most tenuous connections with the general life of the society—which as a consequence has almost ceased to exist. The most obvious victims of this process in our own time are adolescents, who live increasingly in a world all their own. The emergence of the intellectual class in the first couple of decades of the present century reveals the workings of the same process at a somewhat earlier period in time.

The intellectual class, then, is a distinctively modern phenomenon, the product of the cultural fragmentation that seems to characterize industrial and postindustrial societies. It is true that in the United States the agencies of social cohesion (church, state, family, class) were never very strong in the first place. Nevertheless, there existed during the first two and a half centuries of American history a sort of cultural consensus at the heart of which was a common stake in capitalism and a common tradition of patriarchal authority. There were social classes but, compared to Europe or even to American society during the colonial period, remarkably little class-consciousness; and whatever the real opportunities for social advancement, the myth of equal opportunity was sufficiently strong to minimize the tensions and resentments which later came to characterize American society.

> The whole society (wrote Tocqueville in 1831), seems to have melted into a middle class. . . . All the Americans whom we have

[1] For the distinction between classes and status groups (subcultures?), see Max Weber: "Class, Status, Party," in H. H. Gerth and C. Wright Mills, eds., *From Max Weber: Essays in Sociology* (New York: Oxford University Press, 1958), pp. 180–94.

encountered up to now, even to the simplest *shop salesman,* seem to have received, or wish to appear to have received, a good education. Their manners are grave, deliberate, reserved, and they all wear the same clothes. All the customs of life show this mingling of the two classes which in Europe take so much trouble to keep apart.[2]

Divisive influences tended to be local and regional rather than social; and the very intensity of local and regional rivalries enhanced the social solidarity of each particular part of the country, so that Southerners, for instance, found what seemed to be a common interest in resisting the encroachments of the Yankee. Under these conditions men of intellectual inclination had very little sense of themselves as a class. The South—the preindustrial society par excellence—offers a particularly striking example of the degree to which such men shared the general aspirations of the *bourgeoisie,* the highest form of which, as is customary in bourgeois societies, was to set up as country gentlemen on lordly estates.[3]

It was only in the North that writers and thinkers began to acquire a sense of being at odds with the rest of society. The transcendentalists and reformers of the 1830's and 1840's, in their protest against the materialism of a society dominated by the Cotton Whigs, in some respects anticipated the attacks of modern intellectuals on the middle class. But the truth of the matter is suggested by the ease with which the reforming impulse after the Civil War was reabsorbed into the stream of genteel culture. The war itself had a unifying effect on New England, as on the South.[4] Abolitionism petered out in mugwumpery, a form of extreme sectional particularism. Indeed, the whole New England tradition—with which American reform until the twentieth century was so completely bound up—precisely embodied everything against which later intellectuals were in rebellion, everything associated with the cultural ascendancy of the middle class.

The term "middle class" seems nowadays to encounter as much resistance, among historians at least, as the term "intellectual." I have been told by historians that the term means nothing, that indeed the "middle class" is a myth. It is true that the term has often been loosely used. But I do not understand why that should prevent its being used quite precisely. I have used it here simply as a synonym for *bourgeoisie,* to describe a class of people which derives its income from the ownership of

---

[2] George W. Pierson, *Tocqueville and Beaumont in America* (New York: Oxford University Press, 1938), pp. 69–70.

[3] See William R. Taylor, *Cavalier and Yankee* (New York: George Braziller, 1961), especially the chapter on William Wirt, pp. 67–94.

[4] Antislavery politics, wrote Henry Adams (*The Education of Henry Adams* [New York: Modern Library, 1931], p. 26), represented a "violent reaction" which swept New England "back into Puritanism with a violence as great as that of a religious war."

property and in particular from trade and commerce—a definition, when applied to American society in the nineteenth century, which includes most of the farming population as well as the bulk of those who lived in towns. It does not include the salaried employees (clerks, salesmen, managers, professionals), whom C. Wright Mills has called the "new" middle class—itself a creation of the twentieth century. The cultural style of the old as distinguished from the new middle class was characterized by that combination of patriarchal authority and the sentimental veneration of women which is the essence of the genteel tradition. Everything I mean to catch up in the phrase "middle-class culture" seems to me ultimately to derive from these characteristic familial arrangements. It is no wonder that the revolt of the intellectuals so often took the form of a rebellion against the conventional family. The family was the agency which transmitted from generation to generation—and not only transmitted, but embodied, down to the last detail of domestic architecture—the enormous weight of respectable culture; as its defenders would have said, of civilization itself.

Everyone who has studied the history of American reform agrees that the reform tradition underwent a fundamental change around 1900. Some people identify the change with a changing attitude toward government, a new readiness to use government (particularly the federal government) as an instrument of popular control. Others associate it with an abandonment of the old populistic distrust of large-scale institutions, like corporations, and an acceptance of the inevitability of the concentration of wealth and power. Still others define the change as a movement away from the dogma of natural rights toward a relativistic, environmentalist, and pragmatic view of the world.[5] All of these developments, in truth, were going on at the same time, and all of them contributed to the emergence of the new radicalism. Equally important was a tendency to see cultural issues as inseparable from political ones; so that "education," conceived very broadly, came to be seen not merely as a means of raising up an enlightened electorate but as an instrument of social change in its own right. Conversely, the new radicals understood the end of social and political reform to be the improvement of the quality of American culture as a whole, rather than simply a way of equalizing the opportunities for economic self-advancement. It is precisely this confusion of politics and culture, so essential to the new radicalism, that seems to me to betray its origins in the rise of the intellectual class; for such a program, with its suggestion that men of learning occupy or ought to occupy the strategic

[5] See, for instance, Daniel Aaron, *Men of Good Hope* (New York: Oxford University Press, 1951); Charles Forcey, *The Crossroads of Liberalism* (New York: Oxford University Press, 1961); Eric Goldman, *Rendezvous with Destiny* (New York: Alfred A. Knopf, 1952); Morton G. White, *Social Thought in America: The Revolt against Formalism* (New York: Viking Press, 1949); John Braeman, "Seven Progressives," *Business History Review*, 35 (Winter, 1961), pp. 581–92.

loci of social control, has an obvious appeal to intellectuals, and particularly to intellectuals newly conscious of their own common ties and common interests.

What I have called the new radicalism was not the same thing as the so-called progressive movement, though it took shape during the "Progressive Era." Progressivism was influenced by the new radicalism, but it was more deeply indebted to the Populism of the nineteenth century. It was for the most part a purely political movement, whereas the new radicals were more interested in the reform of education, culture, and sexual relations than they were in political issues in the strict sense. Many of them, in fact, rejected progressivism; they saw in "uplift" only another manifestation of middle-class morality. Even those like Jane Addams who did not embrace socialism, and whose political position therefore has to be described, for lack of a better word, as "progressive" (or "liberal"), had more in common with socialists than with the kind of progressives one associates with the initiative and referendum, the campaign against the trusts, and the crusade for "good government." What distinguished her from them was not only her insistence on the preeminence of "education" but her sense of kinship with the "other half" of humanity. The intellectual in his estrangement from the middle class identified himself with other outcasts and tried to look at the world from their point of view. This radical reversal of perspective was still another distinguishing feature of the new radicalism, socialist or progressive. The particular political labels are of little importance. What matters is the point of view such people deliberately cultivated.

That point of view—the effort to see society from the bottom up, or at least from the outside in—seems to me to account for much of what was valuable and creative in the new radicalism. On the other hand, the very circumstance which made this feat possible—the estrangement of intellectuals, as a class, from the dominant values of American culture—also accounted for what seems to me the chief weakness of the new radicalism, its distrust not only of middle-class culture but of intellect itself. Detachment carried with it a certain defensiveness about the position of intellect (and intellectuals) in American life; and it was this defensiveness, I think, which sometimes prompted intellectuals to forsake the role of criticism and to identify themselves with what they imagined to be the laws of historical necessity and the working out of the popular will. . . .

The originality of the new radicalism as a form of politics rested on a twofold discovery: the discovery of the dispossessed by men who themselves had never known poverty or prejudice, and the mutual self-discovery of the intellectuals. The combination of the two accounted for the intensity with which the intellectuals identified themselves with the outcasts of the social order: women, children, proletarians, Indians, and Jews. At the very moment when they became aware of the other half of humanity, they became aware of each other and came to see themselves as yet another class apart. In time, their very sense of kinship with one another made them all the more painfully conscious of their collective isolation from the rest of society. Then the "submerged tenth" came to be seen not only as the visible representation of the unsublimated selfhood of mankind but, more immediately, as a potential political ally. The intellectuals came to court the dispossessed with an ardor doubly endowed.

At the first moment of their mutual self-discovery, however, exhilaration rather than anxiety was the dominant mood. What Edward T. Devine said of the social workers applied to the intellectuals as a whole: "the mutual discovery of one another's existence" constituted one of the "extraordinary developments of the opening decade of the twentieth century."[6] The discovery that others had fought the same fight against bourgeois surroundings, the discovery that one had after all taken part in a general awakening that one's own struggles were the struggles of sensitive people everywhere, endowed the moment with the sense of a thousand possibilities. It suggested hidden treasures of aspiration, yet unfathomed, lying beneath the surface of an outwardly contented and corrupt society. The awareness of their own emancipation made intellectuals see what might be accomplished by the liberation of the repressed energies of the social organism as a whole. "Individuals and groups who represent what might be called the underdog, when they are endowed with energy and life, exert pressures towards modification of our cast-iron habits and lay rich deposits of possible cultural enhancement, if we are able to take advantage of them."[7] The new radicals sought not only justice for the exploited but the enrichment of the cultural life of the whole nation. The terms in which the social workers spoke of their clients made it clear what they expected of them. "More and more," one of them wrote, "I feel how much we have to *learn* from these people whom too often we are expected to teach. They are braver, simpler, better than we are; more generous, more helpful—and it is because they are daily *doing* the things of which we are only thinking."[8]

Where expectations ran so high, disappointment was sure to follow. The new radicals found to their dismay that the poor clung obstinately to the saloon, the church, and the captains of the ward machine—symbols of their unenlightened state which the new radicals, for all their generous understanding of the problems of poverty, never managed to accept with equanimity. Perhaps the intellectuals retained more of their middle-class prejudices than they realized. Or perhaps they were in truth a little frightened by the poor, frightened of the violence of working-class life at the same time that they were charmed by its spontaneity. In any case, the new

[6] Edward T. Devine, *The Spirit of Social Work* (New York: Charities Publication Committee, 1911), p. vi.
[7] Hutchins Hapgood, *A Victorian in the Modern World* (New York: Harcourt, Brace, 1939), p. 567.
[8] Alice Lincoln to Jane Addams, June 29, 1902, Jane Addams MSS.

radicals proposed to extend to the working class the very "advantages" which they themselves professed to reject—as Jane Addams explained, in order "to bring them in contact with a better type of Americans."[9]. . .

It is difficult to understand this second disillusionment [that of the 1920's], unless one remembers the extent to which disillusionment, for many American intellectuals, had early become an end in itself. One of the dogmas of the new radicalism was that appearances were illusory. Behind the political façade was the "invisible government." Beneath the smiling surface of American life was the "submerged tenth." Beneath the moral man was the inner, uncivilized man. Muckraking, history, social work, psychological theory, all seemed to lead to the same conclusion: that reality was precisely what cultured people, respectable people, sought to keep hidden. Disillusionment, therefore—the loss of the illusion that the world actually worked as the official guardians of the social order, parents, preachers, and teachers, pretended it worked—was the necessary beginning of wisdom.

It also tended to become, as I have suggested earlier, a style or attitude, deliberately adopted, in which a certain type of rebellion expressed itself as a matter of convention. One reason why the Twenties seem particularly disillusioned is that the convention had become by that time so general that it was taken up by people whose rebellion went no further than an impatience with parental restraint. But if that was so, it was precisely because older men had already established the pattern, long before the war, the peace, and the excitements of the 1920's. The muckrakers, among others, had already made it clear that a hard-boiled skepticism about the canting morality of the middle class was indispensable equipment for aspiring young rebels; and none of the muckrakers had taken more delight in turning official morality upside down than Lincoln Steffens, whose very first book contained the statement that "the Fourth of July oration is the 'front' of graft" and that "there is no patriotism in it, but treason."[10] The man who could turn out such epigrams was already well advanced toward "disillusionment." Yet so pervasive was the myth of disillusionment in the Twenties that Steffens himself succumbed to it; he spoke of himself, at times, as a man whose illusions had survived intact right down to the end of the war. That he knew better, the *Autobiography* itself makes clear in many places; in spite of which, however, historians persist in reading it as a study of disenchantment and, beyond that, of the way in which a burning sense of injustice drove so many liberals in the postwar years into the regrettable but essentially humanitarian heresy of Communism. Our understanding of the process by which radicals are made remains astonishingly sentimental and crude, and our picture of the cultural

[9] Jane Addams: *Twenty Years at Hull House* (New York: Macmillan, 1910), pp. 231–2.
[10] Lincoln Steffens, *The Shame of the Cities* (New York: Hill & Wang, 1957 [New York, 1904]), p. 8.

history of the Twenties and Thirties, accordingly, seldom rises above the level of a cliché. Thus in Arthur Miller's recent play *After the Fall,* as a reviewer has noted, "all of the ex-Communists . . . are merely 'fighting injustice,' while the friend who commits suicide is 'a decent broken man that never wanted anything more but the good of the world.' "[11] And Richard Rovere has written that "the typical intellectual of the Thirties was a man so shocked by social injustice and the ghastly spectacle of fascism that his brain was easily addled by anyone who proposed a quick and drastic remedy."[12] It is time we began to understand radicals like Lincoln Steffens not as men driven by a vague humanitarian idealism but as men *predisposed* to rebellion as the result of an early estrangement from the culture of their own class; as the result, in particular, of the impossibility of pursuing within the framework of established convention the kind of careers they were bent on pursuing. The intellectuals of the early twentieth century were predisposed to rebellion by the very fact of being intellectuals in a society that had not yet learned to define the intellectual's place. Under such conditions intellectuals were outsiders by necessity: a new class, not yet absorbed into the cultural consensus.

[11] Robert Brustein, "Arthur Miller's Mea Culpa," *New Republic,* 150 (Feb. 8, 1964), p. 28.
[12] Richard H. Rovere, *The American Establishment and Other Reports, Opinions, and Speculations* (New York: Harcourt, Brace & World, 1962), p. 175.

John H. Schaar and Sheldon S. Wolin

Campus Protests: Signals of Discontent in a Technological Society

Writing when the university ferment of the late 1960's was reaching floodtide, political scientists John H. Schaar and Sheldon S. Wolin viewed campus protest less as a response to issues such as Vietnam than as a reaction to a cultural condition: the sense of powerlessness endemic to a technological society. From this perspective, campus disorders become symbolic expressions of "a more general disorder" within a larger technological setting—a setting that changes so quickly as to render past experiences and values almost hopelessly irrelevant. Student rebels, spurning the middle-class legacy that could be theirs, launched counter-movements against a society that seems capable of producing everything except the feeling of individual purpose and power. Professor Schaar is the author of *Escape from Authority* and Professor Wolin has written *Politics and Vision*.

As this is being written, the colleges and universities are digging in for another round of campus troubles. Since the outbreak at Berkeley in 1964, the campuses have become a problem of national concern and, despite the many diagnoses, a matter of puzzlement. Although the head of one major university, responding to a U.S. senator's question whether greater financial aid might not solve the universities' ills, remarked that he knew of no difficulty which would be worsened by more money, the puzzlement remains. Most educators and public officials agree that higher education is in deep financial trouble, but no one believes that lack of funds has produced student unrest, even though it may contribute to the conflicts over black and ethnic studies.

American politicians are not at their best when confronting problems which elude a financial solution, and it was only natural that they should fall back to other familiar positions. The first consisted of forcing the campus problems into legal categories from which, *presto,* they emerged as issues of rule violation and laxity in law enforcement. The obvious solution was to withdraw government aid from disaffected students and to warn the colleges and universities that they would suffer financial loss if they continued to be soft on law and order. The second position was equally predictable: trace the problems to an international Communist conspiracy, and then prove the allegation by introducing hostile witnesses, in this instance some SDS types and a few Yippies.

Although it is likely that higher penalties will tend to discourage campus protests by raising the material and psychic costs to the activists, it is unlikely that such measures will prove to be of more than symbolic significance—interesting testimony to the ways our decision-makers perceive the problem within a framework of public outrage and private anxiety. President Nixon himself has expressed private worry that student discontents might persist even if the Vietnam war ended, which has the merit, at least, of leaving open the possibility of discussing the state of the campuses in other than the conventional terms of public policy. For it may be that we are experiencing a profound crisis in the liberal psyche, broader yet similar to that expressed by John Stuart Mill:

> Suppose that all your objects in life were realized; that all the changes in institutions and opinions which you are looking forward to could be completely effected at this very instant: would this be a great joy and happiness to you? And an irrepressible self-consciousness answered, "No!" At this my heart sank within me: the whole foundation on which my life was constructed fell down.

Suppose no Vietnam, no racial tensions, no poverty . . . .

Perhaps, then, we might think of the student problem, not as a policy question, but as a symbolic fact, as a state of affairs intimating a more general disorder.

Recall the remarkable quality of academic commencement, 1969. Normally commencement is an amiable time, when relatives, friends, and dignitaries gather to honor the graduating students and distinguished recipients of honorary degrees. But last June it was a time of high tension. Administrators and faculty prayed that the ceremonies might be completed without interruption by dissidents or militants. Parents looked on in shock and disbelief at the dress, deportment, and rhetoric of their offspring. The truly remarkable feature of commencement, however, was not the threat of disruption by the young, but the abdication and anxiety of the old. The President of the United States went near no major college or university. He chose, instead, to appear first at a junior college in South Dakota, where he dedicated the Karl Mundt Library and denounced student troublemakers, and then at the Air Force Academy in Colorado, where he affirmed that patriotism was still the highest virtue, and pledged to defend the military against its domestic critics.

Customarily, commencement is a time when notable figures from public and private life invite their youthful audiences into the adult world and seek to describe its promise. But this year, all across the land, and in all manner of academic institutions, student speakers dominated the proceedings, telling the adults what was wrong with the world and what the new generation intended to do about it. They rejected both the austere past symbolized by Dakota and the Cold War anticommunism of Karl Mundt, and the lethal and bleak technological future of the Air Force Academy. They insisted that the world was now theirs, and had to be understood in their terms.

The June events signified a reversal of the rites of passage and a redefinition of the rituals of rebellion. Despite that, they have now been nearly forgotten.

One reason why the events of June were soon forgotten is that the modes of interpreting campus troubles have become fixed within a certain pattern. Placed within that pattern, the June days seemed disturbing, but not surprising. For nearly a half-dozen years now the language and imagery of revolution have been used to describe and analyze events on the campuses—revolt, rebellion, student power, violence, and the like. Once this framework is set, a host of historical associations related to the great revolutions of the past arises, inflating the fears of the threatened, and swelling the dreams of the hopeful. Believing themselves in the midst of revolution, both sides relax their inhibitions about violence.

Bacon once remarked that "even if men went mad all after the same fashion, they might agree one with another well enough." If political and campus officials and large numbers of students agree that they are locked in revolutionary struggle and strive to act accordingly, it is idle to say that they have misunderstood their situation. But it is worth asking, nonetheless, whether inherited notions of revolution are not anachronistic and hence a source of confusion for all parties.

Most of our ideas and images are still shaped by revolutions which happened in pre-industrial societies where differentials of wealth, power, and privilege were deeply and hopelessly etched, and where a small and visible ruling class on the top oppressed and exploited the masses on the bottom. The revolutions of France, Russia, and China were directed against the long historical past and its persistence into the present. Today any lucid discussion of revolution in the advanced states must begin with the fact of technological society, not with ideas fashioned to analyze traditional societies. It must ask whether that fact does not by itself alter the sense in which a revolution is a meaningful possibility; whether social evils do not therefore acquire a novel form; and whether the marks of oppression are not to be sought among groups very different from the oppressed classes described in the classical literature of revolution.

The main feature of technological society is not merely rapid change, but, as its admirers have said, creative destruction. It not only destroys habits, beliefs, and institutions inherited from the past, but those which were created only yesterday. In a society where memory is an irritant because it impedes progress, concepts like "tradition" or categories like "the past" are mostly meaningless. To revolt against such a society means striking against the fluid present rather than against the burdensome past. It means, too, that instead of struggling, as revolutionists usually have, against societies which seemed incapable of moving and growing, today's revolutionist is in the absurd position of protesting against a society in constant movement and capable of promising everything, from the abolition of poverty to the abolition of death—either as a penalty or as a disease.

Talk about "revolution on the campus" is pathetic or mythological, for not only does it overlook the hard fact of technological society, but it also exaggerates the revolutionary potential of the campus. Because universities and colleges are vital to the economy and culture of technological society and because they exercise power over their own members, one may be deluded into believing that they are instrumentalities of power, and hence bases for revolution. Sometimes universities and colleges are able to exercise influence over other parts of society, but by most criteria of power they are weak. As potential centers of revolution they are hopeless, for there is little power to mobilize.

The manifest discontents and chronic disorders on the campuses are important, but their importance is distorted if they are viewed as revolutionary cells in a body politic vulnerable to the classic disorders of revolution. The condition of the campuses is significant because the campus represents the most advanced part of our society, not its most oppressed. It is where the knowledge explosion is happening, where the discontents with our racial, urban, and foreign policies are continuously aired and publicized, and where all manner of experiments are being lived by the new generation. Although student activists are apt to describe students as the "new proletariat" or simply as "niggers," their plight is significant not because they are oppressed but because they are corrupted.

Student discontent first broke out in the economically most advanced and affluent society (something which has been overlooked by social scientists who have warned of the impending "Latin-Americanization of the universities"). Most of the trouble and violence has occurred at the most prestigious institutions. Except for the recent outbreaks by blacks and their "Third World" allies, the rebels have come from comfortable, professional, middle-class and upper middle-class families.

These are familiar facts, but the conclusion from them is what matters: if a revolutionary condition exists on the nation's campuses, it represents a protest by the middle class against the middle class. Or more pointedly, it is a condition created because the middle class has turned against its world and against its own values. How little similarity there is between the politics of the students and classical revolutionary situations is evident in the intense and almost universal hostility of the working classes and rural populations toward the students. The hatred of the "masses" is stirred by the abrasive politics on campus, and by the casual sexuality, drug experimentation, and general slovenliness of the students. It is kept in motion by the continuous spectacle of the sons and daughters of those who have made it in America and who now defile those values of work, achievement, and upward mobility which sustain the city worker and the people of the small towns and rural areas. To claim that the workers and farmers of America are the victims of false consciousness is to miss the main point. What is being expressed on the campuses is a post-Marxian phenomenon, an attempt at change initiated from above and opposed to the aspirations, grievances, and values of those below the middle classes in the social hierarchy. It is, moreover, an attempt at revolution which dares not go into the streets, the factories, and (increasingly) the ghettos.

If the state of the campuses is more reflective of a middle-class revolt than of a revolutionary situation, then the relative ineffectiveness of the students may reveal something important about the possibilities of fundamental change in a liberal, affluent, and technologically advanced society. Tocqueville's conjecture that among democratic nations "great intellectual and political revolutions will become more difficult and less frequent than is supposed" now seems confirmed. A society capable of producing floods of consumer goods, of supporting high levels of employment, or subsidizing those it cannot employ, of practicing a form of politics in which organized groups gain some material satisfaction most of the time, and of providing endless varieties of entertainment and distraction is a difficult target to attack. Such a society lends itself more to "targets of opportunity" than to frontal assaults, *e.g.,* poverty, discrimination, inadequate housing, and exploited fruit-pickers.

The dominant groups of this society are, from the revolutionary point of view, elusive. They prefer the politics of influence and indirect power, rarely flaunt their privileges, and are open to new recruits. It has been a century since they have told the public where it can go. The lack of clearly defined enemies is tacitly recognized in the vocabulary of the rebels: the use of words like "dissent," and of actions like "protest," "resistance," and "demonstration" are an admission that they are reduced to seeking targets of opportunity within a generally benevolent system. Because the liberal, affluent, technological society is characteristically bland, accommodating, and good-natured, it renders the revolutionary powerless, allowing him to act out, outrageously if he wishes, his subversive impulses, encourages him to theatrical revolution, which means that he can shock but never destroy.

The affability of the managers of technological society is encouraged by something more than the fact that they preside over an economy which supplies them, as no other ruling group has ever been supplied, with a generous margin or surplus so that concessions are always possible and mistakes always corrigible. What they have in addition is the enormous power—also without historical precedent—which accrues to those who control a society of consumers, a power owing as much to the powerlessness of the subjects as to the instrumentalities of the rulers. In all previous societies, powerlessness was the consequence of deprivation: deprivation of rights, privileges, property, work, education. Although pockets of material deprivation still exist, the main source of powerlessness is not deprivation but consumption. Technological society lives by consumption, and its members live for it. They allow the quality and tempo of their lives to be set by the changing requirements of technology. They above all acquiesce happily in the reduction of control over the quality and intensity of personal experience which is one of the fruits of technology.

Think of the American who comes to Yosemite in a camper truck with a boat on top, a motorcycle strapped to the front, and a power-boat trailered to the rear. He thinks he has expanded his range of action and his powers of enjoyment, whereas he has really become the prisoner of his technology, restricted to where it can take him and what it can bring him. He suffers a reduction in personal power and experience even while thinking he has extended them. It is instructive that in the same state of nature the sworn enemy of the camper trucker should end in the same state of powerlessness. Deep in the wilderness one may meet a bearded and beaded hippie, totally stoned, incapacitated from encountering nature on its terms. He has renounced the powerlessness of active consumption for the powerlessness of passive consumption.

The powerlessness of the many forms the larger setting for the powerlessness of the campus rebels. The dominant groups in our society do not fear the latter; on the contrary, they find much that is charming and usable in their dress, idiom, and eternal youthfulness—so much so that constant efforts are made to absorb the culture of the young. It may come out wrong, sometimes emerging as *Playboy* culture and commercial advertising. Yet, as we know from recent accounts, the gap between Mrs. Luce and the rebels is not always great. What does alarm the elites, and helps to explain their willingness to support harsh measures against the campuses, is the possibility that the antics of the rebels will intensify and ignite the deep-seated fears and hatreds of broad sectors of the population: urban workers of recent foreign origin, small-town America, and the less sophisticated middle classes in the South, Middle West, Southwest, and Southern California.

The dominant groups *do* fear polarization, but they fear one of the polarities—the student rebels—not so much for what it represents as for the forces it may activate. They fear the other for what it does represent. It brings reminders, often unattractive, of what technological society is always trying to forget and to destroy: its past—a past in which work, self-denial, simplicity, and physical strength were celebrated. Whereas the technological elites can share with the rebels a common fascination for electronic marvels and for the endless movement which modern communications and transportation allow, and can enjoy in private the pleasures which the rebels flaunt in public, those same elites are repelled by honkies, Southerners, and citizens of Orange County. But because they know that the real threat to technological society comes from those who are frightened and confused by incessant change, they are willing to sanction, perhaps reluctantly, firm measures against those who are hip, mod, cool, and really plugged into the future.

The fundamental malady of technological society, then, is the nearly universal sense of powerlessness, disguised as consumption and maintained by rising expectations. That sense of powerlessness is expressed in various ways: in the rage and confusion of the working and lower-middle classes; in the aimlessness of the middle-class hippie; in the despair of the poor and the anger of the blacks; in the fear and harshness of the American Gothics who rallied first to Goldwater and then to [George] Wallace.

Among the many causes which promote our common futility there is one that has gone relatively unnoticed. We may be the first people to experience what it means to live in accordance with the fundamental postulates of the scientific and technological credo. It is one thing to talk, as philosophers and scientists have done for a century, about the differences between scientific beliefs and moral, religious, and political beliefs; about the objective status of the one and the subjective status of the other; about how the one is grounded in empirical realities and the other in prejudice, superstition, or metaphysics; and about how the one gives us power over nature and the future, while the other gives us only solace for our ignorance.

It is quite another thing when an entire society attempts to shape its life by scientific and technical knowledge, making that knowledge the very foundation for the continuance and the security of society, and encouraging its pursuit even to the point of sacrificing the welfare and shattering the memories and hopes of many of its citizens. It is quite another thing because that knowledge is, by the admission of its exponents, silent on the questions of how a man should live, and what he should choose. Those who have interpreted the meaning, presuppositions, and methods of scientific and technical knowledge have insisted that it cannot prescribe ends. They have also asserted that other forms of knowing whose business it is to traffic in "values" lack the characteristics of genuine knowledge, *e.g.*, empirical verification, quantifiability, even rationality.

Once the scientific culture takes hold, there is a scramble to emulate it and thereby avoid the stigma of inferiority; hence its spread to the social studies, history, and the humanities. The end result is the divorce between knowledge and values symbolized by the underlying agreement between the techno-scientist and the hippie, the one declaring that values are subjective preferences, the other mumbling, "Man, I'm only doing my thing." The end result signifies that values are no longer shareable as knowledge, and hence one gets only their functional equivalents: sensation, feeling, spectacle.

But if it is in the nature of the techno-scientific culture to render values private and unshareable, perhaps there is still hope. Perhaps there is

226

one important value crucial to that culture and yet a value to which all can subscribe and even share, the value of knowledge itself.

Knowledge permeates the whole ethos and structure of technological society. This is what mainly distinguishes it from previous forms of society. Consequently, higher education plays a vital role. Its institutions have become the foundation of a society based on scientific knowledge. We must then ask two questions concerning the universities and colleges. Are they succeeding in making knowledge something that can truly be shared? Are they realizing the goal of making knowledge power and hence a means of overcoming human powerlessness?

At first glance it appears that the university has the prerequisites of a community held together by the active sharing of knowledge. Many of the conditions one would want to postulate seem fulfilled. For some time now public universities have been committed to opening their doors to a wide variety of groups and classes. Along with the private institutions, they are now making a serious effort to enroll sizable numbers of students from racial and ethnic groups. Within tolerable limits, the communities of higher education are open; and, despite mounting costs, education is relatively cheap and available. Beyond these and other material conditions conducive to sharing knowledge, there have been the great changes in the nature of knowledge, typified by modern science, which also seem to promote communal ends. Of the many things that might be said to characterize the modern ideal of knowledge, these are the least disputable: it is rational, secular, empirical, cumulative, and public. No secret mysteries, no fixed dogma, no priesthood.

Thus modern knowledge appears uniquely designed to be the stuff from which communities of scholars and students might be formed. In addition, the modern idea of knowledge has promised to help men to a fuller measure of personal freedom, liberating them from ignorance and superstition, and enlarging the efficacy and power of the individual. Unlike those who had trafficked in metaphysics, theology, aesthetics, and the like, the modern man would know something that could be applied directly to the world. He could be equipped to move into the world, confident of his ability to make a place for himself where what *he* did would make a difference in shaping his life.

Yet when we look at what the modern ideal of knowledge has become in the university, we find that at every turn it threatens to diminish what it had promised to enlarge: freedom, efficacy, and sharing. The modern ideal is summed up in the slogan about the "knowledge explosion," which the universities have done so much to detonate. So great is the proliferation of knowledge that the problem now is how to retrieve it from the swelling data banks where it is stored. Realistically, the "knowledge explosion" means that a few know a great deal about how nature and society "work," while the rest of us are about as ignorant as we have always been. Further, as knowledge has become increasingly refined, it becomes more inaccessible to the many, more esoteric, more removed from the world of common experience.

Comparable effects have also been produced in the life of the university by the pursuit of knowledge as a form of power. Repeating the pattern of the outside world, a few university men enjoy great power, while the many are about as powerless as they have always been, perhaps more so. Power within the university depends upon the demands of the "knowledge-market" outside. Those in the university who have knowledge which is in demand, or, equally important, know how to organize those who do have it, come to have superior power and influence. Their superiority is exhibited in countless "special arrangements," higher salaries, lower teaching loads, more research support, more spacious accommodations, and more influence in university councils.

All of this is obvious. It is necessary only to draw the obvious conclusion: the distinction between university and society, the enduring effort of universities to develop a life and culture different from that of society— an effort which began with Plato's Academy and continued into recent times—is now a distinction without a difference. If anything of a difference remains it is a consequence of the reversal which has taken place in the relationships between university and society. Broadly speaking, from the sixteenth century to the end of the nineteenth, universities were frequently criticized for failing to assimilate important types of knowledge, such as modern languages, newer forms of mathematics and science, and various practical arts. In our century, however, it is the other way round. Society is constantly required to adapt to the knowledge being developed in the universities, knowledge not only in the natural sciences and engineering, but in economics, psychology, and sociology as well.

These changes have registered their severest effects upon undergraduate education, especially at the large public universities. Today, undergraduate education is a shambles. Traditionally it has had the task of general education, of defining and transmitting the knowledge appropriate to a "well-educated" or "cultivated" man. When a civilization reaches a fair degree of self-consciousness and self-definition it embodies in a formal curriculum those values which it regards as essential to the best intellect and sensibility: the Greek Academy; the medieval *trivium* and *quadrivium;* the liberal-humanistic curriculum of the nineteenth century.

Moreover, in those earlier societies possession of the knowledge imparted through the college succeeded fairly well in equipping men for understanding themselves and their social order, and for taking positions of influence in church, state, and society. And since virtually all the educated shared a common fund of knowledge, college education enabled all those who had it to converse among themselves about the questions that mattered.

Merely to say these things is to see immediately how far we have moved from them. While all of the older conceptions of the content and purposes of undergraduate education still linger on in more-or-less mutilated form, nobody is very certain of their utility—or, as it is called today, "relevance." Certainly, they provide the stuff of commencement day addresses and college catalog prose, but few will still argue that they provide the knowledge that leads to social power and influence. Nor is anyone really convinced that the liberal arts curriculum teaches values and molds character. About the strongest claim made for education in the arts and humanities today is that the knowledge so gained can enrich one's leisure time: education to solve the "problem of leisure"; and leisure here means recreation, not the fullest use of one's capacities.

The fact is, we simply do not know the form of the highest general culture appropriate to contemporary, largely post-industrial society. Whatever that general culture might come to be and mean, it certainly will not merely be what it always has been. Most colleges occupy the undergraduate years with a kind of pre-professional training and specialization, or a pedantic and uncertain humanism, or an uneasy compromise between the two—some "breadth" courses, followed by concentration in a "major." The result saddens the best teachers, maddens the best students, and gladdens no one.

But the undergraduate curriculum will remain motley and infirm until the colleges decide what those vulnerable years in the lives of the young are for, and what they are not for. The most powerful emerging tendencies are either treating the undergraduate student as a candidate for graduate or professional school, or arranging things so that the student can have the greatest possible latitude for personal search and experiment. Both tendencies, of course, intensify intellectual fragmentation and pluralistic ignorance, leading to privatization rather than to genuine sharing of knowledge and experience. Once again the extremes produce weakness and lead to a society of disconnected particulars. On the one side, increasing professionalization, on the other, a growing tendency to let students go their own ways. Each tendency hurries the student toward his own cocoon.

Compared to the desperate confusions of undergraduate life, the higher reaches of the higher learning—graduate and professional schools and advanced research centers—appear peaceful and well-ordered. A closer look reveals currents which conceal weakness beneath professionalization, atomization beneath organization, powerlessness beneath power.

The proliferation of specialized knowledge, in addition to the availability of research funds, in addition to the tendency to inflate into "professional" status occupations that are really little more than fairly highly skilled jobs, has turned the modern large university into a bewilderingly complex collection of special institutes, centers, bureaus, and schools. These units occupy a semi-autonomous status within the university, enjoying their own budgets, governed by their own officers, adopting their own standards for staff and student performance, and largely oriented toward constituencies outside the university. The resulting centrifugal forces are ungovernably strong, and increasingly the university becomes a holding company with only nominal control over the agencies which bear its name.

These tendencies are strengthened by the multiversitarian ideology of the university as the servant of society. Under this ideology, knowledge is seen as the single most important "growth factor" in modern economies, and universities, as the leading producers within the knowledge industry, become indispensable to all the other productive agencies of society. Universities have always in some sense served society. But never has service been so mundanely conceived or so promiscuously offered as by the modern multiversity.

The precondition of university service to society is professional education. The natural locus of that education is the graduate departments. One expects to find a degree of professionalism in graduate study, but what is now of concern is the tendency to substitute specialization for professionalism and to extend an inflated professionalism into areas of higher education where it does not belong. At its core, the idea of a profession involves a body of knowledge and technique that can be codified, transmitted, and applied in standard ways to socially useful ends. A professional is one who has been certified by other professionals as being in possession of the prescribed knowledge. Specialization as such is not the basic mark of the professional: the lawyer in general practice is as much a professional as the one who specializes in tax law.

The Ph.D. degree most clearly displays the effects of specialization disguised as professionalism. It is no longer regarded as the badge of the man who has acquired competence in a body of knowledge which he wishes to profess to others, whose vocation is scholarship and the pursuit of significant truth, and who gives promise of intellectual creativity. In a growing number of fields, the degree is nothing more than a certification that a man has mastered a limited subject matter and certain techniques of work. The consequences are already apparent, and most are harmful: microspecialization of knowledge, narrowness of outlook, a growing inability to define intellectual significance in any terms other than those set by the techniques of research, and progressive disqualification for the task of teaching undergraduates. His growing expertise closes off much of his subject-field, while surrounding fields are *terrae incognitae*. His capacities for personal growth come to be defined in terms of growing technical mastery. But even this proves illusory: every field is now expected to be in "ferment," and hence the techniques acquired as a graduate student will be superseded in a brief time. The only hope left is that he may some day become a dean.

It remains to point out one general feature of the modern job and income structure that has an important bearing on present student discontent. In simpler and more stable eras, persons who went to college could usually make an early choice of career with fair confidence that the future would contain a place for them. Furthermore, those who went to college

230

could count on a future that would bring them a fair measure of personal independence and social influence and prestige: even the schoolteacher was a figure of considerable standing in the small towns of yesterday. But today, with the vast increase in the college-educated population, these exceptions no longer hold. Furthermore, millions of the college-educated now hold jobs that are far below their skills and ability, and those jobs have all the features of industrial work save one—the need for muscle. The work is repetitive, narrow, and stunting.

The college-educated—including increasing numbers of those formally classified as professional—can no longer confidently look forward to places within the established occupational structure that will bring them independence, challenging work, and social influence. They can count on a fair measure of material comfort and security, but more and more young people are asking whether that is sufficient reward for the sacrifice of autonomy and growth. This long-range change in the shape of work is perhaps one of the basic factors underlying youthful discontent and protest. In often vague and poorly focused ways, students are demanding that education be something more than a union card to job security in the bureaucratic-technological society, where one's talents are exploited for the purposes of others, and where the worker has traded most of the dimensions of genuine freedom enjoyed by former educated and professional classes for clean clothes and comfortable working conditions. But the implementation of that rising demand will require radical changes in the occupational and organizational structure of the technological society itself.

Societies have always been, in part, organizations for the production of the nutrients of life, but modern societies are ruled, as no others have ever been, by the drive for production. Modern production is powerfully oriented toward consumption; and, since consumption is limitless, so too is production. But to produce something means to destroy something else. That is the dynamic of modern production: it must continue as long as there is anything left to destroy.

The evidence of the destructiveness is all around us, both in the realm of nature and in the realm of that "second nature" which is culture. Modern production has obscured the sun and the stars, and it has also made the cities unlivable. It chews up great forests and drinks whole lakes and rivers, and it consumes men's religions and traditions and makes nonsense of their notions of the aims of education. It periodically slays heaps of men in war, and it daily mangles the spirits of millions of others in meaningless labor. The only aim of the civilization is to grow, and to grow it must consume. As Jacques Ellul has shown, the process must run until it consumes those who think they run it—until man is absorbed into technique and process.

The great intellectual task of the present is the task of rethinking every aspect of technological civilization. That this civilization inherently moves toward self-destruction is now clear, and any radical rethinking must start from the premise that its manifest destructiveness will not be stopped by a broader distribution of the values or a more intensive application of the methods and processes which constitute and sustain the evil itself. If the universities were to dedicate themselves to this rethinking, then they would not only serve society in the most valuable way possible, but they might even save themselves.

This task will require more than the opening of the curriculum to miscellaneous "problem courses" on whatever happens to be interesting or bothering people at the moment—with the consequence that the problems of peace, race, poverty, and transcendental meditation all receive equal time. It will require something more of the scientists and technicians than stopping work for a "day of concern." It will require something more of the humanists than a deeper retreat into the sanctuary of ingeniously obscure research, while mumbling incantations about "higher values." What it will require is a new focus, and the courage to withdraw human and material resources from the subjects which have high value on the current market, reallocating them to the task of rediscovering and redefining the humanity and sociability which have become twisted and frustrated by the "single vision" of contemporary modes of organization and public purpose.

The task is in part critical: to examine what technological civilization has done to our language, literature, art, politics, and work. Partly it is retrospective: to expose the historical choices that were made by reference to the putative benefits of science and technology placed in the service of endless growth and power. That study must try to achieve a meaningful assessment of the gains and losses incurred by these choices. Partly it is creative: to reflect upon human history in all of its breadth and diversity in order to acquire the fullest comprehension of the range of human possibilities and, perhaps, a heightened awareness of the crisis which has estranged us from our humanity and our world.

We have preferred to call it a focus rather than a curriculum in order to emphasize the urgency of our condition. Technological civilization encompasses and influences all departments of knowledge, hence it is not just *a* problem: It is *the* problem. There is no subject more relevant, none so important for the renewal of hope for our species.

Samuel P. Hays

Since 1964, when the demonstrations at Berkeley marked a turning point in campus confrontations, American universities have become cultural battlegrounds—fields upon which contending factions, not all necessarily associated with the campuses, have seen their own causes succeeding or failing. Professor Samuel P. Hays examines the Columbia University student strike of 1968 in this context. He shows how a specific protest incident affected the ideological struggles of a variety of right- and left-wing groups, each of which read into the situation its own hopes and fears. Professor Hays, a historian, is the author of *The Response to*

The 1968 Columbia Strike: Ideological Battleground for Right and Left

Industrialism and *Conservation and the Gospel of Efficiency*. He is presently at work on a new synthesis of American history which stresses the concept of social change.

The Columbia student strike played a sharply different role in the life of the two fringes of the political spectrum. Viewing events from the opposite end of politics from which they took place, the right discovered confirmation of its well-established explanations for and cures of the ills of modern America. To the left, however, deeply involved in the events themselves, the strike served not merely to confirm the coercive power of the establishment, but to present a critical stage of self-development. Here we shall be concerned not with the unfolding events of the strike itself, but with the perception of the strike by both right and left.

To the casual observer within the broad center of American politics, including those self-designated as liberals, the political right displays a single uniform set of values. But like the left, the right is deeply fractured and, both in ideology and tactics, sensitive to gradations within it. These distinctions within the right, in fact, form a sub-spectrum from the anti-liberal Buckley-Goldwater-Young Americans for Freedom grouping at the boundary line between the right and the center, through the anti-Communist John Birch Society segment, to the "international conspiracy behind communism" theorists, and, finally, on the outer fringe, to those who speak openly of the threat of black and non-Caucasian peoples to

From Samuel P. Hays, "Right Face, Left Face: The Columbia Strike." Reprinted with permission from the *Political Science Quarterly*, 84 (June 1969), pp. 311–327. Footnotes have been renumbered.

Western civilization. From each of these segments of the right came different reactions to the Columbia strike. Let us consider these reactions, in turn, from the extreme outer fringe to that segment which borders the center.

For those on the extreme outer edge of the spectrum, the struggle for power between students and administration made little dent upon their political consciousness. Those who view the world with a sense of an impending racial crisis between black and white, in which often Jewish influence stands behind the blacks, could have found considerable confirmation of their beliefs in the strike, but, in fact, they paid little attention to it. One of the few such expressions was a letter to the *Thunderbolt,* publication of the National States Rights party: "Now it is the nation's colleges and universities that are being taken over by insane mobs of varmits [*sic*]. The only way to deal with these long-haired, fuzzy-faced faggots and return the campuses to normal is to get rid of the left-wing liberal so-called professors and the Communist Jew students." (June, 1968)

The "conspiracy behind communism" right displayed equally little interest in the strike. When it did, the strike constituted simply another instance of the perennial conspiracy of irreligion to destroy a divinely-inspired social order. Here is a complex of views which suggests a conspiracy far deeper than Communism, which speaks of the Jewish-Masonic inspired secularism of the modern world, which focuses on the Illuminati as the hidden hand behind revolution since the last third of the eighteenth century. A surprisingly large number of groups in America, each small but vocal and prolific in writing, espouses this view of an international conspiracy that cuts deeper in society and deeper in time than Communism. *Don Bell Reports,* a newsletter issued by Marah, Incorporated, in Palm Beach, Florida, expressed a typical reaction from this vantage point:

> We are not suggesting a Communist Conspiracy per se. We are suggesting a far greater kind of conspiracy: a Satan-inspired conspiracy of Man against God which has led to a world-wide defiance of His law and His plans for both societies and governments; a conspiracy that manifests itself on both sides of the so-called Iron Curtain. In the greater sense, this is not a *political* revolution; it is a *religious* revolution: a revolution against God, which is neither new nor old, but *continuing.* . . . (June 7, 1968)

For such segments of the right, Columbia and the rise of Students for a Democratic Society provided weary confirmation of long-held convictions.

The anti-Communist right, most typified by the John Birch Society, viewed the strike as another instance of the Communist conspiracy. . . .

John Reid Kennedy, in *Christian Beacon,* the weekly publication of Reverend Carl McIntyre, called the strike "one of the most successful Marxist strategies ever undertaken in this country and appears to be turning into one of the greatest successes Communism in this country has ever

234

had." Frank Capell cited the quotation of Paul Vilardi, leader of the Columbia student "Coalition of the Majority" in *U.S. News and World Report* that "Communists played an active role in the outbreak," and concluded, "The student uprisings and lawlessness are the result of indoctrination and secret plans carried out by the agents of International Communism." Others stressed simply the penchant for lawlessness as a Communist technique. One writer linked Columbia SDS with Cuba by means of Mark Rudd's visit there two months before the strike, and another implied a tie with Communist China. *Manion Forum* quoted with approval the argument of Drew Pearson and Jack Anderson that Castro, having failed in Latin America, transferred the revolution to Europe and the United States by means of the universities. And columnist John Chamberlain likened the fires during the second Columbia insurrection to the Reichstag Fire. . . .

The Columbia strike's major contribution to right-wing thought was to bring the SDS into center-stage as the symbol of all that was wrong in American student life. A report on SDS by J. Edgar Hoover, which received wide publicity in the mass media, served as authority to bolster the conclusions drawn from the strike events themselves. A large number of right-wing papers reported his remarks with approval. At the same time few segments of the right sought to distinguish among the various segments of the Columbia left. The distinction between SDS and such "student power" manifestations as the Students for a Restructured University was never made. None understood the tensions within SDS itself, and instead of noting the highly tenuous character of cooperation between black and white student groups, they were convinced that the two groups worked together closely. By mid-summer the right was primed to consider SDS as the major focus of its anti-left student thrust; even to Young Americans for Freedom it had almost replaced YAF's traditional student enemy, the National Student Association.

While to the right the Columbia strike merely provided new facts to confirm its previous views, and gradations of reaction conformed precisely with gradations in established outlooks, to the left it presented a more complex challenge. For the strike came at a time when lines of differentiation within the left were in the process of rapid formation. All segments of the left—Old as well as New—shared in the general attack on the Columbia administration and its links with the larger national establishment—with capitalism and imperialism. All recounted the events at Columbia with special emphasis upon the misused power of President Kirk and the trustees, the brutality of the police, and the complicity of the "jocks." But even within these descriptions of the events there were differences in emphasis, in wording, in tone which were to emerge more fully in later weeks and months, as sharp conflicts among forces the left had set in motion.

The transition in this development was the first police action in clearing the campus in the early morning of Tuesday, April 30, for this action sharply increased student support for the strike. The votes on Thursday and Friday of the previous week had indicated strong support for SDS on the substantive issues but not for its tactics. The police bust reversed all this, for now the onus of undesirable tactics was placed upon the police and the administration. The strike leaders suddenly found themselves with a mass of followers with whom they had to cope. But this very success carried with it the seeds of disaster for the strikers; so many new camp followers could not possibly see the strike issues and the proper course of action from here on in the same way. While divergent tendencies had been kept in check during the occupation by the desire of all for success, the bust and the new support provided an opportunity for each one of these tendencies to capture newly radicalized students for its own brand of left-wing politics. It should be emphasized that this sorting out occurred almost entirely within the newer left movement. Although the Communist party and the Socialist Workers party, for example, covered the strike fully and published special material for organizing during it, they remained on the periphery of the subsequent intra-left debate. The same was true of the more recent "sectarian" manifestations of Marxism and Leninism.

One of these sets of divergent tendencies sorted out liberals from radicals with respect to issues, tactics, and student power. SDS's major occupation has been to fashion a radical position among students in opposition to a liberal one. While liberals focused on due process and decision-making within the university, radicals emphasized the substantive issues of war and race and the attendant links between the university and the wider society. For many months SDS had sought to radicalize students from one position to the other; this objective dominated their tactics at Columbia. Even during the first days of the strike SDS sharply distinguished the two positions, but its energies at that time focused on events rather than ideologies to capture potential recruits; its major purpose, in fact, was to guide events, not so much to resolve substantive issues—which it did not believe could be resolved within the Columbia context—but to involve students in radical action and thereby recruit them to the cause. After the bust, however, the ideological tactics came to the fore and divergences appeared. . . .

The decision of New Left leaders in SDS to focus primarily upon the campus battleground has generated a severe dilemma. On the one hand, they must mobilize students in terms of the matters that affect students directly, that is, university conditions that affect their own lives—courses, student hours, the draft. Yet, these matters have little immediate connection with issues of power in society and the world at large, issues to which New Left theoreticians and tacticians are most closely attuned. SDS leaders are fully aware of this problem. Yet the fact remains that the energy they generate among students often serves primarily to change conditions

236

within the university rather than to deal with the extra-university society. Student power symbolizes this problem. To the strike leaders student power was a false issue; students in no way could improve their lives within a university dominated by men whose power was inextricably linked to power in the wider society. To most students, however, changes within the university were real possibilities involving real gains. As soon as the *Columbia Spectator,* immediately after the first bust, called for the heads of Kirk and Truman, strike leaders began to warn against the implications of student power. Although hostile to student power, SDS finds that its actions invariably generate it.

If the strike sharpened differences between liberals and radicals, it also heightened divergent tendencies within radicalism itself. These had been in motion for some time, but the strike provided an opportunity for differences to emerge more sharply. The responsibility of conducting the strike and mobilizing in poststrike ventures those aroused by the events and the struggle for loyalty to different tendencies had the effect of increasing competition among rival radical groups. Although the left, Old and New, appears to many in the center and on the right as monolithic, it is in fact composed of many individuals, groups, tendencies, each with its own brand of radicalism, its own explanations and cures, each seeking a following for its brand of truth. The very success of the Columbia strike spurred each on to new efforts in organizing.

During the twelve to eighteen months prior to the Columbia strike it appears almost as if the left had chosen New York City in which to evolve its internal dialectic. A wide variety of new groupings and publications appeared on the scene. The Progressive Labor party had long been based there; its deep involvement in SDS meant that New York would be the focus of its impact on SDS. The Lower East Side was developing its own brand of youth culture anarchism, with media outlets such as *Black Mask, Anarchos,* and *Rat.* Here also was the *Guardian,* which during the winter of 1967–68 had changed from a "progressive" to a "radical" weekly, and was especially receptive to the "new working class" tendencies within SDS represented by such spokesmen as Carl Davidson and Gregory Calvert. And here, finally, was a rather new tendency which would emerge as the New York SDS Labor Committee, publishing its own periodical, *The Campaigner,* which castigated all anarchist and syndicalist decentralizing groups within SDS and joined PLP in attacking the "youth culture" base of the dominant SDS tendency. The Columbia strike did not generate these divergent views, but it played a major role in shaping them and sharpening the subsequent debates among the New Left.

The sharpest conflict came over the issue of youth culture. Much of the New Left has its roots not in a formulation of concepts of social structure and social change which, in turn, form the groundwork of action, but, instead, in the personal youth rebellion of our time. Rock music, certain styles of dress, pot, and sexual freedom are the outward manifestations of a culture from which the vast number of recruits can be gained and which, in turn, shapes much of the New Left. Personal rebellion gives rise to demands for "control over our own lives" and hostility to cops and authority figures; a systematic analysis of social change recedes into the background. True, those leaders who seek to shape this personal rebellion into a political movement, and thereby expose themselves to the charge of being an "intellectual elite," urge a more highly articulated set of concepts about the "new working class" or "post-capitalist society." But these theories are sustained not by intellectual content but by personal rebellion, and that source of energy not only generates theory but also shapes tactics and organization as well. It propels a theory of participatory democracy into an espousal of decentralization and anarcho-syndicalism in a variety of forms. It asserts the triumph of the individual will over reality, rather than a disciplined movement working with the forces of the external world.[1]

In contrast with this view is one which emphasizes the need to build sustained, disciplined power within a framework of economic inequalities and the industrial discipline which generates and sustains them. There is emphasis on the working class, as in Old Left thought, as a source of power which must be organized, disciplined, directed into action to take power from those who control the system. Decentralization only vitiates this discipline, it is argued; one must seize the power of the state rather than buy the romantic notion held by anarchists that they can destroy all power and live in a purely libertarian condition; individual rebellion must be harnessed, converted into disciplined group action. Student action is not enough, for student action inevitably leads to student power and isolation from the larger world; instead, worker-student alliances should be cemented into a source of disciplined power. While the youth-culture left seeks contacts with blue-collar workingmen in terms of a common youth rebellion, the working-class left seeks those contacts within the context of the work situation. It is hardly surprising that the latter segment of the left is often "straight" in personal behavior and pointedly rejects pot, "hippie" styles, rock music, and sexual freedom. . . .

Within the left, therefore, the Columbia strike constituted a watershed. Into it poured the stream of energy which had been in the making for several years. The details of the strike clearly were not planned, but the fact of confrontation was, and one senses an onrush of New Left forces to the maelstrom of New York City politics during 1967 with a heightened sense of expectation that here is where the action would be. Columbia became the setting for that action in the city, capturing the spotlight from a variety of minor incidents throughout the city's colleges and universities that could have become major ones. But, in turn, the New Left got more than it had bargained for. For it generated not only a strike

[1] A thoughtful analysis of this view and its implications is Irving Louis Horowitz, "Radicals and the Revolt Against Reason," *New Politics*, 6 (1968), pp. 30–41.

which showed its strength in terms of student power, but also stimulated a sharp clarification of tendencies within the amorphous setting of "participatory democracy" which led off into a variety of directions. The immediate impact of these divergent tendencies was to vitiate the movement and to place heavy burdens upon the new SDS ventures which, inspired by the Columbia strike, arose throughout the nation in the fall of 1968.

Right-wing conceptions of politics have in the past decade displayed few innovations; writers continue to restate, add detail, and elaborate, but the perceptions of the right remain basically unchanged. Columbia merely confirmed these views. But during the same time the left has been undergoing considerable ferment; it has, in fact, generated more variety in left thought and action than in any previous time in American history. This complex elaboration has grown out of a variety of circumstances, but it seems clear that among them the Columbia strike was one of the most crucial.

Philip Slater

The Counterculture

"There is a revolution coming," Charles Reich wrote in his controversial bestseller, *The Greening of America* (1970). "It will not be like revolutions of the past. It will originate with the individual and with culture, and it will change the political structure only as its final act." By the 1970's the concept of a counterculture—with a new life style and value system—was subject to much scrutiny, some of

it naive, some hysterical, some loaded with overkill. One of the best analyses came from Philip Slater. He defines here the chief characteristics of the old and new cultures, and stresses the shift from a consciousness predicated upon scarcity to one based upon affluence. Although he is devastatingly critical of the old culture, he is also aware of problems and divisions within the counterculture, as he makes clear in his account of dilemmas separating activist (e.g., Yippie) and dropout (e.g., hippie) factions. Slater, a sociologist, has also written *The Glory of Hera.*

A curious event of the late Sixties was the popularity of the film, *The Graduate,* the viewing of which became almost a ritual for a wide spectrum of middle-class youth, who went to see it over and over. It was a brilliant film, constructed almost entirely of movie clichés, but many middle-aged reviewers were disturbed by its fusion of satire and naive romanticism. With the intolerance for ambiguity that characterizes both the generation and the genre, some critics attempted either to maintain that it was really *all* satire, or to dismiss it as basically callow.

The satire is largely associated with the more modern aspects of the film; reflecting intergenerational hostility, its sources and consequences. But the heart of the film is its celebration of the old American dream of love triumphant over culture. One might even say that it is a revival and a reformation of that Dream. Like Christianity, the Dream has always borne an almost antithetical relation to the everyday life of the society in which it is embedded, yet has still managed to dominate attitudes and even behavior within certain limited spheres. And like Christianity, the Dream became tarnished by this peculiar position in which it found itself.

Mike Nichols, the director of the film, was thus the Martin Luther of the Dream, reviving it and purifying it; clarifying, through satire, its ambiguous relation to the total culture, and restoring its original naive form. It is of no consequence that the hero and his bride will become corrupted

Excerpts from Philip Slater, *The Pursuit of Loneliness: American Culture at the Breaking Point,* pp. 53–56, 60–61, 96–98, 100, 103–04, 106–10, 112–15, 117–18. Copyright © 1970 by Philip E. Slater. Reprinted by permission of Beacon Press.

as time goes by. What is important is that the confrontation has taken place and Love·has won, however briefly. *The Graduate,* like its paler predecessors, is a ritual of purification and cleansing, a celebration of the *capacity* of feeling to triumph over pattern. The interruption of a wedding ceremony—always a popular theme in American films—is not merely a suspense gimmick. It is what the film is all about: the battle between social forms and human feeling. And it is important that human feelings should occasionally win—as important as occasional epiphanies and miracles are for religion. In our society this issue is a matter of life and death (of the society, if not the individual).

In earlier films the basic conflict was usually attenuated, revolving almost exclusively around the question of choosing the more romantic and less conventional of two prospective marital partners. The stop-the-wedding element tended to be approached either comically or in a very muted way (i.e., no disruption of the ceremony). *The Graduate* moves up to its climax with cinematic clichés so densely packed that we feel we have seen the film before. Once in the church, however, we find that the years' accumulations of compromises and dilutions have been ruthlessly cut away. The hero makes no attempt whatever to cover or mask his feelings, the ceremony is totally and irretrievably shattered, and the hero must physically battle the representatives of society's forms. In this scene the old theme is presented with a baldness so complete that it becomes new and revolutionary.

When the old theme is revived in its true form, stripped of its routinizations and redefinitions, it always seems shocking. Raw and literal Christianity has this kind of impact. That *The Graduate* achieved popular success therefore implies some change in values (middle-aged people tended to object to the church scene, while most young people did not). The major change seems to me to be a strengthening of the feeling side of the human-need-versus-social-form conflict. For the older generation rituals, ceremonies, and social institutions have an intrinsic validity which makes them intimidating—a validity which takes priority over human events. One would hesitate to disrupt a serious social occasion for even the most acute and fateful need unless it could be justified in social rather than personal terms. Doris Lessing and Shelley Berman have both observed, in the case of people confronted with aircraft whose integrity has been cast in doubt, that most people would quietly die rather than "make a scene."

The younger generation experiences a greater degree of freedom from this allegiance. They do not see social occasions as automatically having intrinsic and sovereign validity. Their attitude is more secular—social formality is deferred to only when human concerns are not pressing. A well-brought-up young man like the hero of *The Graduate* would have tended, thirty years ago, to stand passively watching while his personal disaster took place—thus the church scene at that time would have seemed much less realistic (or else the hero defined as severely disturbed). Indeed, much of the older cinematic comedy made use of this meek deference—we recall the cops-and-robbers chases in which both participants would briefly interrupt their frantic efforts in order to stand at attention while the flag or a funeral procession passed by.

This change is responsible both for the character of radical protest in the Sixties and for the angry responses of older people to it. Sitting-in at a segregated restaurant, occupying a campus building, lying down in front of vehicles, pouring blood in office files, and all of the imaginative devices emerging from modern protest movements depend heavily on a willingness to make a scene—not to be intimidated by a social milieu. And this is precisely what so enrages their elders, who are shocked not so much by the students' radicalism as by their bad form. That students should be rude to a public figure is more important to their elders than that the public figure is sending their children to their deaths in an evil cause. Students faced with situations in which existing practices are having disastrous consequences (killing people, destroying neighborhoods, cheating the poor, stultifying the minds of children, starving or brutalizing people, or whatever) are skeptical when told they should at all costs go through proper channels, knowing that such channels are typically ineffectual or prohibitively slow.[1] To be told it is better to kill or be killed than to be rude or make a public scene arouses much youthful bitterness and disillusionment, deftly captured in the protest song, "It Isn't Nice." . . .

Before leaving *The Graduate* we should take note of the hostile reaction of older adults in the society to the cross incident, which was widely criticized as being "unnecessary" and "in bad taste." That they should pick up this issue of "taste" and ignore the meaning of the incident exemplifies a characteristic tendency toward irrelevance that exasperates their children. In the midst of a dramatic confrontation between the generations they are distracted by the unorthodox use of a religious symbol. In the midst of a dramatic confrontation between blacks and whites they are distracted by a four-letter word. In the midst of a dramatic confrontation between those who espouse and those who oppose the Vietnam war, they are distracted by the long hair of some of the participants.

The young are baffled, amused, and enraged by these bizarre responses. They alternately view the middle-aged as hopelessly detached from reality and as willfully perverse. What they overlook is the terror. The young are challenging the fundamental premises on which their elders have based their lives, and they are attacking at all of the weakest points. No one likes to admit that they have spent their lives in a foolish, evil, or crazy manner. Furthermore, the elders were always taught to lie about their feelings. They are not likely to say: "You frighten and depress us.

---

[1] At my own university recently a proposal for curriculum reform was passed after seven years of moving through "normal faculty procedures," and of course long after those students who had sought the change were graduated.

We are afraid we have spent our lives in narrow self-aggrandizement, neglecting and brutalizing our neighbors, pursuing useless and trivial artifacts, and creating a joyless environment. It always seemed the right thing to do, but now we are a little unsure, and anyway we wouldn't know how to behave differently." Instead, they suppress their doubts and fears about themselves by refusing to perceive the meaning of the stimulus. When their children cry for peace or social justice they say, "don't talk dirty" or "get a haircut." This is a way of saying, "There is nothing important or disturbing going on here—this is just my child who is mischievous or careless at times—it is just a family affair" ("But Mother, I'm going to jail—I'm a political prisoner.". . . "Well, at least they'll give you a decent haircut"). It is a desperate attempt to view the world as unchanging—to convert the deep social unrest of the day into the blank torpor of suburban life—to translate Watts into "Julia," Berkeley and Columbia into "Dobie Gillis," Chicago into "Mayberry," and Vietnam into "McHale's Navy."

*   *   *

In the new there is always an admixture of the old, and this is true of the protean counterculture now burgeoning in the United States. This makes it very difficult . . . to tell what is a true counterculture and what is simply a recruiting outpost for the old culture. But the mere fact that the old culture tries to gobble up something new does not invalidate the potential revolutionary impact of this novelty. At some point a devourer always overreaches himself, like the witch or giant in folk tales who tries to drink up the sea and bursts, or like the vacuum monster in *Yellow Submarine* who ultimately devours himself and disappears. This seems to me the most probable future for the old culture in America.

When I talk of two separate cultures in America I do not mean rich and poor, or black and white (or science and humanism), but rather the opposition between the old scarcity-oriented technological culture that still predominates and the somewhat amorphous counterculture that is growing up to challenge it. At times this distinction may seem synonymous with old-versus-young, or radical-versus-conservative, but the overlap is only approximate. There are many young people who are dedicated to the old culture and a few old people attracted to the new; while as to politics, nothing could be more old-culture than a traditional Marxist. . . .

For the older generation, the ultimate moral reference group is the far right—authoritarian, puritanical, punitive, fundamentalist. Such views are of course considered extreme, impractical, and "moralistic," but they are accorded an implicit and unquestioned *moral* validity. The liberal majority generally feel uncomfortable and awkward defining issues in moral terms, but when it becomes inescapable it is this brand of morality that they tend to fall back upon. They are practical and "realistic" as long as possible, but when accused of moral flabbiness or being too compromising they feel called upon to pay homage to a kind of Bible Belt morality. They tend to view their position as one of sensible men mediating between hypermoralistic conservatives and amoral radicals, bending the rigid rules of the former to accommodate and indulge the latter. . . .

There are an almost infinite number of polarities by means of which one can differentiate between the two cultures. The old culture, when forced to choose, tends to give preference to property rights over personal rights, technological requirements over human needs, competition over cooperation, violence over sexuality, concentration over distribution, the producer over the consumer, means over ends, secrecy over openness, social forms over personal expression, striving over gratification, Oedipal love over communal love, and so on. The new counterculture tends to reverse all of these priorities. . . .

The core of the old culture is scarcity. Everything in it rests upon the assumption that the world does not contain the wherewithal to satisfy the needs of its human inhabitants. From this it follows that people must compete with one another for these scarce resources—lie, swindle, steal, and kill, if necessary. These basic assumptions create the danger of a "war of all against all" and must be buttressed by a series of counter-norms which attempt to qualify and restrain the intensity of the struggle. Those who can take the largest share of the scarce resources are said to be "successful," and if they can do it without violating the counter-norms they are said to have character and moral fibre.

The key flaw in the old culture is, of course, the fact that the scarcity is spurious—man-made in the case of bodily gratifications and man-allowed or man-maintained in the case of material goods. It now exists only for the purpose of maintaining the system that depends upon it, and its artificiality becomes more palpable each day. Americans continually find themselves in the position of having killed someone to avoid sharing a meal which turns out to be too large to eat alone.

The new culture is based on the assumption that important human needs are easily satisfied and that the resources for doing so are plentiful. Competition is unnecessary and the only danger to humans is human aggression. There is no reason outside of human perversity for peace not to reign and for life not to be spent in the cultivation of joy and beauty. Those who can do this in the face of the old culture's ubiquity are considered "beautiful."

The flaw in the new culture is the fact that the old culture has succeeded in hiding the cornucopia of satisfactions that the new assumes —that a certain amount of work is required to release the bounty that exists from the restraints under which it is now placed. Whereas the flaw in the old culture has caused it to begin to decompose, the flaw in the new culture has produced a profound schism in its ranks—a schism between activist and dropout approaches to the culture as it now exists. We will return to this problem a little later.

244

It is important to recognize the internal logic of the old culture, however absurd its premise. If one assumes scarcity, then the knowledge that others want the same things that we have leads with some logic to preparations for defense, and, ultimately (since the best defense is offense), for attack. The same assumption leads to a high value being placed on the ability to postpone gratification (since there is not enough to go around). The expression of feelings is a luxury, since it might alert the scarce resources to the fact that the hunter is near. . . .

Another logical consequence of scarcity assumptions is structured inequality. If there is not enough to go around then those who have more will find ways to prolong their advantage, and even legitimate it through various devices. The law itself, although philosophically committed to equality, is fundamentally a social device for maintaining structured systems of inequality (defining as crimes, for example, only those forms of theft and violence in which lower class persons engage). One of the major thrusts of the new culture, on the other hand, is equality: since the good things of life are plentiful, everyone should share them: rich and poor, black and white, female and male.

It is a central characteristic of the old culture that means habitually become ends, and ends means. Instead of people working in order to obtain goods in order to be happy, for example, we find that people should be made happy in order to work better in order to obtain more goods, and so on. Inequality, originally a consequence of scarcity, is now a means of creating artificial scarcities. For in the old culture, as we have seen, the manufacture of scarcity is the principal activity. Hostile comments of old-culture adherents toward new-culture forms ("people won't want to work if they can get things for nothing," "people won't want to get married if they can get it free") often reveal this preoccupation. Scarcity, the presumably undesired but unavoidable foundation for the whole old-culture edifice, has now become its most treasured and sacred value, and to maintain this value in the midst of plenty it has been necessary to establish invidiousness as the foremost criterion of worth. Old-culture Americans are peculiarly drawn to anything that seems to be the exclusive possession of some group or other, and find it difficult to enjoy anything they themselves have unless they can be sure that there are people to whom this pleasure is denied. For those in power even life itself derives its value invidiously: amid the emptiness and anesthesia of a power-oriented career many officials derive reassurance of their vitality from their proximity to the possibility of blowing up the world.

The centrality of invidiousness offers a strong barrier to the diffusion of social justice and equality. But it provides a *raison d'être* for the advertising industry, whose primary function is to manufacture illusions of scarcity. In a society engorged to the point of strangulation with useless and joyless products, advertisements show people calamitously running out of their food or beer, avidly hoarding potato chips, stealing each other's cigarettes, guiltily borrowing each other's deodorants, and so on. In a land of plenty there is little to fight over, but in the world of advertising images men and women will fight before changing their brand, in a kind of parody of the Vietnam war.

The fact that property takes precedence over human life in the old culture also follows logically from scarcity assumptions. If possessions are scarce relative to people they come to have more value than people. This is especially true of people with few possessions, who come to be considered so worthless as to be subhuman and hence eligible for extermination. Many possessions, on the other hand, entitle the owner to a status somewhat more than human. But as a society becomes more affluent these priorities begin to change—human life increases in value and property decreases. New-culture adherents challenge the high relative value placed on property, although the old priority still permeates the society's normative structure. It is still considered permissible, for example, to kill someone who is stealing your property under certain conditions. This is especially true if that person is without property himself—a wealthy kleptomaniac (in contrast to a poor black looter) would probably be worth a murder trial if killed while stealing.[2] . . .

. . . It should be stressed that affluence and economic security are not in themselves responsible for the new culture. The rich, like the poor, have always been with us to some degree, but the new culture has not. What is significant in the new culture is not a celebration of economic affluence but a rejection of its foundation. The new culture is concerned with rejecting the artificial scarcities upon which material abundance is based. It argues that instead of throwing away one's body so that one can accumulate material artifacts, one should throw away the artifacts and enjoy one's body. The new culture is not merely blindly reactive, however, but embodies a sociological consciousness. In this consciousness lies the key insight that possessions actually generate scarcity. The more emotion one invests in them the more chances for significant gratification are lost—the more committed to them one becomes the more deprived one feels, like a thirsty man drinking salt water. To accumulate possessions is to deliver pieces of oneself to dead things. Possessions can absorb an emotional cathexis, but unlike personal relationships they feed nothing back. Americans have combined the proliferation of possessions with the disruption, circumscription, and trivialization of most personal relationships. An alcoholic becomes malnourished because drinking obliterates his hunger. Americans become unhappy and vicious because their preoccupation with amassing possessions obliterates their loneliness. This is why production in America seems to be on such an endless

---

[2] A more trivial example can be found in the old culture's handling of noise control. Police are called to prevent distraction by the joyous noises of laughter and song, but not to stop the harsh and abrasive roar of power saws, air hammers, power mowers, snow blowers, and other baneful machines.

upward spiral: every time we buy something we deepen our emotional deprivation and hence our need to buy something. This is good for business, of course, but those who profit most from this process are just as trapped in the general deprivation as everyone else. The new-culture adherents are thus not merely affluent—they are trying to substitute an adequate emotional diet for a crippling addiction.

The new culture is nevertheless a product of the old, not merely a rejection of it. It picks up themes latent or dormant or subordinate in the old and magnifies them. The hippie movement, for example, is brimming with nostalgia—a nostalgia peculiarly American and shared by old-culture adherents. This nostalgia embraces the Old West, Amerindian culture, the wilderness, the simple life, the utopian community—all venerable American traditions. But for the old culture they represent a subordinate, ancillary aspect of the culture, appropriate for recreational occasions or fantasy representation—a kind of pastoral relief from everyday striving —whereas for the new culture they are dominant themes. The new culture's passion for memorabilia, paradoxically, causes uneasiness in old-culture adherents, whose future-oriented invidiousness leads to a desire to sever themselves from the past. Yet for the most part it is a question of the new culture making the old culture's secondary themes primary, rather than simply seeking to discard the old culture's primary theme. Even the notion of "dropping out" is an important American tradition—neither the United States itself nor its populous suburbs would exist were this not so.

Americans have always been deeply ambivalent about the issue of social involvement. On the one hand they are suspicious of it and share deep romantic fantasies of withdrawal to a simple pastoral or even sylvan life. On the other hand they are much given to acting out grandiose fantasies of taking society by storm, through the achievement of wealth, power, or fame. This ambivalence has led to many strange institutions— the suburb and the automobile being the most obvious. But note that both fantasies express the viewpoint of an outsider. Americans have a profound tendency to feel like outsiders—they wonder where the action is and wander about in search of it (this puts an enormous burden on celebrities, who are supposed to know, but in fact feel just as doubtful as everyone else). Americans have created a society in which they are automatically nobodies, since no one has any stable place or enduring connection. The village idiot of earlier times was less a "nobody" in this sense than the mobile junior executive or academic. An American has to "make a place for himself" because he does not have one.

Since the society rests on scarcity assumptions, involvement in it has always meant competitive involvement, and, curiously enough, the theme of bucolic withdrawal has often associated itself with that of cooperative, communal life. So consistently, in fact, have intentional communities established themselves in the wilderness that one can only infer that society as we know it makes cooperative life impossible.

Be that as it may, it is important to remember that the New England colonies grew out of utopian communes, so that the dropout tradition is not only old but extremely important to our history. Like so many of the more successful nineteenth-century utopian communities (Oneida and Amana, for example) the puritans became corrupted by involvement in successful economic enterprise and the communal aspect was eroded away—another example of a system being destroyed by what it attempts to ignore. The new culture is thus a kind of reform movement, attempting to revive a decayed tradition once important to our civilization. . . .

I pointed out earlier . . . that children are taught a set of values in earliest childhood—cooperation, sharing, equalitarianism—which they begin to unlearn as they enter school, wherein competition, invidiousness, status differentiation, and ethnocentrism prevail. By the time they enter adult life children are expected to have largely abandoned the value assumptions with which their social lives began. But for affluent, protected, middle-class children this process is slowed down, while intellectual development is speeded up, so that the earlier childhood values can become integrated into a conscious, adult value system centered around social justice. The same is true of other characteristics of childhood: spontaneity, hedonism, candor, playfulness, use of the senses for pleasure rather than utility, and so on. The protective, child-oriented, middle-class family allows the child to preserve some of these qualities longer than is possible under more austere conditions, and his intellectual precocity makes it possible for him to integrate them into an ideological system with which he can confront the corrosive, life-abusing tendencies of the old culture. . . .

Up to this point we have (rather awkwardly) discussed the new culture as if it were an integrated, monolithic pattern, which is certainly very far from the case. There are many varied and contradictory streams feeding the new culture, and some of these deserve particular attention, since they provide the raw material for future axes of conflict.

The most glaring split in the new culture is that which separates militant activism from the traits we generally associate with the hippie movement. The first strand stresses political confrontation, revolutionary action, radical commitment to the process of changing the basic structure of modern industrial society. The second involves a renunciation of that society in favor of the cultivation of inner experience and pleasing internal feeling-states. Heightening of sensory receptivity, commitment to the immediate present, and tranquil acceptance of the physical environment are sought in contradistinction to old-culture ways, in which the larger part of one's immediate experience is overlooked or grayed out by the preoccupation with utility, future goals, and external mastery. Since, in the old culture, experience is classified before it is felt, conceptualization tends here to be forsworn altogether. There is also much emphasis on aesthetic expression and an overarching belief in the power of love.

248

This division is a crude one, and there are, of course, many areas of overlap. Both value systems share an antipathy to the old culture, both share beliefs in sexual freedom and personal autonomy. Some groups (the Yippies, in particular) have tried with some success to bridge the gap in a variety of interesting ways. But there is nonetheless an inherent contradiction between them. Militant activism is task-oriented, and hence partakes of certain old-culture traits such as postponement of gratification, preoccupation with power, and so on. To be a competent revolutionary one must possess a certain tolerance for the "Protestant ethic" virtues, and the activists' moral code is a stern one indeed. The hippie ethic, on the other hand, is a "salvation now" approach. It is thus more radical, since it remains relatively uncontaminated with old-culture values. It is also far less realistic, since it ignores the fact that the existing culture provides a totally antagonistic milieu in which the hippie movement must try to survive in a state of highly vulnerable parasitic dependence. The activists can reasonably say that the flower people are absurd to pretend that the revolution has already occurred, for such pretense leads only to severe victimization by the old culture. The flower people can reasonably retort that a revolution based to so great a degree on old-culture premises is lost before it is begun, for even if the militants are victorious they will have been corrupted by the process of winning.

The dilemma is a very real one and arises whenever radical change is sought. For every social system attempts to exercise the most rigid control over the mechanisms by which it can be altered—defining some as legitimate and others as criminal or disloyal. When we examine the characteristics of legitimate and nonlegitimate techniques, however, we find that the "legitimate" ones involve a course of action requiring a sustained commitment to the core assumptions of the culture. In other words, if the individual follows the "legitimate" pathway there is a very good chance that his initial radical intent will be eroded in the process. If he feels that some fundamental change in the system is required, then, he has a choice between following a path that subverts his goal or one that leads him to be jailed as a criminal or traitor.

This process is not a Machiavellian invention of American capitalists, but rather a mechanism which all viable social systems must evolve spontaneously in order to protect themselves from instability. When the system as it stands is no longer viable, however, the mechanism must be exposed for the swindle that it is; otherwise the needed radical changes will be rendered ineffectual. . . .

Closely related to the activist-hippie division is the conflict over the proper role of aggression in the new culture. Violence is a major theme in the old culture and most new-culture adherents view human aggression with deep suspicion. Nonviolence has been the dominant trend in both the activist and hippie segments of the new culture until recently. But more and more activists have become impatient with the capacity of the old culture to strike the second cheek with even more enthusiasm than the first, and have endorsed violence under certain conditions as a necessary evil.

For the activists the issue has been practical rather than ideological: most serious and thoughtful activists have only a tactical commitment to violence. For the dropout ideologues, however, aggression poses a difficult problem: if they seek to minimize the artificial constriction of emotional expression, how can they be consistently loving and pacific? This logical dilemma is usually resolved by ignoring it: the love cult typically represses aggressive feelings ruthlessly—the body is paramount only so long as it is a loving body.

At the moment the old culture is so fanatically absorbed in violence that it does the work for everyone. If the new culture should prevail, however, the problem of human aggression would probably be its principal bone of contention. Faced with the persistence of aggressiveness (even in the absence of the old culture's exaggerated violence-inducing institutions), the love cult will be forced to reexamine its premises, and opt for some combination of expression and restraint that will restore human aggression to its rightful place as a natural, though secondary, human emotion.

A third split in the new culture is the conflict between individualism and collectivism. On this question the new culture talks out of both sides of its mouth, one moment pitting ideals of cooperation and community against old-culture competitiveness, the next moment espousing the old culture in its most extreme form with exhortations to "do your own thing." I am not arguing that individualism need be totally extirpated in order to make community possible, but new-culture enterprises often collapse because of a dogmatic unwillingness to subordinate the whim of the individual to the needs of the group. This problem is rarely faced honestly by new-culture adherents, who seem unaware of the conservatism involved in their attachment to individualistic principles.

It is always disastrous to attempt to eliminate any structural principle altogether; but if the balance between individualistic and collective emphases in America is not altered, everything in the new culture will be perverted and caricatured into simply another bizarre old-culture product. There must be continuities between the old and the new, but these cannot extend to the relative weights assigned to core motivational principles. The new culture seeks to create a tolerable society within the context of persistent American strivings—utopianism, the pursuit of happiness. But nothing will change until individualism is assigned a subordinate place in the American value system—for individualism lies at the core of the old culture, and a prepotent individualism is not a viable foundation for any society in a nuclear age.

Peter L. Berger and Brigitte Berger

Peter and Brigitte Berger do not doubt that a growing number of individuals are moving into a counterculture; indeed, they believe this is a fact. Moreover, they agree that the end result may bring "power to the people." But the process, they contend, will strengthen rather than challenge the technological society. As "beautiful people" join the counterculture, the blue-collar masses who have been waiting in the wings will move to center stage; the actors, in effect, will change but the act will not, and "the system" will again demonstrate its ability to adjust to social change. The authors are both sociologists. Peter Berger has

The Counterculture and "The Blueing of America"

also written *Invitation to Sociology, A Rumor of Angels* and *The Sacred Canopy,* and co-authored *Movement and Revolution* and *The Social Construction of Reality.* Brigitte Berger has written *Societies in Change.*

A sizable segment of the American intelligentsia has been on a kick of revolution talk for the last few years. Only very recently this talk was carried on in a predominantly left mood, generating fantasies of political revolution colored red or black. The mood appears to have shifted somewhat. Now the talk has shifted to cultural revolution. Gentle grass is pushing up through the cement. It is "the kids," hair and all, who will be our salvation. But what the two types of revolution talk have in common is a sovereign disregard for the realities of technological society in general, and for the realities of class and power in America.

Only the most religious readers of leftist publications could ever believe that a political revolution from the left had the slightest prospects in America. The so-called black revolution is at a dividing fork, of which we shall speak in a moment. But as to the putatively green revolution, we think that the following will be its most probable result: It will accelerate social mobility in America, giving new opportunities for upward movement of lower-middle-class and working-class people, and in the process will change the ethnic and religious composition of the higher classes. Put differently: far from "greening" America, the alleged cultural revolution will serve to strengthen the vitality of the technological

From Peter L. Berger and Brigitte Berger, "The Blueing of America," *The New Republic* (April 3, 1971), pp. 20–23. Reprinted by permission of THE NEW REPUBLIC, © 1971, Harrison-Blaine of New Jersey, Inc.

society against which it is directed, and will further the interests of precisely those social strata that are least touched by its currently celebrated transformations of consciousness.

The cultural revolution is not taking place in a social vacuum, but has a specific location in a society that is organized in terms of classes. The cadres of the revolution, not exclusively but predominantly, are the college-educated children of the upper-middle class. Ethnically, they tend to be WASPs and Jews. Religiously, the former tend to belong to the main-line Protestant denominations, rather than to the more fundamentalist or sectarian groups. The natural focus of the revolution is the campus (more precisely, the type of campus attended by this population), and such satellite communities as have been springing up on its fringes. In other words, the revolution is taking place, or minimally has its center, in a subculture of upper-middle-class youth.

The revolution has not created this subculture. Youth, as we know it today, is a product of technological and economic forces intimately tied to the dynamics of modern industrialism, as is the educational system within which the bulk of contemporary youth is concentrated for ever-longer periods of life. What is true in the current interpretations is that some quite dramatic transformations of consciousness have been taking place in this sociocultural ambience. These changes are too recent, and too much affected by distortive mass-media coverage, to allow for definitive description. It is difficult to say which manifestations are only transitory and which are intrinsic features likely to persist over time. Drugs are a case in point. So is the remarkable upsurge of interest in religion and the occult. However, one statement can be made with fair assurance: the cultural revolution has defined itself in diametric opposition to some of the basic values of bourgeois society, those values that since Max Weber have commonly been referred to as the "Protestant ethic"—discipline, achievement, and faith in the onward-and-upward thrust of technological society. These same values are now perceived as "repression" and "hypocrisy," and the very promises of technological society are rejected as illusionary or downright immoral. A hedonistic ethic is proclaimed in opposition to the "Protestant" one, designed to "liberate" the individual from the bourgeois inhibitions in all areas of life, from sexuality through aesthetic experience to the manner in which careers are planned. Achievement is perceived as futility and "alienation," its ethos as "uptight" and, in the final analysis, inimical to life. Implied in all this is a radical aversion to capitalism and the class society that it has engendered, thus rendering the subculture open to leftist ideology of one kind or another.

Its radicalism, though, is much more far-reaching than that of ordinary, politically defined leftism. It is not simply in opposition to the particular form of technological society embodied in bourgeois capitalism but to the very idea of technological society. The rhetoric is Rousseauean rather than Jacobin, the imagery of salvation is intensely bucolic, the troops of the revolution are not the toiling masses of the Marxist prophecy but naked children of nature dancing to the tune of primitive drums.

When people produce a utopia of childhood it is a good idea to ask what their own childhood has been like. In this instance, the answer is not difficult. As Philippe Ariès has brilliantly shown, one of the major cultural accomplishments of the bourgeoisie has been the dramatic transformation of the structure of childhood, in theory as well as in practice. Coupled with the steep decline in child mortality and morbidity that has been brought about by modern medicine and nutrition, this transformation is one of the fundamental facts of modern society. A new childhood has come into being, probably happier than any previous one in human society. Its impact, however, must be seen in conjunction with another fundamental fact of modern society—namely, the increasing bureaucratization of all areas of social life. We would see the turmoil of youth today as being rooted in the clash between these two facts—paraphrasing Max Weber, in the clash between the new "spirit of childhood" and the "spirit of bureaucracy." However one may wish to judge the merits of either fact, both are probably here to stay. Logically enough, the clash almost invariably erupts when the graduates of the new childhood first encounter bureaucracy in their own life—to wit, in the educational system.

We cannot develop this explanation any further here, though we would like to point out that it is almost exactly the opposite of the Freudian interpretations of the same clash provided, for example, by Lewis Feuer or Bruno Bettelheim: Rebellious youth is not fighting against any fathers; on the contrary, it is outraged by the *absence* of parental figures and familial warmth in the bureaucratic institutions that envelop it. The point to stress, though, is that the transformation of childhood, born of the bourgeoisie, today affects nearly all classes in American society—*but it does not affect them equally.* As, for example, the work of John Seeley and Herbert Gans has demonstrated, there exist far-reaching differences between the childrearing practices of different classes. The transformation, and with it the new "spirit of childhood," developed most fully and most dramatically in the upper-middle class—that is, in the same social context that is presently evincing the manifestations of "greening."

To say this is in no way to engage in value judgments. If value judgments are called for, we would suggest calibrated ones. Very few human cultures (or subcultures) are either wholly admirable or wholly execrable, and the intellectuals who extol this particular one are as much *terribles simplificateurs* as the politicians who anathematize it. In any case, our present purpose is to inquire into the probable consequences of the cultural changes in question.

The matrix of the green revolution has been a class-specific youth culture. By definition, this constitutes a biographical way station. Long-haired or not, *everyone*, alas, gets older. This indubitable biological fact has been used by exasperated over-thirty observers to support their hope that the new youth culture may be but a noisier version of the old American pattern of sowing wild oats. Very probably this is true for many young rebels, especially those who indulge in the external paraphernalia and gestures of the youth culture without fully entering into its new consciousness. But there is evidence that for an as yet unknown number, the way station is becoming a place of permanent settlement. For an apparently growing number there is a movement *from youth culture to counterculture*. These are the ones who drop out permanently. For yet others, passage through the youth culture leaves, at any rate, certain permanent effects, not only in their private lives but in their occupational careers. As with the Puritanism that gave birth to the bourgeois culture of America, this movement too has its fully accredited saints and those who only venture upon a *halfway covenant*. The former, in grim righteousness, become sandal makers in Isla Vista. The latter at least repudiate the more obviously devilish careers within "the system" —namely, those in scientific technology, business and government that lead to positions of status and privilege in the society. They do not drop out, but at least they shift their majors—in the main, to the humanities and the social sciences, as we have recently seen in academic statistics.

The overall effects of all this will, obviously, depend on the magnitude of these changes. To gauge the effects, however, one will have to relate them to the class and occupational structures of the society. For those who become permanent residents of the counterculture, and most probably for their children, the effect is one of downward social mobility. This need not be the case for the halfway greeners (at least as long as the society is ready to subsidize, in one way or another, poets, encounter-group leaders and humanistic sociologists). But they too will have been deflected from those occupational careers (in business, government, technology and science) that continue to lead to the higher positions in a modern society.

What we must keep in mind is that whatever cultural changes may be going on in this or that group, the personnel requirements of a technological society not only continue but actually expand. The notion that as a result of automation fewer and fewer people will be required to keep the technological society going, thus allowing the others to do their own thing and nevertheless enjoy the blessings of electricity, is in contradiction to all the known facts. Automation has resulted in changes in the occupational structure, displacing various categories of lower-skilled labor, but it has in no way reduced the number of people required to keep the society going. On the contrary, it has increased the requirements for scientific, technological and (last but not least) bureaucratic personnel. (The recent decline in science and engineering jobs is due to recession, and does not affect the long-term needs of the society.) The positions disdained by the aforementioned upper-middle-class individuals

254

will therefore have to be filled by someone else. The upshot is simple: *There will be new "room at the top."*

Who is most likely to benefit from this sociological windfall? It will be the newly college-educated children of the lower-middle and working classes. To say this, we need not assume that they remain untouched by their contact with the youth culture during their school years. Their sexual mores, their aesthetic tastes, even their political opinions might become permanently altered as compared with those of their parents. We do assume, though, that they will, now as before, reject the anti-achievement ethos of the cultural revolution. They may take positions in intercourse that are frowned upon by Thomas Aquinas, they may continue to listen to hard rock on their hi-fi's and they may have fewer racial prejudices. But all these cultural acquisitions are, as it were, functionally irrelevant to making it in the technocracy. Very few of them will become sandal makers or farmers on communes in Vermont. We suspect that not too many more will become humanistic sociologists.

Precisely those classes that remain most untouched by what is considered to be the revolutionary tide in contemporary America face *new prospects of upward social mobility*. Thus, the "revolution" (hardly the word) is not at all where it seems to be, which should not surprise anyone. The very word *avant-garde* suggests that one ought to look behind it for what is to follow—and there is no point asking the *avant-gardistes*, whose eyes are steadfastly looking forward. Not even the Jacobins paid attention to the grubby tradesmen waiting to climb up over their shoulders. A technological society, given a climate of reasonable tolerance (mainly a function of affluence), can afford a sizable number of sandal makers. Its "knowledge industry" (to use Fritz Machlup's term) has a large "software" division, which can employ considerable quantities of English majors. And, of course, the educational system provides a major source of employment for nontechnocratic personnel. To this may be added the expanding fields of entertainment and therapy, in all their forms. All the same, quite different people are needed to occupy the society's command posts and to keep its engines running. These people will have to retain the essentials of the old "Protestant ethic"—discipline, achievement orientation, and also a measure of freedom from gnawing self-doubt. If such people are no longer available in one population reservoir, another reservoir will have to be tapped.

There is no reason to think that "the system" will be unable to make the necessary accommodations. If Yale should become hopelessly greened, Wall Street will get used to recruits from Fordham or Wichita State. Italians will have no trouble running the RAND Corporation, Baptists the space program. Political personnel will change in the wake of social mobility. It is quite possible that the White House may soon have its first Polish occupant (or, for that matter, its first Greek). Far from weakening the class system, these changes will greatly strengthen it, moving new talent upward and preventing rigidity at the top (though, probably, having little effect at the *very* top). Nor will either the mechanics or the rewards of social mobility change in any significant degree. A name on the door will still rate a Bigelow on the floor; only there will be fewer WASP and fewer Jewish names. Whatever other troubles "the system" may face, from pollution to Russian ICBMs, it will not have to worry about its being brought to a standstill by the cultural revolution.

It is, of course, possible to conceive of such economic or political shocks to "the system" that technological society, as we have known it in America, might collapse, or at least seriously deteriorate. Ecological catastrophe on a broad scale, massive malfunction of the capitalist economy, or an escalation of terrorism and counterterror would be cases in point. Despite the currently fashionable prophecies of doom for American society, we regard these eventualities as very unlikely. If any of them should take place after all, it goes without saying that the class system would stop operating in its present form. But whatever else would then be happening in America, it would *not* be the green revolution. In the even remoter eventuality of a socialist society in this country, we would know where to look for our greeners—in "rehabilitation camps," along the lines of Castro's Isle of Pines.

We have been assuming that the children of the lower-middle and working classes remain relatively unbitten by the "greening" bug—at least sufficiently unbitten so as not to interfere with their aspirations of mobility. If they too should drop out, there would be literally no one left to mind the technological store. But it is not very easy to envisage this. America falling back to the status of an underdeveloped society? Grass growing over the computers? A totalitarian society, in which the few remaining "uptight" people run the technocracy, while the rest just groove? Or could it be Mongolian ponies grazing on the White House lawn? Even if the great bulk of Americans were to become "beautiful people," however, the rest of the world is most unlikely to follow suit. So far in history, the uglies have regularly won out over the "beautiful people." They probably would again this time.

The evidence does not point in this direction. The data we have on the dynamics of class in a number of European countries would suggest that the American case may not be all that unique. Both England and West Germany have been undergoing changes in their class structures very similar to those projected by us, with new reservoirs of lower-middle-class and working-class populations supplying the personnel requirements of a technological society no longer served adequately by the old elites.

What we have described as a plausible scenario is not terribly dramatic, at least compared with the revolutionary visions that intellectuals so often thrive on. Nor are we dealing with a process unique in history. Vilfredo Pareto called this type of process the "circulation of elites." Pareto emphasized (rightly, we think) that such circulation is essential if a society is going to survive. In a Paretian perspective, much of the green revolution would have to be seen in terms of decadence (which, let us remark in passing, is not necessarily a value judgment—some very impressive flowerings of human creativity have been decadent in the same sociological sense).

But even Marx may, in a paradoxical manner, be proven right in the end. It may be the blue-collar masses that are, at last, coming into their own. "Power to the people!"—nothing less than that. The "class struggle" may be approaching a new phase, with the children of the working class victorious. These days we can see their banner all over the place. It is the American flag. In that perspective, the peace emblem is the old bourgeoisie, declining in the face of a more robust adversary. Robustness here refers, above all, to consciousness—not only to a continuing achievement ethos, but to a self-confidence not unduly worried by unending self-examination and by a basically intact faith in the possibilities of engineering reality. Again, it would not be the first time in history that a declining class leaned toward pacifism, as to the "beautiful things" of aesthetic experience. Seen by that class, of course, the blue-collar masses moving in suffer from considerable aesthetic deficiencies.

"Revolutionary" America? Perhaps, in a way. We may be on the eve of its blueing.

R. Serge Denisoff

Protest Songs: Muted Music of the Revolution

Slave songs and the blues are prime examples of musical forms that have served as vehicles of protest, articulating grievances and discontent. But the rise of the "Woodstock culture" intensified discussion of the role of music as an instrument of peaceful revolution, effecting a subtle but profound change in human consciousness and values. R. Serge Denisoff contends, however, that while popular protest songs may reinforce listeners' attitudes, they probably do little to change them. After distinguishing between the social roles of hit-parade protest songs and the "freedom songs" of the civil rights movement, he concludes that music may be a weak weapon in the struggle to change men's minds. Denisoff is a sociologist who is author of *Great Day Coming: Folk Music and the American Left,* co-author of *The Sounds of Social Change* and has published widely in scholarly journals on the content, function and trends of popular music. He is editor of the *Journal of Society and Popular Music.*

I care not who makes the nation's laws," so the cliché goes, "so long as I can make its songs." This proposition has on occasion resounded in the White House, in the Communist party and in the world of show biz. Herbert Hoover, at the height of the Depression, told jazz-age crooner Rudy Vallee, "If you can sing a song that would make people forget their troubles and the Depression, I'll give you a medal." Woody Guthrie—the Marxist Will Rogers—inscribed "This Machine Kills Fascists," on his guitar. Several decades later, during the folksong revival, Peter Yarrow of Peter, Paul, and Mary, exclaimed to an interviewer, "we could mobilize the youth of America today in a way that nobody else could." As these diverse statements indicate, song is viewed as a potent weapon in the propaganda arsenal. Nevertheless, there is little, if any, concrete or empirical evidence that songs *do* in fact have an independent impact upon attitudes in the political arena. . . .

Both practitioners and critics have, despite this fact, tended to see music as an effective external weapon. *Fortune* magazine, at one time,

From R. Serge Denisoff, "Protest Songs: Those on the Top Forty and Those of the Streets," *American Quarterly,* 22 (Winter, 1970), pp. 807–23. Copyright, 1970, Trustees of the University of Pennsylvania. Reprinted by permission of the Trustees of the University of Pennsylvania and the author. Footnotes have been renumbered.

announced that picket-line songs were comparable to corporation public relations efforts. Other antagonists have labeled these ditties "subversive ploys." The activities of Congressional committees and vigilante groups aided by *Red Channels*, a magazine devoted to "identifying Reds," and the [Joe] McCarthy atmosphere banned socially significant compositions from the mass media for a decade. Protest songs were submerged and segregated to New York City "hoots" and liberal university campuses. The folk music revival, however, did reintroduce protest material into the commercial music media, but on a highly selective basis.

While People's Artists partisans were socially isolated in the 1950's, another segment of the folk-music scene was not barred from the mass media. Traditional folk songs were injected into the pop music complex by Burl Ives, Oscar Brand, John Jacob Niles, Harry Belafonte and the Weavers, and received some exposure. The Weavers, with their recordings of "Goodnight, Irene," "So Long, It's Been Good To Know You," and "Tzena," were the first urban singing group to reach the much sought-after number-one ranking on the Country and Western charts and the Hit Parade since Vernon Dalhart's 1924 recording of the "Wreck of the 97." Right-wing zealots curtailed the career of the Weavers, perhaps postponing for nearly a decade a revival which would wed protest songs and the mass media.

Prior to the boom triggered by the Kingston Trio's rendition of "Tom Dooley," folk music enjoyed sporadic bursts of success with the record-buying public. It was generally considered a novelty item until the late 1950's. Commercial revivals, as students of mass communication note, exhibit a self-destructive consumption. Following the introduction of southern-white ballads and Negro blues material, satirical songs were incorporated into the repertoires of folk-singing groups and, finally, traditional and contemporary protest songs, hidden away all these years, caught the attention of a large mass of young people. Protest songs became a means of expressing personal disdain for the events of the early 1960's. One of these dissenters in the folk idiom was Bob Zimmerman who changed his name, in emulation of his favorite literary figure, to Dylan.

Bob Dylan, since his first show business success in a Greenwich Village coffeehouse, has gone through a number of musical styling changes: topical and political songs; symbolic and expressionist poetic songs in the folk genre; and later, folk-rock, a variant of rock 'n' roll. This pacesetter was catapulted into the world of the Top Forty more by his song-writing ability than by his prowess as a singer. His early compositions were recorded by popular folk singers Peter, Paul, and Mary, who placed his ballad "Blowin' in the Wind" on the best-seller charts of *Billboard*. During this period Trini Lopez's rock version of the "Hammer Song," written by People's Songsters Pete Seeger and Lee Hays, sold over a million copies. Dylan's direct audience was at this time substantially limited to folkniks and a body of teenagers who identified with the sentiments expressed in his lyrics. All of this was altered by the release of "Subterranean Homesick Blues," a rock 'n' roll number with, at first hearing, nearly unintelligible lyrics. The electrified piece was a "hit" and some went so far as to suggest that it was all one glorious put-on. One prominent folk music publication, *Sing Out*, issued an open letter to the "folk poet" stating that he was losing sight of the fundamental purpose of music, social protest. Dylan had chosen drums, electric Fender guitars and amplifiers over Guthrie's inscription to convey his thought. The end product of this transition was that a proponent of social dissent became a force in popular music. Dylan was the trailblazer. It was, however, a former member of an apolitical commercial group, the Christy Minstrels —one Barry McGuire—who exploded the "art is a weapon" ethos upon the Top Forty.

A song prophetic of the nuclear annihilation of mankind unless social conditions were to change became the best-selling record in the country in the fall of 1965, introducing the pessimism of existential and Russelian thought into an area of musical expression previously confined to the problems of going steady and "purple people eaters." "The Eve of Destruction" was written by a nineteen-year-old and designed to make people face the facts of "where the world is at." The song was more in keeping with [Bertolt] Brecht's notion of art than with the trials and tribulations of teenage romantic love. The theme of the song was that man was half an hour away from global extinction:

> Can't you see the fear that I'm feelin' today?
> If the button is pushed there's no running away . . .

This piece, whatever its musical merits, was a breakthrough in a medium whose range of lyrical dissatisfaction was restricted to generational conflict. For the adolescent, the Top Forty was *his* music as opposed to the "straight" or "square" compositions preferred by his parents. Covertly, the genre itself was a form of protest. Explicitly, some rock 'n' roll numbers did fleetingly point to the banalities of going to school and the interference of parents in adolescent love rites. Eddie Cochran's "Summertime Blues," the Coasters' "Yakety Yak" and Chuck Berry's "Almost Grown" may have protested against parental control, yet none hinted at even the slightest possibility of altering this relationship except by the inevitability of growing up. The structure of "The Eve of Destruction" incorporated these elements with political sentiments to create a mild furor.

The emergence of "art is a weapon" in the rock idiom was received with mixed emotions. Tom Paxton, a major contemporary topical song writer, stated:

> The fact that there has been a response by the young to these "protest" songs is no cause for rejoicing. Anyone who asks of these idols that they probe a bit deeper will be disappointed, because these

songs never intended to tell them anything more than Mom and Dad don't understand them.[1]

A teenage folknik in northern California protested that "This new concept of uniting rock 'n' roll and folk music is a debauchery of all the ideals which made folk music unique and thought-provoking." Brecht's philosophical presence on the Top Forty and the growth of social awareness in American youth did not escape the gaze of the radical right. In 1963, prior to the blossoming of the folk-rock syndrome, the Fire and Police Research Association of Los Angeles called for an investigation of folk music as a tool in the subversion of American youth. A protest song on the Top Forty was a resounding call to arms. David Noebel, of the Christian Crusade, wrote that the lyrics of "Eve" "are obviously aimed at instilling fear in our teenagers as well as . . . [inducing] the American public to surrender to atheistic, international Communism." Groups such as Citizens for Conservative Action and the Young Republicans for a Return to Conservatism in California filed a complaint with the Federal Communications Commission arguing that "Eve" and similar songs violated the equal time provision, and contacted popular rock 'n' roll aggregates in an attempt either to ban or refute the message of the controversial song. Decca Records jumped on the political bandwagon with the "Dawn of Correction" by the Spokesmen. The ideological antithesis of "Eve" was not a commercial success. As this outcry illustrates, neither the advocates of the Guthrie-Seeger tradition nor the radical right were overjoyed with this type of protest on the airwaves. The left objected to the aesthetic while supporting the sentiment. The right partially discounted the idiom and concentrated on the content. Both agreed that music was a powerful opinion-forming device. The popularity of "The Eve of Destruction" raised a question which has not generally been treated by social scientists: "Is art an effective weapon?" More specifically, do protest songs on the Top Forty have any measurable impact upon their generalized audiences? The mass exposure of "The Eve of Destruction" provided an excellent opportunity to gain some insights in this sphere.

During the period that "The Eve of Destruction" received extensive air-play a questionnaire was administered to a random sample of students at a junior college in the San Francisco area. The school was chosen for several features. First, the subjects were either freshmen or sophomores, thus presumed to be more attuned to the offerings of the Top Forty. Secondly, due to the wide range of programs offered by the college a representative sample of the general population was possible. The curriculum included both vocational and academic courses. Finally, the student body was generally conservative and apolitical in contrast to the four-year schools in the region such as the University of California at Berkeley and

[1] Tom Paxton, "Folk Rot," *Sing Out,* 15 (Jan. 1966), pp. 103–4.

San Francisco State College. For example, only the Young Republicans existed on the campus, and even that organization operated *sub rosa,* for political groups were banned. During the previous semester, the spring of 1965, students had overwhelmingly rejected the attempts of a small band of on- and off-campus radicals to institute free speech reforms at the junior college. This latter factor appeared to make the sample ideal to measure the impact of a song considered left of center.

The students were posed questions to determine the following aspects of propaganda songs: 1) exposure, 2) intelligibility of lyrics, and 3) the responses of listeners.

The injection of protest material into the offerings of the Top Forty did, as expected, greatly increase the audience for this material. Of those sampled, 88 percent (158) had heard "The Eve of Destruction." Eighty-six percent of the total sample were first exposed to the song on the radio. Because of radio broadcasting, the Top Forty proved to be an excellent medium for bringing political ideology to teenagers and young adults. "The Eve of Destruction" reached a sizable portion of the sample, suggesting that it far outstripped the folk genre of earlier decades in gaining the attention of a mass audience. . . .

A substantial number of negative respondents were concerned about the content of the songs. They criticized such songs for lacking patriotism during wartime and for being part of a generalized subversive plot. The "hawks" felt that social criticism was inopportune while the Vietnam conflict was in progress:

> . . . songs come at a bad time. We're in Vietnam and they are getting much more play than they should.
> . . . they are made by guys who are afraid to help their country.
> . . . Anti-American in view of U.S. involvement in Vietnam.
> . . . when I listen to these songs, I feel another page in the story of anti-war pacifists has been written. We have a tradition to keep up, and it won't be kept up by lying down in the middle of the street or lighting yourself on fire at the Pentagon.
> . . . I don't like Peace Marchers.

A more extreme presentation of the unpatriotic view was the "Communist plot" motif:

> . . . Put them in one big pile then put the pacifists on top of the pile and either burn them or drop them in North Vietnam with the rest of the REDS.
> . . . they're pinko.

Several others, concurring with opinions that the songs were of a subversive nature, stated that these ditties "should not be *played* on the radio." A majority of the students who responded negatively objected on political or philosophical grounds to protest songs. . . .

Protest songs disseminated by the mass media do not appear to transcend the reaffirmation function, that is, confirming previous intellectual commitments. The facts that only 24 percent of those queried advocated the use of political material on "pop music" stations and that only 36 percent correctly interpreted the meaning of the song under consideration suggest that protest songs outside of a supportive context are not overtly effective as agitational weapons. This is a far cry from the role of so-called "freedom songs" of the civil rights movement.

In 1966 urban black militants such as Julius Lester were saying, "man, the people are too busy getting ready to fight to bother with singing anymore." Prior to the popularization of the black power slogan, in civil rights circles the "freedom song" was an extremely effective weapon if printed accounts and observations of Negro rights activists are correct. A number of observers, including the late Martin Luther King, Jr., have credited "freedom songs" with unifying the movement, giving it the will to continue, and creating new courage in the rank-and-file members. As one writer put it:

> They are dramatic emblems of the struggle and mighty weapons in it. Their steady, surging rhythms, their lilting melodies, and their simple, inspirational words, repeated over and over again, generate a fervor that can only be described as religious in its intensity. Even the least articulate of people can join in these group songs and respond to them fully; often the music serves as the best, even the primary, means of communication between the people and their leaders.[2]

The majority of these songs were adaptations of songs familiar to their constituents. They were based on the hymns sung weekly in southern churches. They, like the Psalms, were directed at believers. An examination of the lyrics of "freedoom songs" indicates that unlike "The Eve of Destruction" and other popular songs, these tunes are directed to those within a movement or picket line rather than to a general audience. The lyrics are specific, repetitive and simplistic. They do not use abstract concepts as does "Eve" but rather evoke immediate situations and solutions for those in the movement. "We Shall Overcome" has been particularly effective in marches and other situations of confrontation, since it reaffirms the valor of the marchers and the righteousness of the cause in a highly repetitive manner:

> We are not afraid, we are not afraid
> We are not afraid today.
> Oh, deep in my heart, I do believe,

[2] Robert Sherman, "Sing A Song of Freedom," *Saturday Review,* 66 (Sept. 28, 1963), pp. 65, 67.

We shall overcome someday . . .
We are not alone . . . [3]

Songs like "Oh Freedom," "We Shall Not Be Moved," "Ain't Gonna Let Nobody Turn Me Round" and many more all stress the role of a collectivity, a group, in achieving social goals. As I have reported elsewhere, 95 percent of the songs from the SNCC songbook (1964) were directed internally to those already in the movement or on a picket line. Freedom songs were, therefore, aimed at the committed at a time when social action was in progress or contemplated. Labor songs of the 1930's exhibited a similar character. They were spontaneous and appropriate in terms of a given conflict situation. The songs of the civil rights movement of the South were what members of People's Songs, Inc. would call "zipper songs"—songs that were repetitive and so structured that verses could be improvised to meet any contingency. "Ain't gonna let _____ turn me round" could be sung for any occasion on the streets of any community. The simplicity and repetitiveness made the song easy to learn within a matter of minutes.

In contrast, "The Eve of Destruction" was not conducive to group singing, because of its narrative quality and the number of disjointed verses. Civil rights songs were structured for group singing, as opposed to "Eve," which was primarily suited for a professional entertainer. Furthermore, popular protest songs are not collective statements of discontent, but rather individualized sentiments as to what is wrong with society. Solutions are not offered, social action is not advocated and, most important, the songs are impersonal statements sandwiched in between other Top Forty selections of a totally apolitical nature, not to mention commercials. As such, propaganda songs on the radio primarily are entertainment-oriented. Indeed, some singers of "protest material" do not accept the sentiments of the songs themselves. To illustrate, Glen Campbell, who recorded the antiwar song "Universal Soldier," is reported to have stated that "draft card burners should be hanged.". . .

Propaganda songs, both in social movements and on the Top Forty, stress the notion of reaffirmation of existent belief systems. Nevertheless, it would appear that, outside of an organizational structure or a demonstration, protest songs function primarily at the intellectual level when positively received. An emotional response is generally associated with a negative reaction. Surprisingly, despite the exposure afforded protest songs on the Top Forty radio, this medium does not have the impact some observers have suggested. For example, the radical right's conten-

---

[3] "We Shall Overcome," new words and music arrangement by Zilphia Horton, Frank Hamilton, Guy Carawan and Pete Seeger. TRO—Copyright © 1960 and 1963 by Ludlow Music, Inc., New York, N.Y. Used by permission. (Royalties derived from this composition are being contributed to the Freedom Movement under the trusteeship of the writers.)

tion that "mass hypnosis" protest songs on the Top Forty are potent weapons does not appear justified. Instead, the most striking aspect of this probe is that a large portion of college students were totally unconcerned with protest songs. This is possibly due to the transitory nature of the Top Forty. Songs come and go, fads change, hit songs last for a month or two and are rarely revived. Another interpretation is suggested by several performers. Singer Neil Diamond, for one, estimates that only 10 percent of the Top Forty audience listens to the lyrics of popular songs. While the responses to "Eve" do not support this contention, it would appear that the protest song is primarily seen as an entertainment item rather than one of political significance. Perhaps Marxists (the only ones to give the subject serious consideration) are correct in pointing to popular music as basically an obscurantist tool. However, a great deal more research is called for.

Furthermore, it appears that for maximum effectiveness, protest songs must be linked to some supportive organizational form such as a social movement. Otherwise, the message is intellectualized without any possible social action.

Protest on the Top Forty appears to reach a large audience. Once the message has been received, it is subjected to a number of responses, of which only a minority are affirmative.

The opinion formation function of protest songs on the Top Forty remains unsubstantiated with the burden of proof still in the hands of the advocates of "music is a weapon." As Pete Seeger observed in 1968: "No song I can sing will make Governor Wallace change his mind."

Suggestions
for further reading

THE PROTEST
OF
VALUES AND STATUS

Outstanding examples of historical analyses of cultural and status conflict in the American past include John Higham, *Strangers in the Land: Patterns of American Nativism, 1860–1925* (New Brunswick, N.J., 1955); Richard Hofstadter, *The Paranoid Style in American Politics and Other Essays* (New York, 1965); David Brion Davis, "Some Themes of Counter-Subversion: An Analysis of Anti-Masonic, Anti-Catholic, and Anti-Mormon Literature," *Mississippi Valley Historical Review*, 47 (September, 1960), 205–24; Stanley Coben, "A Study in Nativism: The American Red Scare of 1919–1920," *Political Science Quarterly*, 79 (March 1964), 52–75; and William W. Freehling, "Paranoia and American History," *The New York Review of Books* (September 23, 1971), 36–39. An excellent overview of the 1960's from such a perspective is Dan Wakefield, *Supernation at Peace and War* (New York, 1968). Garry Wills, *Nixon Agonistes: The Crisis of the Self-Made Man* (Boston, 1969, 1970), also offers a number of insights into the subject.

David M. Chalmers, *Hooded Americanism: The History of the Ku Klux Klan* (New York, 1965) includes many examples of the "our country" viewpoint; but see also Robert Moats Miller's penetrating analysis of the Klan as "a study in anxiety" in John Braeman, Robert Bremner and David Brody (eds.), *Change and Continuity in Twentieth-Century America: The 1920's* (Columbus, Ohio, 1968). Kenneth T. Jackson, *The Ku*

Klux Klan in the City, 1915–1930 (from which "The Urban Klansman" has been excerpted in this section) is a superior work that contains a very helpful bibliographical essay. Also noteworthy is Charles C. Alexander, *The Ku Klux Klan in the Southwest* (Lexington, Ky., 1965), which stresses the KKK's concern for "moral and social conformity."

On the "radical right," see Seymour Martin Lipset and Earl Raab, *The Politics of Unreason: Right-Wing Extremism in America, 1790–1970* (New York, 1970), and Daniel Bell (ed.), *The Radical Right* (Garden City, N.Y., 1963), both of which make provocative use of social science techniques. However, for a critical analysis of key assumptions that inform the Lipset-Raab-Bell viewpoint, one should also consult Michael P. Rogin's superb study, *The Intellectuals and McCarthy: The Radical Specter* (Cambridge, Mass., 1967). J. Allen Broyles describes the organizational structure and membership of *The John Birch Society* (Boston, 1964). Essays that have been of particular value in capturing the attitudes of various groups on the right in recent years are Joseph C. Goulden, "Voices from the Silent Majority," *Harper's Magazine* (April, 1970), 67–78; and Peter Schrag, "America's Other Radicals," *Harper's Magazine* (August, 1970), 35–46. Elizabeth Hardwick, "Mr. America," *The New York Review of Books* (November 7, 1968), deals with George Wallace and his supporters. Richard Rogin, "Joe Kelly Has Reached His Boiling Point," *The New York Times Magazine* (June 28, 1970), discusses the New York construction workers. Ward Just, *Military Men* (New York, 1970), probes into sources of right-wing enthusiasm in the military. David Riesman, "America

Moves To the Right," *The New York Times Magazine* (October 27, 1968), provides an excellent overview.

The counterculture has been a subject of considerable recent attention. Theodore Roszak, *The Making of a Counter Culture* (Garden City, N.Y., 1968), may well be a minor classic; the book is an informative and provocative analysis of this phenomenon as well as an expression of it. Also useful is William Braden, *The Age of Aquarius: Technology and the Cultural Revolution* (Chicago, 1970). More important in popularizing the idea of a counterculture is Charles A. Reich's bestselling *The Greening of America* (New York, 1970); Reich posits a changing American consciousness that is moving ineluctably toward "Consciousness III" of the youth culture. Paul Lauter and Florence Howe, *The Conspiracy of the Young* (New York, 1970), discusses several manifestations of the youth culture and concludes that "no administration can control the social and political force of the insurgent counterculture." The writings of Kenneth Keniston provide some of the most useful insights into the youth culture; see especially his *Youth and Dissent: The Rise of a New Opposition* (New York, 1971). Paul Goodman, *New Reformation, Notes of a Neolithic Conservative* (New York, 1970) suggests an analogy between the "protest, conflict, disgust with the Establishment" in 1510 and at present. For sympathetic descriptions and photographs of one aspect of the counterculture, see William Hedgepeth, *The Alternative: Communal Life in New America* (New York, 1970). For reports from Rainbow Farm and other communitarian experiments, see the "Culture/Counter Culture" section of *Ramparts* magazine. Other statements from diverse parts of the counterculture include Abbie Hoffman, *Woodstock Nation: A Talk-Rock Album* (New York, 1969); Jerry Rubin, *We are Everywhere* (New York, 1971); and Raymond Mungo, *Total Loss Farm; A Year In the Life* (New York, 1970).

Commentary magazine has been among those dubious about the counterculture; see, especially, the issue on "The Counter-Culture and Its Apologists" (December, 1970). Philip Nobile (ed.), *The Con III Controversy: The Critics Look At the Greening of America* (New York, 1971), includes a number of devastating responses to Charles Reich's version of the counterculture. James Hitchcock, "Comes the Cultural Revolution," *The New York Times Magazine* (July 27, 1969), and Robert Brustein, *Revolution As Theatre; Notes on the New Radical Style* (New York, 1971), are highly skeptical of the much-heralded "cultural revolution."

Among the more important interpretations that place campus unrest in social and cultural context are Sheldon Wolin and John Schaar, *The Berkeley Rebellion and Beyond* (New York, 1970); Irving Louis Horowitz and William H. Friedland, *The Knowledge Factory: Student Power and Academic Politics in America* (Chicago, 1970), which views "students as a social class"; and Michael Miles, *The Radical Probe: The Logic of Student Rebellion* (New York, 1970), an examination of the student movement within a "super-industrial society." Mark Gerzon, *The Whole World is Watching* (New York, 1970), speaks as a participant in the defection among the postwar generation from the old culture. Two provocative essays are Diana Trilling, "On the Steps of Low Library:

v *Suggestions for further reading*

Liberalism and the Revolution of the Young," *Commentary* (November, 1968), 29–55, which examines the Columbia University uprising as part of "a revolution in and of modern culture," and George Kateb, "The Campus and its Critics," *Commentary* (April, 1969), 40–48, which argues from the view that "the major source of student malaise is the larger society."

Christopher Lasch, *The New Radicalism in America, 1889–1963: The Intellectual As a Social Type* (New York, 1965), is a major work that draws connections between radicalism and the intellectual's estrangement from his culture. For related interpretations, see David Felix, *Protest: The Intellectuals and the Sacco-Vanzetti Case* (Bloomington, Indiana, 1965); Daniel Aaron, *Writers on the Left* (New York, 1961); Warren Susman, "A Second Country: The Expatriate Image," *Texas Studies in Literature and Language,* III (Summer, 1961), 171–83; R. Jackson Wilson, *In Quest of Community: Social Philosophy in the United States, 1860–1920* (New York, 1968), especially chapter 1; Richard Hofstadter, *Anti-Intellectualism in the United States* (New York, 1963); Henry F. May, *The End of American Innocence* (New York, 1959); and Andrew M. Greeley, "Intellectuals As an 'Ethnic Group,' " *The New York Times Magazine* (July 12, 1970). For an example of recent splits within the intellectual community over protest and the intellectuals' role, see Hans Morgenthau, "Truth and Power: The Intellectuals and the Johnson Administration," *The New Republic* (November 26, 1966), 8–14; and

for divisions within university faculties on the matter of protest, see Stanley Diamond and Edward Nell, "The Old School at the New School," *The New York Review of Books* (June 18, 1970), 38–43.

On music as a vehicle for cultural protest, see R. Serge Denisoff and Richard A. Peterson, *The Sounds of Social Change* (Chicago, 1972); Lawrence W. Levine, "The Concept of the New Negro and the Realities of Black Culture," in Nathan I. Huggins, Martin Kilson, and Daniel M. Fox (eds.), *Key Issues in the Afro-American Experience* (New York, 1971); Jerome L. Rodnitzky, "The Evolution of the American Protest Song," *Journal of Popular Culture,* 3 (Summer, 1969), 35–45; R. Serge Denisoff and Mark H. Levine, "Generations and Counter-Culture: A Study in the Ideology of Music," *Youth and Society,* 2 (September, 1970), 33–58, and "The Popular Protest Song; The Case of 'Eve of Destruction,' " *Public Opinion Quarterly,* 35 (Spring, 1971), 117–22; Denisoff, "Protest Movements: Class Consciousness and the Propaganda Song," *Sociological Quarterly,* 9 (Summer, 1968), 228–47; Marcello Truzzi, "The 100% American Songbag: Conservative Folksongs in America," *Western Folklore* (January, 1969), 27–40; and Robert A. Rosenstone, "The Times They are A-Changin': The Music of Protest," *The Annals of the American Academy of Political and Social Science,* 382 (March, 1969), 131–44. John Seelye, "The Sound of Money," *The New Republic* (June 27, 1970), 21–24, is a suggestive interpretation of left- and right-wing protests within country music.

268

The Continuity
of Protest
and the New Left

During the 1960's America witnessed, and was shaken by, the rise of the New Left. As earlier selections in this volume have indicated, protest is not new to American society; some writers have already explicitly or implicitly tied very recent protest to the past. These earlier articles, such as the ones by Martin Duberman and Melvyn Dubofsky, along with the first three readings in this section which directly seek past precedent for recent radicalism, all raise the question of how "new" is the New Left. Does the term have substantive meaning or is it merely chronological? In what ways does the New Left differ from the Old Left? In what manner do the protest and protesters of the 1960's and early 1970's diverge from prior dissent and dissenters? In an attempt to answer these questions, the New Left is compared by Bertram Wyatt-Brown to the nineteenth-century antebellum abolitionists, by Howard Zinn to the Old Left of the 1930's, and by William Lee Miller to the cultural protesters of the 1920's and the political-economic protesters of the 1930's.

Because of its amorphous nature and the twists and turns in the movement's evolution from inception to the present, it is difficult to pinpoint the characteristics of the New Left. Yet it can be reliably stated that at various points in its development the New Left adhered to one, some, or all of the following: the doctrine of participatory democracy, engagement in confrontation politics, distrust of bureaucracy, loss of faith in the university as an institution of learning, opposition to the Vietnam War and a general distrust of American foreign policy, desire for advancement of the undergroups in our society, black power, pursuit of new life styles and cultural departures, and preference for action as opposed to intellectualizing. For some it was a movement, a religion, a way of life—all rolled into one. Typically, Howard Zinn has proclaimed in an essay other than the one printed herein,

> Because of our vision of how men *should* live and the contrast with our knowledge of how they *do* live. . . , the most urgent theoretical question for the New Left (in which traditional Marxism gives least guidance) is: How do we change society? How do we redistribute power in order to redistribute wealth? How do we overcome those who enjoy power

and wealth and won't give them up? How do we stop the fanaticism of civilian and military leaders who feel it is America's duty to establish its power (or its puppets) wherever possible in the world, and do not care how many people, Americans or other, they kill in process?[1]

In varied form, such questions have been asked throughout American history. The New Left, from its birth sometime during the early 1960's, began its inquiry into the nature of American society. Building on the sit-in confrontation techniques of the civil rights movement, apprenticing in the Mississippi Summer Project of 1964, graduating to the Berkeley Free Speech Movement, the New Left gathered greatest momentum with its opposition to the Vietnam War. From the teach-in movement, which began in the spring of 1965, to the October Moratorium and November Mobilization which drew several hundred thousand protesters to Washington in 1969, to the student strike over the Cambodian invasion which closed down 437 colleges and universities during its first week of protest in the spring of 1970, the New Left was in the vanguard of the discontented society.

Some time during this period, probably in 1967, the movement—as described in Section V—spawned its cultural counterpart, or as some observers proclaimed, its counterculture to traditional American society. First, as hippies, counterculture youth seemed to be politically apathetic—dropping out—then, with the formation of the Youth International Party by Jerry Rubin and Abbie Hoffman, Yippies combined politics and counterculture to produce what was for some, as the title of one of Hoffman's books indicated, "revolution for the hell of it." Yet, the discontent, midwifed by the New Left, that welled up in America during the 1960's and early 1970's, was not the product of an isolated few, but of a large and vocal segment of American life.

Whether, like Howard Zinn, one welcomed recent radicalism and was "glad to be with it," or like liberal William Lee Miller rejected the New Left, not only for its sometimes "violent, illegal, coercive, defamatory" tactics but for its "underlying social analysis, . . . cultural revolt, . . . and political objectives," something seemed to be wrong with life in the United States. Even Miller, who contends that America is far superior to the way the New Left has pictured it, accepts "as accurate most of the particular criticism of American society." For him, however, its evils could not be "corrected by a holistic rejection of that society or by tactics of violence and abuse." The question at the beginning of the 1970's was whether others, and in what numbers, would accept what Miller could not. What would be the future of protest?

[1] Howard Zinn, "Marxism and the New Left," in *Dissent: Explorations in the History of American Radicalism,* edited by Alfred F. Young (De Kalb, Ill.: NIU Press, 1968), p. 369.

The final selection by Peter Drucker, while not aimed directly at the issue of protest, provides one economic analyst's answer to that question. Drucker's prediction agrees with Bertram Wyatt-Brown's conclusion that

> The climax of radical frustration is yet to come, but declension of religious zeal and yearnings for order and tranquility have always followed in the cycle of human affairs. At some point, the temples must empty, the participant—refreshed, worried, bored, touched, and exasperated—must turn home to the humdrum and familiar, remembering sadly that the dreams of youth become the broken promises of maturity.

If there is such a "cycle of human affairs," if the only constant in history is change, then how soon will the New Left become old and the protest of today fade into the memory of tomorrow? Will it all matter and will America be changed for the better?

Bertram Wyatt-Brown

New Leftists and Abolitionists: A Comparison of American Radical Styles

Bertram Wyatt-Brown finds conditions during the 1830's and in recent years producing similar cases of "righteousness fever" among the former era's abolitionists and the latter's New Left. Drawing on psychological studies such as Kenneth Keniston's *Young Radicals* and his own and other work on abolitionists, Wyatt-Brown highlights the resemblance between both groups of protesters in terms of social backgrounds, family structure, mobility, and attitudes toward communal living. Moreover, he sees the style of both representing the American impulse for moral regeneration and the habit of setting goals impossible to achieve, yet necessary to proclaim. Professor Wyatt-Brown is the author of *Lewis Tappan and the Evangelical War against Slavery*.

F rom John Winthrop's sermon to the Puritan travelers to the last, pious pronouncement from the White House, Americans have felt a compulsive urge to preach—to be prophets of doom and evangels of inspiration. Lately there have been so many Jeremiahs crowding into the national pulpit that there is hardly anyone left in the pews to listen. Demands for national repentance are heard on every side—from the columns of *Barron's* to the revolutionary chitchat of Stokely Carmichael on the Dick Cavett Show. So devoted are we to the irresistible pleasures of catechizing each other that the preaching of revolution becomes a substitute for the hard work of planning it. Dynamiting empty office buildings in New York, occupying a dean's office, razzing a Daley judge, or blowing up Rodin's Thinker outside the "establishment's" Cleveland Museum are all sermons, not revolutionary acts. They are not preludes to truly revolutionary incidents like the storming of the Bastille, the Potemkin mutiny, or the assassination of General Trujillo. Instead, they are theatrical versions of those fundamentalist billboards throughout the South—"Prepare to Meet Thy God," "The Wages of Sin is Death." Both reactionaries and radicals harken to calls for moral regeneration. Our

From Bertram Wyatt-Brown, "New Leftists and Abolitionists: A Comparison of American Radical Styles," *Wisconsin Magazine of History,* 53 (Summer 1970). Reprinted by permission of the State Historical Society of Wisconsin and the author.

religious impulses are not introspective; we advertise convictions as if they were toothpaste. But *self-repentance* is always in short supply in the marketplace of indignation.

"Righteousness fever" seems to strike like a recurring illness at different times in American history. Two of the most notable examples, though, are our present situation and that of the 1830's. Like conditions do not always produce similar consequences. Yet, one can discern a pattern of events that link these two periods of moral outrage, alienation, and romantic extravagance. Both belong to ages of foreign revolutions and domestic unrest. Both were preceded by a decade or so of relative stability and social calm—the post-Napoleonic era and the Eisenhower years. Men who lived through the trauma of French Revolution and Napoleonic militarism on the one hand, and the Second World War, the rise of Stalinism, and the fall of Nationalist China on the other, yearned for public order, release from the "terrors of ideological politics," and the pursuit of private, domestic interests. Desperately these men—the fathers of the upcoming radicals of the next generation—tried to check the decline of what Hannah Arendt has described as "the old Roman trinity of religion, tradition, and authority." Grand visions of revolutionary utopias, which only seemed to lead to totalitarian, self-defeating results wearied and frightened them.

At first glance, Americans of the 1820's and 1950's seemed to have overcome their fears of ideology. Both postwar eras celebrated a national consensus about politics and social aims. After the outward menaces of foreign ideologies receded somewhat, Americans settled quite comfortably for a benign religious orthodoxy, stable republicanism, and social and political compromises necessary for sectional harmony. Pragmatic, low-keyed goals of economic expansion occupied their thoughts and time. Just as Charles Wilson could boast that what was good for General Motors was also good for the country, so, too, a businessman of 1825 could swell with pride in American manufacturing: "Poor mother earth was never so beat and exercised as now, and she must think a new race dwells on her surface." Superficially, the world seemed relatively well-ordered with developing institutions, prosperity, increasingly rapid communications, and a concern for religious and social orthodoxy.

Not far below the surface, however, anxieties about the stability of society and the uncertain state of traditional values hid beneath such comforting characterizations of their times as the "era of good feelings" and "the silent generation." A conservative of 1830 grumbled: "The men of the present generation must decide the momentous question, whether this great Christian Republic shall move on in the path explored and recommended by the patriots of '76, under the healthful influence of her Bible and Sabbaths: or be thrown upon the ocean of experiment, with no other compass than that by which the leaders of the French Revolution were guided, in their bloody and disastrous course. . . ." Memories of the Bastille, the guillotine, the desecration of Notre Dame lingered like an immense shadow upon the American imagination. Southerners, faced with the examples of the Gabriel, Denmark Vesey, and Nat Turner threats of massive black insurrection, could hardly forget the French Revolutionary example of Toussaint L'Ouverture and Dessalines.

Against this setting in the early republic with its modern equivalent, the next generation of Americans took its cues. The upcoming zealots felt no terrors of international ideologies. The classic enemies of freedom—Jacobinism and Communism—had to be learned from textbooks and teachers, parents, and aging spokesmen. Neither Jacobinism nor Communism were to be perfect models for the youngsters, but they at least represented points of reference by which to judge contemporary society. French and Russian (or preferably Cuban) revolutionary systems symbolized a break with the past and demonstrated the power of absolute principle to move men's hearts, even if they had little application as systems of economy or government to American needs. At the same time, the young noticed that adults did not live up to their own orthodox standards of conduct. As Barrington Moore recently observed, the present-day radicals "have been both acting upon their elders' ideals and rebelling against their betrayal, struggling to see what went wrong, and searching desperately for substitutes." Slavery could not be squared with the sacred rhetoric of the Declaration of Independence; traditional American concepts of self-determination for colonial peoples were obviously betrayed in the interventions in Santo Domingo, the Cuban Bay of Pigs, and Indochina.

Cruelty, oppression, war, and institutional violence of all kinds became highly visible, monolithic, and impervious to the ameliorative plans that the older generation had devised for controlling them. Raised to believe that men were rational creatures, that society had designed safeguards to protect liberty of action, that material progress indicated divine favor, these young radicals of the 1830's and 1960's were impatient with the ancient paradox of human sin. Institutions, not the human condition, must explain the origin of evil. "Immediacy" replaced "progress" as the catchword for change: immediate withdrawal from Vietnam, immediate emancipation for the slaves. Supreme faith in human possibility took the place of institutional gradualism. . . .

Examining radicals involved in the nonviolent "Vietnam Summer" of 1967, [Kenneth] Keniston discovered that most of them belonged to middle-class and college-trained families with Stevensonian or left-wing leanings. The centers of family life were the close-knit family unit itself and the community's affairs. Parents of young radicals took their places in PTA, church, civic drives, and other charitable and political activities. Turning to [David] Donald's information about the abolitionists, we find that this breed of committed youth came from families of farmers, teachers, ministers, and storekeepers of New England. By and large, abolitionists' parents were pious Quakers, Congregationalists, Presbyterians, Unitarians, and Baptists. Keniston found that some of these faiths also appear quite prominently in the New Leftists' backgrounds, but he included Reform Judaism. Unhelpfully Keniston presents no statistics nor any control group data.

Keniston's chief point, however, is that a sense of moral uprightness dominated the young agitator's home life, a kind of rectitude that stressed social responsibility. Donald argues quite accurately along similar lines regarding abolitionists. These young men and women of both eras were usually taught to free themselves from overt biases against the less fortunate. Usually, the modern radical's mother assumed a role of moral preceptor, not the father, according to Keniston's study. The relation between the young radical and his mother was very intimate, warm, and intense, Keniston suggested. Immediately one is reminded of the strong-willed, quietly intense, religious mothers of William Lloyd Garrison, Lewis and Arthur Tappan, Thomas Wentworth Higginson, Theodore Weld, and James G. Birney's Aunt Doyle. According to Tilden Edelstein's excellent biography of Thomas W. Higginson, young Higginson's father confessed "that his wife supervised the children's moral training," holding daily prayers, reading sermons aloud, and preparing them for the divine life after death.

If the modern radical was a girl, Keniston surmised, she was likely to look to her father for spiritual and ethical advice. Thus, Angelina and Sarah Grimké, Elizabeth Cady Stanton, and Harriet Beecher Stowe received their moral lessons from their fathers. In any case, one of the parents seemed to be the focus of childhood attention. Richard Hildreth and Elizur Wright, for example, learned spiritual duty from their schoolmastering fathers. In such instances, the abolitionist sometimes spoke of a relatively cool relationship with the overshadowed parental partner. This psychological factor might lead to a feeling of neglect from the more indifferent parent. Keniston found that frequently modern radical youths with strong maternal ties complained about their fathers' absorption in business, their willingness to compromise with principle, and their conventional beliefs. It is difficult to calculate the results of Oedipal ambiguities upon the nonconformist; Keniston in other writings convincingly denies that such Freudian speculations have much validity in assessing radical motivation. Despite a "split image" of the father, radicals have a generally healthy, well-structured relationship with their parents. . . .

For youths raised up to believe in their own superiority, their ability to master the normal hurdles and to search for underlying values, these visible marks of arrival at adulthood could become unsatisfying when the occupation involved as well as the ceremony symbolizing it was no longer integrated in the larger social context. Thus to the ordinary agonies about reaching the career or moral goal would be added doubts about its relevance. With institutions and vocations losing old functions and taking on new ones, questions about their value were not easy to answer. For the radical today the issue involves the role of student. Scornfully but pertinently, a Young Socialist Alliance broadside declared: "The best student is the obedient, docile student who dutifully collects credits until he reaches the magical number when he is considered 'educated.'"

The reaction of abolitionists to the changes in their most significant institution, the church, was as intense as the radicals' response to theirs—the university. The young man could no longer feel that society honored the life of divinity as much as new careers in business or the law. By the 1820's the minister was not the most learned, most respected individual in his community as he once had been. As Daniel Calhoun has shown, he was merely another atomistic entrepreneur, so to speak, seeking always the better salary and the approval of equally acquisitive, equally transient laymen. For some, this state of affairs intensified youthful feelings of inferiority and confusion about an ultimate career....

The origins of abolitionist migration from orthodoxy must be traced to the uncertain state of that orthodoxy in their adolescence. When faced with his parents' anxieties about an acquisitive world, a community's fear of nonconformity, a national horror of revolution and sectional conflict, and a world's indifference to and doubt of divinity, the young radical-to-be was bound to have difficulty locating himself, his career, and his own set of beliefs. The society around him, entangled in cruel oppressions against all kinds of unfortunate groups, institutional hypocrisies, and empty symbols, indeed seemed "sick." In no area was the dream for American order, fidelity to principle, and that integrating force of "liberty" for all so clearly denied in actuality than in the expanding, slaveholding South.

The cold war atmosphere, national complacency, and technocratic changes of the 1950's posed similar problems for the young idealist. Both eras were ones of rapid mobility. Families not only moved into new neighborhoods, they also moved up and sometimes down the social ladder within them. This "uprootedness," as Erikson remarked, is typical of American life, but for these young persons it led to questioning of the legitimacy of the social order. Such migrations belied the family insistence upon stability and community loyalty. Surely, too, migrations of high school and college administrators and teachers, loyal to themselves and their fields of specialization alone, and not to the local "community of scholars and students"—more mobile in fact than the four-year student himself—might have similar effects upon radical youth today....

Radicals may discover in their work for the "cause" a sufficient satisfaction of their need for mutuality, but many seek more formal ties. Thus, in both antebellum and modern periods, cooperative enterprises and communitarian experiments flourished, based upon the assumed social failures of competition and upon the presumed superior character of radical inner life....

The speculations offered herein suggest that present unrest, especially on the nation's campuses, will result in no completion of the revolution *manqué* that the abolitionists began. It must be remembered that anti-slavery purists did not arouse a northern constituency for a holy war against slavery in the old states. Charles Beard's economic analysis may have been overly simple, but, as Eugene Genovese has explained, slavery was economically incompatible with industrial, commercial, and agricultural free labor. The Civil War was a struggle for economic and political unification, analogous to that of Germany and Italy, in which southern agrarian elites capitulated to aggressive northern capitalism. The Union army and Republican party policies, not the abolitionist forces, destroyed slavery as a necessary reordering of power. The slave moved from bondage to serfdom, as he usually has throughout the history of the institution. Radical idealists were instrumental in the complex evolution of northern and southern polarity; their influence as polemical watchdogs continued through war and Reconstruction, as James McPherson has shown, but the utopian new world of racial brotherhood remained an unfulfilled dream.

Like the antebellum agitators, modern radicals seek only to reach those within their cultural milieu. Although antihistorical in aims and approach, they are bound by the chains of their own past. "From the bourgeoisie," declared one radical, "you have come, and to them you shall go." Efforts to collaborate with white workers and downtrodden ethnic minorities have not enjoyed much more than temporary success here and there. Garrisonians were separated from poor whites and blacks, but, as Benjamin Quarles has wisely observed, even the Northern free Negro abolitionists found it difficult to cooperate with even the most egalitarian abolitionists. In that more paternalistic age, with its emphasis upon conformity of dress and decorum, abolitionists seldom felt it necessary to break with custom as a way of showing solidarity with the poor. But simulated poverty by style of hair and clothes cannot disguise the gap between the educational radical "elite"—the children of the establishment—and the traditional bases of revolution, the worker-peasant classes. Instead, stress is given to the "politicizing" of middle-class institutions, especially the universities and colleges, just as abolitionists sought the same moral goal for the national churches. Echoing Garrison's demands for a "true church" of "integrity and purity," Tom Hayden in equally romantic terms declared that the Columbia radicals wanted "a new and independent university standing against the mainstream of American society, or they want no university at all." Such dreams have little place in the search for genuine power that must animate the true revolutionary.

We return to the original point. Americans love to preach, to clothe their personal fears and aspirations in the language of the apocalypse, to stage battles between the forces of good and evil, "to make the world safe for democracy," and, in the words of Carl Oglesby, SDS president in 1965, to "change the system that needed slaves in the first place and could 'emancipate' them only into ghettos in the second . . . to liberate for the conquest of joy . . . to go inside yourself first to rediscover the feeling of your own possible freedom, and from there to the feeling of the possible freedom of others." The community of the alienated faithful—an "elect" that rejects all compromises and complicities—strenuously believes in a cosmology embracing all men, all institutions, a vision impossible to achieve but essential to proclaim if the American covenant is to survive.

It is the tragedy and also the hope of the American experience in its age-old search for meaning that radical sentiments and experimentations should arise and have their influence upon events. The climax of radical frustration is yet to come, but declension of religious zeal and yearnings for order and tranquility have always followed in the cycle of human affairs. At some point, the temple must empty, the participant—refreshed, worried, bored, touched, and exasperated—must turn home to the humdrum and familiar, remembering sadly that the dreams of youth become the broken promises of maturity.

Howard Zinn

A Comparison of the Militant Left of the Thirties and Sixties

Comparing the Old and New Left, Howard Zinn, an adherent of the latter group, finds more differences than similarities between the two movements. While both have faulted America for its poverty, racism, foreign policy, and sometime repression of dissenters, the New Left, according to Zinn, is less ideological, bureaucratic and hero-worshipping. This essay, first published in 1968 and written before the Chicago Democratic party convention, the formation of the Weathermen, and the advent of the Yippies, uses SDS, SNCC and the general anti-Vietnam War movement as prototypes of the New Left. One should consider whether events since the essay's original publication outdate or reinforce Zinn's conclusions. Howard Zinn has authored several books including *The Politics of History, SNCC: The New Abolitionists,* and *La Guardia in Congress.*

It is with the Communist-influenced militant left of the Thirties that I would like to compare the New Left of the Sixties. To represent this New Left, while recognizing that there are other groups which might be considered part of it, I would discuss those elements I know best: the Student Nonviolent Coordinating Committee, which is the most aggressive of the civil rights groups working in the South; Students for a Democratic Society, which carries on a variety of activities on campuses, in depressed urban areas, on civil rights and foreign policy; and that assorted group of intellectuals, civil rights workers and just ordinary draft-card burners who have become active in the opposition to the war in Vietnam.

Before noting the differences between the Old Left and the New Left, we should recognize the common ground which they share. Both have been sharply, angrily critical of American society, at home and abroad. Both movements of the Thirties and of the Sixties have pointed to poverty in the midst of wealth, to sins committed against the Negro, to limitations on free expression by congressional committees and public prosecutors, to shameful behavior in foreign policy. And in this, both movements I believe—despite many characteristics which I find distasteful in the Old Left

Reprinted by permission of the publisher from "A Comparison of the Militant Left of the Thirties and Sixties" by Howard Zinn, pp. 30–34, 36–43, originally published in *The Thirties,* edited by Morton J. Frisch and Martin Diamond, copyright © 1968 by Northern Illinois University Press.

and mostly missing in the New Left—have made vital contributions to values in American society which almost all of us claim to cherish.

I see, first, in the new militants, a lack of ideology unthinkable in the Old Left. Alfred Kazin has spoken (in his book *Starting Out in the Thirties*) of many leftists in his time as "ideologues." They were always attending classes on Marxist theory, buying or selling or arguing about works by the Big Four (Marx, Engels, Lenin, Stalin), engaging in endless discussions on surplus value, dialectical materialism, the absolute impoverishment of the working class, Plekhanov's theory on the role of the individual, Stalin's views on the national question, Engels on the origin of the family, Lenin on economism, or imperialism, or social democracy, or the state as the executive committee of the bourgeoisie.

The people in SNCC, by and large, know little about Marx. They have no Manifesto or any other infallible guide to the truth. Their discussions are rarely abstract or theoretical, and deal mostly with day-to-day practical problems: the tent city in Lowndes County, hunger in Greenville, the Freedom Democratic Party, how to meet the next payroll for the 130 field secretaries. SDS people I have met are more white than SNCC, more middle-class, more intellectual, and thus have read more of Marx—but they don't seem to take it as the Gospel. I recently read a book of essays by SDS people, and found very little theorizing in it, above the level of the immediate. The Old Left would have had a quotation from Lenin on the headquarters wall. In the dilapidated SNCC offices, you will find odd bits of prose and poetry pinned on the walls, like this, which I saw recently in Atlanta:

> Ever danced out on a limb
> It doesn't always break.
> And sometimes when it does you fall
> into a grassy meadow.

All this means there is an open-mindedness and a flexibility in the New Left which was rare in the Thirties. There is a refreshing lack of pompous intellectuality, of quotations from the great, of hewing to a "line." To some people on borders of the left today, like Michael Harrington, the lack of ideology is disturbing. I admit I have some tremors from time to time, but on the whole I find it heartening.

The Old Left was rigidly committed to a nation and to a system: the nation was the Soviet Union, and the system was socialism. Some adherents were disillusioned by Stalin's purges of old Bolsheviks in the Thirties; others dropped away after the non-aggression pact between the USSR and Germany. But many stood fast, held by the power of an earlier vow which they were unwilling to renounce. This new generation of radicals starts with no such commitment. They have no illusions about the purity of any nation, any system. They have seen Stalinism unmasked, by

Khrushchev himself. They have watched aggression, subversion, and double-dealing engaged in by all sides, West as well as East, "free world" as well as "communist world." They are very much aware of Russian aggression in Hungary, Chinese repression in Tibet, and the desire of Communists everywhere to support revolution in the world. But they also know that the American CIA overthrew a democratically-elected government in Guatemala, that the United States secretly conspired in the invasion of Cuba, that our marines invaded the Dominican Republic in violation of the Rio Pact. The new radicals are quite persuaded that the Communist nations will use *any* means to gain their ends. Yet, when they see American planes bombing Vietnamese villages, and marines throwing grenades down tunnels in which crouch helpless women and children, they see that the United States will use any means to gain *its* ends. They have grown up in a world where force and deception are found on all sides; and so they have what I believe is a healthy disposition to call the shots as they see them, no matter who looks bad.

The Old Left was sectarian, suspicious, and exclusive: the Socialists would expel Communists, the Trotskyists would expel Socialists, and the Communists would expel almost everyone. While there is some silly backbiting in SNCC against other civil rights groups, both SNCC and SDS are open organizations, welcoming anyone regardless of affiliation or ideology who will work. One result is a succession of head-shakings and warnings from various people about Communist infiltrators (this is the liberal counterpart of Communist suspiciousness), but SNCC and SDS have remained cool on this subject. Bob Moses of SNCC, in the fall of 1963, responded to an article by Theodore White in *Life* magazine, where White referred accusingly to a "penetration" of SNCC by "unidentified elements." White seemed bashful about saying he meant Communists. Moses replied: "It seems to me that . . . we have to throw what little weight we have on the side of free association and on the side of autonomy within our group to pick and choose those people whom we will work with, on relevant criteria, and one of the criteria which is not relevant is their past political associations." Another SNCC veteran, Charles Sherrod, said: "I don't care who the heck it is—if he's willing to come down on the front lines and bring his body along with me to die—then he's welcome!"

The radicals of the Thirties were dutiful bureaucrats: over-organized, over-prompt, and quite parliamentary. If a SNCC worker cited Roberts' Rules of Order, nonviolence would probably be ditched for that moment. The B'nai Brith or the Elks have been known to start their meetings fifteen minutes late, and the Young Democrats of Waukegan an hour late, but SNCC often starts meetings a day late, sometimes two. I am not citing this as a virtue, but rather as a sign of that human carelessness about organization which seemed to be lacking in the Old Left. A bureaucratic sense of "responsibility" is largely a product of middle-class upbringing, and SNCC is more proletarian-peasant in background than either SDS, the teach-in crowd, or the Old Left.

The radicals of the Thirties indulged in a good deal of hero-worship, from Stalin over there to Earl Browder over here. Today's militants, on the other hand, are suspicious of individuals who set themselves up, or are set up by others, as heroes of the movement. That is one reason SNCC is critical of Martin Luther King, Jr. Neither SNCC nor SDS nor the New Left as a whole has some one person immediately identifiable as *the* leader. It is hard to fit Bob Moses or John Lewis or Tom Hayden or Carl Oglesby into the pattern of a charismatic figure, and while the mass media have tried to do this with Staughton Lynd, both he and others in the New Left have derided this.

There is an existential quality to current radicalism which distinguishes it sharply from that of the Thirties. Marxists, particularly the dogmatic ones, are rather unhappy with existentialism, even though Jean-Paul Sartre has made an attempt to reconcile his existentialism with his Marxism. (Walter Odajnyk's study of this attempt finds it unsuccessful.) To discover what separates the orthodox left of the Thirties from existentialism, see a new book by a Marxist, Sidney Finkelstein, called *Existentialism and Alienation in American Literature.* Finkelstein finds the existentialist insufficiently aware of the binding force of history, incredulous of the idea of progress, excessively emotional, overly individualist, and, as he puts it, "the modern counterpart of the ancient rebel against a world he saw as corrupt, who withdrew to a cave or monastery." . . .

The radicals of the Thirties believed fervently in the power of historical forces churning away, moving the world inexorably towards a glorious future. This came from the historical materialism of Marxism, with its confident laying-out of the stages of history. Capitalism would be followed by socialism just as surely as it had followed feudalism. Socialism would be the first stage of communism which would be a return in one sense to an earlier primitive communalism, but in a more important sense would represent a complete break with the impoverished past. All would be pre-history; man's life as a free human being would truly begin now, with communism, and he would for the first time take charge of his own destiny, become the prime motive power in the movement of history. It was a ferocious determinism, and yet, oddly enough, it was accompanied by the most vigorous calls to action. This should have made its adherents suspicious of the notion of "inevitability" which pervades Marxism, but they accepted this dialectical "unity of opposites" as dutifully as Calvinists accompanied the notion of predestination with exhortations to moral behavior.

The radicals I know today are not bound by history. They accept neither the Marxist nor the biblical nor any other interpretation of history. What they know best is the present, and they consider it malleable by the power of their own hands. When you have *made* history, when you have *forced* social change, the magic of a philosophy of history fades. In eleven years, if we date the movement from the Montgomery bus boycott of 1955, or six years, if we date it from the sit-ins of February, 1960, the militant youngsters of the Southern movement have moved mountains— not very far, true, but to move a mountain even a few inches gives a sense of power. "The Deep South Says Never," a journalist wrote after the Supreme Court decision. But Negroes are defying guns and subterfuge in Alabama and Mississippi, organizing their own parties, preparing to elect their own sheriffs, mayors, congressmen. In Georgia, Negroes are sitting in the state legislature, and the expulsion of Julian Bond can be seen not only as a patriotic move to support the Vietnamese war by the freedom-loving members of the Georgia General Assembly, but also as a belated outburst of anger at the thought of so many Negroes sitting among them in their formerly sacrosanct, all-white chamber. Southern Negroes are still poor, but they dare to strike in the Mississippi Delta against the plantation owner. They are still afraid, but not as afraid as they used to be. The active ones know that the changed atmosphere is not the result of beneficence from the succession of great white fathers in Washington, but the result of their own willingness to risk their lives, to march, to demonstrate, to go to jail; they know that Johnson and Kennedy did not act for them, but reacted to them. These Southern militants feel free to change history. And although they know they have only scratched the surface of a social order which keeps them poor and harassed, they are off their knees; they have stretched their limbs, and are ready to do more, undeterred by notions of what history does or does not permit them to do.

Yet, when the hold of history is weakened, it allows not only awareness of freedom, but a sense of despair. This is very much in the existentialist mood, and quite different from the radicalism of the Thirties. To the old radicals, revolution was always around the corner; the proletariat was always about to rise and smite the foe; capitalism was always about to collapse in one of its periodic economic crises; every bloody nose received by the left was received not with a call for a handkerchief, but with joy that here was a sign of the desperation of the reactionaries, and so the day of socialism was not far off.

The New Left is not afraid to say it is unsure of victory. Tom Hayden . . . makes no cheery predictions about how SDS will transform America, and says: "Radicalism then would go beyond the concepts of optimism and pessimism as guides to work, finding itself in working despite odds. Its realism and sanity would be grounded in nothing more than the ability to face whatever comes." Michael Harrington, commenting on this, is unhappy; he needs to know he will win, and right away, and so seeks desperately to create a coalition which will have a majority of Americans in it. Harrington still has much of the Old Left in him. The new radical is more in tune with Wendell Phillips, the abolitionist orator, who wrote: "The reformer is careless of numbers, disregards popularity, and deals only with ideas, conscience, and common sense. . . . He neither expects, nor is overanxious for immediate success." Phillips contrasted the reformer with the politician, who "dwells in everlasting now. . . ." Similarly, James Russell Lowell, the abolitionist poet, wrote: "The Reformer must expect comparative isolation, and he must be strong enough to bear it." The new radicals' strength comes from the other side of existentialist despair, a supreme sense of responsibility, an unrelenting activism.

The radicals of the Thirties were very active in traditional politics. They ran candidates and sought entry into legislative bodies. William Z. Foster and Earl Browder were the Communist candidates for president at various times; Norman Thomas was the perennial Socialist candidate. Their realism about parliamentary democracy did not seem to be even as penetrating as that of conservative political scientists, who quietly point out the flaws in the electoral process. It is a fact of American political life that the cards are stacked against minority candidates in our electoral college system, and in the single-district system by which we elect congressmen. And even if a radical should break through, mysterious things begin to happen. Socialist Victor Berger, twice elected, was twice excluded from Congress, in 1918 and 1919. Five Socialists elected to the New York State Legislature were expelled also just after World War I. And when Communists began electing members to the City Council in New York under the system of proportional representation, the system was abolished, and the Communists were out. With all this, the Communist and Socialist parties retained a touching faith in the ballot box.

Militants of today have worked very hard in the South registering Negroes to vote, forming the Freedom Democratic party in Mississippi, the Black Panther party in Alabama, trying to oust the Mississippi congressmen from their seats and replace them with black Mississippians. However, this is accompanied by a basic mistrust of politics, and what seems to me, anyway, to be a sharper awareness than was shown in the Thirties of the limitations of parliamentary democracy. The vote, today's radicals know, is only an occasional flicker of democracy in an otherwise elitist system; the voice of the people therefore must be manifested in other ways, by day-to-day activity, by demonstrative action, by a constant politics of protest rather than the traditional politics of the ballot.

The left of the Thirties had its organized gods: the Soviet Union, the Party, the body of Marxist theory. The left of today distrusts the crystallization of power in any form which becomes rigid and commanding. Only a few have read Robert Michels, but they seem to instinctively sense his thesis, that there is an "iron law of oligarchy" in any organization, with power flowing toward the top. And so, in both SDS and SNCC, there is distrust of leadership, an anxiety for what is called "participatory democracy," an almost romantic notion that "the people" must decide things for themselves. Hence, SNCC has always emphasized that local people in the towns and hamlets of the Black Belt must be brought along to become the leaders; the SNCC people prod and stimulate and start things, and then move on.

284

The Old Left was humorless, it is often said, and this is hard to check up on, because historical records tend to squeeze the juices out of the past; but there are enough vestiges of the Old Left around to indicate that this is probably accurate. The Old Left was square. The new radicals are more cool, have more fun, are less puritanical, less inhibited, more irreverent. I remember Julian Bond showing me one of his first poems in the early days of the Atlanta student movement, a tiny couplet which went like this:

> Look at that gal shake that thing;
> We can't all be Martin Luther King.

In the Thirties, Communists and their friends juggled deftly the categories of "just wars" and "unjust wars," using Marxist scripture and analyses from on high to help decide which was which. The Germans, Italians, and Japanese were denounced for their acts of war against helpless peoples. The Russian attack on Finland was justified as a case of self-defense. World War II was unjust and imperialistic until the invasion in June 22, 1941 of the Soviet Union by Hitler; it then became a people's war. It must be said that here the Communists were very much in the modern liberal tradition: both Communists and liberals see war as an extension of the internal benevolence of the system they favor, so that to the Sovietophiles wars waged by the Soviet Union will be *ipso facto,* just, and to American patriots, wars waged by the liberal United States, must by that fact, be wars for freedom. The New Left, on the other hand, is very much influenced by the nonviolent approach of the civil rights movement, joined to an ancient American streak of pacifism which goes back to Thoreau and the abolitionist movement. It is not a pure nonviolence, as attested by the movement's general approval of the Deacons in the deep South; and I would guess that if a revolution broke out in South Africa there would be support among the New Left for it, as there has been a good deal of sympathy for the Castro revolution in Cuba. The abolitionists too were not pure in their pacifism; when the war came they decided to support it. I would guess that the distinctions which the New Left makes are, in the first instance (that of the Deacons), between aggressive violence and self-defense; and in the second instance (South Africa, Cuba, Algeria), between traditional wars for national power and revolutionary uprisings for social goals. I think the strong strain of feeling for the Vietcong in the present conflict stems from the belief that the United States is acting on behalf of its national power, and that the guerrillas in South Vietnam (despite the fact that China may be trying to augment its own power, and Ho Chi Minh his) are themselves conducting a revolutionary war against a foreign invader which manipulates a militaristic, and elitist puppet government.

While most old categories of radical thought do not neatly fit the New Left, I find a cluster of *anarchist* ideas at its core. There is the suspicion of organized power in any form, even the power of radical groups themselves. There is the fear of centralization, and so a tendency for decisions to be made in the field rather than by executive committees; and there is the creation of parallel organizations inside the old structure, as a tiny fire around which people gather to keep warm as a way of *showing,* rather than just talking about, what the future might be like. Hence the freedom parties, the freedom schools, the freedom houses (radical versions of frat houses, I suppose), the freedom labor union (intended to put the AFL-CIO to shame), the free university, the Congress of Unrepresented People, and who knows what next.

The militants of the Thirties and those of today have a common ground of concern: the abolition of war, poverty, racial discrimination, and political imprisonment. Both groups looked ultimately to a society where cooperation and affection would replace the scramble for money and power, while leaving the individual free to determine his own way of enjoying life and love. These were marvelously desirable ends. But what the leftists of the Thirties did was to commit a deadly ethical error: they made absolutes of the means which would be used to achieve these ends. And so they absolutized Marxism, the Party, the Soviet Union, socialism. When the means become absolutes, then immediately the possibility, even the probability appears, that the original ends will be forgotten or distorted. In doing this, the radicals of that day lost the chance to break new ethical ground, and followed the example of other social currents in modern times: a loving Christ-centered religion, absolutized in the church, in ritual, in dogma; liberalism, absolutized in the modern parliamentary, capitalist, jingoistic state; education and intellect absolutized in the Ph.D., the university, the scholarly monograph, and the mass media; the joy of life, absolutized in spectator sports, in television, in credit-cards, first-class passage, and success measured by money income.

The militant left of the Sixties has so far been fluid and free-wheeling, refusing to deify any nation, any person, any ideological system; and yet holding fast—to the point of prison, defamation, even death—to a core of beliefs about the value of the individual human being. This is not to say there are not lapses, faults, aberrations, irrationalities, pettinesses, absurdities, or that the danger of creating absolutes is not there every moment. And no one can predict what will happen tomorrow. But right now the New Left to me looks not only concerned, but honest and open, free of icons and gods, full of courage, and very much alive. So, I personally welcome the radicalism of the Sixties. And, while I want always to keep a small thinking part of me outside *any* movement, I am glad to be with it.

William Lee Miller

Writing from a liberal perspective at the close of the Sixties, William Lee Miller finds the roots of that decade's cultural protest in the Twenties and the base of its political-economic protest in the Thirties. For him, the protest, dissent, and radicalism of the late 1960's was a native form of anti-Americanism, previously the province of other nations. While the decade at its beginning contained a serious side of social reform and national self-criticism, Miller believes its later New Left manifestation to be an unfortunate attack against the entire

The New Anti-Americanism of the 1960's

sweep of the American experience, an attack which has polarized the country ideologically. Miller is author of *The Fifteenth Ward and the Great Society, Piety along the Potomac,* and *Morals in the Fifties.*

In the 1960's, especially in the latter part of the decade, several forms of American protest, dissent, and radicalism came simultaneously into public view. They reenforced each other, and created a new spirit of native anti-Americanism—a heresy against the American creed in culture, politics, and economics—that seems to me to go beyond anything I have read about in our past.

I said the "American creed." Perhaps I should use instead the vague and rather fatuous phrase that was widely heard in the very different decade that preceded this one, and say that in the nineteen-sixties there was a new level of both serious criticism and nose-thumbing directed against the "American way of life." A predominant mood of the Sixties kicked the national pieties of the Fifties in the seat of the pants. A significant part of the protest movement of the Sixties also took up serious social reform and national self-criticism, again in contrast to the comparative complacency of the years that had gone before. And then toward the end of the decade there developed, on the left, something else: a movement that went beyond irreverence, reform, and national self-criticism in the direction of what it called revolution. It stood in opposition not only to the national failings but also to the national ideals and established procedures. It was in protest not just against the Fifties but against the whole sweep of the American experience, at least according to its most ferocious spokesmen. It stood in opposition not to particular injustices, not to the ex-

Reprinted with permission from the September, 1969 issue of *The Center Magazine,* a publication of the Center for the Study of Democratic Institutions in Santa Barbara, California.

cesses of capitalism, not even precisely to American capitalism as a whole, but to the entire system, the entire, vaguely defined and virtually all-inclusive "establishment"; in other words, not only to the specific faults of America but to America itself, including its moral core, constitutional procedures, and liberal democracy. As I write, the division between the reformers and these new revolutionaries is still taking shape, and meanwhile a reaction on the part of ordinary citizens against all this anti-Americanism is gathering strength. I write this on July 4th, with decals of the American flag on every other car that passes by.

Some of the feeder streams that flow into the floodtide of dissent, protest, and radicalism in the Sixties may be identified, at least symbolically, with decades of the past. To start with, we may say that the Sixties saw the simultaneous return of the cultural protest of the Twenties and the political-economic protest of the Thirties. . . .

One of these streams comes from the Twenties. It has mainly to do with culture, higher and lower: with items of behavior and attitude, of manners and morals, of values and leisure activities.

The affinities of the Twenties with the Sixties have been noticed fairly often by now. I believe there has even been a popular song on this subject, one sexy prosperous era of short skirts and youthful revolt calling out to another. If you reread *Only Yesterday* you will find much that reminds you of the Sixties; endless discussions about the Younger Generation with middle-class young people in rebellion against the middle-class standards of their middle-class parents; endless discussions of sex, with a rapid change in the role of women and in mating mores and morals; endless fascination with popular culture: the Jazz Age, radio, Paul Whiteman's orchestra playing "It's Three O'Clock in the Morning." The standard word for the Twenties, as we have noted, is "disillusionment"; there is an important aspect of the later Sixties to which that word applies, too. In both periods there are widespread and visible evidences of escapism, hedonism, frivolity, dropping-out: the hip-flask and the speakeasy in one period, the drug culture, the hippies, the pot party in another. In both periods it is not only the young who reject the authority figures and mock the representative national characters; celebrated intellectual leaders do the same. It marks quite a shift in national mood when H. L. Mencken supplants William Dean Howells as the literary arbiter. In both decades the most talked about of the intelligentsia mock, criticize, deplore, and satirize national institutions and prevailing national standards. One might say that the most vocal of the youth and the intellectuals of the Twenties, interrupted by historical distractions, had to leave George Babbitt standing there half beaten, and only in the Sixties were their counterparts able to pick up the clubs and start in again on this—as he would now be called —this uptight square.

The 1920's saw a rebellion against the middle-class family; a "revolt against the village"; a rejection of what was rather mistakenly called

288

"puritanism." These dissenting movements opened fissures in the national culture that were then more or less papered over during each of the three decades that followed, for reasons which each of the decades provided. Then in the Sixties the cultural divisions burst open again.

Both these decades saw the city asserting its values against those of the small town and countryside; each has seen the old stock and conventional cast of American characters lose visibility and prestige. In the Twenties they were called puritans or the booboisie or tiresome spokesmen for gentility; Mencken assaulted, among all these others, the "Anglo-Saxons," whose heritage had been celebrated by some during World War I. It is probably in the Twenties that, in the phrase of the senior Arthur Schlesinger, the sturdy yeoman turns into the hick. In the Sixties there came into widespread and not flattering use a tag for the hitherto predominant ethnic-religious group—the WASP—as well as the ubiquitous pejorative for the putative rulers of the nation—the Establishment.

Although the Ku Klux Klan was strong in the early Twenties and a force at the Democratic Convention of 1924, the Democratic Convention of 1928 nominated an unequivocally urban figure, a Wet, an Irish Catholic, a man whose higher education, as he said, had taken place at the Fulton Fish Market. Although in 1959-60 there was much somber discourse about whether the nation could survive a Catholic president, by 1968 that discussion seemed as remote as Moses and the fact that two of the three Spring contenders for the Democratic nomination were Irish Catholics passed virtually unnoticed. The Harvard-Catholic-Boston-sophisticated figure of John F. Kennedy, who, of course, is immensely important for the spirit of the Sixties, was not only the first president born in this century but perhaps the most remote in all recent American history from the ethos of Main Street. He calmly explained to a farm audience on his Western tour in the autumn before his death that he was a city boy who had never milked a cow or plowed a furrow, straight or crooked.

In the Twenties American literature completed its break with Protestant propriety; in the Sixties white Northern Gentiles no longer wrote novels. The writers of the 1920's who came from that kind of a background were fleeing it or attacking it: Sinclair Lewis satirizing Sauk Center; Willa Cather preferring European immigrants and Southwestern Spanish to decaying Anglo-Saxon Midwesterners; Ernest Hemingway staying a million miles away from his mother's Congregational Church in Oak Park, Illinois. In the Sixties the Protestant Middle West just vanished from sight. In the Twenties there was a distinctive Negro cultural movement, with some whites paying attention to Harlem's cultural riches; in the Sixties black became beautiful.

In these two decades the urban variety of the real United States made itself felt against the uniformities of the mythical United States of Main Street, the New England Yankee, and suburbia. In these two decades American culture seemed livelier, richer, more heterogenous than in the rather stuffy periods that preceded them. At the same time there came—

especially in the late Sixties—a sweeping repudiation of authority and of standards that may not prove as welcome a development as the other one.

As with the Sixties and the Twenties, there is also a connection between the Sixties and the Thirties, when the Depression brought quite another kind of criticism of the nation's institutions.

The characteristic protesters of the Twenties had not been much concerned with politics and economics. They went to Paris. They read H. L. Mencken and laughed at the American boob. They satirized *Main Street*. They may have laughed at Harding, Coolidge, and Hoover, but not out of any very clearcut contrary political judgment. They were contemptuous of the nation's Babbitts, but not out of any very clearcut contrasting economic ethic. If you reread *The Great Gatsby* you will find a good deal in it that reminds you of the Sixties (of the motion picture phenomenon *The Graduate,* for example), but except for some incidental disapproval of the reactionary opinions of Tom Buchanan you won't be able to make out Fitzgerald's political and economic views. He disapproves of the behavior of Tom and Daisy, who smash things and retreat back into their money, but his attitude toward Jay Gatsby is an undefined sentimental mixture. Fitzgerald himself was later to say that he did not then have any developed political and economic views of his own. Neither, apparently, did the Hemingway of the Twenties. Sinclair Lewis was a social and cultural satirist who really did not give big Republicans and big bankers very much to worry about; even the people of Zenith themselves seemed to read his books without much pain. Some of the figures of the Twenties turned out to be unalloyed political conservatives: Willa Cather and, in his own way, of course, Mencken. The itch for political and economic reform was, in fact, an expression of the "bilge of idealism" of people like the "Archangel Woodrow," and then in the Thirties of a certain Presidential "radio crooner" that Mencken and the supermen of *The American Mercury* looked down upon.

The crash, the coming of the Depression, the "American earthquake," as Edmund Wilson was to call it, changed all that. In the spring of 1932 Wilson looked back at the attitudes of the Twenties, which he said already "seemed a long way off"; from the Thirties, he said, "we can see how superficial they were." The first of these attitudes was that of the "Menckenian gentleman, ironic, beer-loving, and 'civilized,' living principally on the satisfaction of feeling superior to the broker and enjoying the debauchment of American life as a burlesque show or a three-ring circus. . . ." Further along in his article Mr. Wilson said that it could now be seen that all the suddenly outdated attitudes from the Twenties

represented attempts on the part of the more thoughtful Americans to reconcile themselves to a world dominated by "salesmen and brokers" . . . that they all involved compromises with the salesman and the broker. Mencken and Nathan laughed at the broker, but they justified the system which produced him and they got along with him very well, provided he enjoyed George Moore and had pretensions to a taste in liquor. . . .

In the Thirties these "more thoughtful Americans" no longer made any compromise with "the salesman and the broker"; before the decade was over too many made compromise instead with the hard-line revolutionaries of the Communist party. Many others hoped for a democratic socialism; what they got instead was—so to speak—the Federal Deposit Insurance Corporation. But during this decade the criticisms of America did turn to a sober examination of politics and economics.

C. Vann Woodward wrote about this period:

> In the Thirties and well into the following decade there occurred the most thoroughgoing inquest of self-criticism that our national economy has ever undergone—not even excepting that of the muckraking and Progressive era. No corner nor aspect nor relationship of American capitalism was overlooked, and no shibboleth of free enterprise went unchallenged. The prying and probing went on at every level from the sharecroppers to holding companies and international cartels. Subpoenas brought mighty bankers and public-utility empire-builders to the witness stand. Nor was this activity merely the work of the wild-eyed and wooly-haired, nor the exclusive concern of one of the major parties. It was a popular theme of the radio, the press, the theater, and even the pulpit. . . . Universities hummed and throbbed with it. . . . Then in the mid-40's something happened. It happened rather suddenly. The floodstream of criticism dwindled to a trickle and very nearly ceased altogether. It was as if some giant sluice-gate had been firmly shut.

The shutting of that sluice-gate by the celebrational atmosphere of the Forties and Fifties perhaps helped to make the backed-up floodstream more of a torrent when the sluice-gate opened and that criticism flowed out again in the Sixties, as it certainly did.

That the American economy is again the object not only of criticism but of attack in the Sixties is evident in every one of the institutions Professor Woodward mentions, and also in television and especially in books and magazines. He referred to muckraking and the Progressive era, which might stand as the next previous historical antecedent to the thoroughgoing criticism of capitalism in the Thirties. The muckraking magazine article reappeared everywhere in the Sixties, including publications in which it was quite incongruous: in *The New Yorker,* that prestigious survivor of the spirit of the Twenties ("not for the Old Lady from Dubuque"), which ran long columns of social criticism side by side with advertisements for two-thousand-dollar diamond clips from Van Cleef & Arpels; in such an all-American entry as that hinterland Bible, the *Saturday Evening Post,* in its last days; and even in the flagship of the American Century, Henry Luce's *Life* magazine. Crusaders and crusading books and articles tumbled over each other. Church and university had a new leftward flavor. As to the theater, the cinema, and books—I have already suggested that one reason for the severity of the rebellion of the late Sixties may be the coinciding of different kinds of protest, antipuritan and anticapitalist. In the legitimate theater of the Sixties one gets them at once, at full whistle, and it has to be said that what has happened there is beyond the power of the present writer to comment on. The same is almost true of movies and books. I remember that George Bernard Shaw somewhere tells the story of the man, famous for his swearing, who when he saw all of his worldly goods spilling out of the wagon down the hill into a river had to say, after a pause, "I cannot do justice to this situation." So also one has to say about the state of these arts at the end of the Sixties, and pass on without another word.

I have come this far without mentioning the most obvious, important, and widely discussed causes of the moral-political mood of the Sixties: the black man's movement; the Vietnam war; and the "unrest," as it is called, with comic inadequacy, on the part of college students. I assume these ubiquitous topics have been enough commented upon elsewhere.

"Unrest" of contemporary students around the world suggests the parochial limitation of the remarks I have been making: the protest of the Sixties may be a part of a worldwide phenomenon. But the United States, as the heaven of the bourgeoisie, the leader of technological development, and the only nation so far to have used nuclear weapons, may be the object of a distinct antagonism, from within and without, that goes beyond that directed toward other nations. In a way, what has happened in the late Sixties is that a worldwide anti-Americanism has developed a powerful local branch.

The Vietnam war is the most important single cause, among white citizens at least, of the protest of the Sixties, but it is not the only one; there are aspects that preceded the enlarged American participation in the war, and presumably will continue after that is ended. In line with my remarks about the decades, and with all those fluvial metaphors I used, we may observe that there was another stream of dissent that was dammed in 1939 or 1941—the protest against war and the military. The revulsion against "merchants of death" in the aftermath of World War I, and the very strong pacifist and isolationist movements of the Thirties, were thoroughly discredited by Munich, Pearl Harbor, the unity of the nation fighting Hitler, the revelations about the concentration camps and, then, after the war, by Stalin's activities in the developing Cold War. The debacle of Vietnam has made a kind of antiwar view intellectually and morally respectable again, and has made it politically possible to challenge the military seriously.

Antimilitarism, antipuritanism, anticapitalism—and antiracism. When you speak of America's treatment of the black man you have to deal, alas, not in decades but in centuries. I think this stream of reform was dammed in 1876. That does not mean one should ignore or deprecate—as some of the fierce new fellows do—the long steady battle by (for example) the NAACP, through almost all of this century, for Negro rights; but it is true that the battle has not been in the center of the nation's politics. In the nineteenth century, of course, it was—from the abolitionism of the 1830's to the end of Reconstruction. But then it was dropped, even by reform movements. After a brief interracial beginning Populism did not help the Negro's cause, and finally some of the worst racist demagogues came from a Populist background. The Progressive movement doesn't seem to have had much to say for the Negro beyond Theodore Roosevelt's entertaining of Booker T. Washington in the White House; during Woodrow Wilson's presidency social segregation was *instituted* in federal government buildings in Washington, and the early years of the century—the Progressive era—are sometimes called the nadir of the struggle for Negro rights since emancipation. Certainly the cultural critics of America during the Twenties did not make any serious campaign for racial equality; Mencken, who regretted that he missed a chance to report the lynching of a "blackamoor," surely would not have regarded such a campaign as a suitable occupation for gentlemen. The New Deal does not have as impressive a record on racial equality as one might expect; F.D.R. won over the votes of the traditionally Republican Negro electorate primarily on economic issues. I think it can be said that racial equality was not a chief feature of any progressive movement that played a large role in American politics from 1876 until 1948 or 1954 (I say 1948 because of the Truman civil-rights program, the partial desegregation of the armed services and the fight over the civil-rights plank in the 1948 Democratic Convention.)

It is as though the nineteenth-century trauma over this moral paradox at the heart of American democracy exhausted the nation, exhausted even the reformers, some of whom quite explicitly checked off slavery on their list of "social questions," and turned to other matters like the labor question, the woman question, the temperance question. It is as though Americans, during this "lost century of civil rights," looked back upon the Emancipation Proclamation in something of the way they look at the Declaration of Independence, as a complete declaratory accomplishment that made real its objectives at a stroke. For whatever the reasons may be, the broad white American public, from the end of Reconstruction until these past few years, has suppressed the truth about the treatment of the black man. As the civil-rights movement and the Black Power movement force this historic injustice upon the attention of the white Americans, they raise also in the minds of the young and the critical other questions about a nation that could so long have tolerated so manifest an evil. The Vietnam war and the Negro movements have had the side effect of making more plausible the criticisms of the nation in other fields. In the eyes of some, America is morally discredited, and the national evils are not particular, separable items but a general condition.

Among many other criticisms of the nation, those directed against "conformity" and "mass society" and big bureaucratic organization, which became very common in the Fifties, are now still present, along with all these other themes, in the Sixties. Now they have a sharper anti-American edge than they did fifteen years ago: the ills of technological society, too, are the faults somehow of "America" and of the "Establishment."

I suppose the way one groups and interprets and makes distinctions about these disturbing and significant years represents a kind of ideological test. If I may dramatize my own evaluation (that of a liberal, if you want to say so), I would describe the first part of the decade as the best period in American history that I have lived through, and the last part of the decade as potentially the worst. I say "potentially" because the full results of the late Sixties have not yet been felt. This period is not yet worse than that dominated by Senator Joseph McCarthy; it might soon become so. But it must be added that the dangerous trends of these last years—the trends toward nasty, closed-minded, antidemocratic attitudes, toward new levels of violence, toward polarization—are still accompanied to some extent by a continuation of the healthy developments of the earlier years of the decade in social reforms and national self-criticism. So as the decade ends it is a confusing period, with the stakes all raised. Where it will end, knows God.

The two parts of the decade that I have graded up and down in this rather simplified way actually overlap. The first extended from the sit-in movement in the Spring of 1960 and the election of John Kennedy in the Fall, more or less down to the congressional elections of 1966. Its high points came after the Cuban missile crisis in October of 1962, President Kennedy's American University speech in the following June, and then the ratification of the nuclear test-ban treaty in the late Summer, changing the international atmosphere. In that same June the civil-rights movement for the first time had the full moral support of the Presidency; in August came the most remarkable of demonstrations, the "I Have a Dream," Jobs and Freedom march in Washington; during Kennedy's presidency the Keynesian economic outlook was consolidated in governmental policy (a much more significant development than is realized by the young radicals, who are subsidized by the prosperity that has resulted from it). The early Sixties saw a new "dialogue" among the religious communities; the remarkable civil-rights coalition of the Spring of 1964, and the enactment of the laws of 1964 and 1965; a new national interest in, and legislation for, the poor and the cities; and in the period from the assassination in November, 1963, until the elections of November, 1966, the most remarkable outpouring of social legislation in recent political history.

But meanwhile the Berkeley outburst and Harlem disorders of 1964 had been the first big signs of something else; the escalation of the Vietnam war and the Watts riot of 1965 brought it fully into American politics, and it reached what is so far its worst expression in the terrible period of 1967–68, from the Newark and Detroit riots through the march on the Pentagon in the Autumn, the assassinations of Martin Luther King and Robert Kennedy and the Columbia riots of the Spring, to the Chicago confrontation in August. This phenomenon—not new, of course, but now expressed at a new level of intensity—was the politics of violence, provocation, confrontation, the polarizing and potential unraveling of the nation. The ideological accompaniment of this phenomenon on the far left (if it makes sense still to use the ancient spectrum of left and right) was a hard-line and explicit anti-Americanism that rolled all the objections to different parts and aspects of American society into one big ball and saw in it one evil plan of an "establishment." Ironically this new anti-Americanism was very "American" in its style: moralistic, antipolitical, anti-intellectual, contemptuous of the past, a simplistic crusade against a conspiracy. It is especially difficult to deal with because the cultural revolt is joined with the political one. There is a repudiation of authority, a defiance of standards of behavior, an elite contempt for the common man, a rejection of received values, which give to the present a dimension going beyond mere political reform.

A liberal like the present writer, who rejects this New Left, might object not only—as is commonly said—to the tactics sometimes employed (violent, illegal, coercive, defamatory) but also to the underlying social analysis, the cultural revolt, and the political objectives; in my view, America, despite all its particular ills, is not as they have pictured it. Moreover, I do not want this nation to be made over according to their goals, whatever they may be (one may assume them to be implicit in the methods they employ and the attitudes they exhibit).

I have to admit that the inadequacy of the heritage of liberal reform is one cause of the present American distress. And I accept as accurate most of the particular criticism of American society. But I certainly do not believe the evils in it will be corrected by a holistic rejection of that society or by tactics of violence and abuse.

Meanwhile, there are those decals on the windshields. Perhaps they represent in some cases just a critical patriotism of a kind that I share. But I don't think they do in most cases. I'm afraid they represent a gathering repressive reaction against the outbursts of these last years.

Peter F. Drucker

The Seventies
and the
Future of Protest

In the final selection of this volume,
Peter F. Drucker, social scientist,
economic analyst, and one of the
nation's leading management
consultants, looks to the future of
America in the 1970's. Basing his
analysis primarily on population
dynamics and economic indicators,

Professor Drucker forecasts the end of
the youth culture, a preoccupation with
economic matters, and in general, "a
traditional, old-fashioned decade." If
correct, this by no means marks the
end of protest in America, but it may
indicate another turn in the
never-ending cycle of satisfaction and
discontent in American society. Are
there any elements omitted from
Professor Drucker's analysis which
might point to another conclusion?
Peter F. Drucker is the author of
Technology, Management and Society,
The Age of Discontinuity, and *Men,*
Ideas and Politics.

A great many people, especially the better educated, take it for
granted that today's "youth culture" is the wave of the future. They assume that as the present generation of college students become the young
adults of tomorrow, their new life-styles will come to dominate American
society and our economy. Practically all of the popular forecasters have
been telling us that this will mean a dwindling concern with affluence and
the production of material goods.

Maybe so. But the only facts that we know for sure about the future
make these predictions look quite unreliable. To me it seems far more
probable that during the Seventies this country will return to a preoccupation with the traditional economic worries. Indeed, during the next
decade economic performance—with jobs, savings, and profits at the center—may well become more important than it was in the Sixties. Productivity rather than creativity is likely to be the key word. Charles Reich's
Consciousness III, in my view, is a description of what happened in the
recent past, rather than a forecast of what will happen in the future. No
doubt the next ten years will be turbulent; but their central issues and
concerns may be familiar ones.

For the only thing we can know with certainty about America's near
future—the next ten or twenty years—are a few facts about its population. We can foresee its size, its structure, and its dynamics, because

From Peter F. Drucker, "The Surprising Seventies," *Harper's Magazine,* 243 (July
1971), pp. 35–39. Reprinted by permission of publisher and author.

everyone who will enter college or the work force between now and the late Eighties already is alive. We know, for example, that this year marks a true watershed. It is the last year, for as long as we can see ahead, in which teen-agers—that is, 17- and 18-year-olds—will form the center of gravity of our population. Consequently, tomorrow's population dynamics are sure to be radically different from those of the past ten years, the decade of the Youth Revolution.

Everyone knows that the United States had a baby boom after World War II, but few people realize how violent and unprecedented it was. Within a few short years, mainly between 1948 and 1953, the number of babies born in this country rose by almost 50 percent. This is by far the biggest increase in births ever recorded here or, up until then, in any other country. It destroyed the axiom on which population forecasts had always been based: the assumption that birthrates change only at a snail's pace, except in times of major castastrophe, such as war, pestilence, or famine.

We still have no explanation for this extraordinary baby boom. It may never happen again. But it did happen—not only in the United States, but also in the Soviet Unon and in all of the other industrially developed states but one. Great Britain was the sole exception.

AN ERUPTION OF TEEN-AGERS

If the baby boom was unprecedented, so was the baby bust ten years later. The boom crested in 1953. For the next six years the number of births still increased, but at a much slower rate. By 1955 one- and two-year-olds made up a smaller proportion of the total population than they had in the preceding years, and by 1960 the total number of births had started to drop sharply. It kept on dropping for seven years. Like the preceding rise, this was the sharpest fall recorded in population history. Almost 4.3 million babies were born in 1960, but only 3.5 million in 1967 —a drop of 20 percent. Today the birthrate is still bumping along at about the same low level and shows little sign of going up.

Because of the violent fluctuations, seventeen-year-olds became in 1964 the largest single age group in the country. For the next seven years—that is, until 1971—the seventeen-year-old group has been larger every year than it was the year before. Throughout that period, then, age 17 has been the center of population gravity in this country.

Now, seventeen is a crucial age. It is the age at which the youngster generally moves out from the family. Until this time, he has taken much of his behavior, and many of his attitudes and opinions—indeed, his way of life—from the family. At seventeen, however, he is likely to make his first career decisions and to take his opinions, attitudes, and concerns increasingly from his peer group, rather than from his family. Seventeen, in other words, has for centuries been the age of the youth rebellion.

In 1960 the center of population gravity in this country was in the thirty-five-to-forty age group—older than it had ever been before. Suddenly, within five years, the center shifted all the way down to age 17—younger than it had been in our history since the early nineteenth century. The psychological impact of this shift proved unusually strong because so many of these seventeen-year-olds—almost half of the young men—did not join the work force but instead stayed on in school, outside of adult society and without adult responsibilities.

The youth revolution was therefore predictable ten or twelve years ago. It was in fact predicted by whoever took the trouble to look at population figures. No one could have predicted then what form it would take; but even without Vietnam or racial confrontation, something pretty big was surely bound to result from such a violent shift in age structure and population dynamics.

We are now about to undergo another population shift, since the seventeen-year-olds will no longer be the largest single group in the population. Perhaps more importantly, this is the last year in which this group will be larger than the seventeen-year-old group of the year before. From now on, the center of population gravity will shift steadily upward, and by 1975 the dominant age year will be twenty-one or twenty-two. From 1977 to 1985, the total number of seventeen-year-olds in the population will drop sharply.

THE SHOCK OF GROWING UP

In urban and developed economies such as ours, the four years that separate age 17 from age 21 are the true generation gap. No period in a man's life—except perhaps the jump from fulltime work at age 64 and eleven months to complete retirement at sixty-five—involves greater social or psychological changes. Seventeen-year-olds are traditionally (and for good reasons) rebellious, in search of a new identity, addicted to causes, and intoxicated with ideas. But young adults from twenty-one to thirty-five—and especially the young adult women—tend to be the most conventional group in the population, and the one most concerned with concrete and immediate problems. This is the time of life when the first baby arrives, when one has to get the mortgage on one's first house and start paying interest on it. This is the age in which concern with job, advancement, career, income, furniture, and doctors' bills moves into the fore. And this is the age group which, for the next fifteen years, is increasingly going to dominate American society and to constitute its center of gravity.

This group is even more likely than comparable age groups in the past to concern itself with the prosaic details of grubby materialism. For the shift between the economic reality they knew when they dominated our population as seventeen-year-olds, and the economic reality they will experience when, still dominant in terms of population, they become young marrieds, is going to be unusually jarring. In the past, most seventeen-year-olds went to work, began to earn a living and to think about money, jobs, prices, and budgets. The affluent seventeen-year-old of the past ten years—especially the very large proportion that went to college (half of the males, and almost two-fifths of the females)—have never known anything but what the economists call "discretionary income." They may not have had a great deal of money in their jeans, but however much it was they could spend it any way they wanted without worrying about the consequences. It made little difference whether they blew it on the whims of the moment or put it into a savings account. The necessities—shoes, the dentist, food, and, in most cases, tuition—were still being provided by their parents. Now, within a few short years, they will suddenly have to take care of these things themselves. Even if a young woman marries a young man with a good income—an accountant, for instance, a college professor, or a meteorologist in the Weather Bureau—she will suddenly feel herself deprived. Suddenly she will have no discretionary income at all. The demands on her purse will inevitably be much greater than her resources because her expectations have risen much faster than her income will. She now expects health care, decent schools, housing, a clean environment, and a hundred other things her grandmother never dreamed of and even her mother did not take for granted when she first started out in married life.

She and her husband, therefore, will probably demonstrate a heightened concern with economics. Ralph Nader, rather than the Weathermen, is likely to foreshadow the popular mood. And no matter how radical Ralph Nader may sound, his is a highly conventionl view of the "system." Indeed, his are the values of our oldest tradition: populism. Nader believes in economic performance above all; he makes it the central touchstone of a good society.

Many sociologists and psychologists in the past few years have pointed out that the significant gap in society today may be not that between generations—that is, between middle-class, affluent parents and their college-age children—but that between the kids in college and the young hard-hats who have gone to work after high school. Usually it is the kids in college, the kids of the youth revolution, who are touted as the harbingers of tomorrow, with the hard-hats representing yesterday. But it may well be the other way around. It is just conceivable that the nineteen-year-old hard-hat—precisely because he is already exposed to the realities of economic life which are soon to shock college graduates—prefigures the values, the attitudes, and the concerns to which today's rebellious youth will switch tomorrow.

JOBS WILL BECOME MORE IMPORTANT

The shock the individual college graduate will feel on entering the job market may be severe. The shock to the job market itself may be even stronger. During each year of the next decade, we will have to find jobs for 40 percent more people than in each of the past ten years. The babies of the baby boom are only now entering the work force in large numbers, because so many of them delayed going to work by entering college.

There has been a great deal of talk about the "young, educated employee," but he is only now beginning to come out of the colleges, and the full impact his group will make is still three or four years away.

The first implication of this is, of course, that jobs are likely to be of increasing concern to the young during the next ten years. The shift from "abundant jobs for college graduates" in 1969 to a "scarcity of jobs for college graduates" in 1971 is not, as most commentators believe, merely a result of the 1970–1971 mini-recession. It is a result of the overabundance of college graduates, which will continue until the end of the decade even if the economy starts expanding again at a fast clip.

At the same time that many more young, college-trained people are out looking for jobs, the largest single source of jobs available to them in the Sixties—that is, teaching jobs—will almost completely dry up.

During the past two decades the number of children in school expanded at an unprecedented rate, and, as every anguished taxpayer well knows, new schools had to be built to accommodate them. The reason, obviously, was that the babies born during the postwar boom were then reaching school age. Yet the teachers in the schools during the Fifties and early Sixties were mostly elderly; the last period of massive hiring had been in the Twenties, an era when high schools grew as fast as colleges have recently. Between 1955 and 1970, therefore, an unusually large number of teachers reached retirement age, became disabled, or died. As a result, some five million college-educated young people found teaching jobs available during this period.

During the next ten years, however, no more than two million teaching jobs will open up; some forecasts put the figure as low as one million. One reason is that the school-age population will be smaller, as a result of the decline in birthrates that began a decade ago. Another reason is that teachers today are the youngest group of workers in the country, so fewer vacancies will occur because of death and retirement.

This decreasing demand for teachers will be partly offset by an increasing demand for computer programmers, medical technologists, and employees of local governments. These jobs, like teaching, traditionally have attracted women with technical training. But an education in the liberal arts, which is what many college women choose, does not qualify them for such positions.

Some college-educated girls will probably not even enter the work force but make straight for marriage, home, and a family. If they do, however, this will only increase the economic pressure on them and their husbands, and intensify their concern with incomes, prices, and jobs. A good many young women will decide to work and, as they look for jobs in fields other than teaching, they will begin to compete with young men; it is hardly coincidence that there has been a sharp increase these past two years in the number of women applicants in law and accounting, for instance. (There are fewer women in management or the professions today than there were twenty years ago—a staple of Women's Libbers' complaints—

but the explanation may lie as much in the tremendous demand for teachers since the Fifties as in male chauvinism.) The woman who looks for work in business or government because there is no place for her in the public school is, of course, increasing the pressure for jobs.

THE COMING DEMAND FOR CAPITAL

If we hope to succeed in creating a vast number of new jobs for the young people coming into the labor market during the years just ahead, the country will have to find a great deal of new capital somewhere. For every additional job requires a capital investment. This is particularly true of the jobs we will need the most—jobs for highly educated people who are supposed to work with knowledge rather than with their hands. The greater the skill or knowledge demanded by a job, the greater the capital investment needed to make it possible.

A computer operator can't work without a computer. A doctor can't function efficiently without a substantial investment by somebody in a nearby hospital, equipped with everything from X-rays to artificial heart-lung machines—not to mention the costly equipment in his own office and in the laboratories on which he depends. A writer (or editor) needs not only his own typewriter, but an investment somewhere in printing presses and the facilities for nationwide distribution of books and magazines. An atomic physicist may need at least part-time access to a nuclear accelerator costing billions. A professor needs not only a classroom, but a good library, perhaps a laboratory, and probably housing for his students. A business executive's job depends on a going business, his own or a corporation's, and anyone who has ever tried to start even a small enterprise knows how much capital that eats up. So on the average a "knowledge job" in the American economy today—whether in business, education, or government—requires a prior investment of something like $20,000. (Even the hippies who go off to live the simple, close-to-nature life on a commune discover, alas, that they need some capital to buy land, spades, seeds, fencing, and liniment for their aching backs. And if they ever try to become truly efficient farmers, they will need a great deal of expensive equipment; for modern agriculture has become a knowledge industry requiring both specialized training and a high degree of mechanization.)

The rate of capital formation, therefore, will have to go up very sharply if this country is to escape massive unemployment. Capital formation is, of course, simply the economists' term for the savings and profits which become available to create new jobs.

We cannot hope to get this new capital by drawing on fat in the economy—by "reducing excess profits," as youthful rhetoric sometimes bids us to do. Whatever their persuasion or politics, all economists agree that we have not been building up capital reserves in recent years. In fact, we have barely been maintaining our existing capital resources.

For inflation always eats up capital. Last year American wage earners laid away 7½ percent of their incomes in savings, one of the highest savings rates on record in this country. Yet this was barely enough to offset what was lost through inflation on the savings they had set aside earlier. Few businesses in this country would have shown any profit at all during the past few years if they had adjusted their earnings figures to take into account the effect of inflation on their fixed assets. (The Securities Exchange Commission requires them to do this with their foreign subsidiaries, but not on their domestic operations.)

WHAT GOVERNMENT CAN'T DO

These are ominous facts, because new capital can come from only two sources: savings and profit. The government can act in a number of ways to encourage—or discourage—savings and profit; but nothing it can do will create capital directly. Deficit spending, no matter how large, cannot create a "full employment economy" when capital is in short supply. (John Maynard Keynes demonstrated that deficit spending by the government *can* create jobs under certain special circumstances—that is, when capital already in existence is not being invested in job-creating enterprises. The reason this is so is too complicated, and too familiar to economists and most businessmen, to be reviewed here. But even the most devoted Keynesians do not argue that these circumstances exist today, or are likely to in the foreseeable future.)

The problem ahead of us is one we have never faced before. Only once in the past—in the shift to a total war economy in 1942–43—have we encountered such a sudden jump in the need for capital. And then we were able to shift a massive amount of existing capital from peacetime facilities into war production by government decree. Today that possibility does not exist, although an end to the war in Indochina should free some capital resources for a return to better uses, such as building homes and cleaning up our environment. Even so, it is impossible to predict whether we can meet the demand for new capital formation, or even how. The situation suggests possibilities for the most sustained boom in American history. It may also produce one of the most severe unemployment crises.

In either case, economics is not likely to fade out of the public consciousness. The graduates from today's youth culture are likely to find themselves far more worried about jobs and money than they now suspect.

THE PUZZLE OF PRODUCTIVITY

Productivity will also be a major challenge and a major concern of the next ten years. Productivity, we have all heard a good many times by now, is the key to managing the inflation which plagues all developed countries today. To have price stability, wages must not rise faster than productivity. But all attempts to gear wages to productivity—guidelines, Mr. Nixon's "jawboning" in the construction industry, and the productivity bargaining which the British are advocating—have concerned themselves primarily with manual workers in manufacturing, transportation,

302

mining, and construction. But manual workers are, increasingly, a minority. The majority of the young are acquiring advanced educations and are unlikely to go into manual work. The bulk of tomorrow's employment will be in service trades, knowledge jobs—in health care, teaching, government, management, research, and the like. And no one knows much about the productivity of knowledge work, let alone how to improve it. About the only thing we can be sure of is that it has not been going up very fast. The salesgirl in today's department store does not sell more than the salesgirl of thirty or forty years ago did, if the change in the purchasing power of money is taken into account. Hospitals forty years ago had three employees for every ten patients and a very low investment per patient. Today they have up to thirty employees for every ten patients and their investment is high. Yet judged by the most primitive yardstick— the percentage of patients who leave the hospital alive—there has been little increase in productivity. Surely few of us would hold that today's schools are more productive than schools were forty years ago, no matter how one defines or measures the productivity of education. The same is true of government and research. Large businesses, these past twenty years, have added layer upon layer of management and all kinds of specialized staffs, from market research to personnel and from cost analysis to long-range planning. Whether there has been any corresponding increase in productivity and performance of management is, however, by no means proved.

We learned, some seventy years ago, how to define, how to measure, and how to raise the productivity of manual work. But we have yet to learn what productivity really means in any other kind of work. Yet the sales clerk and the college teacher, the nurse and the marketing manager, the policeman and the accountant all expect their incomes to rise as fast as that of the manual worker. In fact, the knowledge workers among them expect their incomes to rise faster and be higher in absolute terms than those of the manual worker.

The "cost-squeeze" of today, on governments, universities, and business, is the first warning—it is really a productivity squeeze. The only way out of it is for the nonmanual employee, whether he is a knowledge worker or a policeman, to become more productive. In his own interest, he will find he has to push for this. It is the only way, in the long run, for him to enjoy a comfortable, let alone a rising, standard of living. As the economy, therefore, employs more and more nonmanual and, especially, more knowledge workers, we should increasingly expect concern with productivity to become central. And whatever else productivity may be— and it is a very elusive concept—it is clearly a conventional, an old-fashioned, and, above all, an economic value.

I do not assert that population dynamics will determine the psychology, politics, or even economics of the years to come. I would consider that absurd. No one factor, I am convinced, is decisive. But it seems equally absurd to omit population as an important factor in determining the characteristics of any era, especially of a time marked by swings as extreme as those we are going through now. The new big issues that emerged these past twenty years—race and civil rights, the urban crisis, the environment —will not go away. For this reason alone, the Seventies will surely not be at all like the Fifties or the Thirties. But a study of population dynamics indicates that they will not be like the Sixties either.

Whether they will be conservative in their mood or liberal, reactionary or revolutionary, no one can yet foresee. But in the issues that matter to them, in their values, and, above all, in their needs, the Seventies may be a very traditional—indeed, a quite old-fashioned—decade.

Essentially, all of the readings in this volume and the books and articles mentioned in the bibliographies at the end of each section are appropriate for the study of "the continuity of protest and the New Left." In the final analysis, it is for the reader to make his or her own comparisons, analogies and interpretations. The following few suggestions may aid in this analysis.

Insight into the Old Left of the 1930's is provided by the appropriate chapters in Daniel Aaron, *Writers on the Left* (New York, 1961). James Gilbert, "The Left Young and Old," *Partisan Review,* 36 (1969), 343–363, is informative. In addition to Howard Zinn's article on the Old and New Left reprinted herein, one should see his "Marxism and the New Left" in Alfred F. Young (ed.), *Dissent: Explorations in the History of American Radicalism* (DeKalb, Illinois, 1968), which is in itself a significant anthology of essays helpful for understanding protest in American society. The characteristics of the New Left are studied in Penina Migdal Glazer, "The New Left: A Style of Protest," *Journal of Higher Education,* 38 (March 1967), 119–130; its history is traced in James P. O'Brien, "The Development of the New Left," *The Annals of the American Academy of Political and Social Sciences,* 395 (May 1971), 15–25. Massimo Teodari's *The New Left: A Documentary History* (Indianapolis, 1969) offers a collection of writings on the subject.

The more violent side of recent protest is highlighted in Jerome H. Skolnick, *The Politics of Protest* (New

THE CONTINUITY
OF
PROTEST

York, 1969), a reprint of Skolnick's report to the National Commission on the Causes and Prevention of Violence dealing with antiwar demonstrations, student riots and black militancy. The Commission's attempt to place violent protest in historical perspective can be found in Hugh Davis Graham and Ted Robert Gurr, *Violence in America: Historical and Comparative Perspectives* (New York, 1969). A similar, but less effective, attempt is made in Thomas Rose (ed.), *Violence in America: A Historical and Contemporary Reader* (New York, 1969). Nonviolent protest is usefully investigated in Staughton Lynd (ed.), *Nonviolence in America: A Documentary History* (Indianapolis, 1966).

Finally, just as the New Left has made history during the 1960's and early 1970's, it has also interpreted history. Two anthologies are especially helpful in studying this perspective; they are Barton J. Bernstein (ed.), *Towards A New Past: Dissenting Essays in American History* (New York, 1969) and Irwin Unger (ed.), *Beyond Liberalism: The New Left Views American History* (Waltham, Mass., 1971). One should also consult the periodicals *Studies on the Left* (1959–1967) and *Radical America* for this view of American history and society.

INDEX

Dubofsky, Melvyn, 148, 151–55, 269
Du Bois, W. E. B., 34, 50
Duncan, Isadora, 77
Dunne, Finley Peter, 129n
Dylan, Bob, 194, 259, 260

Easley, Ralph, 106
East, Henry Clay, 180–85 *passim*
Eastern Europeans, 74
Easy Rider, 19, 196
Economic Research and Action Project,
  101
Edelstein, Tilden, 275
Educational Issues Coordinating Coun-
  cil, 59
Einstein, Albert, 142, 142n
Eisenhower, Dwight D., 143, 144, 273
Elks, 281
Ellul, Jacques, 231
El-Shabazz, El-Hajj Malik (Malcolm
  X), 32–42
Embree, A. S., 155
Emerson, Ralph Waldo, 12, 13
End of the American Era, The, vii
Engels, Friedrich, 280
English, 199
Erikson, Erik, 276
Escape from Authority, 220
Ethical Culture Society, 116
"Eve of Destruction, The," 260–65
Ex-Communists, 219
*Existentialism and Alienation in Amer-
  ican Literature,* 282

Fairbank, John K., 129, 129n
Fair Employment Practices Committee,
  44, 46
Fall, Bernard B., 128n
Farm Bureau, 178
Farmer-Labor party, 107, 108
Farmers' Alliance, 149, 174
Farmers' Holiday Association, 149, 168–
  73
Farmers' Protective Association, 169
Farmers' Union, 169, 173
Fascism, 6
Fascists, 258
Federalists, 192
Federalists, New England, 93
Fellowship, 141, 144
Fellowship of Reconciliation, 122, 124,
  139, 140, 141
Fellowship of Youth for Peace, 116
Feuer, Lewis, 253

*Fifteenth Ward and the Great Society,
  The,* 287
Filipinos, 93, 132–35 *passim*
Finch, Robert, viii
Fine, Sidney, 148, 148n
Finkelstein, Sidney, 282
Finnish Immigrants in America, 175
Fitzgerald, F. Scott, 290
Five Easy Pieces, 82
Foran, U. S. Attorney Thomas, 196
Forcey, Charles, 215n
Fortune, 258
Foster, William Z., 103, 108, 284
Franklin, John Hope, 35n
Freedom Democratic Party, 280, 284
Freehling, William W., 195, 195n
Freeman, Joseph, 109, 109n
Free Speech Movement, 101
Freud, Sigmund, 82
Freudian, 253, 275
Frick, Henry Clay, 10, 11
Friends, Society of, 141
Frisch, Morton, 279n
Fritzen, Judy, ix
Fulbright, J. William, 127, 129, 129n,
  134, 137
Fuller, Henry Blake, 133
Futrell, J. Marion, 186

Gadola, Paul V., 159, 160
Galbraith, John Kenneth, 136
Gandhi, Mohandas K., 157
Gans, Herbert J., 17, 17n, 253
Gardner, John, 8
Garrison, William Lloyd, 26, 27, 275,
  277
Garrisonians, 277
Garvey, Marcus, 17, 32–47, 50
Gates, John, 109, 109n
Gatsby, Jay, 290
Gay Activist Alliance, 18, 83
Gay Liberation, 17, 20, 79–86
Gay Liberation Front, 80, 83
Gays, 20
Genovese, Eugene, 277
Gentiles, 289
Germans, 199, 285
Gerth, H. H., 213n
"Gillis, Dobie," 243
Gilman, Charlotte Perkins, 113
Glory of Hera, The, 240
Godey's Lady's Book, 71
Godkin, E. L., 130, 132, 135
Godkinesque, 136
Goldman, Emma, 11, 29

Jewish, 234, 256
Jewish Daily Forward, 109
Jews, 23, 46, 65, 131, 173, 183, 199, 204, 211, 216, 234, 252
Jim Crow, 34, 66
John, Vera, 54
John Birch Society, 202, 233–34
John Birch Society Bulletin, 209
Johnson, Sen. Hiram, 193
Johnson, John, 171
Johnson, Lyndon B., 127, 131, 137, 283
Jones, Jack, 64
Jones, LeRoi, 40*n*, 41, 41*n*
Jones, Marvin, 187
Joplin, Janis, 194
Jordan, David Starr, 134
Journal of Negro History, 34
Journal of Society and Popular Music, 258
Judaism, Reform, 275
"Julia," 243
Jung, Harry, 172

Katayami, Sen, 106
Kazin, Alfred, 280
Kefauver, Estes, 143
Kempton, Murray, vii
Keniston, Kenneth, 272, 274, 275
Kennan, George, 137
Kennedy, John F., 283, 289, 294
Kennedy, John Reid, 234
Kennedy, Robert, 7, 65, 133, 136, 295
Kestner, Cecil, 170
Keynes, John Maynard, 302
Keynesian, 294
Khrushchev, Nikita, 123, 281
King, Martin Luther, Jr., 263, 282, 285, 295
King, Mrs. Martin Luther, Jr., 3
Kingston Trio, 259
Kinney, Anne, 74, 75
Kiowa Tribe, 62, 63
Kipnis, Ira, 103
Kirk, Grayson, 235, 237
Klansmen, 202
Knights of Labor, 99
Know-Nothing Party, 100
Know-Nothings, 192
Knudsen, W. S., 159
Kollantai, Alexandra, 106
Kopkind, Andrew, 3, 5–9, 23
Korean War, 121, 122, 123, 140, 143, 144
Kuhn, Margaret, 20

Ku Klux Klan, viii, 183, 192–94, 197–201, 288
Ku Klux Klan in the City, The, 197
Kunen, James, 2

Labor and Liberty, 180
LaFollette, Robert, 107
LaFollette Civil Liberties Committee, 186
LaGuardia in Congress, 279
Langer, Sen. William L., 171
La Raza, 54–60
La Raza, 59
La Raza: The Mexican Americans, 52
Larkin, James, 106
Larson, Louis, 170
Lasch, Christopher, 129, 129*n*, 193, 194, 212–19
Lawyers' Committee on American Policy Toward Vietnam, 137
League for Industrial Democracy, 114, 123, 156
League of Nations, 116, 199
Left, 233–39
Left, New, ix, 5, 27–30, 80, 101–03, 117, 123, 129, 235–38, 269–87, 295
Left, Old, 102, 235, 237, 238, 269, 279–86
Lemars Globe-Post, 172
Lenin, V. I., 194, 202, 280
Leninism, 236
Leninists, 102, 106, 110
Leon, D. H., 92
Lerner, Max, 116
Lesbians, 83
Lessard, Suzannah, 79–86, 193
Lessing, Doris, 241
Lester, Julius, 263
Lewis, John L., 282
Lewis, Michael, 18, 43–51
Lewis, Oscar, 152, 152*n*
Lewis, Sinclair, 289, 290
Lewis Tappan and the Evangelical War Against Slavery, 272
Liberal Party, 75
Liberty Amendment Committee, 202
Life, vii, 281, 292
Like a Conquered Province, 1
Lincoln, Abraham, 25, 93
Lincoln, Alice, 217*n*
Lippmann, Walter, 113, 129, 129*n*
Little Red Songbook, 148
Locke, John Galen, 198
London, Jack, 113
Long, Huey, 180, 182

Longfellow, Henry Wadsworth, 140
Looking Backward, 152
Lopez, Trini, 259
Los Angeles Teachers' Association, 59
Los Angeles *Times,* 53
Lost Found Nation of Islam in the Wilderness of North America, 36, 37, 40. *See also* Black Muslims
L'Ouverture, Toussaint, 274
Lowell, James Russell, 283–84
Lozada, Froben, 56, 60
Lubell, Samuel, 140
Luce, Clare Booth, 225
Luce, Henry, 292
Luddites, 97
Luther, Martin, 240
Lynd, Staughton, 282

MacAlpine, Eadmonn, 106
McCarran, Patrick, 140
McCarthy, Eugene, 5, 6, 7, 8, 133
McCarthy, Joseph, 79, 93, 122, 139–44, 259, 294
McCarthyism, 122, 139–44
McCarthyites, 7
McCarthy, Mary, 129, 129*n*
McCloud, Janet, 69
McDermott, John, 129
McDonald, Ramsey, 96
McGovern, George, 128, 128*n,* 133
McGuire, Barry, 260
"McHale's Navy," 243
Machiavellian, 249
McIntire, Carl, 202, 206, 234
McKinley, William, 11, 131, 132, 133, 134, 137
McKnight, Joe, 57
McPherson, James, 277
MacPherson, Myra, 20*n*
Mailer, Norman, 130
Main Street, 290
March on Washington Movement (MOWM), 43–50
Malays, 135
Malcolm X, 32–42
Manion Forum, 235
Marcuse, Herbert, 8
Martin, Herbert, 171
Marx, Karl, 6, 8, 257, 280
Marxian, 118, 224
Marxism, 84, 109, 236, 269, 270, 286
Marxist, 152, 234, 243, 253, 258, 265, 280, 282, 284, 285
Masonic, 234
Mattachine Society, 80

Maurer, James H., 107, 110
"Mayberry," 243
Means, La Nada, 65–69
Melville, Herman, 13, 212
Men, Ideas and Politics, 296
Mencken, H. L., 288, 290, 293
Methodists, 198, 211
Mexican-Americans, viii, 1, 17, 18, 52–61. *See also* Chicanos, Mexicans
Mexican American Unity, Council of, 59
Mexicans, 20, 77. *See also* Chicanos, Mexican-Americans
Michels, Robert, 284
Midnight Cowboy, 82
Mill, John Stuart, 28, 221
Miller, Arthur, 219
Miller, William Lee, 269, 270, 287–95
Millett, Kate, 82
Mills, C. Wright, 213*n,* 215
Mills, Sid, 63
Minnesota Holiday Association, 170
Mississippi Freedom Democratic Party, 39
Mitchell, Harry L., 180–88 *passim*
Mohawk, 64
Momaday, N. Scott, 62
Monroe Doctrine, 135
Montez, Philip, 58
Montgomery, Robert, 140
Moore, Barrington, 274
Moore, George, 291
Morals in the Fifties, 287
Morgan, Robin, 70*n*
Morgenthau, Hans, vii, 130
Moses, Bob, 281, 282
Mott, Lucretia, 72
Movement and Revolution, 251
Muchlup, Fritz, 255
Mugwumps, 130
Muhammad, Elijah, 36, 37
Mumford, Lewis, 140
Mundt, Karl, 221, 222
Murphy, Frank, 160
Muste, A. J., 141, 143, 144

Nader, Ralph, 5, 299
Napoleon Bonaparte, 273
Nathan, George, 290
Nation, The, 122, 124, 135, 141, 212
National Advisory Committee on Mexican American Education, 56
National Assembly of Student Christian Groups, 118

National Association for the Advancement of Colored People (NAACP), 43, 45, 46, 47, 59, 124, 293
National Committee for a Sane Nuclear Policy (SANE), 124
National Conference of Students in Politics, 118
National Farmers' Organization, 177, 178, 179
National Guard, 165, 186
National Liberation Front (NLF), 128
National Negro Business League, 33
National States Rights party, 234
National Student Association, 121, 122, 235
National Student Committee for the Limitation of Armaments, 116
National Student Federation of America, 116, 118, 120
National Student Forum, 116
National Student League, 118, 119
National Women's Suffrage Association, 74, 76
Native Americans, 19, 68. *See also* Indians
Nava, Julian, 59
Navajo, 63, 69
Nazi party, 23
Nazis, 65
Nef, Walter, 153
Negroes, viii, 19, 20, 22–31, 43–51, 101, 131, 135, 166, 182, 183, 197–201, 204, 259, 263, 283, 284, 289, 293. *See also* Afro-Americans; Blacks
Nero, 133
New Deal, 91, 92, 103, 110, 150, 168, 173, 179, 180, 183, 185–88, 293
New Flag, The, 133
New Indians, The, 52
New Radicalism in America, The, 212
New Republic, The, vii, 52, 122, 141, 198
New Student, 115, 116
Newsweek, vii
New University Thought, 123
New Yorker, The, 141, 291
New York Herald, 130
New York Herald Tribune, 140
New York Review of Books, The, 212
New York Times, 6, 130, 132, 140, 184
New York Times Magazine, 1
Nichols, Mike, 240
Niles, John Jacob, 259
Nixon, Richard M., vii, viii, 2, 133, 221, 302

Noebel, David, 261
Non-Caucasians, 233
Nonpartisan League, 149
Norcross, Hiram, 182
North American Student, 114
Novak, Michael, 18, 18n, 19
November Moratorium, 270

Oakes, Richard, 64, 65
O'Connor, Edward L., 172
October Moratorium, 270
Odasnyk, Walter, 282
Oedipal, 275
Oglesby, Carl, 277, 282
One Big Union, 153
Only Yesterday, 288
Onondaga Indians, 140
Oppenheimer, J. Robert, 142
Organization of American Historians (OAH), 18
Owen, Chandler, 50

Pacific Southwest Council of the Union of Hebrew Congregations, 59
Pankhurst, Christabel, 74, 75
Pankhurst, Emmeline, 74. *See also* Pankhurst, E. Sylvia
Pankhurst, E. Sylvia, 75n. *See also* Pankhurst, Emmeline
Pareto, Vilfredo, 256
Passing of the Great Race, 199
Paterson, Thomas G., ix
Paxton, Tom, 260, 261n
Peacher, Paul, 187
Pearson, Drew, 235
Pena, Albert, 54
People's Artists, 259
Peter, Paul and Mary, 258, 259
Peterson, Patti, viii, 93, 112–26, 156
Peterson, Robert, ix
Pfaff, William, 129, 129n
Philadelphia Peace Caravan, 140
Philbrick, Herbert, 140, 141
Phillips, Wendell, 283
Pickett, Clarence, 144
Pierson, George W., 214n
Piety Along the Potomac, 287
Pilgrims, 18, 192
Pinkertons, 10, 13
Pitts, C. W., 171, 172
Plato, 228
Playboy, 70, 78, 225
Plekhanov, George, 280
Poles, 199, 200
Polish, 255

Tucker, Benjamin, 29
Turner, Nat, 274
Twentieth Century America, 94
Twentieth Century Reformation, 202, 206

Un-Americanism, viii, 202–11
"Uncle Tom-Tom," 62
Unitarians, 211, 274–75
United Automobile Workers of America (UAW), 24, 148, 157, 159, 164
United Daughters of the Confederacy, 141
United Farmers' League, 170, 173
United Farm Workers Organizing Committee, 150
United Federation of Teachers (UFT), 24
United Mexican American Students, 59
United Nations, 205
United Native Americans, 63
United States Civil Rights Commission, 58
U. S. News and World Report, 235
United World Federalists, 120–21, 142
Universal Negro Improvement Association (UNIA), 17, 47, 50
Urban League, 18, 43, 45

Valdez, Luis, 57, 61
Vallandigham, C. L., 93
Vallee, Rudy, 258
Vanzetti, Bartolomeo, 116
Verba, Sidney, 131*n*
Vesey, Denmark, 274
Vietcong, 285
Vietnam, 7, 63, 85, 101, 129, 130, 137, 191, 193, 220, 262, 274, 279, 298
Vietnamese, 281, 283
Vietnam War, vii, 19, 93, 127, 128, 131, 221, 242, 246, 269, 270, 292, 293
Vigilante Federation, 173
Vilardi, Paul, 235
Vladeck, Charney, 109
Volodorsky, V., 106

WACS, 82
Wallace, George, 6, 194, 226, 265
Wallace, Henry, 121, 182
Wallace, Lew, 133
Ward, John William, 3, 4, 10–14
Warren, Josiah, 29
Warren, Robert Penn, 19
War Resisters' League, 139, 140

Washington, Booker T., 28, 33, 34, 35, 293
Washington Monthly, The, 79
Waskow, Arnold, 150
Watson, Thomas, 8
WAVES, 82
Wayne, John, 18
Weathermen, 279, 299
Weavers, The, 259
Weber, Max, 213*n*, 252, 253
Weinstein, James, 93, 101–11, 112
Weisberger, Bernard A., 20, 20*n*
Welch, Robert, 202
Weld, Theodore, 275
We Shall Be All, 151
Westfield, Casper, 170
When Workers Organize, 151
Whig Party, 93
White Anglo-Saxon Protestants (WASPs), 199, 252, 256, 289
White, E. B., 141
White, Morton G., 215*n*
White, Theodore, 281
White, Walter, 43, 45
Whiteman, Paul, 288
Whites, 166, 182
Wilson, Charles, 273
Wilson, Edmund, 290
Wilson, Woodrow, 103, 104, 105, 293
Winstanley, Gerrard, 98
Winthrop, John, 272
Wirt, William, 214*n*
Wittner, Lawrence S., 93, 139–44
Wobblies, 147–48, 151–55. *See also* International Workers of the World
Wolcott, Thomas, 160
Wolin, Sheldon S., viii, 193, 194, 220–32
Women, vii, 20, 70–78
Women's Emergency Brigade, 159
Women's International League for Peace and Freedom, 141
Women's Liberation, 17, 19, 70–78, 300
Women's Social and Political Union, 74, 75
Women's Trade Union League, 76
Woodson, Carter G., 34
Woodward, C. Vann, 291
World Court, 114
World War I, viii, 43, 77, 101, 103, 113, 114, 147, 154, 157, 192, 199, 284. *See also* Great War
World War II, 49, 102, 120, 141, 143, 153, 175, 273, 296

Wright, Elizur, 275
Wright, Quincy, 137
Wyatt-Brown, Bertram, 269, 271, 272–78

Xerxes, 133

Yakima, 63
Yarrow, Peter, 258
Yellow Submarine, 243
Yippies, 2, 5, 221, 240, 249, 279. *See also* Youth International Party
Young, Alfred F., 270
Young Americans for Freedom (YAF), 122, 233, 235
Young Communist League, 119
Young Democrats, 281
Young Men's Christian Association (YMCA), 114, 116, 118, 122, 125

Young People's Socialist League, 114, 115, 116, 119, 122, 125
Young Progressives of America, 121
Young Radicals, 272
Young Republicans, 262
Young Republicans for a Return to Conservatism in California, 261
Young Socialist Alliance, 276
Young Women's Christian Association (YWCA), 114, 116, 118, 122, 125
Young Worker's League, 116
Youth International Party, 270. *See also* Yippies

Zapata, Sons of, 52, 54
Zieger, Robert H., ix
Zimmerman, Bob, 259. *See also* Dylan, Bob
Zinn, Howard, 269, 270, 270n, 279–86